Discourse Analysis
An Introduction
2nd edition

A companion website to accompany this book is available online at:
http://www.bloomsbury.com/discourse-analysis-9781441167620

Please type in the URL above and receive your unique password for access to the book's online resources.

If you experience any problems accessing the resources, please contact Bloomsbury at: companionwebsites@bloomsbury.com

Bloomsbury Discourse Series

Series Editor:
Professor Ken Hyland, University of Hong Kong

Discourse is one of the most significant concepts of contemporary thinking in the humanities and social sciences as it concerns the ways language mediates and shapes our interactions with each other and with the social, political and cultural formations of our society. The *Bloomsbury Discourse* Series aims to capture the fast-developing interest in discourse to provide students, new and experienced teachers and researchers in applied linguistics, ELT and English language with an essential bookshelf. Each book deals with a core topic in discourse studies to give an in-depth, structured and readable introduction to an aspect of the way language in used in real life.

Other titles in the series:
The Discourse of Online Consumer Reviews
    Camilla Vásquez
News Discourse
    Monika Bednarek and Helen Caple
The Discourse of Text Messaging
    Caroline Tagg
The Discourse of Twitter and Social Media
    Michele Zappavigna
Workplace Discourse
    Almut Koester
The Discourse of Blogs and Wikis
    Greg Myers
Professional Discourse
    Britt-Louise Gunnarsson
Academic Discourse
    Ken Hyland
School Discourse
    Frances Christie
Historical Discourse
    Caroline Coffin
Using Corpora in Discourse Analysis
    Paul Baker
Metadiscourse
    Ken Hyland

Discourse Analysis
An Introduction

2nd edition

Brian Paltridge

BLOOMSBURY

LONDON · NEW DELHI · NEW YORK · SYDNEY

Bloomsbury Academic

An imprint of Bloomsbury Publishing Plc

50 Bedford Square	1385 Broadway
London	New York
WC1B 3DP	NY 10018
UK	USA

www.bloomsbury.com

Bloomsbury is a registered trade mark of Bloomsbury Publishing PLC

First published in 2012
Reprinted 2013 (twice), 2014

British Library Cataloguing-in-Publication Data
A catalogue record for this book is available from the British Library.

ISBN: HB: 978-1-4411-7373-7
PB: 978-1-4411-6762-0
EPDF: 978-1-4411-5820-8
EPUB: 978-1-4411-3335-9

Library of Congress Cataloging-in-Publication Data
Paltridge, Brian.
Discourse analysis: an introduction/Brian Paltridge. – 2nd ed.
p. cm. – (Continuum discourse series)
Includes bibliographical references and index.
ISBN 978-1-4411-7373-7 (alk. paper) – ISBN 978-1-4411-6762-0 (pbk.: alk. paper) –
ISBN 978-1-4411-5820-8 (eBook pdf) – ISBN 978-1-4411-3335-9 (eBook epub)
1. Discourse analysis. I. Title.
P302.P23 2012
401'.41–dc23
2012005161

Typeset by Newgen Imaging Systems Pvt Ltd, Chennai, India
Printed and bound in India

Contents

List of Figures

List of Tables

Preface to the Second Edition

The second edition of this book is an updated and expanded version of the book that was published in 2006. In my revisions, I have taken account of feedback from reviews of the first edition that were commissioned by the publisher as well as reviews that have been published in academic journals. Each of these has been extremely helpful to me in my thinking about this second edition of the book. More recent research has also been added to each of the chapters and I have added a new chapter on multimodal discourse analysis. In-text references have also been updated as have the further readings section at the end of each chapter. I have added exercises and sample texts for readers to analyse in each of the chapters and provided suggested answers to these exercises in the appendix at the back of the book. A further addition that comes with this edition is a companion website where I have placed extended reading and reference lists for each of the chapters, as well as set of PowerPoint slides that people who are using my book for teaching a course on discourse analysis might find useful.

A link to the companion website is shown by the ⌖ icon in the margin of the text. A link to the *Continuum Companion to Discourse Analysis* (Hyland and Paltridge, 2011) is shown by the 📖 icon in the text.

Brian Paltridge

Acknowledgements

I would like to thank the editor of this series Ken Hyland for the detailed and helpful feedback he gave on each of the chapters of this book. I also wish to thank the reviewers of the first edition of this book for their suggestions, which have been incorporated into this second edition of the book.

Thank you also to Gurdeep Mattu, Colleen Coalter and Laura Murray at Bloomsbury for their helpfulness and advice at each of the stages of the book's development, also to Srikanth Srinivasan at Newgen Knowledge Works for managing the production of the book so smoothly. I also wish to thank two people who taught me so much about discourse analysis: Winnie Crombie and Joy Phillips. I am grateful to my many very good students whose work I have cited in this book, especially Peng Hua, Jianxin Liu, Jun Ohashi, Joanna Orr, Carmel O'Shannessy, Kirsten Richardson, Wei Wang and Lan Yang. Thank you also to Eunjoo Song for the Korean example in Chapter 3 and Angela Thomas and Jianxin Liu for their reading of Chapter 8. My thanks also to Emi Otsuji, Ikuko Nakane and Helen Caple for their feedback on how I have represented their work in the book.

In addition, thank you to Ken Hyland for agreeing to let me include the glossary of terms that we wrote for the *Continuum Companion to Discourse Analysis* in this book. Also to Marie Stevenson and Aek Phakiti for the work they did in compiling the glossary of terms for the *Continuum Companion to Research Methods in Applied Linguistics* which I have also drawn on in this book.

The students who took my course in discourse analysis at the University of Sydney gave me valuable feedback on the exercises that are included in this book for which I especially thank them. The Language and identity network meetings at the University of Sydney were also invaluable for providing a context in which people with similar interests could get together to talk about things of common interest.

1

What is Discourse Analysis?

This chapter provides an overview of *discourse analysis*, an approach to the analysis of language that looks at patterns of language across texts as well as the social and cultural contexts in which the texts occur. The chapter commences by presenting the origins of the term discourse analysis. It then discusses particular issues which are of interest to discourse analysts, such as the relationship between language and social context, culture-specific ways of speaking and writing and ways of organizing texts in particular social and cultural situations.

The chapter continues with a discussion of different views of discourse analysis. These range from more textually oriented views of discourse analysis which concentrate mostly on language features of texts, to more socially oriented views of discourse analysis which consider what the text is doing in the social and cultural setting in which it occurs. This leads to a discussion of the *social constructionist* view of discourse; that is, the ways in which what we say as we speak contributes to the construction of certain views of the world, of people and, in turn, ourselves. The relationship between language and identity is then introduced. This includes a discussion of the ways in which, through our use of language, we not only 'display' who we are but also how we want people to see us. This includes a discussion of the ways in which, through the use of spoken and written discourse, people both 'perform' and 'create' particular social, and gendered, identities.

The ways in which 'texts rely on other texts' is also discussed in this chapter; that is the way in which we produce and understand texts in relation to other texts that have come before them as well as other texts that may follow them. This chapter, then, introduces notions and lays the ground for issues that will be discussed in greater detail in the chapters that follow.

1.1 What is discourse analysis?

> *Discourse analysis* examines patterns of language across texts and considers the relationship between language and the social and cultural contexts in which it is used. Discourse analysis also considers the ways that the use of language presents different views of the world and different understandings. It examines how the use of language is influenced by relationships between participants as well as the effects the use of language has upon social identities and relations. It also considers how views of the world, and identities, are constructed through the use of discourse.

The term *discourse analysis* was first introduced by Zellig Harris (1952) as a way of analysing connected speech and writing. Harris had two main interests: the examination of language beyond the level of the sentence and the relationship between linguistic and non-linguistic behaviour. He examined the first of these in most detail, aiming to provide a way for describing how language features are distributed within texts and the ways in which they are combined in particular kinds and styles of texts. An early, and important, observation he made was that:

> connected discourse occurs within a particular situation – whether of a person speaking, or of a conversation, or of someone sitting down occasionally over the period of months to write a particular kind of book in a particular literary or scientific tradition. (3)

There are, thus, typical ways of using language in particular situations. These *discourses*, he argued, not only share particular meanings, they also have characteristic linguistic features associated with them. What these meanings are and how they are realized in language is of central interest to the area of discourse analysis.

The relationship between language and context

By 'the relationship between linguistic and non-linguistic behaviour' Harris means how people know, from the situation that they are in, how to interpret what someone says. If, for example, an air traffic controller says to a pilot *The runway is full at the moment*, this most likely means it is not possible to land the plane. This may seem obvious to a native speaker of English but a non-native speaker pilot, of which there are many in the world, needs to understand the relationship between what is said and what is meant in order to understand that he/she cannot land the plane at that time. Harris' point is that the expression *The runway is full at the moment* has a particular meaning in a particular situation (in this case the landing of a plane) and may mean something different in another situation. If I say *The runway is full at the moment* to a friend who is waiting with me to pick someone up from the airport, this is now an explanation of why the plane is late landing (however I may know this) and not an instruction to not land the plane. The same discourse, thus, can be understood differently by different language users as well as understood differently in different contexts (van Dijk 2011).

Van Dijk provides two book length accounts of the notion of context. He argues that context is a subjective construct that accounts not only for the uniqueness of each text but also for the common ground and shared representations that language users draw on to communicate with each other (van Dijk 2008). Van Dijk (2009) argues, further, that the link between society and discourse is often indirect and depends on how language users themselves define the genre or communicative event in which they engaged. Thus, in his words, '[i]t is not the social situation that influences (or is influenced by) discourse, but the way the participants *define* (original emphasis)' the situation in which the discourse occurs (van Dijk 2008: x). In his view, contexts are not objective conditions but rather (inter)subjective constructs that are constantly updated by participants in their interactions with each other as members of groups or communities.

The relationship between language and context is fundamental to the work of J. R. Firth (1935, 1957a, 1957b), Michael Halliday (1971, 1989a) and John Sinclair (2004), each of whom has made important contributions to the area of discourse analysis. Firth draws on the anthropologist Malinowski's (1923, 1935) notions of *context of situation* and *context of culture* to discuss this relationship, arguing that in order to understand the meaning of what a person says or writes we need to know something about the situational and cultural context in which it is located. That is, if you don't know what the people involved in a text are doing and don't understand their culture 'then you can't make sense of their text' (Martin 2001: 151).

Halliday (1971) takes the discussion further by linking context of situation with actual texts and context of culture with potential texts and the range of possibilities that are open to language users for the creation of texts. The actual choices a person makes from the options that are available to them within the particular context of culture, thus, take place within a particular context of situation, both of which influence the use of language in the text (see Hasan 2009, Halliday 2009a, van Dijk 2011 for further discussion of the relationship between language and context). The work of J. R. Firth has been similarly influential in the area of discourse analysis. This is reflected in the concern by discourse analysts to study language within authentic instances of use (as opposed to made-up examples) – a concern with the inseparability of meaning and form and a focus on a contextual theory of meaning (Stubbs 1996). Sinclair also argues that language should be studied in naturally occurring contexts and that the analysis of meaning should be its key focus (Carter 2004).

Discourse analysis, then, is interested in 'what happens when people draw on the knowledge they have about language . . . to do things in the world' (Johnstone 2002: 3). It is, thus, the analysis of language in use. Discourse analysis considers the relationship between language and the contexts in which it is used and is concerned with the description and analysis of both spoken and written interactions. Its primary purpose, as Chimombo and Roseberry (1998) argue, is to provide a deeper understanding and appreciation of texts and how they become meaningful to their users.

The discourse structure of texts

Discourse analysts are also interested in how people organize what they say in the sense of what they typically say first, and what they say next and so on in a conversation or in a piece of writing. This is something that varies across cultures and is by no means the same across languages. An email, for example, to me from a Japanese academic or a member of the administrative staff at a Japanese university may start with reference to the weather saying immediately after *Dear Professor Paltridge* something like *Greetings! It's such a beautiful day today here in Kyoto*. I, of course, may also say this in an email to an overseas colleague but is it not a ritual requirement in English, as it is in Japanese. There are, thus, particular things we say and particular ways of ordering what we say in particular spoken and written situations and in particular languages and cultures.

Mitchell (1957) was one the first researchers to examine the *discourse structure* of texts. He looked at the ways in which people order what they say in buying and selling interactions. He looked at the overall structure of these kinds of texts, introducing the notion of *stages* into discourse analysis; that is the steps that language users go through as they carry out particular interactions. His interest was more in the ways in which interactions are organized at an overall textual level than the ways in which language is used in each of the stages of a text. Mitchell discusses how language is used as, what he calls, *co-operative action* and how the meaning of language lies in the situational context in which it is used and in the context of the text as a whole.

If, then, I am walking along the street in Shanghai near a market and someone says to me *Hello Mister, DVD*, I know from the situation that I am in that they want to sell me DVDs. If I then go into a market and someone asks what seems to me to be a very high price for a shirt, I know from my experience with this kind of interaction that the price they are telling me is just a starting point in the buying and selling exchange and that I can quite easily end up buying the shirt for at least half the original price. I know from my experience how the interaction will typically start, what language will typically be used in the interaction and how the interaction will typically end. I also start to learn other typical characteristics of the interaction. For example, a person will normally only say *Hello Mister, DVD* (or *Hello Mister, Louis Vuitton*, etc.) when I am between stalls, not when I am in a stall and have started a buying and selling interaction with someone.

Hasan (1989a) has continued this work into the analysis of service encounters, as has Ventola (1984, 1987). Hasan and Ventola aim to capture obligatory and optional stages that are typical of service encounters. For example, a greeting such as *Hi, how are you?* is not always obligatory at the start of a service encounter in English when someone is buying something at the delicatessen counter in a busy supermarket. However, a sales request such as *Can I have . . .* or *Give me . . .* etc. where you say what you want to buy is. Hasan and Ventola point out, further, that there are many possible ways in which the stages in a service encounter (and indeed many genres) can be realized in terms of language. For example, a request for service might be expressed as *Could you show me . . .* or *Have you got . . .* (etc.). The ways in which these elements are expressed will vary, further, depending on where the service encounter is taking place; that is whether it is in a supermarket, at the post office or at a travel agent etc. It will also vary according to variables such as the age of the people involved in the interaction and whether the service encounter is face-to-face or on the phone, etc. (Flowerdew 1993). There is, thus, is no neat one-to-one correspondence between the structural elements of texts and the ways in which they are expressed through language.

Other researchers have also investigated recurring patterns in spoken interactions, although in a somewhat different way from Mitchell and others following in that tradition. Researchers working in the area known as *conversation analysis* have looked at how people open and close conversations and how people take turns and overlap their speech in conversations, for example. They have looked at casual conversations, chat, as well as doctor–patient consultations, psychiatric interviews and interactions in legal settings. Their interest, in particular, is in fine-grained analyses of spoken interactions such as the use of overlap, pauses, increased volume and pitch and what these reveal about how people relate to each other in what they are saying and doing with language.

Cultural ways of speaking and writing

Different cultures often have different ways of doing things through language. This is something that was explored by Hymes (1964) through the notion of the *ethnography of communication*. Hymes' work was a reaction to the neglect, at the time, of speech in linguistic analyses and anthropological descriptions of cultures. His work was also a reaction to views of language which took little or no account of the social and cultural contexts in which language occurs. In particular, he considered aspects of speech events such as who is speaking to whom, about what, for what purpose, where and when, and how these impact on how we say and do things in culture-specific settings.

There are, for example, particular cultural ways of buying and selling things in different cultures. How I buy my lunch at a takeaway shop in an English-speaking country is different, for example, from how I might do this in Japan. In an English-speaking country there is greater ritual use of *Please* and *Thanks* on the part of the customer in this kind of interaction than there is in Japan. How I buy something in a supermarket in an English-speaking country may be more similar to how I might do this in Japan. The person at the cash register in Japan, however, will typically say much more than the customer in this sort of situation, who may indeed say nothing. This does not mean that by saying nothing the Japanese customer is being rude. It simply means that there are culturally different ways of doing things with language in different cultures. The sequence of events I go through may be the same in both cultures, but the ways of using language in these events and other sorts of non-linguistic behaviour may differ.

A further example of this can be seen when companies decide to set up a braches of their business overseas. A number of years ago the Japanese department store Daimaru opened a branch in Melbourne. Each year the store had a spring sale and sent out circulars to its customers to let them know about it. It was interesting to see how differently the company wrote their promotional materials for their Japanese-speaking and their English-speaking customers. The Japanese texts commenced with 'seasonal greetings' (as in the emails above) referring to the warm spring weather and the sight of fresh flowers in the gardens whereas the English texts went straight to the point of the message, the sale that would be starting shortly. In the Japanese texts it would have been impolite not to do this whereas in the English texts it would have been unnecessary and, indeed, may have hidden the point of the text for the English readers if they had done this.

1.2 Different views of discourse analysis

There are in fact a number of differing views on what discourse analysis actually is. Social science researchers, for example, might argue that all their work is concerned with the analysis of discourse, yet often take up the term in their own, sometimes different, ways (Fairclough 2003). Mills (1997) makes a similar observation showing how through its relatively short history the term discourse analysis has shifted from highlighting one aspect of language usage to another, as well as being used in different ways by different researchers.

Fairclough (2003) contrasts what he calls 'textually oriented discourse analysis' with approaches to discourse analysis that have more of a social theoretical orientation. He does not see these two views as mutually exclusive, however, arguing for an analysis of discourse that is both linguistic and social in its orientation. Cameron and Kulick (2003) present a similar view. They do not take these two perspectives to be incompatible with each other, arguing that the instances of language in use that are studied under a textually oriented view of discourse are still socially situated and need to be interpreted in terms of their social meanings and functions.

David Crystal's (2008) analysis of Barack Obama's victory speech when he won the US presidential election is an example of textually oriented discourse analysis. One of the features Crystal notes in Obama's speech is the use of *parallelism*, where he repeats certain grammatical structures for rhetorical effect. In the following extract from the opening lines of his speech Obama repeats 'who clauses' (highlighted below) lowering the processing load of the speech so that listeners will focus on the content of each the clauses that follow. Crystal also shows how Obama follows the rhetorical 'rule of three' in this section of his speech in a way that mirrors the speeches of former political leaders such as Winston Churchill.

> If there is anyone out there *who still doubts* that America is a place where all things are possible, *who still wonders* if the dream of our founders is alive in our time, *who still questions* the power of our democracy, tonight is your answer. (CNNPolitics.com 2008)

Obama also uses lists of pairs in his speech to rhetorical effect, as in:

> It's the answer spoken by young and old, rich and poor, Democrat and Republican, black, white,
> Hispanic, Asian, Native American, gay, straight, disabled and not disabled. (ibid.)

Higgins' (2008) analysis of Obama's speech is an example of more socially oriented discourse analysis. Higgins traces Obama's speech back to the oratory of the ancient Greeks and Romans showing how the use of the 'tricolon' (series of threes), as in the example above, was one of Cicero's, as well as Julius Caesar's, rhetorical techniques, as in Caesar's 'Veni, vidi, vici' (I came, I saw, I conquered). In doing this, Obama recalls both the politics and traditions of ancient Athens where oratory was 'the supreme political skill, on whose mastery power depended' (ibid., online). Williams (2009) discusses Obama's speech within the context of the political (and economic) moment of his victory, highlighting the central message of optimism in his speech captured in the repetition of the refrain 'Yes, we can'. Higgins (2008) also discusses how this 'Yes, we can' relates, intertextually, to the call-and-response preaching of the American church and the power that effective preachers have on their congregations. Obama's reference in his speech to previous leaders, thus, draws on the *social stock of knowledge* (Luckmann 2009) he shares with his audience and their social and cultural histories.

We can see, then, that discourse analysis is a view of language at the level of text. Discourse analysis is also a view of language in use; that is, how people achieve certain communicative goals through the use of language, perform certain communicative acts, participate in certain communicative events and present themselves to others. Discourse analysis considers how people manage interactions with each other, how people communicate within particular groups and societies as well as how they communicate with other groups, and with other cultures. It also focuses on how people do things beyond language, and the ideas and beliefs that they communicate as they use language.

Discourse as the social construction of reality

The view of discourse as the *social construction of reality* see texts as communicative units which are embedded in social and cultural practices. The texts we write and speak both shape and are shaped by these practices. Discourse, then, is both shaped by the world as well as shaping the world. Discourse is shaped by language as well as shaping language. It is shaped by the people who use the language as well as shaping the language that people use. Discourse is shaped, as well, by the discourse that has preceded it and that which might follow it. Discourse is also shaped by the medium in which it occurs as well as it shapes the possibilities for that medium. The purpose of the text also influences the discourse. Discourse also shapes the range of possible purposes of texts (Johnstone 2007).

Wetherell's (2001) analysis of the BBC *Panorama* interview with the late Diana, Princess of Wales (BBC 1995) provides an example of the role of language in the construction (and construal) of the social world. She shows how, through the use of language, Diana 'construes' her social world, presenting herself as a sharing person and Prince Charles as 'a proud man who felt low about the attention his wife was getting' (Wetherell 2001: 15). That is, as she speaks, the Princess creates a view of herself and the world in which she lives in a way that she wishes people to see. As Wetherell points out:

> As Diana and others speak, on this and many other occasions, a formulation of the world comes into being. The world as described comes into existence at that moment. In an important sense, the social reality constructed in the Panorama interview and in other places of Diana's happy marriage bucking under media pressure did not exist before its emergence as discourse. (16)

A further example of this *social constructivist* view of discourse can be seen in the text on the cover of the December 2004 Asian edition of *Business Week*:

> The three scariest words in U.S. industry: 'The China Price'

The feature story in this issue discusses China's ability to undercut production costs to the extent that, unless US manufacturers are able to cut their prices, they can 'kiss their customers goodbye'. This special report states that for decades economists have insisted that the US wins from globalization. Now they are not so sure. China, a former US trade representative says, 'is a tiger on steroids'. A labour economist from Harvard University says in this series of articles that the wages of white collar workers in the United States 'could get whacked' as a result of this shift and that white collar workers in the United States have a right to be scared that they may lose their jobs as they are displaced by this 'offshoring'. Ultimately, the report argues, more than half the 130 million US workforce could feel the impact of this change in global competition (Engardio and Roberts 2004).

Harney (2009) in her book *The China Price* continues this discussion, showing how this reality is changing with regional labour shortages and rising wages. While 'the China Price' has become a brand that means the lowest price possible, there are Chinese factories that have had to close, have moved their business to other parts of China where labour costs are lower or have sent their work outside of China because they have not been able to maintain their earlier level of pricing (ibid.). This outsourcing of work has led to increases in manufacturing in neighbouring countries such as Malaysia where some regions have increased their productivities enormously. Penang, for example, increased its manufacturing in 2010 by 465 per cent compared to 2009 because of this, due to what is now being called 'the China effect' (Chowdhury 2011). For someone reading about this for the first time, this becomes not just part of their social stock of knowledge but also part of their social reality, a reality constructed (in part) through discourse.

Smart's (forthcoming) discussion of climate change provides an example of the use of a term, *climate change*, and accompanying arguments to create different realities for different people. He demonstrates how both advocates and sceptics of climate change draw on their own particular take on the work of the same person, Dr James Hansen, an outspoken climate change researcher to argue both for (the advocates) and against (the sceptics) climate change. Smart shows how advocates draw on Hansen's credentials as a leading climatologist with NASA and the standing of the journal in which he has published, *Science*, to support his argument for the irreversibility of climate change. The sceptics, however, make connections between Hansen's arguments, fiction and horror movies to argue against his point of view. Here, we have opposing discourses on the same person's work to make cases both for and against the same phenomenon.

Cameron and Kulick (2003: 29) in their discussion of the history of the terms 'gay', 'lesbian' and 'queer' provide a further example of the connections between words and the meanings that become associated with them. As they argue:

> words in isolation are not the issue. It is in *discourse* – the use of language in specific contexts – that words acquire meaning.
>
> Whenever people argue about words, they are also arguing about the assumptions and values that have clustered around those words in the course of their history of being used. We cannot understand the significance of any word unless we attend closely to its relationship to other words and to the discourse (indeed, the competing discourses) in which words are always embedded. And we must bear in mind that discourse shifts and changes constantly, which is why arguments about words and their meanings are never settled once and for all.

As Firth argued 'the complete meaning of a word is always contextual' (Firth 1935: 37). These meanings, however, change over time in relation to particular contexts of use and changes in the social, cultural and ideological background/s to this use.

Discourse and socially situated identities

When we speak or write we use more than just language to display who we are, and how we want people to see us. The way we dress, the gestures we use and the way/s we act and interact also influence how we display social identity. Other factors which influence this include the ways we think, the attitudes we display and the things we value, feel and believe. As Gee (2011) argues, the ways we make visible and recognizable *who* we are and *what* we are doing always involves more than just language. It involves acting, interacting and thinking in certain ways. It also involves valuing and talking (or reading and writing) in appropriate ways with appropriate 'props', at appropriate times and in appropriate places.

The Princess of Wales, for example, knows in the *Panorama* interview not only how she is expected to speak in the particular place and at the particular time but also how she should dress, how she can use body language to achieve the effect that she wants as well as the values, attitudes, beliefs and emotions it is appropriate for her to express (as well as those it is not appropriate for her to express) in this situation. That is, she knows how to enact the *discourse* of a Princess being interviewed about her private life in the open and public medium of television. This *discourse,* of course, may be different from, but related to, the *discourses* she participated in in her role as mother of her children, and the public and private roles and identities she had as wife of the Prince of Wales. A given discourse, thus, can involve more than just the one single identity (ibid.).

Discourses, then, involve the *socially situated identities* that we enact and recognize in the different settings that we interact in. They include culture-specific ways of performing and culture-specific ways of recognizing identities and activities. Discourses also include the different styles of language that we use to enact and recognize these identities; that is, different *social languages* (Gee 1996). Discourses also involve characteristic ways of acting, interacting and feeling, and characteristic ways of showing emotion, gesturing, dressing and posturing. They also involve particular ways of valuing, thinking, believing, knowing, speaking and listening, reading and writing (Gee 2011).

Discourse and performance

As Gee explains:

> a Discourse is a 'dance' that exists in the abstract as a coordinated pattern of words, deeds, values, beliefs, symbols, tools, objects, times, and places in the here and now as a performance that is recognizable as just such a coordination. Like a dance, the performance here and now is never exactly the same. It all comes down, often, to what the 'masters of the dance' will allow to be recognised or will be forced to recognize as a possible instantiation of the dance. (36)

This notion of performance and, in particular, *performativity*, is taken up by authors such as Butler (1990, 1991, 1997, 1999, 2004), Cameron (1999), Eckert and McConnell-Ginet (2003), Hall (2000) and Pennycook (2004, 2007). The notion of performativity derives from speech act theory and the work of the linguistic philosopher Austin. It is based on the view that in *saying* something, we *do* it (Cameron and Kulick 2003). That is, we bring states of affairs into being as a result of what we say and what we do. Examples of this are *I promise* and *I now pronounce you husband and wife*. Once I have said I promise I have committed myself to doing something. Once a priest, or a marriage celebrant, says *I now pronounce you husband and wife*, the couple have 'become' husband and wife. Performance, thus, brings the social world into being (Bucholtz and Hall 2003).

Butler, Cameron and others talk about doing gender in much the way that Gee talks about discourse as performance. Discourses, then, like the performance of gendered identities, are socially constructed, rather than 'natural'. People 'are who they are because of (among other things) the way they talk' not 'because of who they (already) are' (Cameron 1999: 144). We, thus, 'are not who we are because of some inner being but because of what we do' (Pennycook 2007: 70). It is, thus, 'in the doing that the identity is produced' (Pennycook 2011).

Social identities, then, are not pre-given, but are formed in the use of language and the various other ways we display who we are, what we think, value and feel, etc. The way, for example, a rap singer uses language, what they rap about and how they present themselves as they do this, all contributes to their performance and creation of themselves as a rap singer (Pennycook 2007). They may do this in a particular way on the streets of New York, in another way in a show in Quebec, and yet another way in a night club in Seoul. As they *do* being a rap singer, they bring into existence, or repeat, their social persona as a rap singer.

Nor are we who we are because of how we (physically) look or where we were originally born. Otsuji (2010: 189) gives the example of asking a student (in a Japanese class) with an Indonesian name and Indonesian appearance 'How is it in Indonesia?' to which the student simply replied (in Japanese) 'I am Australian'. Similarly, she asks another student 'Where are you from?' to which the student replies 'Well, maybe China . . . my parents are from Shanghai but I don't know much about China. Cause I grew up here'. Otsuji's parents are ethnically Japanese. She was born, however, in the United States. She has lived in Japan, as well as in Scotland, Singapore, Holland and Australia. When she tells this to a Japanese person in a casual meeting a frequent reply is 'Then you are not Japanese'. Otsuji, however, is Japanese in appearance, she speaks Japanese, she has lived in Japan and she has strong family connections in Japan. So what, then, does it mean 'to be Japanese', or to have a 'Japanese' identity? (see Choi 2010, Otsuji 2010 for further discussions of this).

Discourse and intertextuality

All texts, whether they are spoken or written, make their meanings against the background of other texts and things that have been said on other occasions (Lemke 1992). Texts may more or less implicitly or explicitly cite other texts; they may refer to other texts, or they may allude to other past, or future, texts. We thus 'make sense of every word, every utterance, or act against the background of (some) other words, utterances, acts of a similar kind' (Lemke 1995: 23). All texts are, thus, in an *intertextual* relationship with other texts. As Bazerman (2004: 83) argues:

> We create our texts out of the sea of former texts that surround us, the sea of language we live in. And we understand the texts of others within that same sea.

Umberto Eco (1987) provides an interesting discussion of intertextuality in his chapter 'Casablanca: Cult movies and intertextual collage'. Eco points out that the film *Casablanca* was made on a very small budget and in a very short time. As a result its creators were forced to improvise the plot, mixing a little of everything they knew worked in a movie as they went. The result is what Eco (1987) describes as an 'intertextual collage'. For Eco, *Casablanca* has been so successful because it is not, in fact, an instance of a single kind of film genre but a mixing of stereotyped situations that are drawn from a number of different kinds of film genres. As the film proceeds, he argues, we recognize the film genres that they recall. We also recognize the pleasures we have experienced when we have watched these kinds of films.

Wang's (2007) study of newspaper commentaries in Chinese and English on the events of September 11 provides an example of how writers in different languages and cultural settings draw on intertextual resources for the writing of their texts and how they position themselves in relation to their sources. One of the most striking differences Wang found was that in the Chinese texts he examined the writers often drew their views from other sources but made it clear they were not the authors of the texts. They did not attempt to endorse these views or take a stance towards them, thereby keeping a distance from the views that they had presented. In the English language texts, however, the writers took the points of view they were presenting as widely held within the particular community and did not try to distance themselves from them. Wang then discusses how many of the differences he observed can be traced back to the different sociocultural settings in which the texts occurred, and especially the role of the media in the two different settings. Thus, while media discourses are often global in nature, they are, at the same time, often very local (Machin and van Leeuwen 2007) and draw on other texts for different purposes and often in rather different ways (see Paltridge and Wang 2010, 2011 for further discussion of this study).

1.3 Summary

Discourse analysis, then, considers the relationship between language and the social and cultural contexts in which it is used. It considers what people mean by what they say, how they work out what people mean and the way language presents different views of the world and different understandings. This includes an examination of how discourse is shaped by relationships between participants, and the effects discourse has upon social identities and relations.

Discourse analysis takes us into what Riggenbach (1999) calls the 'bigger picture' of language description that is often left out of more micro-level descriptions of language use. It takes us into the social and cultural settings of language use to help us understand particular language choices. That is, it takes us beyond description to explanation and helps us understand the 'rules of the game' that language users draw on in their everyday spoken and written interactions. There are many ways in which one could (and can) approach discourse analysis. What each of these ways reveals is, in part, a result of the perspective taken in the analysis, and the questions that have been asked. The aim of this book is to provide an introduction to some of these perspectives.

1.4 Discussion questions

(1) Think of examples of how people recognize your socially situated identity through your use of language. For example, in what ways does your use of language reflect your age, social class, gender, ethnic background or nationality? This might be through your use of vocabulary, your accent

or the things you talk about and how you talk about them. Try to think of specific examples of each of these.

(2) Think of a situation you have been in where someone has meant more than what they said in their use of language. For example, you may have asked someone a favour and not got a direct answer from them. How would the other person have expected you to work out their answer to your request? Or perhaps someone wanted to complain to you about something but thought it would not be polite to do this directly. How did they do this indirectly, yet still feel sure you would get the point of what they are saying?

(3) Think of rules of communication that people seem to follow when they are using language. For example what are some of the rules that students follow when talking to their teachers? Do they use a typical level of formality and typical forms of address (such as 'Sir', or 'Miss') when they speak to their teachers? Are there typical topics they talk to their teachers about, and some topics they do not talk about? Are there typical ways they start and end a conversation with a teacher? Do some of these depend on the setting in which the conversation takes place, such as in a classroom, or in the teacher's office?

(4) Think of some of the kinds of spoken or written discourse that you participate in, such as lunchtime conversations with your friends, tutorial discussions with other students or email messages to friends. What are some of the characteristic ways in which you interact in this kind of situation? How do you typically express yourself in these situations? Is the way in which you communicate the same or different in each of these situations? Why do you think this is the case?

1.5 Exercise

Exercise 1: Definitions of discourse analysis

Below are a number of definitions of the term 'discourse analysis'. Read each of these definitions and summarize the main features they list as being characteristic of discourse analysis.

Discourse analysis examines how stretches of language, considered in their full textual, social, and psychological context, become meaning and unified for their users. (Cook 1989: viii)

Discourse analysis is concerned with the study of the relationship between language and the contexts in which it is used . . . Discourse analysis is not only concerned with the description and analysis of spoken interaction . . . discourse analysts are equally interested in the organisation of written interaction. (McCarthy 1991: 12)

Discourse analysis is the analysis of language in use. Better put, it is the study of language at use in the world, not just to say things, but to do things. (Gee 2011: ix)

While some discourse analysts focus on how meaning and structure are signaled in texts, others, especially since the early 1990s, have used discourse analysis more critically to examine issue relating to power, inequality and ideology. (Baker and Ellece 2011: 32)

Discourse is language use relative to social, political and cultural formations – it is language reflecting social order but also language shaping social order, and shaping individuals' interaction with society. (Jaworski and Coupland 2006: 3)

Discourse analysis is not just one approach, but a series of interdisciplinary approaches that can be used to explore many different social domains in many different types of studies. (Phillips and Jorgenson 2002: 1)

1.6 Directions for further reading

Baker, P. and Ellece, S. (2011), *Key Terms in Discourse Analysis*. London: Continuum.

This book provides a very useful set of definitions of terms in the area of discourse analysis. It also provides short biographies of key researchers as well as summaries of key books in the area of discourse analysis.

Gee, J. and Handford, M. (eds) (2011), *The Routledge Handbook to Discourse Analysis*. London: Routledge.

This Handbook contains chapters on a wide range of areas including conversation analysis, genre analysis, corpus-based studies, multimodal discourse analysis and critical discourse analysis. Educational and institutional applications of discourse analysis are discussed as well as topics such as identity, power, ethnicity, intercultural communication, cognition and discourse.

Hall, C. J., Smith, P. H. and Wicaksono, R. (2011), *Mapping Applied Linguistics. A Guide for Students and Practitioners*. London: Routledge. Chapter 4. Discourse analysis.

This chapter is a very accessibly written overview of discourse analysis. Topics covered include linguistic approaches to discourse analysis, social approaches to discourse analysis and current themes in discourse analysis including conversation analysis, corpus linguistics, discursive psychology, multimodality and critical discourse analysis.

Hyland, K. and Paltridge, B. (eds) (2011), *Continuum Companion to Discourse Analysis*. London: Continuum.

This collection of chapters discusses a range of approaches and issues in researching discourse. Assumptions underlying methods and approaches are discussed as are research techniques and instruments appropriate to the goal and method of the research. The second part of the book provides an overview of key areas of discourse studies. In each chapter the authors include a sample study which illustrates the points they are making and identify resources for further reading on the particular approach or issue under discussion.

Jaworski, A. and Coupland, N. (2006), 'Introduction: Perspectives on discourse analysis', in A. Jaworski and N. Coupland (eds), *The Discourse Reader* (2nd edn). London: Routledge, pp. 1–37.

Jaworski and Coupland's introduction to the second edition of their book provides further details on a number of topics that have been presented in this chapter. This includes definitions of the term 'discourse', traditions in the analysis of discourse, speech act theory and pragmatics, conversation analysis, and critical discourse analysis. Strengths and limitations of discourse studies are also discussed.

1.7 Useful website

A list of introductory texts on discourse analysis prepared by Teun van Dijk, editor of *Discourse & Society, Discourse Studies* and *Discourse & Communication*.

www.discourses.org/introductions.pdf

For an extended list of references and further readings see the companion website to this book.

2

Discourse and Society

The previous chapter discussed the social-situatedness of discourse; that is, that spoken and written discourse occurs in particular social and cultural settings and is used and understood in different ways in different social and cultural settings. This chapter will discuss, in more detail, important aspects of the social and cultural settings of spoken and written discourse. It will start with a discussion of the notion of *discourse communities*. It will then discuss the various ways we express our *social identity* through discourse. One of the identities we express is our *gendered identity*. This is a topic that has been discussed at great length (and in changing ways) in the area of discourse analysis and is discussed along with *discourse and identity* in this chapter. The issue of *ideology and discourse*, a further important topic in the area of discourse analysis, is also discussed in this chapter.

2.1 Discourse communities

A key notion in the area of discourse analysis is the concept of *discourse community* (see box on the next page for definition). Swales (1990) provides a set of characteristics for identifying a group of people as members of a particular discourse community. The group must have some set of shared common goals, some mechanisms for communication and some way of providing the exchange of information among its members. The community must have its own particular genres, its own set of specialized terminology and vocabulary and a high level of expertise in its particular area. These goals may be formally agreed upon (as in the case of clubs and associations) 'or they may be more tacit' (24). The ways in which people communicate with each other and exchange information will vary according to the group. This might include meetings, newsletters, casual conversations or a range of other types of written and/or spoken communication. That is, the discourse community will have particular ways of communicating with each other and ways of getting things done that have developed through time. There will also be a threshold level of expertise in the use of the genres the discourse community uses for its communications for someone to be considered a member of that community.

> A *discourse community* is a group of people who share some kind of activity. Members of a discourse community have particular ways of communicating with each other. They generally have shared goals and may have shared values and beliefs. A person is often a member of more than one discourse community. Someone may be a university student, a member of a community volunteer organization and a member of a church group, for example. The ways in which they communicate in each of these groups, and the values and beliefs that are most prominent in each of these groups may vary. There may also be discourse communities within discourse communities. Academic departments, for example, may differ in the ways that they do things and the beliefs and values that they hold, as indeed may other parts of the university.

A telephone call centre is an example of a discourse community. Cameron's (2000) study of telephone call centres in the United Kingdom suggests what some of the characteristics of this kind of discourse community might be. She found, for example, that the telephone operators in the call centres she examined were trained to communicate with customers on the phone in very particular ways. They were trained to answer the phone 'with a smile in their voice'. They were asked to pay attention to the pitch of their voice so that they conveyed a sense of confidence and sincerity in what they said. They were required to talk neither too loudly nor too quietly. They were trained not to drag out what they said, or to speed through what they were saying. They were also required to provide sufficient feedback to their callers so that the callers knew they had been understood.

Call centre workers also have common goals, that of providing the service or making the sales for which the centre is set up, common ways of sharing information among telephone workers, their own particular service call genres and their own terminology and vocabulary for the product or service they are dealing with. There is also a specific level of expertise required for successful call centre workers, both in the knowledge of the product or service, and in the way call centre workers deal with their callers. New workers may be hired for a probationary period, for example, until it is clear that they have met the threshold level of performance required to be members of the particular call centre discourse community. If they do not meet this threshold level, their position with the company may be terminated.

People do, however, have different degrees of membership of discourse communities and at times the borders between them may not always be clear cut. That is, discourse communities may consist of close-knit networks of members such as writers of poetry and their readers, or loose-knit groups of members such as advertising producers, consumers and contributors to online discussion boards. Discourse communities may also be made up of several overlapping groups of people. People, further, may be (and normally are) members of more than just the one single discourse community. A person, thus, may be a call centre operator, a member of a poetry group, a member of a school parent–teacher group and a contributor to an online discussion board. A person may also have to operate in a number of different roles in the same discourse community. For example, a person may be working towards a doctoral degree in one part of a university and in another part of the university be a new (or indeed long-standing) member of academic staff. The 'ways of belonging' may be quite different in each of these parts of the discourse community, as may be the genres that people use and the social relations within the different parts of the discourse community (see Ohashi, Ohashi and Paltridge 2008 for an example of this). Discourse communities also interact with wider speech *communities*. For example, the academic discourse community of students and academics also interacts with the wider speech community of the town or city in which the academic institution is located (Swales 1993). It is for these reasons that some people prefer the term *communities of practice* (Lave and Wenger 1991, Wenger 1998, 2006; Meyerhoff 2002, Eckert and McConnell-Ginet 2007) to the term 'discourse community'.

Devitt (2004: 42–4) adds to this discussion by proposing three types of groups of language users: *communities*, *collectives* and networks. Communities are 'groups of people who share substantial amounts of time together in common endeavors', such as a group of people who all work in the same office. Collectives are groups of people that 'form around a single repeated interest, without the frequency or intensity of contact of a community', such as people who are members of a bee-keeping group, or voluntary members of a community telephone advice service. Networks are groups of people that are not as tightly knit as speech communities with connections being made by one person 'who knows another person, who knows another person', such as connections that are made through email messages sent and received by people who may never have met each other (and perhaps never will), but are participating in a common discourse.

2.2 Language as social and local practice

Speakers, then, often have a repertoire of social identities and discourse community memberships. They may also have *a linguistic repertoire* that they draw on for their linguistic interactions. That is, they may have a number of languages or language varieties they use to interact in within their particular communities. This kind of situation is common in many parts of the world. The choice of language or language variety may be determined by the domain the language is being used in, such as with family, among friends and in religious, educational and employment settings. Social factors such as who we are speaking to, the social context of the interaction, the topic, function and goal of the interaction, social distance between speakers, the formality of the setting or type of interaction and the status of each of the speakers are also important for accounting for the language choice that a person makes in these kinds of settings (Holmes 2008).

The US legal drama *The Good Wife* (CBS 2011) provides an example of the use of language by the same speaker in different social, professional and personal settings. The lead character in the show, Alicia Florrick, returns to the legal profession after many years of being a homemaker when her husband goes to jail following a sex and corruption scandal.

In the show, she is a lawyer, a mother, the wife of a disgraced former state attorney and has a romantic relationship with a colleague in the law firm in which she works. She behaves, and uses language differently, when she is in each of these different situations, depending on whether she in her office, in a court of law or at home in her apartment. The way she speaks also depends on the role which is most prominent at the time, who she is speaking to, and the purpose of the interaction in which she is engaged.

A further example of the connection between language variation and group membership can be seen is Qing Zhang's research (2005, 2008) into the language of managers in state-owned and foreign-owned businesses in Beijing. In her (2005) paper 'A Chinese yuppie in Beijing', she identifies a number of pronunciation features in the use of language by managers of the foreign-owned companies that, she argues, are signs of the development of a cosmopolitan variety of Mandarin Chinese that is associated with a new transnational professional identity. She argues that the possession of this variety gives the speakers *linguistic capital* that, in turn, brings them both material and symbolic rewards in their particular setting.

Zhang (2012) further discusses emerging varieties of Chinese in her study of the use of language by Chinese television talk show hosts. She shows how, through the use of innovative phonological, lexical and syntactic features, as well as a mixing of English and Mandarin, a new cosmopolitan style of Mandarin is employed. This particular style indexes the cool, trendy and cosmopolitan personae of the two hosts. This is a key part of the symbolic repertoire of people who are part of this new cosmopolitan Chinese lifestyle.

Each of these examples highlights the point made by Litossoleti (2006), Eckert (2008) and Pennycook (2010) that language is both a social (Litossoleti and Eckert) and local (Pennycook) practice, and the meanings that are made through the use of language are based in the ideologies, activities and beliefs of what it means to be in a particular place, at a particular time and in a particular setting. In the words of Eckert:

> people fashion their ways of speaking, moving their styles this way or that as they move their personae through situations from moment to moment, from day to day, and through the life course. (2008: 463)

In this process, she argues, 'people do not simply use social meaning – they both produce and reproduce it' (ibid.).

2.3 Discourse and gender

Early work in the analysis of gender and discourse looked at the relationship between the use of language and the biological category of sex. This has now moved to an examination of the ways language is used in relation to the social category, or rather the *socially constructed category*, of *gender*. Thus, from the moment a female child is born and someone says 'It's a girl!' that child learns how to *do* being a girl in the particular society and culture, from the way she talks through to the way she walks, smiles, dresses and combs her hair (Butler 1993, Livia and Hall 1997).

Gender, then, is not just a natural and inevitable consequence of one's biological sex (Weatherall 2002). It is, rather, 'part of the routine, ongoing work of everyday, mundane, social interaction'; that is, 'the product of social practice' (Eckert and McConnell-Ginet 2003: 5). Gender, further, as Swann (2002: 47) has pointed out:

> has come to be seen as highly fluid, or less well defined than it once appeared. In line with gender theory more generally, researchers interested in language and gender have focused increasingly on plurality and diversity amongst female and male language users, and on gender as performativity – something that is 'done' in context, rather than a fixed attribute.

Simone de Beauvoir famously said 'one is not born, but rather becomes a woman'. *Performativity* is based on the view that in saying something, we do, or 'become' it. A person learns, for example, how to do and, in turn 'display', being a woman in a particular social setting, of a particular social class. People perform particular identities through their use of language and other ways of expressing themselves in their interactions with each other. Mostly, this is done unconsciously as we 'repeat acts' such as gestures, movement and ways of using language that signify, or index a particular identity. These acts are not, however, natural nor are they part of the essential attributes of a person. They are part of what people acquire in their interactions with each other

---

Many of the conversations in the TV show *Sex and the City* are examples of the way the lead characters, through their use of language, do gender. In the following extract, Miranda asks Carrie why she accepted her boyfriend's proposal of marriage. In her response, Carrie both enacts and affirms, through her use of language, her gendered identity, that of a woman who, because she loves her boyfriend, has to accept his proposal of marriage:

Miranda: I'm going to ask you an unpleasant question now. Why did you ever say yes?
Carrie: Because I love him . . . a man you love kneels in the street, and offers you a ring. You say yes. That is what you do. (King 2002)

The discussion of how men and women speak, and what they do as they speak, has also been extended to how people speak about men and women. Holmes (2004), for example, compared the use of the terms *woman* and lady and found that the social significance of these terms has changed over the last 30 years. She found *woman*, for example, has moved from being marked as impolite to a situation where this is no longer the case (although *woman* is more frequently used in written British English than in spoken British English). She also found that while *lady/ladies* may be used as a politeness marker in formal settings nowadays, however, in informal settings it is also used to trivialize and patronize (see Mills 2008, Mills and Mullany 2011 for further discussion of sexist language). As Holmes (2004: 156) argues, language choices are often enactments of who's in charge and 'whose values will prevail'.

Identity is, equally, conveyed through writing as well as through speech. Richardson's (2000) study of the use of disparaging language and sexually humiliating formulae by male members of a cricket club in their newsletter to talk about women provides an example of this. Richardson found that the men in her study used their language and the traditional 'women only' discourse of gossip to create solidarity as a group, and to construct their heterosexual masculinity, as did Cameron (1999) in her study of talk between fraternity brothers in the United States. The students writing in Richardson's cricket club newsletter used a language they called 'Dross' as a way of creating an in-group identity as members of the club. One of the members she interviewed said 'It's the one thing that really does set [the Club] apart from other Clubs' (60). The members also gossiped about women, sex and alcohol in the newsletter as a way of creating solidarity among themselves. This was often done through the use of formulaic language such as *Rumour has it that . . .* to indicate that what was about to be said was gossip, and may not necessarily be true. Richardson argues that the members' identities presented in the newsletter are constructed through differentiation. That is, the members of the cricket club defined themselves 'by that which they are not' (65). They wrote, they said, in ways that are different from members of other cricket clubs. They also described the club as a heterosexual-only zone by using terms such as 'poofter' and 'poofs' (derogatory terms for gay men) as out-group naming strategies, reinforcing the expectation that members of the club will be heterosexual and that the identity of homosexual male is not appropriate for membership of the club. The following extract from the newsletter illustrates this:

> [The Cricket Club]'s Presentation Night for 97/98 will be at the MCG [a cricket stadium] on April 3. Players, partners, parents, patriarchs, presenters, poofs (sorry, no poofs) are all welcome to attend. (Richardson 2000: 70)

Hall's (1995) study of the use of language by telephone sex workers in the United States provides a further example of how speakers create gendered identities through their use of language. Not all of the sex workers in Hall's study were heterosexual, although this was the persona they were projecting; nor were they all female. One was a male Mexican American who took pride in being able to 'replicate' Asian, Latina and Black women's personas though his use of accent, intonation, voice quality and choice of vocabulary. The workers, thus, used 'gendered styles to construct sexual meaning' (Cameron and Kulick 2003: 59).

Gender, then, is 'not something a person "has", but something that a person does' (Cameron 2005a: 49). Gender (and in turn other identities) is not a result of what people (already) are but a result of, among other things, the way they talk and what they do.

As Eckert and McConnell-Ginet (2003: 4) argue:

> gender doesn't just exist, but is continually produced, reproduced, and indeed changed through people's performance of gendered acts, as they project their own claimed gender identities, ratify or challenge other's identities, and in various ways support or challenge systems of gender relations and privilege.

Sex and the City provides many examples of the lead characters *doing gender identity* of a certain kind (among other things, independent successful professional New York City women of a certain age and certain social class) not only in the way they talk but also in the way they dress, and the way they behave as they speak to each other, their lovers and their friends. What to some people, then, may seem natural in their interactions is a result of what Butler (1990: 33) calls 'a set of repeated acts' and a 'repeated stylisation of the body'. These gendered identities are then 'reaffirmed and publicly displayed by repeatedly performing particular acts' (Cameron 1999: 444) in accordance with historically and socially constructed cultural norms which define (this particular view of) femininity.

Gender identity then is a complex construction. All levels of language and discourse, as well as aspects of nonverbal and other kinds of behaviour are involved in doing gender (Butler 2004). Gender, further, interacts with other factors such as social class and ethnicity (Eckert 2011). As Holmes observes:

> gender is only one part of a person's social identity, and it is an aspect, which will be more or less salient in different contexts. In some contexts, for example, it may be more important to emphasise one's professional expertise, one's ethnic identity, or one's age than one's gender. (1997: 9)

As Cameron and Kulick (2003: 57) argue, 'the relationship between language and gender is almost always indirect, mediated by something else'. The ways that people speak are, in the first instance, associated with particular roles, activities and personality traits, such as being a mother, gossiping and being modest (Cameron and Kulick 2003). The extent to which these roles, activities and personality traits become associated in a particular culture with being *gendered* lead to these ways of speaking pointing to, or *indexing* (Ochs 1992, Bucholtz and Hall 2005, Bucholtz 2009) a particular gender in the same way that particular ways of speaking may point to, or index, a person's social class or ethnic identity (Litosseliti 2006, Baker 2008). The features of language use which do this are not at a single level such as a particular vowel quality, choice of vocabulary item, grammatical structure or language variety. This occurs, rather, at multiple levels, all at the same time. The use of language may be, in part, intentional and it may, in part, be habitual. Identity, further, is not something that is pre-assigned in fixed social categories. It, rather, is something that emerges in practice, through the use of discourse (Bucholtz 1999, Bucholtz and Hall 2005).

In some cases, a person's different identities may be difficult to separate. As Cameron and Kulick (2003: 58) point out:

> The actual balance between them is not determined in advance by some general principle, but has to be negotiated in specific situations, since meaning is not only in the language itself, but also in the context where language is used by particular speakers for particular purposes.

A person, then, will have a *multiplicity of identities* or *personae* (Eckert 2002) which may be at play all at the same time, at different levels of prominence. They may not all be equally salient at a particular moment (Sunderland and Litosseliti 2002). Rather, one or more of these identities may be foregrounded at different points in time and for different (conscious or unconscious) reasons. Different aspects of identity, further, may be inseparable from each other (Bucholtz 2011). Cameron's (2000) study of the use of language in telephone call centres in the United Kingdom is an example of this. Here there is a mix of both professional and gendered identities, both of which are salient at the same time. Cameron talks about a process of styling the worker where male and female workers are trained to use what is popularly thought of as a feminine communication style and expressive intonation to project rapport and to establish empathy with their callers. The worker's supervisors, managers and 'mystery outside callers' in some cases use checklists as they listen to the workers' calls to ensure the training they have been given is producing a particular gendered style of speech.

The point here, then, is that:

> no way of speaking has only one potential meaning: the meanings it conveys in one context are not necessarily the same ones it conveys in another, and it may also acquire new meanings over time. (Cameron and Kulick 2003: 57)

People, further, '*do* perform gender differently in different contexts, and do sometimes behave in ways we would normally associate with the "other" gender' (Cameron 1999: 445) such as the case of the workers in Cameron's call centre study and the telephone sex workers in Hall's (1995) study.

The relationship between language and sexuality further complicates the topic of gender and discourse by adding the notion of *desire* to the discussion. While gender is something that is socially constructed, sexuality has a much more unconscious basis, based in the notion of desire; that is, a person's intimate desire for connection to others that exceeds their conscious control (Cameron and Kulick 2003). The lead characters' conversations about men in *Sex and the City*, for example, are guided by their sexual desire in just the same way as a personal ad on a gay website is guided by the gay man's desire for intimate connection with another man. So while Carrie and her friends' conversations index their gender, it is their unconscious desire that motivates their desire for intimate connections with men and heterosexual men in general, an identity that they express through their language. Identities, thus, are built moment by moment in social and linguistic interaction (Bucholtz 2011).

A person may, however, perform a certain identity in their conversation, as Carrie and her friends do in *Sex and the City*, where this may not, in fact, be the case. Rock Hudson, for example, did this famously in many of his movie roles (and in the performance of his public persona) where he 'played the straight man', displaying and maintaining male heterosexuality in his discourse when he was actually gay (Kiesling 2002). Jude Law gives a similar simulated gendered performance in the film *Closer* when he has online sex with Julia Roberts' future boyfriend. Masquerading as a heterosexual woman, Jude Law simulates (his view of) a woman having cybersex in an internet chat room. The character at the other end of the line, played by Clive Owen, believes Jude Law's performance to the extent that he makes a date to meet his online sex object the next day, with the view of going to a hotel and having sex with 'her'.

Discussions of language and sexuality, then, take us beyond discussions of language and gender and into the world of language and desire. These desires, further:

> are not simply private, internal phenomena but are produced and expressed – or not expressed – in social interaction, using shared and conventionalised linguistic resources. (Cameron and Kulick 2003: 125)

Carrie and her friends do just this in *Sex and the City*. The meanings that they express are not just the result of their intentions, but are shaped by forces they 'have no conscious awareness of, let alone willed control over' (ibid.). Thus, whereas gendered identities may be socially inducted (and capable of being simulated or, indeed, faked as we have seen above), sexual desires are not, even though these desires and associated identities may be displayed in linguistically recognizable (and regularly repeated) ways (Cameron and Kulick 2003).

Saunston and Kyratzis (2007) discuss how people use language to construct sexual identities and relationships, how this varies across cultures and how people express love and desire through language. Morrish and Leap (2007) discuss 'desire-centred' approaches to the study of language and sexuality, as in the work of Cameron and Kulick (2003) and 'identity-centred' approaches to the study of language and sexuality, as in the work of Bucholtz and Hall (2004) and Morrish and Saunston (2007). Morrish and Saunston (2007) and the other contributors to their volume *New Perspectives on Language and Sexual Identity* present data which illustrates the interrelationship between language, gender and sexuality, arguing that both gender and sexuality are inseparable. In making statements about one, including how it is both performed and constructed through discourse, we are also making statements about the other. Bucholtz and Hall (2004) argue that the move, in some research, to replace identity with desire in language and sexuality research 'is founded on an overly narrow and restrictive vision of what sexuality is, and it misses how sexuality is negotiated beyond the individual psyche in the social, cultural, and political world' (507) (see Wilkinson and Kitzinger 2007, McConnell-Ginet 2011 for further discussion of the relationship between gender, sexuality and discourse).

2.4 Discourse and identity

A person may have a number of *identities*, each of which is more important at different points in time. They may have an identity as a woman, an identity as a mother, an identity as someone's partner and an identity as an office worker, for example. The ways in which people display their identities includes the way they use language and the way they interact with people. Identities are not natural, however. They are constructed, in large part, through the use of discourse. Identity, further, is not something that is fixed and remains the same throughout a person's life. It is something that is constantly constructed and re-constructed as people interact with each other. Part of having a certain identity is that it is recognized by other people. Identity, thus, is a two-way construction.

The earliest studies into the relationship between language and identity were based on a variationist perspective; that is, they looked at the relationship between social variables such as social class in terms of variation in the use of linguistic variables such as certain features of pronunciation, or the use of non-standard grammar. More recent work, however, has taken a *poststructural* perspective on language and identity, seeing identity 'as something that is in constant process' (Swann et al. 2004: 140–1) arguing that it is through language, or rather through discourse, that identity is principally forged.

The information a person 'gives off' about themselves, and in turn, their identity, depends very much on the context, occasion and purpose of the discourse. It also depends on the 'space' and 'place' of the interaction (Blommaert 2005). Cameron (1999) gives an example of this in her discussion of how a group of male US college students construct heterosexual masculinity through the talk that they engage in while watching TV in their college dorm. Richardson (2000) shows something similar in her analysis of the language male cricket club members use to talk about women in the cricket club newsletter they contribute to. In both these studies the men involved perform and enact particular gendered (and sexual) identities which for that moment in time are, for them, socially salient.

It is not just through the performance of identities that they are created, however. It is also by the fact that they are recognized by other participants in the interactions. In Blommaert's (2005: 205) words, 'a lot of what happens in the field of identity is done by others, not by oneself'. In some cases this identity may only be temporary. Equally '[n]ot every identity will have the same range or scope' (211) nor be the same across time and physical space. As Blommaert says, people speak both in and from a place. Place, he argues, 'defines people, both in their eyes and in the eyes of others' (223) as well as attributes certain values to their interactions. People can (and do) he argues, shift places 'frequently and delicately, and each time, in very minimal ways, express different identities' (224). No single aspect of identity (such as gender, race and ethnicity), further, is independent of other aspects of identity (such as social class, occupation and sexuality). Identity, rather, is a social accomplishment that 'operates as a repertoire of styles, or ways of doing things that are associated with culturally recognized social types' (Bucholtz 2010: 2).

Thomas (2007) has explored the issues of language and identity in online chat environments, a very particular place and space. With a focus on adolescent 'cybergirls', she examines how girls use words and images to establish online identities which reflect both their fantasies and their desires in this particular setting. She does an analysis of both the words and the images that they use to create their identities. In their online environment, the cybergirls interacted with words, symbols for words, as well as various other symbols such as emoticons and 'avatars' (visual characters which express a certain identity) in order to establish their online identities. One of her participants, Violetta, talked about how she wrote online to convey a particular persona:

> Violetta: i'd have whole typing styles for people. like, if i were trying to trick someone i knew into thinking i was someone else, i'd type a lot differently than i do normally. a person's typing style can give them away like their voice does. (114)

Thomas found that 'the girls who gain and exercise power in their online worlds are those who know how to use and manipulate words, images and technology' (Thomas 2004: 359). She found that some of what they did online reflected the kind of 'learned social accomplishments' that researchers in the area of language and gender have referred to. Some of what they did, however, reflected fantasies they had about themselves and their desired personae, the online medium giving them a safe and private place to establish these fantasized-about identities.

The identities that people establish online, then, provide an interesting example of how people create identities through their use of language (and other visual devices) that may, in some cases, be separate and distinct from their offline identity. Each of these identities is part of the ongoing process of establishing who we are, and who we want (at least at certain times) to be. It is for this reason that authors such as Thurlow, Lengel and Tomic (2004) prefer to talk about *identity online* rather than *online identity*. Some people communicating online may, indeed, change essential characteristics about themselves (such as their age, ethnicity, race or physical appearance) in order to present an identity online that will be more appealing to the audience they are wanting to communicate with. A Taiwanese user of online chat rooms in Tsang's (2000) study, for example, found he had more success in getting people to chat with him if he said he was Caucasian, rather than Chinese (see Liu 2010a, 2010b; Varis, Wang and Du 2011 for a discussion of online identities in China).

Identity and casual conversation

Many of the interactions in the show *Sex and the City* are examples of the use of discourse to create, express and establish social (and other) identities. A common way in which the characters in the show do this is through their use of the genre casual conversation. As Eggins and Slade (1997: 6) argue:

> Despite its sometimes aimless appearance and apparently trivial content, casual conversation is, in fact, a highly structured, functionally motivated, semantic activity. Motivated by interpersonal needs continually to establish who we are, how we relate to others, and what we think of how the world is, casual conversation is a critical linguistic site for the negotiation of such important dimensions of our social identity as gender, generational location, sexuality, social class membership, ethnicity, and subcultural and group affiliations.

Eggins and Slade argue that people do not engage in casual conversations just to 'kill time', but rather to negotiate social identities as well as to negotiate, clarify and extend interpersonal relations. As they put it:

> The apparent triviality of casual conversation disguises the significant interpersonal work it achieves as interactants enact and confirm social identities and relations. (16)

They describe this as the central paradox of casual conversation. As they argue, casual conversation is the type of talk in which people feel most relaxed, most spontaneous and most themselves, 'yet casual conversation is a critical site for the social construction of reality'. Casual conversations do a number of things which are crucial to discussions of language and identity. They establish solidarity 'through the confirmation of similarities', and they assert autonomy 'through the exploration of differences' (ibid.).

The way in which language is used in casual conversations, like all spoken interactions, is influenced by the relationship between the people speaking, the frequency with which they come into contact with each other, the degree of involvement they have with each other and their sense of affiliation for each other. In the case of *Sex and the City*, each of the four female characters knows each other extremely well. Although they are the best of friends, they are each quite different and from quite diverse backgrounds. As they meet together, they share their experiences and negotiate their understandings of (among other things) life, love, men and sex. As Carrie and her friends talk, they construct themselves in a way which signifies (their view of) desirable Western women of a certain social class in a certain physical and social setting through their use of the genre of casual conversation.

Understanding the social and cultural context of the *Sex and the City* conversations is critical to understanding the identities that are being expressed and negotiated in many of the conversations. What to some people may seem natural in their interactions is a result of Butler's (2004) 'sets of repeated acts' and 'repeated stylisations of the body'; that is, the acts that they repeatedly perform which reaffirm and publicly display their views of themselves, and in turn their social identities as, among other things, independent successful professional New York City women of a certain age and certain social class (see Paltridge, Thomas and Liu 2011 for further discussion of this; also Richardson 2010, Piazza, Rossi and Bednarek 2011 for further discussion of television dramatic dialogue).

When we speak (or write), then, we are telling other people 'something about ourselves' (Cameron 2001: 170) and relating to people in particular ways. Identity, thus, is a joint, two-way production. Identity, further, is not just a matter of using language in a way that reflects a particular identity. It is rather a socially constructed self that people continually co-construct and reconstruct in their interactions with each other. This leads to different ways of doing identity with different people in different situations. A person's identity then:

> is not something fixed, stable and unitary that they acquire early in life and possess forever afterwards. Rather identity is shifting and multiple, something people are continually constructing and reconstructing in their encounters with each other in the world. (ibid.)

Identity is a 'negotiated experience' in which we 'define who we are by the way we experience our selves . . . as well as by the ways we and others reify our selves' (Wenger 1998: 149). Identities are not fixed, but constantly being reconstructed and negotiated through the ways we do things and ways of belonging (or not) to a group (Casanave 2002). Our identities are further developed as we increase our participation in particular communities of practice. These identities, further, are based on shared sets of values, agreed-upon cultural understandings and the ideologies which underlie our use of spoken and written discourse.

These communities of practice, further, may be imagined (Anderson 1991) or they may be virtual (Meadows and Waugh 2010). Pavlenko and Norton (2007) discuss the notion of *imagined communities* in relation to English language learners arguing that learners' desired memberships of imagined communities influence their motivation for learning and the investment they make in their learning. Meadows (2009) uses the notion of *imagined national communities of practice* in his discussion of the ways in which students may invest in this notion as a way of maintaining their position, and privilege, in their more local (and actual) community. Thomas' (2007) *Youth Online* provides many examples of how people in online worlds create and establish identities that may be quite different, at times, from their offline 'actual' identities.

Identity and written academic discourse

Identity is as much an issue in written discourse as it is in spoken discourse. This is particularly the case in student academic writing. Hyland (2002c) discusses the view that is often presented to students that academic writing is faceless, impersonal discourse. Students are told, he says, 'to leave their personalities at the door' when they write and not use personal pronouns such as 'I' which show what is being said is the student's view or place in things. As Hyland (2002c: 352) argues, 'almost everything we write says something about us and the sort of relationship that we want to set up with our readers'. Indeed, one of the ways that expert academic writers do this, in some academic disciplines at least, is through the use of the pronoun 'I'.

Establishing writer identity is, however, something that is often difficult for second language writers. This is often complicated by students bringing a different writer 'voice' from their first language setting to the second language writing situation (Fox 1994). Students may come from backgrounds where they have considerable standing in their field of study and find it difficult to be told they need to take on the voice of a novice academic writer, and hide their point of view, as they write in their second language. Hirvela and Belcher (2001) argue that teachers need to know more about the ways students present themselves in their first language writing and about their first language and culture identities so they can help students deal with the issue of identity in their second language writing.

As Casanave (2002: 23) argues in her book *Writing Games*, learning to belong to a community of practice can take time and a great deal of effort. It can be filled with tensions and conflict. As she points out:

> Newcomers inevitably feel the foreignness of unfamiliar practices, the unwieldiness of new forms and tools of communication, and relationships with more experienced practitioners that are not necessarily harmonious.

Work in the area of *academic literacies* (Lea and Street 2006, Lillis and Scott 2007, Blommaert, Street and Turner 2008, Street 2010, Wingate and Tribble 2011) provides a way of thinking about some of these issues. An academic literacies perspective on academic writing sees learning to write in academic settings as learning to acquire a repertoire of linguistic practices which are based on complex sets of discourses, identities and values. Here, students learn to switch practices between one setting and another, learning to understand, as they go, why they are doing this, and what each position implies. This means understanding what is required of writers at a particular level of study in terms of attitudes to knowledge and how this is revealed through language. This also involves how a writer, at the particular level, shows their command of their subject matter and their ability to critically reflect on it. That is, students need to show both their authorial identity and authority through the text they are writing in such a way that their reader will recognize and respond to this (see Paltridge and Starfield 2007, Paltridge et al. 2009 where this is discussed further).

Ivanic (1998) discusses the notion of self-representation in academic writing and, in particular, the concept of the *discoursal self*. As she points out, there are always a range of alternatives writers can choose from in order to represent themselves in a text, their relationship with their readers, and their relationship to the knowledge they are discussing. This can be through the use of *stance* features such as *self mentions* (*I, we, my*), *hedges* (*might, perhaps*), *boosters* (*definitely, in fact*) and *attitude markers* such as *unfortunately* and *surprisingly*, which express their attitude towards a proposition (Hyland 2005b). Writers also draw on *engagement* strategies such as *reader pronouns, personal asides, appeals to shared knowledge, directives* and *questions*. Examples of each of these strategies are shown in Table 2.1. Through the use of these strategies, writers both acknowledge and recognize the presence

Table 2.1 Examples of stance and engagement strategies in academic writing (based on Hyland 2005c)

Strategy	Examples
Stance	
Hedges	*Our results suggest* that rapid freeze and thaw rates during artificial experiments in the laboratory *may* cause artificial formation of embolism.
Boosters	With a few interesting exceptions, we *obviously* do not see a static image as moving. This seems *highly* dubious.
Attitude markers	The first clue of this emerged when we noticed a *quite extraordinary* result.
Self-mentions	This experience contains ideas derived from reading *I* have done.
Engagement	
Reader pronouns	Although *we* lack knowledge about a definitive biological function for . . .
Personal asides	And – *as I believe many TESOL professional will readily acknowledge* – critical thinking has now begun to make its mark.
Appeals to shared knowledge	Of course, *we know* that the indigenous communities of today have been reorganized by the catholic church . . .
Directives	*It is important to note* that these results do indeed warrant the view that . . .
Questions	*Is it, in fact, necessary to choose between nature and nurture?*

of their readers at the same time as they position themselves in relation to the outcomes of their research (Hyland 1998a, 1998b, 2002a, 2005c, 2009a, 2009b, 2010, 2011).

As Hyland (2009a, 2012) points out, in order to be successful students need to represent themselves in a way that is valued by their discipline as well as adopt the values, beliefs and identity of a successful academic writer in their area of study. It involves 'negotiating a self which is coherent and meaningful to both the individual and the group' (Hyland 2011a: 11). This identity, further, is only successful by the extent to which it is recognized by the discipline and the group (Hyland 2010). Students, thus, need to choose ways of expressing themselves that will resonate with members of the group so that their claims to be one of them will be seen to be credible and valid (Hyland 2011a). This kind of writing, thus, is highly situated (Barton, Hamilton and Ivanic 2000) and requires an in-depth understating of the values and ideologies of the discipline in which the student is working, the subject of the next section of this chapter (see Hyland 2012 for further discussion of identity and academic writing).

2.5 Discourse and ideology

The values and ideologies which underlie texts tend to be 'hidden' rather than overtly stated. As Threadgold (1989) observes, texts are never ideology-free nor are they objective. Nor can they be separated from the social realities and processes they contribute to maintaining. For Threadgold, spoken and written genres are not just linguistic categories but 'among the very processes by which dominant ideologies are reproduced, transmitted and potentially changed' (107). In her view, a spoken or written genre is never just the reformulation of a linguistic model, but always the performance of a politically and historically significant process.

There are a number of ways in which ideology might be explored in a text. The analysis may start by looking at textual features in the text and move from there to explanation and interpretation of the analysis. This may include tracing underlying ideologies from the linguistic features of a text, unpacking particular biases and ideological presuppositions underlying the text and relating the text to other texts, and to readers' and speakers' own experiences and beliefs (Clark 1995).

One aspect that might be considered in this kind of analysis is the *framing* (Gee 2004, Blommaert 2005) of the text; that is, how the content of the text is presented, and the sort of angle or perspective the writer, or speaker, is taking. Closely related to framing is the notion of *foregrounding*; that is, what concepts and issues are emphasized, as well as what concepts or issues are played down or backgrounded (Huckin 1997, 2010) in the text. The following scene from *Sex and the City* is an example of this. Carrie had just discovered an engagement ring in her boyfriend, Aiden's, overnight bag. She then went into the kitchen and vomited. She is telling her friends about this incident:

Charlotte:	You're getting engaged!
Carrie:	I threw up. I saw the ring and I threw up. That's not normal.
Samantha:	That's my reaction to marriage.
Miranda:	What do you think you might do if he asks?
Carrie:	I don't know.
Charlotte:	Just say yessss!!!
Carrie:	Well, it hasn't been long enough has it?
Charlotte:	Trey and I got engaged after only a month.
Samantha:	How long before you separated?
Charlotte:	We're together now and that's what matters. When it's right you just know.
Samantha:	Carrie doesn't know.
Carrie:	Carrie threw up.
Samantha:	So it might not be right . . .

(King 2001)

A key cultural value is foregrounded in this conversation: if a man asks a woman to marry him she should 'Just say yes' (also the title of the episode). Other values are backgrounded, or rather omitted, such as Carrie's views on Aiden's occupation, ethnic background and social class, possibly because the audience of the show already knows this (not because, in this case, they are not relevant).

Equally important is what attitudes, points of view and values the text presupposes. A *presupposition* present in this conversation is that Aiden will formally propose to Carrie (which he later does). A further presupposition is that Aiden will ask her this directly and that she should give a direct response. This is very much an (English) culture-based assumption. Saville-Troike (2003), for example, discusses marriage proposals in Japanese showing that, in Japanese a marriage proposal is not always directly stated and, if it is, it is not always directly responded to. An example of this is when the Japanese Crown Prince Naruhito proposed to his bride-to-be Masako (on a hunting trip). Masako did not accept the proposal immediately but took nearly 3 months to give a reply. When she did she said 'Will I really do?' and 'If I can be of any help to you, I will humbly accept'. The Crown Prince replied 'I will protect you throughout your life' (Asahi Newspaper 1993).

A further example of presupposition is the view expressed in the *Sex and the City* scene of marriage being based (among other things) in romantic love and desire. This is also a very culture-specific view of marriage. Farrer (2002) describes how this is only a recent phenomenon in China, for example, where marriage was until recently a family business, arranged by parents in accordance with social hierarchies, as Zhang in her (1986) book *Love Must Not be Forgotten* says, 'part of a mind-set passed down from feudal times'. Arranged marriages (as opposed to 'love marriages') are still surprisingly popular in Japan. In earlier times, in Japan, as in China, marriage was a community-centred rather than a person-centred matter. Even today there is an Arranged Marriages Association in Japan, which promotes the benefits of this kind of marriage (Davies and Ikeno 2002).

More recently, however, there has been a romantic revolution in China (Farrer 2002) with young urban people now expecting to be able to choose their own marriage partners and to marry for love. The award-winning movie *House of Flying Daggers* by the Chinese filmmaker Zhang Yimou (2005), for example, is a glorification of romantic love and desire, telling the story of three people who sacrifice everything for love. The overlying theme of this film suggests a change in the social *semiotic of desire* in present day Chinese society, in Eckert's (2002: 109) words, 'the most powerful force in the maintenance of gender order'.

A further presupposition underlying the Sex *and the City* conversation is the issue of who will propose to whom; that is, the *agency* of the action being discussed in the conversation. It is a clear assumption here that the man will propose to the woman, not the other way round. As independent as Carrie and her friends are, it is less likely that they would propose to a man (or that they would refuse him, should he ask). Even though the leading characters in the show take an active role in their pursuit of sex and many of the other things they want from life, it is the man who initiates the action and who has the most power in the situation. Carrie waits for Aiden to propose, not the other way round.

This, of course, is just a single reading of *Sex and the City*. People from other cultures and with different social, cultural and political points of view will, of course, read Sex *and the City* in quite different ways from how I have read it here. For some people, a show such as *Sex and the City* mirrors their social identities and ideologies. For others, however, it challenges social identities and ideologies. What may seem natural and unsurprising to some people as they view a show such as *Sex and the City* is by no means 'natural' and for many people may be far from unsurprising. It is also important to point out that, as Negra (2004) suggests, some of the concerns it discusses 'would be utterly unrecognisable to whole groups of American women', and others. Notwithstanding, *Sex and the City* provides an excellent example of its lead characters doing gender (and many other identities) as they negotiate, clarify and extend their multiple gendered identities in their conversations about living in the particular place and space of the city.

The critical framing of texts, then, can help us unpack some of the assumptions underlying the use of language and what the text is aiming to do where we stand back and look at them in relation to their social and cultural values. It also helps remind us of the importance of considering the social, political underpinnings of spoken and written discourse, as well as helping us unpack the ideological thrust of seemingly ordinary, everyday genres (Johns 2006).

Written texts are, of course, as similarly ideologically loaded as spoken texts. An area of research where this has been taken up in particular is in the examination of media discourse. KhosraviNik (2005), for example, discusses discourses of refugees, asylum seekers and immigrants in the UK press. He shows how while *The Times* refrains from explicitly reproducing stereotypes in its discussion of these groups, the *Daily Mail*, in general, perpetuates existing stereotypes, thus, reproducing negative attitudes among its readers. In KhosraviNik's view, while the *Daily Mail* reflects existing prejudices, *The Times* creates and introduces newer versions of prejudice.

Montgomery (2011) focuses on different representations of the 'war on terror', showing how in UK newspapers the expression *war on terror* is often cited in quotation marks, suggesting the newspapers treat the term as being somewhat problematic, attributing the term to leading politicians rather than taking it on as part of their own discourse. Kandil and Belcher (2011) examine reports on the Israeli-Palestinian conflict in CNN, BBC and Al-Jazeera web-based news pages. They found a commonly occurring term in the web pages was the word *terrorism*. Al-Jazeera, they observed, frequently problematized the term by prefacing it with *so-called* and *described as*. The BBC, like the newspapers in Montgomery's (2011) study, put the term in quotes, while CNN did not distance itself from the term in either of these ways, suggesting more support for this notion than the other two sources, and thereby encouraging their readers to view it this way as well.

Wang (2009) examines gender stereotypes in Taiwanese tabloid gossip columns showing how female performing artists are typically presented as being concerned with their appearance and social pressures in relation to marriage and sexuality whereas portrayals of male performing artists in Taiwanese tabloids often focus on their (very many) love affairs. Wang conducted a survey in order to uncover the extent to which these values were representative of views that were held in the broader community. He found that many of the stereotypes he had identified in his analysis were reflective of widely held views in the community, highlighting what he calls 'the intense relationship between sensationalism and Taiwanese tabloid culture' (768) and the connection between giving readers what they want to read and increasing the audience and market share of the newspaper.

Analyses of this kind, then, take us beyond the level of description to a deeper understanding of texts and provides, as far as might be possible, some kind of explanation of why a text might be as it is and what it is aiming to do. They look at the relationship between language, social norms and values and aim to describe, interpret and explain this relationship. In doing so, they aim to provide a way of exploring and perhaps challenging some of the hidden and 'out of sight' social, cultural and political values that underlie the use of spoken and written discourse.

2.6 Summary

This chapter has looked at discourse analysis from a number of social and other perspectives. It has introduced several notions that are important for discussions of language from a discourse perspective. It has also aimed to show how some of these notions have changed since they were first introduced (such as language and gender and language and identity) and how these notions are currently viewed in discussions of the use of spoken and written discourse. The chapter which follows looks at discourse from a *pragmatics* perspective and provides further detail on how language does what it does and means more than it says in the context of our day-to-day communications.

2.7 Discussion questions

(1) What discourse communities are you a member of? Do any of these communities overlap? How similar, or different, is your use of language in each these communities? Complete the chart below as you carry out your discussion.

Discourse community	Use of language

(2) What factors influence the way you use language when you speak? For example, is your use of language influenced by your ethnic identity, your level (or kind) of education, your age, your gender or your occupation? How do you think your use of language reflects these sorts of categories? Complete the chart below as you carry out your discussion.

Factor	Use of language
Ethnic identity	
Education	
Age	
Gender	
Occupation	
Other identity	

(3) Think of ways in which your identity has been constructed through ways of doing things and ways in which you use language in a group. You may look at your identity as a student in your class, or as a member of another social group that you belong to. Complete the chart below.

Group	Ways of doing things in the group	Ways of using language that shows you belong to the group

2.8 Data analysis projects

(1) Think of ways in which how your use of language reflects the identity you have of yourself. Tape-record a conversation between you and someone else. Analyse your conversation and identify aspects of the conversation which you think reflect the way you are presenting yourself to the other person. These might, for example, include the use of particular vocabulary, the use of a particular voice quality or through the way in which you express a particular point of view.

(2) Can you think of situations in which the way(s) you interact is influenced by your gender? Tape-record a conversation between you and someone else where you think this is relevant. Analyse your conversation and identify aspects of the conversation which you think reflect your 'gendered identity'. This might, for example, be through the use of a particular voice quality, or the ways in which you interact linguistically with the person you are speaking to.

(3) Think of a situation where your gender is less important than other factors in the way you interact. Tape-record a conversation between you and someone else where you think this is relevant. Analyse your conversation and identify aspects of the conversation which you think reflect your most prominent identity in the conversation.

(4) Choose a spoken or written text which you think reflects certain stereotyped (or otherwise) views of how people interact and their views on certain issues. Analyse the text according to the following categories:
- foregrounding
- backgrounding
- presuppositions
- agency

To what extent do you think the text reflects certain presuppositions and ideologies?

2.9 Exercises

Exercise 1: Discourse and gender

The following extract is from Holmes's (2006: 196–7) *Gendered Talk at Work*. The context is a regular weekly meeting of an IT project team in a large commercial organization. There are six male speakers at the meeting. They are discussing a company dinner they will be holding soon. One of the speakers, Eric, has a reputation for getting drunk and misbehaving at company functions. There is considerable overlap in this conversation, shown by the symbols / \. The symbols ( ) indicate an unintelligible word or phrase. Paralinguistic features (e.g. laughing) are in square brackets, colons indicate start/finish. In what ways do the speakers seem to be doing stereotypical masculinities in this interaction?

1	Callum	you'll be off to the kitchen pretty quickly though, /won't you?\
2	Eric	/yeah I \ know yeah
3	Barry	cooking
4	Eric	after that third bottle of wine I'll be in there / ( ) \
5	Barry	/[laughs]\ [laughs]: making dinner: [laughs]
6	Eric	/I haven't\ I haven't done that kitchen so /that'll\ be one
7	Callum	/yeah\
8	Eric	for the collection
9	Barry	[laughs] [laughs] you /can't you can't\ remember it
10	Eric	/ ( ) [laughs]\
11	Marco	there's a lot of kitchens he doesn't remember

(Source: Holmes 2006: 196–7)

Exercise 2: Second language identities

The following extract is from Schmidt's (1983) study of Wes, a Japanese photographer living in Hawai'i. Wes is a capable second language speaker of English in that he is able to produce language that is sociolingistically appropriate to a situation. He has few communication breakdowns and is able to negotiate most speech situations. There are some features of his speech that mark him as a second language speaker of English, however, notably his use of grammar and his pronunciation. There are, though, strategies that he employs that make up for this. Look at the following extract and identify what these strategies might be. (In this data / indicates the end of a chunk of talk, NS refers to the native speaker (Doug) Wes is talking to.)

1	Wes	Doug / you have dream after your life?
2	NS	whaddya mean?
3	Wes	OK / everybody have some dream / what doing / what you want / after your life / you have it?
4	NS	you mean after I die?
5	Wes	no no / means next couple years or long time / OK / before I have big dream / I move to States / now I have it / this kind you have it?
6	NS	Security I suppose / not necessarily financial / although that looms large at the present time

(Source: Schmidt 1983: 165)

Exercise 3: Identity online

Look at the following extract from Thomas' (2007) book *Youth Online*. What features does Violetta employ when she writes online that are typical of online discourse?

1	Violetta	Well. I sprinkle lots of my typing with stuff like '*grins*' (which I've found myself doing on notes irl. ppl must thnk I'm crazy! heheheh)
2	Violetta	You also have to make use of actions such as raising eyebrows, and rolling your eyes
3	Violetta	Uses it wayyyyyy too much

(Source: Thomas 2007: 114)

What do you do when you write online to show you are part of the group in English, or in another language?

Exercise 4: Academic writing and identity

Read the section in this chapter on academic writing and identify stance features such as *hedges*, *boosters*, *attitude markers* and *self mention* in the following examples of academic writing.

1	We propose several possible reasons of this.
2	On this point, we must definitely follow Hegel's intuitions.
3	Still, I believe that Dworkin's investment model has remarkable resonance and extraordinary potential power.
4	What we found interesting about this context, however, is the degree of uniformity of their norms and attitudes.
5	There is a strong tendency for the bubbles to redissolve at the time of thaw.
6	Of course, I do not contend that there are no historical contingencies.

(Source: Hyland 2009a: 75–6)

2.10 Directions for further reading

Benwell, B. and Stokoe, E. (2006), *Discourse and Identity*. Edinburgh: Edinburgh University Press.

Benwell and Stokoe's book takes an interdisciplinary view on discourse and identity drawing on work in the areas of sociology, ethnomethodology, critical theory, feminism, philosophy, cultural studies and human geography. The book looks at texts across a wide variety of discourse contexts.

Block, D. (2010), 'Researching language and identity', in B. Paltridge and A. Phakiti. (eds), *Continuum Companion to Research Methods in Applied Linguistics*. London: Continuum, pp. 233–349.

This chapter provides an overview of issues in researching language and identity. It discusses research strategies for doing identity research and, in particular, narrative analysis. Block provides a sample study to show how the issues he has discussed can be taken up in this kind of research.

Cameron, D. (2007), *The Myth of Mars and Venus: Do Men and Women Really Speak Different Languages?* Cambridge: Cambridge University Press.

The Myth of Mars and Venus is an accessible review and critique of the literature on language and gender. Cameron shows how many popular writers have been both selective and inaccurate in their discussions on this topic. Cameron (2010) continues this argument in her paper 'Sex/gender, language and the new biologism'.

Deckert, S. and Vickers, C. H. (2011), *An Introduction to Sociolinguistics*. London: Continuum. Chapter 2. Identity as central theme in linguistics.

This chapter is an overview of the notion of identity in sociolinguistics research. The co-construction of identity through language as well as gendered, social and cultural identities are discussed. Identity is also discussed in relation to multilingual speakers, native and non-native speakers, and migration.

Lin, A. and Kubota, R. (2011), 'Discourse and race', in K. Hyland and B. Paltridge (eds), *Continuum Companion to Discourse Analysis*. London: Continuum, pp. 277–90.

Lin and Kubota discuss the discursive construction of race, drawing on critical race theory, whiteness studies, positioning theory and storyline analysis. They discuss how racist ideologies are produced and reproduced in elitist discourses. They then describe a study which examined messages posted on a Hong Kong-based online discussion forum of *Dae Jang Geum*, a Korean TV drama, looking at how the Self and Other are constructed in the discourse.

Meyerhoff, M. (2011), *Introducing Sociolinguistics* (2nd edn). London: Routledge.

Meyerhoff's book contains excellent chapters on language and social class, social networks, communities of practice, language and gender and politeness. The development of each of these issues is discussed in detail, in both linguistic and social terms. Key terms are explained alongside the main text in each of the chapters.

Talbot, M. (2010), *Language and Gender* (2nd edn). Cambridge: Polity Press.

This second edition of Talbot's book is an excellent review of research in language and gender as well as issues more broadly related to discourse and identity research. The book is strongly influenced by the notions of construction and performance in language and identity research. Examples are given of language, gender and consumerism; language and masculinities; language, gender and sexualities and critical perspectives on gender identity.

For an extended list of references and further readings see the companion website to this book.

3
Discourse and Pragmatics

This chapter presents an overview of research in the area of *pragmatics* that is of relevance to people interested in looking at language from a discourse perspective. It discusses the relationship between language and context, a key issue in the area of pragmatics as well as in the area of discourse analysis. It also looks at ways in which people typically perform *speech acts* (such as apologizing or requesting, etc.) in spoken and written discourse. The chapter discusses the reasons we choose to perform a speech act in a particular way such as, for example, reasons of *politeness*. The ways in which people perform speech acts across cultures is also discussed, as well as what happens when people do not follow culture-specific expectations for performing particular speech acts.

3.1 What is pragmatics?

> *Pragmatics* is the study of meaning in relation to the context in which a person is speaking or writing. This includes social, situational and textual context. It also includes background knowledge context; that is, what people know about each other and about the world. Pragmatics assumes that when people communicate with each other they normally follow some kind of cooperative principle; that is, they have a shared understanding of how they should cooperate in their communications. The ways in which people do this, however, varies across cultures. What may be a culturally appropriate way of saying or doing something in one culture may not be the same in another culture. The study of this use of language across cultures is called *cross-cultural pragmatics*.

The relationship between linguistic form and communicative function is of central interest in the area of pragmatics and, as Cameron (2001) argues, is highly relevant to the field of discourse analysis. We need to know the communicative function of an utterance, that is, what it is 'doing' in the particular setting in order to assign a discourse label to the utterance in the place of the overall discourse. For example, if someone says 'The bus was late' they may be complaining about the bus service (and so we label the stage of the conversation 'complaint'), they may be explaining why they are late as a follow up to an apology (and so we label the stage of the conversation 'explanation') or they may be doing something else. We also need to know what this meaning is in order to understand, at a broader level, what people typically say and do as they perform particular genres in particular social and cultural settings.

3.2 Language, context and discourse

An understanding of how language functions in context is central to an understanding of the relationship between what is said and what is understood in spoken and written discourse. The *context of situation* (see Chapter 1) of what someone says is, therefore, crucial to understanding and interpreting the meaning of what is being said. This includes the physical context, the social context and the mental worlds and roles of the people involved in the interaction. Each of these impacts on what we say and how other people interpret what we say in spoken and written discourse.

A conversation between two people in a restaurant may mean different things to the actual people speaking, something different to a 'side participant' in the conversation (such as someone sitting next to one of the speakers), something different to a 'bystander' (such as the waiter) and again something different to someone who may be eavesdropping the conversation (Verschueren 1999). Equally, a student's assignment written for a law course takes on a different meaning if it is re-typed on the letterhead of a law firm and addressed to a client. The text then takes on the status and function of 'a piece of legal advice' and the reader's interpretation of the text is significantly different from the way in which it would have been read by the student's professor (Freedman 1989). The linguistic context in terms of what has been said and what is yet to be said in the discourse also has an impact on the intended meaning and how someone may interpret this meaning in spoken and written discourse.

There are, then, a number of key aspects of context that are crucial to the production and interpretation of discourse. These are the *situational context* in terms of what people 'know about what they can see around them', the *background knowledge context* in terms of what people 'know about each other and the world' and the *co-textual context* in terms of what people 'know about what they have been saying' (Cutting 2008: 5). Background knowledge context includes cultural knowledge and interpersonal knowledge. That is, it includes what people know about the world, what they know about various areas of life, what they know about each other (Cutting 2008) and what they know about the norms and expectations of the particular *discourse community* (see Chapter 2) in which the communication is taking place. Contextual knowledge also includes social, political and cultural understandings that are relevant to the particular communication (Celce-Murcia and Olshtain 2000).

As Thomas (1995: 22) explains:

> meaning is not something that is inherent in the words alone, nor is it produced by the speaker alone or the hearer alone. Making meaning is a dynamic process, involving the negotiation of meaning between speaker and hearer, the context of utterance (physical, social and linguistic), and the meaning potential of an utterance.

Meaning, thus, is produced in interaction. It is jointly accomplished by both the speaker and the listener, or the writer and their reader. It involves social, psychological and cognitive factors that are relevant to the production and interpretation of what a speaker (or writer) says, and what a hearer (or reader) understands by what is said (Thomas 1995).

3.3 Speech acts and discourse

Two influential works in the area of pragmatics relevant to the area of discourse analysis are Austin's (1962) *How to Do Things With Words* and Searle's (1969) *Speech Acts*. Austin and Searle argued that language is used to 'do things' other than just refer to the truth or falseness of particular statements. Their work appeared at a time when logical positivism was the prevailing view in the philosophy of language. The logical positivist view argued that language is always used to describe some fact or state of affairs, and unless a statement can be tested for truth or falsity it is basically meaningless. Austin and Searle observed that there are many things that we say which cannot meet these kinds of truth conditions but which are, nevertheless, valid and which do things that go beyond their literal meaning. They argued that in the same way that we perform physical acts, we also perform acts by using language. That is, we use language to give orders, to make requests, to give warnings or to give advice; in other words, to do things that go beyond the literal meaning of what we say.

A central issue which underlies this is the relationship between the literal meaning, or *propositional content*, of what someone says and what the person intends by what he/she says. Thus, if someone says 'It's hot in here' they are not only referring to the temperature, they may also be requesting someone to do something such as turn on the air conditioning. What we say, then, often has both a literal meaning and an *illocutionary meaning* (or *illocutionary force*); that is, a meaning which goes beyond what someone, in a literal sense, has said.

Austin argued that there are three kinds of acts which occur with everything we say. These are the *locutionary act*, the *illocutionary act* and the *perlocutionary act*. The locutionary act refers to the literal meaning of the actual words (such as 'It's hot in here' referring to the temperature). The illocutionary act refers to the speaker's intention in uttering the words (such as a request for someone to turn on the air conditioning). The perlocutionary act refers to the effect this utterance has on the thoughts or actions of the other person (such as someone getting up and turning on the air conditioning).

The following example on a bus illustrates this.

Bus driver: This bus won't move until you boys move in out of the doorway.

Clearly the bus driver is doing more than making a statement. He is also telling the boys to move. The locutionary act, in this case, is the driver saying he won't start the bus with people standing in the doorway, the illocutionary act is an order and the perlocutionary act is the boys moving inside the bus.

It is not always easy, however, to identify the illocutionary force of what someone says, as it may also depend on the stage in the discourse as well as the social context in which the person is speaking. An illocutionary force, further, might be spread over more than one utterance. The example below, where the sales request is spread over several utterances, illustrates this:

A:	Hello, welcome to Hungry Jack's. Can I take your order please?
B:	Can I have a Whopper with egg and bacon . . .
A:	Would you like cheese with that?
B:	Yes please . . . and a junior Whopper with cheese . . . and large fries please.
A:	Would you like any drinks or dessert with that?
B:	No thank you.
A:	OK . . . that's a Whopper with cheese, egg and bacon, a Whopper junior with cheese and large fries.
B:	Yes. Thank you.
A:	OK . . . Please drive through.

It is also not unusual for what someone says to have more than a single illocutionary force. For example, 'What are you doing tonight?' might be both a question and an invitation. A person might reply 'I still haven't finished my homework' treating the utterance as both a question and invitation which they decide not to accept. They may equally reply 'Nothing special. What do you feel like doing?' providing an answer to the question but this time accepting the (as yet unspoken) invitation.

Direct and indirect speech acts

Sometimes when we speak we do mean exactly what we say. The following example from the BBC *Panorama* interview with the Princess of Wales is an example of this. Here, the interviewer asks Diana if she allowed her friends to talk to the author of her biography, Andrew Morton:

Bashir: Did you allow your friends, your close friends, to speak to Andrew Morton?
Diana: Yes I did. Yes I did. (BBC 1995)

Often we do, however, say things indirectly. That is, we often intend something that is quite different from the literal meaning of what we say. For example a common expression on an invitation to a party is 'to bring a plate'. This may, to someone who is not familiar with this kind of cultural convention, be interpreted as a request to bring an (empty) plate to the party. In fact, it is asking someone to bring food to the party, not necessarily on a plate. Equally, if someone calls someone to ask them to come to their home for dinner and the person being asked says 'Can I bring anything?' in many countries the host will say 'No, just bring yourself' whereas, in fact, they expect the guest to bring wine (or in some countries something such as flowers for the host) with them to the dinner.

The example above of 'Can I have a Whopper with egg and bacon . . .?' also illustrates this. Here, the customer is not asking about their ability to buy a hamburger – the literal meaning of the sentence – but making a sales request. This is very common in service encounters where 'can' is often used to refer to something other than ability or permission.

Felicity conditions and discourse

An important notion in speech act theory is the concept of *felicity conditions*. For a speech act to 'work', Austin argued that there are a number of conditions that must be met. The first of these is that there must be a generally accepted procedure for successfully carrying out the speech act, such as inviting someone to a wedding through the use of a formal written wedding invitation, rather than (for many people) an informal email message. Also the circumstances must be appropriate for the use of the speech act. That is, someone must be getting married. The person who uses the speech act must be the appropriate person to use it in the particular context – such as the bride or groom's family, or in some cases the bride or groom, inviting the person to the wedding. A friend of the couple getting married cannot, for example, without the appropriate authority invite someone to the wedding.

Austin argued that this procedure must be carried out correctly and completely. And the person performing the speech act must (in most circumstances) have the required thoughts, feelings and intentions for the speech act to be 'felicitous'. That is, the communication must be carried out by the right person, in the right place, at the right time and, normally, with a certain intention or it will not 'work'. If the first two of these conditions are not satisfied, the act will not be achieved and will 'misfire'. If the third of these conditions does not hold, then the procedure will be 'abused'.

Rules versus principles

Searle took Austin's work further by arguing that the felicity conditions of an utterance are 'constitutive rules'. That is, they are not just something that can 'go right' (or wrong) or be 'abused' – which was Austin's view – but something which makes up and defines the act itself. That is, they are rules that need to be followed for the utterance to work.

Thomas (1995) critiques this notion of constitutive rules and suggests that the notion of *principles* is perhaps more helpful to this discussion. She points out that it is extremely difficult to devise rules which will satisfactorily account for the complexity of speech act behaviour. She presents five basic differences between rules and principles to support her argument. The first of these is that rules are 'all or nothing', whereas principles are 'more or less'. That is, rules are 'yes/no' in their application whereas principles can be applied partially. Thus, you can speak extremely clearly, fairly clearly, or not at all clearly, rather than simply 'clearly'.

Thomas also argues that rules are exclusive whereas principles can co-occur. Thus, using one rule precludes another whereas a number of principles (rather than rules) might apply at the same time. Rules aim to define a speech act whereas principles describe what people do. Further, whereas rules are definite, principles are 'probabilistic'; that is, they describe what is more or less likely to be the case, rather than something which either does or does not apply. Finally Thomas argues that rules are arbitrary, whereas principles are 'motivated'. That is, people follow them for a reason, or purpose, to achieve a particular goal.

If, for example, someone apologizes for something (in English) there is the assumption that they were responsible for what has been done (or in a position to represent this on someone else's behalf), have actually said 'I'm sorry', are sincere in what they say and will do something to rectify the situation, if this is required (or possible). The person may not be completely responsible for what was done, however, so it is more helpful to see this as a case of more or less, rather than yes or no. Equally, an apology is often more ritual than 'sincere' but has been carried out for a very important reason, so that the person being apologized to will feel better about the situation and the tension that was there will be resolved. Taking a principles-based view of speech act performance, rather than a rule-based one, thus, describes what people often do, or are most likely to do, when they apologize, rather than what they 'must' do.

Presupposition and discourse

A further important notion in the area of speech act theory and pragmatics is *presupposition*. Presupposition refers to the common ground that is assumed to exist between language users such as assumed knowledge of a situation and/or of the world. This may come from sources such as books, television and the internet, or through personal experiences with the world. A speaker says something based on their assumption (or presupposition) of what the hearer is likely to 'know', and what they will infer from what they say.

Two main kinds of presupposition are discussed in the area of pragmatics: conventional presupposition and pragmatic presupposition. Conventional presuppositions are less context-dependent than pragmatic presuppositions and are typically linked to particular linguistic forms. For example 'Would you like *some* coffee?' suggests the coffee is already prepared whereas 'Would you like *anything* to drink?' does not suggest a drink has already been prepared (Lo Castro 2003).

Pragmatic presuppositions, however, are context-dependent and arise from the use of an utterance in a particular context. The following example in the delicatessen section of a supermarket illustrates this. The customers know they need to take a ticket from the ticket machine and wait their turn to be served. The person with the ticket with '2' on it is the next person to be served. B implicates what A has said as an offer of service to them (alone).

A: Customer number two!
B: Ah . . . could I have 250 grams of the honey smoked ham please?

Presuppositions are crucial to an understanding of what people mean by what they say in spoken and written discourse. Often, we presuppose a person will have a similar understanding to us in terms of what we mean by what we say. It is indeed because people make this assumption that discourse (normally) proceeds as smoothly as it does.

3.4 The cooperative principle and discourse

In his paper, 'Logic and conversation' Grice (1975) argues that in order for a person to interpret what someone else says, some kind of *cooperative principle* must be assumed to be in operation. People assume, he argued, that there is a set of principles which direct us to a particular interpretation of what someone says, unless we receive some indication to the contrary. The cooperative principle says we should aim to make our conversational contribution 'such as is required, at the stage at which it occurs, by the accepted purpose or direction' (45) of the exchange in which we are engaged.

Thus, when someone is speaking to us, we base our understanding of what they are saying on the assumption that they are saying what needs to be said rather than more than needs to be said (as in the delicatessen example above), they are saying it at an appropriate point in the interaction (such as when the person working in the delicatessen has finished serving one person and is ready to serve another) and they have a reason for saying what they say (as both an offer of service as well as to make it clear whose turn it is to be served). The person working in the delicatessen follows these assumptions, assuming that customers will follow them as well. In this way, both people involved in the service encounter cooperate in its production and interpretation.

Grice based his cooperative principle on four sub-principles, or *maxims*. These are the maxims of *quality*, *quantity*, *relation* and *manner*. The maxim of quality says people should only say what they believe to be true and what they have evidence for. Grice's maxim of quantity says we should make our contribution as informative as is required for the particular purpose and not make it more informative than is required. The maxim of relation says we should make our contribution relevant to the interaction, or we should indicate in what way it is not. His maxim of manner says we should be clear in what we say, we should avoid ambiguity or obscurity and we should be brief and orderly in our contribution to the interaction.

In the following example both speakers observe all of these maxims. Both say all that is required at the appropriate stage in the conversation. They both observe the purpose and direction of the conversation. What they say is relevant to the conversation and they are each brief, orderly and unambiguous in what they say:

A: Hi. What would you like?
B: Two hundred grams of the shaved ham thanks.

We, thus, expect a person's contribution to an interaction to be genuine, neither more nor less than is required as well as being clear and appropriate to the interaction. Grice argues that we assume a speaker is following these maxims and combine this with our knowledge of the world to work out what they mean by what they say.

In the BBC *Panorama* interview, many of the people Diana is referring to need to be inferred from what has gone before in the interview. In the following extract Diana makes her contribution 'as informative as is required for the current purpose of the exchange' (Grice 1999: 78) showing she is obeying the maxim of quantity. Her interviewer Martin Bashir and the audience, she assumes, can clearly derive from her answer who she is talking about (Kowal and O'Connell 1997). Here Diana uses 'people around me' and 'people in my environment' to refer to the royal household, expecting her audience will know who she is talking about:

Diana: People's agendas changed overnight. I was now the separated wife of the Prince of Wales, I was a problem, I was a liability (seen as), and how are we going to deal with her? This hasn't happened before.

Bashir: Who was asking those questions?

Diana: People around me, people in this environment, and . . .

Bashir: The royal household?

Diana: People in my environment, yes, yes.

At other points in the interview, Diana uses 'people' to refer to the press and at other points the British public. When she wants to make it clear exactly who she is referring to (and is obeying the maxim of quality) she adds a clarification, as in the extracts below:

Diana: I'd like to be a queen of people's hearts, in people's hearts, but I don't see myself being Queen of this country. I don't think many people will want me to be Queen.

. . . .

Diana: The people that matter to me – the man on the street, yup, because that's what matters more than anything else.

There are times, however, when being truthful, brief and relevant might have different meanings. Indeed different contexts and situations may have different understandings of what 'be truthful, relevant and brief' means. There are, further, occasions where we cannot be brief and true at the same time (Cook 1989). This leads us to the 'flouting' of the cooperative principle and its maxims.

3.5 Flouting the cooperative principle

On some occasions speakers flout the cooperative principle and intend their hearer to understand this; that is, they purposely do not observe the maxim and intend their hearer to be aware of this. In the following example a student goes to the library to collect books he had asked to be put on hold for him. The librarian knows, in his final line, what he is saying is not true (or physically possible), and intends the student to know this:

Librarian: (raises his eyes, looks at the student with no facial expression)
Student: Hi. Could you check for me whether I have any books to collect?
Librarian: (swipes the student's card, clears his throat, wipes his nose with a tissue, glances at the computer screen, turns to the shelf to get a book, then another book)
Student: Any more?
Librarian: (turns and gets a third book, stamps them all with the return date)
Student: Is that all?
Librarian: Are you going to borrow all the books in the library?
Student: OK . . . I see . . . thank you very much

People may also flout the maxim of relation, or be told they are flouting this maxim, in similar ways. The following extract is an example of this. An American student has asked a Chinese student directions to the station. As they are walking to the station, the following conversation occurs:

Chinese student: What do you do in America?
American student: I work in a bank.
Chinese student: It's a good job isn't it?
American student: Well, just so so.
Chinese student: Then, how much is your salary every month?
American student: Oh no
Chinese student: What's wrong?
American student: Why are you asking that?
Chinese student: Just asking, nothing else . . .
American student: The station isn't far is it?

Here the question the Chinese student has asked does not observe the maxim of relation for an English conversation of this kind. He is not aware of this, although the American student clearly is. He then asks her if she is travelling alone and if she is married. The American student quickly hails a taxi and takes it to the station.

In the next example the serving person politely suggests the customer is flouting the maxim of quantity, saying more than is necessary, as the ham is already thinly sliced.

A: Can I get six thin slices of Danish ham please?
B: Six thin slices. . . .
A: Yep.
B: They're all really thin, so. . . .

Differences between flouting and violating maxims

Thomas (1995) and Cutting (2008) discuss differences between flouting and violating maxims. A speaker is flouting a maxim if they do not observe a maxim but has no intention of deceiving or misleading the other person. A person is 'violating' a maxim if there is a likelihood that they are liable to mislead the other person. For example 'Mummy's gone on a little holiday because she needs a rest' meaning 'Mummy's gone away to decide if she wants a divorce or not' violates, rather than flouts, the maxim of manner (39). Here, the speaker intends the hearer to understand something other than the truth, on purpose.

A speaker may also 'infringe' a maxim when they fail to observe a maxim with no intention to deceive, such as where a speaker does not have the linguistic capacity to answer a question. A speaker may also decide to 'opt out' of a maxim such as where a speaker may, for ethical or legal reasons, refuse to say something that breaches a confidentiality agreement they have with someone or is likely to incriminate them in some way (Thomas 1995; Cutting 2008).

Overlaps between maxims

There is also often overlap between each of Grice's maxims. An utterance may be both unclear and longwinded, flouting the maxims of quality and quantity at the same time (ibid.). Equally it may be socially acceptable, and indeed preferred, to flout a maxim (such as quality) for reasons of tact and politeness, such as when I ask someone if they like something I am wearing, and they don't.

It is important, then, for both the production and interpretation of spoken and written discourse to understand to what extent people are following these maxims, or not, in what they say. The interview with the Princess of Wales is a good example of this. While Diana's contribution to the conversation is indeed cooperative, she very skillfully exploits Grice's maxims (especially the maxims of quality and quantity) to get her points across. Even when she pauses, or remains silent in the interview, she is observing the maxim of quantity, showing an appropriate reflectiveness and seriousness in her approach to the interview and not saying more than she should, or needs to (Kowal and O'Connell 1997). That is, she is making her contribution 'such as is required, at the stage at which it occurs', by the purpose and direction of the conversation.

3.6 Cross-cultural pragmatics and discourse

The ways in which people perform speech acts, and what they mean by what they say when they perform them, often varies across cultures. One of my Japanese students complained, for example, that he had had work done by a local (English-speaking) builder that was unsatisfactory and no matter how much he pushed the matter he could not get the builder to apologize. On reflection, he realized that this was, in part, due to the different implications that might be drawn from an apology in English as opposed to an apology in Japanese. For my Japanese student, he expected the builder to apologize as a matter of course and he was very disturbed that the builder would not do this. This did not mean for him, however, that the builder would be taking responsibility for the unsatisfactory work, or that, having apologized, he would then be obliged to do anything about it. In English, he discovered, the apology, for the builder, would mean that he was both taking responsibility for the faulty work and agreeing to do something about it – a situation the builder was most likely keen to avoid given the financial, and other, implications this might have had for him. In Japan, the apology would not necessarily have had these implications.

Communication across cultures

Different languages and cultures, then, often have different ways of dealing with pragmatic issues, as well as different ways of observing Grice's maxims (Wierzbicka 2003). For example, speakers of different languages may have different understandings of the maxim of quantity in conversational interactions. Be'al (1992) found in a communication in the workplace study that communication difficulties occurred between English and French speakers because the English speakers saw questions such as 'How are you?' or 'Did you have a good weekend?' as examples of 'phatic' communication and expected short, standard answers such as 'Fine thanks'. The French speakers, however, saw the questions as 'real' requests for information and, in the English speakers' eyes, flouted the maxim of quantity, by talking at length about their health or what they did at the weekend.

Austin's (1998) discussion of letters of recommendation in academic settings is a further example of cross-cultural pragmatic differences. As she points out, in English academic settings letters of recommendation may vary in strength of recommendation. Readers also take into account the prestige of the person writing the letter, where they work and the content and tone of the letter. They might also notice 'what has not been said' in the letter. In Japanese academic settings, however, the situation is quite different. Japanese letters of recommendation are often much shorter than they are in English and often there is no particular relationship between the length of the letter and the quality of recommendation. A reader may need to ask for more information about a candidate, rather than rely on the letter alone. An English-speaking academic, thus, may misread a Japanese letter of recommendation if he/she is not aware of the different pragmatic role and values these texts have in their particular cultural setting (see Bargiela-Chiappini and Harris 2006 for further discussion of issues that arise in multicultural and multilingual encounters).

Cross-cultural pragmatics

Studies which investigate the cross-cultural use of speech acts are commonly referred to as *cross-cultural pragmatics*. As Wierzbicka (2003) points out, different pragmatic norms reflect different cultural values which are, in turn, reflected in what people say and what they intend by what they say in different cultural settings. Wierzbicka gives the example of thanking in Japanese and English. The concepts encoded in the English word *thanks*, she argues, do not really fit Japanese culture. In English, she says, to thank someone means, roughly, to say we feel something good towards them because of something good they have done and we want them to feel good in return. But in Japanese culture with its stress on social hierarchy, moral duty and the repayment of favours, this situation is somewhat different. Japanese speakers of English, further, may frequently say *sorry* when they mean *thank you*, leading to a completely different interpretation of what they mean, from what they intend to mean (Ide 1998). As Cameron (2001: 74) explains, the act of thanking is an expression of indebtedness in both English and Japanese. In the case of Japanese, however, 'a debt not yet repaid calls for an apology from the debtor'. Apologizing, thus, for a Japanese speaker is one way of expressing indebtedness, and thanking someone.

Kim (2008) shows how the term *mainhada* can mean both *sorry* and *thanks* in Korean. *Mainhada* is used less often than *sorry* in English, however, as South Koreans often express an apology implicitly or nonverbally. Also, *mainhada* is not the only way of thanking in Korean. If the speaker thinks they are not able to return the benefit they have received from the person they are thanking, they will say *mainhada*. If they think they can return the benefit, however, they will say *gamsahada*. *Mainhada* is also used for requesting in Korean. It is used within a group when the speaker thinks fulfilling the request will be difficult. It is also used with people outside the group to incorporate them into the group but an honorific will be added to the word (i.e. *mainhabnida*) to show particular respect to that person.

Spencer-Oatley (2008) discusses the speech act of requests showing how these vary depending on factors such as the speaker's wish to maintain rapport with their addressee, relations of power and social distance between participants. These, of course, can be quite different across languages and cultures. When I was teaching in Japan I asked my students to complete a task which highlighted how different this speech act can be across cultures. The task I set my students was:

> You are writing your graduation thesis (in English). You want to ask your (English) professor to read one of your chapters for you. What would you say in an email to your professor?

This is how one of my students completed the task:

> Dear Jim
>
> Hello, I am currently working on my graduation thesis, and would like to know if it is good or not. Would you mind reading one of the chapters for me? I would really appreciate it.
>
> Thanks
> Tetsuya Fujimoto
> (not his real name)

I then asked the students to carry out the same task, this time asking a Japanese professor to read one of their chapters for them. Below is how the same student completed the task (I asked the students to write the request in Japanese as well as give me an English translation of their text).

> Greetings, Professor Nakamura
>
> Early spring, in this sizzling day, how are you spending your day? This time, I would like you to do me a favor, and this I why I take up my pen (In Japanese this means 'to write' in a formal way).
>
> I am now writing my graduation thesis, and even though I am afraid to ask, would you mind seeing my work . . . of course, as long as it does not bother you. If it is not inconvenient for you, could you please consider it?
>
> I beg you again
>
> Sincerely
> Tetsuya Fujimoto

Then I asked the students to explain the differences between the texts. This is what Tetsuya said:

> In a formal Japanese letter, there is reference to the weather or season, but in English letters, there is nothing like that. The reason why Japanese start letters with irrelevant topics is because it is too blunt to say what you want to say without putting seasonal words first. Also, in the English one, we can say 'thank you' or 'I will appreciate it . . .' but in the Japanese one, it should be avoided because if we say 'thank you', it imposes and sounds as if we were expecting the professor to do the task.

This was another student's explanation:

> In English, I could ask the professor just like asking my friends to do me a favour. But in Japanese, I have to use an indirect sentence to say what I want the professor to do. So it is hard to get the point of what I want to say. This is because in English speaking countries, the relationship between students and professors are close so that it is easy for the student to ask questions. But in Japan, we don't usually talk to the professor, or form a relationship with the professor on a one-to-one basis, so we have to ask the question just like asking a complete stranger.

It is clear, then, that the students were aware of relations of power and social distance between themselves and their professors and that the different cultural values and relations required different approaches to the same act.

3.7 Conversational implicature and discourse

A further key notion in pragmatics which has implications for both the production and interpretation of discourse is the concept of *conversational implicature*. Conversational implicature refers to the inference a hearer makes about a speaker's intended meaning that arises from their use of the literal meaning of what the speaker said, the conversational principle and its maxims. For example, if I say 'There's nothing on at the movies' I do not mean 'nothing at all', but rather 'nothing that I'm interested in seeing'. The person I am speaking to will assume this and 'implicate' my meaning. Implicature is not the same, however, as inference. As Thomas (1995: 58) explains, an implicature 'is generated intentionally by the speaker and may (or may not) be understood by the hearer'. An inference, on the other hand, is produced by a hearer on the basis of certain evidence and may not, in fact, be the same as what a speaker intends.

To calculate an implicature, Grice (1975) argues, hearers draw on the conventional meanings of words, the cooperative principle and its maxims, the linguistic and non-linguistic context of the utterance, items of background knowledge and the fact that all of these are available to both participants and they both assume this to be the case. Given this basic process, implicature can be created in one of three ways. A maxim can be followed in a straightforward way and the hearer implicates what the speaker intends. The following example, where a customer orders a beer, illustrates this:

A: What'd you like?
B: A beer thanks.

Here, B has followed the maxim of quality by saying what he wants, the maxim of manner by answering clearly, the maxim of quantity by saying enough and no more and the maxim of relation by providing an answer that is clearly relevant to the question. Here, no implicature is generated that is necessary for the interpretation of the utterance.

A maxim might also be flouted because of a clash with another maxim as in:

A: What time did your flight get in this morning?
B: Seven (when it actually arrived at 7.04 am)

Here B flouts the maxim of quality (the truth) in order to obey the maxim of quantity (be brief).

Or a maxim might be flouted in a way that exploits a maxim as in:

A: How are we getting to the airport tomorrow?
B: Well . . . I'm going with Peter.

Here, B has given less information than is required and is flouting the maxim of quantity – from which B derives that he or she may have to make their own way to the airport.

Conventional and particularized conversational implicatures

Grice describes two kinds of conversational implicature: *conventional* and *particularized conversational implicatures*. With conventional implicatures, no particular context is required in order to derive the implicature. In the above example, the use of 'well' can conventionally implicate that what the speaker is about to say is not what the hearer is hoping to hear. Similarly, the use of 'anyway' conventionally implicates a return to the original topic of a conversation (Lo Castro 2003). The use of 'but' and 'on the other hand' to express contrast, 'even' to suggest something is contrary to expectation and 'yet' to suggest something will be different at a later time, are further examples of conventional implicatures.

Particularized conversational implicatures, however, are derived from a particular context, rather than from the use of the words alone. These result from the maxim of relation. That is, the speaker assumes the hearer will search for the relevance of what is said and derive an intended meaning. For example in:

A: You're out of coffee.
B: Don't worry there's a shop on the corner.

A derives from B's answer that they will be able to buy coffee from the shop on the corner. Most implicatures, in fact, are particularized conversational implicatures.

Scalar implicatures

A further kind of implicature is *scalar implicature*. These are derived when a person uses a word from a set of words that express some kind of scale of values. A speaker may choose one item from a scale, then correct it while speaking to cancel out another item in the scale. The following extract from the BBC *Panorama* interview is an example of this. Here Diana cancels out 'full' with 'some', then cancels 'some' with 'half of', adding an explanation as to why she has done this (Abell and Stokoe 1999):

Bashir: Looking back now, do you feel at all responsible for the difficulties in your marriage?
Diana: Mmm. I take full responsibility, I take some responsibility that our marriage went the way it did. I'll take half of it, but I won't take any more than that, because it takes two to get in this situation.

3.8 Politeness, face and discourse

Two further key notions in the area of pragmatics and discourse are *politeness* and *face*. The notion of 'face' comes from Goffman's (1967) work on face and from the English 'folk' notion of face, which ties up with notions of being embarrassed, humiliated or 'losing face' (Brown and Levinson 1987). Politeness and face are important for understanding why people choose to say things in a particular way in spoken and written discourse.

Politeness principles and cooperative principles, however, are often in conflict with each other. There are also situations in which one principle might become more important than another. In an emergency, for example, there is less need to be polite than, say, in a normal situation.

Involvement and independence in spoken and written discourse

Two further issues in discussions of face and politeness are the notions of *involvement* and *independence* (Scollon and Wong-Scollon 2001). The term involvement refers to the need people have to be involved with others and to show this involvement; that is a person's right and need to be considered a normal, contributing, supporting member of society; in other words, to be treated as a member of a group. We might show this involvement by showing our interest in someone, by agreeing with them, by approving what they are doing or by using in-group identity markers such as given names, or nicknames. The independence part of face refers to a person's right not be dominated by others, not to be imposed on by others and to be able to act with some sense of individuality, or autonomy. We do this, for example, by not presuming other people's needs or interests, by giving people options, by not imposing on other people and by apologizing for interruptions. In order to maintain social relationships people acknowledge both of these aspects of a person's face at the same time. People thus aim to build up closeness and rapport with each other, while at the same time trying to avoid being a threat to each other's social distance; that is, maintaining each other's involvement and independence (Scollon and Wong-Scollon 2001).

Choosing a politeness strategy

We draw on a number of considerations when we decide on a choice of politeness strategy. We may consider how socially close or distant we are from our hearer. For example, are we close friends, is the hearer older than I am and are we 'social equals'? We may consider how much or how little power the hearer has over us. For example, am I talking to my boss or to my employee, to a policeman, to a service employee or to a judge? We may also consider how significant what I want is to me, and to the person I am talking to. For example, am I asking for change, for a loan or to borrow a car? We may consider how much emphasis both of us (in our culture or cultures) place on involvement and independence in circumstances like the one we are in. And we may consider whether both of us would have the same answers to these questions (Gee 1993).

3.9 Face and politeness across cultures

It is important to point out that the specific nature of face and politeness varies from society to society and from culture to culture. For example, in some cultures the idea of personal space and independence may vary. In some societies, parents have more right to interfere in the domestic affairs of adult children than in others. In some cultures a bedroom is private and cannot be entered and in others it is not. In some cultures refusal of an offer may be merely polite (even if to an English speaker a refusal may seem like refusing involvement) and in others the opposite may be true (Cook 1989).

Gu (1990) discusses politeness in relation to Chinese culture while Ide (1982) discusses politeness in Japanese. Gu sees politeness in Chinese not so much in terms of psychological wants, but rather in terms of social norms. Face is threatened he argues, not when someone's needs are not met, but when someone fails to live up to social standards. Ide sees politeness in Japanese as something which helps to maintain communication. In Japanese politeness is less strategic and more a matter of socially obligatory linguistic choices through which social harmony is achieved (Eelen 2001). It is important to remember, then, that the use of language will very often vary across cultures and in relation to the social realities of these cultures (Leech 2009).

Gift-giving is an example of a politeness strategy that varies across cultures. Brown and Levinson list gift-giving as a positive politeness strategy in English, or in Scollon and Wong-Scollon's (2001) terms an involvement strategy; that is, a strategy by which we show our closeness and rapport with someone else. We may spend a lot of time deciding what to buy for the gift, think about what the person receiving the gift will feel about what we have bought them and what their reaction to our gift might be. In Japanese culture, however, there are times when gift-giving may mean something quite different from this and be more of a social ritual rather than a positive politeness strategy. Japanese have many gift-giving occasions throughout the year that cover many events in Japanese life where gift-giving is more ritual, or an expression of duty. The gift-giving may still have the function of maintaining social relationships, but be much less an expression of intimacy and rapport than it might be in an English speaking country (Davies and Ikeno 2002).

The ways in which people express politeness also differs across cultures. On one occasion I asked a group of bilingual Japanese/English students how they would ask a friend to close the window if they were in the car with them and they were feeling cold. These students had all lived in an English-speaking country and were fluent in both English and Japanese. These are some of the examples they gave me of what they would say in English to an English speaking friend:

Could you close the window for me?
Can I close the window?
Hey yo, close the window, would you?

This is what they said they would say in Japanese to a Japanese friend:

Isn't it a little chilly?
It's cold don't you think?
I wonder why it's so cold today?

In the Japanese examples none of the students actually mentioned the window. When I asked them about this, one of the students told me that that in Japanese indirectness is a sign of intimacy and is often used between friends as a sign of mutual understanding and friendship. Indirectness, then, is often an involvement, or positive politeness, strategy in Japanese whereas in English it is often an independence, or negative politeness, strategy. My students also told me that in Japanese culture, involvement is much more important than independence. Thus, whereas in English a speaker may weigh up what they are saying in terms of both involvement and independence, a Japanese speaker may give much greater weight to what they are saying in terms of involvement, rather than independence (see Kadar and Mills 2011 for further discussion of politeness in East Asian cultures).

3.10 Politeness and gender

Politeness strategies have also been shown to vary according to gender. Holmes (1995) discusses this at length, showing differences in the use of politeness strategies between men and women. Her work reveals that the relationship between sex, politeness and language is a complex one and that while research shows that, overall, women are more polite than men, it also depends on what we mean by 'polite' as well as which women and men are being compared and what setting or *community of practice* the interaction occurs; that is, the particular local conditions in which the man or woman is speaking (Cameron 1998).

In her book *Gender and Politeness*, Mills (2003) points out that context has an important role to play in terms of whether what someone says is interpreted as polite or not. She gives the example of 'street remarks' to illustrate this. If, for example, I say 'Hello gorgeous' to a long-time friend when I see her, this can be taken as an expression of intimacy and rapport; that is, as a positive politeness, or involvement strategy. If, however, someone calls this out from a building site to a woman walking by this can have the opposite effect. For the woman, it may be an act of harassment. For the men on the building site, it may be an act which shows solidarity and rapport among the group. It is not always the case that 'Hello gorgeous' is a positive politeness strategy, at least for the person it is being said to. We need, then, to consider who is saying what, to whom, from what position, where and for what purpose in order to come to a closer understanding of this (Cameron 1998).

This communities of practice view of politeness and gender is also discussed by Christie (2002) and Mills (2008). Christie looks at politeness and gender in parliamentary debate in the United Kingdom. Christie argues that while there are many instances of men and women publicly criticizing, ridiculing and challenging each other in parliamentary debates, these are not so much instances of gender specific impoliteness, but rather *politic verbal behaviour* (Watts 2003). In this case, Christie argues, the insults, etc. are part of the discourse expectations of a good parliamentary speaker, regardless of whether they are male or female. She also found in her data that female Members of Parliament rarely apologize, a finding that runs counter to other, more general politeness and gender research that suggests that women apologize more than men. Indeed, as with the work on language and identity, politeness and gender research suggests that it may not always be a person's gendered identity that is the most salient in a particular situation but perhaps some other aspect of their identity that more influences their linguistic behaviour (Mullany 2002). It is also important to remember that a community of practice does not exist in isolation from other cultural groups and cultural values. There are always connections between individuals, groups, social norms and communicative practices. None of these work in isolation from the other. There will, further, always be a range of norms and views on appropriateness within a community of practice and, indeed, within a culture as a whole (Mills 2008).

A *community of practice* is a group of people who come together to carry out certain activities with each other. Parents doing volunteer work in a childcare centre, a group of high-school friends with a shared interest and Members of Parliament are examples of communities of practice. Members of a community of practice interact with each other in particular ways, have a common endeavour and share ways in which they express their group identity. The ways they talk, the ways they do things and their common knowledges, values and beliefs emerge and develop as they carry out their activities. Researchers in the area of linguistic politeness argue for a communities of practice view of politeness; that is, an examination of the ways in which politeness is typically expressed, its function and what it means, in the particular social and communicative setting, place and time.

3.11 Face-threatening acts

Some acts 'threaten' a person's face. These are called *face-threatening acts*. Often we use *mitigation devices* (Fraser 1980) in conversations to take the edge off face-threatening acts. One example is the use of a 'pre-sequence' as in the following invitation:

A: Are you doing anything after work? (a pre-sequence)
B: Why are you asking?
A: I thought we might go for a drink. (an indirect speech act)
B: Well, no, nothing in particular. Where would you like to go?

This example also uses an *insertion sequence* in the middle to take the edge off the face-threatening act of 'inviting someone out'.

We might also use an *off-record speech act* as in:

A: I'm dying for a drink (an off-record invitation)
B: Yes it's really hot isn't it? (an off-record rejection of the invitation)

Here, A never actually asked B to go for a drink so doesn't lose any face by being rejected. Equally, B hasn't rejected the invitation on record but simply 'commented' on the weather in their off-record rejection of the invitation.

A person may, equally, feel that their face has been threatened and make this clear to their audience. An example of this is when the US Secretary of State Hilary Clinton on a visit to the Congo in 2009 was asked by a student what her husband thought of the issue she was discussing. (The student actually meant Mr Obama but the translator had mistakenly said Mr Clinton.) In her response 'You want me to tell you what my husband thinks?' she makes it clear that her face had been threatened. She was in the Congo as the Secretary of State, not the wife of the former US president, and the question that she had been asked was inappropriate. This, of course, also led to loss of face for the student, having been reprimanded by the Secretary of State in such a public setting. After the event the student approached Hilary Clinton and explained the mistake. She smiled at the student, rather embarrassedly, and told him not to worry about it (Harnden 2009).

3.12 Politeness and cross-cultural pragmatic failure

It is important to remember that the particular nature of face varies across cultures and that politeness strategies are not necessarily universal. Equally, what may be a face-threatening act in one culture may not be seen the same way in another. Matsumoto (1989), for example, argues that the use of deference in Japanese is an indication of social register and relationship and not a politeness strategy. Gu (1990) and Mao (1994), equally, argue that the politeness model proposed by Brown and Levinson (1987) in their *Politeness: Some Universals in Language Usage*, for example, does not suit Chinese. As Gu (1990: 256) observes, while politeness, of itself, may be a universal phenomenon, 'what counts as polite behaviour (including values and norms attached to such behaviour) is . . . [both] culture-specific and language-specific'.

Clearly, the ways in which politeness is expressed is not the same across languages and cultures and might mean different things in different linguistic and cultural settings. Even though people may draw on similar notions such as face, there may be gradations of politeness in terms of the importance of involvement, independence, tact and modesty, etc. in the particular setting. The interpretation and linguistic encoding of these, however, can sometimes vary enormously across languages and cultures (Leech 2007).

A lack of understanding of ways of expressing politeness in different languages and cultures can be a cause of cross-cultural pragmatic failure (Thomas 1983). As Tanaka (1997) and others have pointed out, native speakers of a language are often less tolerant of pragmatic errors in cross-cultural communication contexts than they are, for example, of grammatical errors. Different views of pragmatic appropriateness, then, can easily lead to misunderstandings and inhibit effective cross-cultural communication. In cross-cultural settings, in particular, people need an awareness as well as an expectation of sociopragmatic differences as much as they need an understanding of how these differences might be expressed linguistically.

3.13 Summary

This chapter has discussed key notions in the analysis of discourse from a pragmatics perspective. While many researchers discuss the importance of pragmatic competence, much of the research in the area of pragmatics and language learning has examined pragmatic development in terms of the acquisition of particular speech acts or issues of politeness, rather than some of the other issues discussed in this chapter. What research there is, however, shows that language learners have difficulties in the area of pragmatics, regardless of their level of grammatical ability. As Tanaka argues, the development of second language learners' pragmatic competence needs to remain an important goal of language learning classrooms as pragmatic failure can 'deny learners access to valuable academic or professional opportunities' (15). Pragmatic competence, then, 'is not extra or ornamental, like the icing on the cake'. It is a crucial part of discourse competence and, in turn, communicative competence (Kasper 1997).

It is important, however, not to take English as the default target language in second language pragmatics research (Lo Castro 2011). Communication between speakers of Asian languages such as Chinese, Japanese and Korean can be as complicated, if not more so, than between English and one of these languages, especially when one thinks of the seemingly similar cultural values between these languages when this may not, indeed, be at all the case (see Lo Castro 2011 for further discussion of this, also Taguchi 2011 for a discussion of post-structural perspectives on pragmatics).

3.14 Discussion questions

(1) Think of possible speech acts for each of the following situations. Compare the three sets of speech acts. In what ways are they different and why? For example is what you say influenced by your relationship with the person you are speaking to, their age or their gender? Or is it influenced by things such as how well you know the other person, or your view of their social position in relation to yours? If the person is your boss is that different, for example, than if the person you are speaking to is a co-worker? Or is what you say influenced by what you are talking about?

- You and a close friend are having dinner together and you suddenly realize you have left your money at home. Ask your friend to lend you some money to pay for dinner.
- You want to take a week off work to see a friend who is visiting you from overseas and you have no holidays owing to you. You go to your boss' office to ask for the week's leave.
- You are in a restaurant. Your steak is over-cooked. You wanted it cooked rare. Ask the waiter to bring you another steak.

(2) Choose a speech act (such as asking someone for a favour, or complaining about something) and discuss how it is performed in English and in another language. Discuss cross-cultural differences in the way the speech act is performed and how it is responded to, and why. For example, is what you say influenced by different views of politeness? Is it influenced by different views of appropriate social behaviour? Or is it influenced by different views of social relationships?

(3) Think of a situation where you have experienced cross-cultural pragmatic failure; that is, a situation you think there has been a misunderstanding and the reason for this is cross-cultural. Explain what happened, why you think it happened and what you would tell someone else who found themselves in a similar situation.

(4) Think of examples of face-threatening acts; that is acts (such as complaining, or refusing someone who has asked you out on a date). What are some ways you might respond to these acts, and why?

3.15 Data analysis projects

Collect several examples of spoken or written language. In each case, try to collect a complete example of the text, rather than just a section of it. Transcribe (in the case of spoken texts) and analyse the data you have collected from one of the following perspectives.

(1) Carry out a speech act analysis of your texts to identify direct speech acts and indirect speech acts. Analyse in what way the speakers 'mean more than what they say'; that is, what is the difference between the literal meaning of what they say and what you think they mean by what they say. Why do you think they chose to use a direct or an indirect speech act?

(2) Carry out an analysis of your sample texts concentrating on Grice's maxim of cooperative behaviour. Find examples where people are observing (or not) his maxims of quality (tell the truth), quantity (say no more than you need to), relation (be relevant in what you say) and manner (be clear and unambiguous in what you say). Look at Chapter 6 in Schiffrin (1994) for examples of this kind of analysis.

(3) Carry out an analysis of your sample texts concentrating on involvement and independence. That is, look for strategies which show closeness, intimacy, rapport and solidarity (involvement strategies) and strategies which give the other person choices and allow them to maintain their freedom (independence strategies). How do the speakers use language to do this?

(4) Carry out a cross-cultural pragmatic analysis of a particular speech act. That is, look at how someone performs a particular speech act in English and in another language. In what way(s) are they similar and in what way(s) are they different? Why do you think this might be the case? Chapter 11 in Lo Castro (2003) is a useful starting point for this analysis.

3.16 Exercises

Exercise 1: Sentence types and speech acts

Analyse the following set of answer phone messages for kinds of speech acts (e.g. request, apology, etc.), and whether the speech acts are direct or indirect:

A: This is 9457 1769. I can't answer the phone right now. Please leave a message after the tone.

B: It's me again. I'm trying to organize the barbeque for John's birthday on Saturday. Can you give me a call and let me know if you'll be coming?

Exercise 2: Different meanings of the same utterance

Richards and Schmidt (1983) give the example of 'Hello' as an utterance which can have different meanings in different contexts. Think of another utterance which can have different meanings depending on the context.

Exercise 3: Speech acts across cultures

Look at Wierzbicka's (2003: 157–8) analysis of thanking in English in Chapter 5 of her book *Cross Cultural Pragmatics: The Semantics of Human Interaction*. Discuss this analysis with a native speaker of a language other than English to see if this is the same or different in their language and culture.

Exercise 4: Indirect speech acts and Grice's maxims

(1) Look at the following extract from a conversation in a coffee shop in the United States. Find examples of indirect speech acts in the conversation.
   (In this extract S = sales person and C = customer)

1	S:	Hi. Can I help you?
2	C:	Can I get a grande frappe with vanilla?
3	S:	Did you want that blended or on the rocks?
4	C:	Blended, I guess.
5	S:	2% or skimmed?
6	C:	Uhm 2%
7	S:	2% OK. Any whipped cream?
8	C:	Sorry?
9	S:	Did you want whipped cream on that?
10	C:	Yes.
11	S:	Anything else?
12	C:	No, that's it.

(Source: Bartlett 2006: 338)

(2) Look at the conversation in a coffee shop again and find examples of where the speakers follow the maxims of *quality*, *quantity*, *relation* and *manner*.

Exercise 5: Flouting maxims

Think of situations in which Grice's maxims are flouted.

Exercise 6: Conversational implicature

Think of some exchanges in which people understand each other because of conversational implicature.

3.17 Directions for further reading

Archer, D. and Grundy, P. (eds) (2011), *The Pragmatics Reader*. London: Routledge.

This collection of classic texts and newer extracts contains work by authors such as Austin, Searle, Grice, Levinson, Blakemore, Goffman, Watts, Kasper and Schegloff. Topics covered include linguistic pragmatics, historical pragmatics, politeness, face, impoliteness, cross-cultural and intercultural pragmatics and pragmatics and conversation.

Cutting, J. (2008), *Pragmatics and Discourse: A Resource Book for Students* (2nd edn). London: Routledge.

Cutting's book provides a very clear review of issues in the area of pragmatics research. The topics covered include context and co-text, speech acts, the cooperative principle, politeness and culture and language learning.

Jaworski, A. and Coupland, N. (eds) (2006), *The Discourse Reader* (2nd edn). London: Routledge.

Jaworski and Coupland's book contains extracts from the seminal work of Austin and Grice in the area of pragmatics – Austin's (1962) *How to do Things with Words* and Grice's (1975) paper Logic and conversation.

Kasper, G. (2008), 'Data collection in pragmatics research', in H. Spencer-Oatey (ed.), *Culturally Speaking: Culture, Communication and Politeness Theory*. London: Continuum, pp. 279–303.

In this chapter, Kasper outlines research strategies for carrying out pragmatics research. These include the use of questionnaires, interviews, diaries and verbal reports. She discusses the limitations of self-report data and especially discourse completion tasks (DCTs). She argues that researchers need a clear understanding of what self-report data can, and cannot, deliver.

LoCastro, V. (2011), 'Second language pragmatics', in E. Hinkel (ed), *Handbook of Research in Second Language Teaching and Learning* (Vol. 2). London: Routledge, pp. 319–44.

LoCastro's chapter is an overview of second language pragmatics research. She discusses pronunciation and second language pragmatics, politeness and moving beyond speech acts to extended talk and discourse. She also discusses second language pragmatic transfer, pointing out that this is an area of research which has important, real-world consequences.

O'Keefe, A., Clancy, B. and Adolphs, S. (2011), *Introducing Pragmatics and Use*. London: Routledge.

This is an introductory text which covers topics such as speech theory, Gricean maxims, politeness, cross-cultural pragmatics and pragmatics and language teaching. Many examples of real-life language use are provided to illustrate the points being made.

Spencer-Oatey, H. (ed.) (2008), *Culturally Speaking: Culture, Communication and Politeness Theory* (2nd edn). London: Continuum.

This book describes a wide range of studies of communication across cultures. These include apologies in Japanese and English, British and Chinese reactions to compliment responses, Greek and German telephone conversations, interactions in Japanese–American workplaces and face in Chinese–English business meetings. The chapter by Meredith Marra gives advice on recording and analysing talk across cultures and the chapter by Gabrielle Kasper discusses data collection in pragmatics research.

For an extended list of references and further readings see the companion website to this book.

4

Discourse and Genre

One of the key ways in which people communicate with each other is through the participation in particular communicative events, or genres. A letter to the editor is an example of a genre. Letters to the editors occur in a particular setting such as in newspapers and magazines. They have distinctive and recognizable patterns of organization and structure. That is, they typically have a heading at the top, the body of the letter and the name of the author of the letter at the end. They are typically fairly short and they usually aim to comment, or present a particular point of view on a topic of current interest to the readers of the newspaper or magazine. Other examples of genres are news reports, business reports, parliamentary speeches, summing up in a court of law and weather reports. Each of these occurs in a particular setting, is organized in a particular way and has a distinctive communicative function, or purpose.

The example in Figure 4.1 of a letter to the editor shows the discourse structures of a sample text. It has a *generic structure* that is typical of letters to the editor and a *rhetorical structure* which is typical of argument-type texts (see Section 4.8 below for further discussion of generic structures and rhetorical structures).

4.1 What is a genre?

What indeed then are genres? Genres are ways in which people 'get things done' through their use of spoken and written discourse. In the text shown in Figure 4.1 Sally Sartain chose a letter to the editor to make her point, rather than a phone call to the editor of the newspaper, or indeed a letter or phone call to the reviewer she is complaining about as this is a very typical way of responding in a situation such as this.

> *Genres* are activities that people engage in through the use of language. Academic lectures and casual conversations are examples of spoken genres. Newspaper reports and academic essays are examples of written genres. Instances of a genre often share a number of features. They may be spoken or written in typical, and sometimes conventional, ways. They also often have a common function and purpose (or set of functions and purposes). Genres may typically be performed by a particular person

aimed at a particular audience, such as an academic lecture being delivered by a lecturer to a group of undergraduate students. There may be certain contexts in which a genre typically occurs, such as a lecture taking place in a university lecture theatre, and certain topics that are typically associated with the use of a genre, such as particular academic course content. Genres change through time. This may, for example, be in response to changes in technologies or it may be as a result of changes in values underlying the use of the particular genre. The office memo is an example of a genre that has changed in response to technological changes. An office meeting may change when a new person takes over chairing the meeting who has a different idea from their predecessor as to how the meeting should be run, what is important to discuss and how this should be discussed.

Sender's address	34 Victoria St	
	Lake's Entrance 3099	
Telephone number	Tel – 9380 7787	
Date	20 April 1995	
Receiver's address	Letters to the Editor	
	The Sunday Age	
Salutation	Dear Sir/Madam	
Body of the letter	I feel compelled to write to you about the appalling way Stephen Downes denigrates restaurants and, in fact, the very food which he is, sadly, in the position of 'judging'.	Thesis statement
	He has a happy knack of putting the reader completely off by his disgusting descriptions. He also completely disregards the joy that simplicity brings to the customer, who after all are the whole reason for the restaurants in the first place.	Argument
	I do speak with a great deal of knowledge as my husband and I, until recently, owned and were chefs at our two restaurants, Sartain's at Metung and Sally's, Lakes Entrance.	Evidence 1
	Mr Downes' snide remarks about the entrees at the Pavilion, St Kilda Beach, just indicate he has absolutely no idea of the wishes of even the most discerning customers. Then, when he mentioned the 'subtle slime' to go with the 'massive scrum' of yabbies, I felt it was time to act! How dare he describe a dish so badly, then call it a quality product. He insults the chef.	Evidence 2
	The Main Event. Well, I was sad to hear that for $21.50 the garfish were not boned, but that is the restaurant's choice and I don't criticise. He describes two tiny potatoes as being 'tired', when obviously it is the receiver who is 'spoilt' and 'tired' of judging so much food.	Evidence 3
	Don't let Stephen Downes destroy descriptions of good food. Having made these derogatory remarks about the restaurant, he then awards them three stars. Very strange.	Summing up
Sign off	Yours faithfully	
Signature	*Sally Sartain*	
Sender's name	Sally Sartain	

Figure 4.1 The discourse structure of a letter to the editor (based on Sartain 1995)

We use language in particular ways according to the content and purpose of the genre, the relationship between us and the person we are speaking to or the audience we are writing for or speaking to. The way we use language in a particular genre also depends on whether the text is written or spoken, and the social and cultural context in which the genre occurs. When we do this, we draw on our previous experience with the genre to know how we should normally do this, as Sally Sartain has clearly done in her letter to the editor. This does not mean, however, that every instance of a genre is the same, nor that genres do not change. Genres, further, vary in terms of their typicality. That is, a text may be a typical example of a genre, or a less typical one, but still be an example of the particular genre.

Examples of genre change can be seen in the way the internet has influenced existing forms of communications such as internal office memos, and has introduced new forms of communication such as internet chat rooms, blogs and online discussion forums. The introduction of new technologies can also bring with it new genres, such as the way mobile phones have introduced the new genre of text messaging.

Defining genre

Martin's (1984: 25) definition of genre as 'a staged, goal-oriented, purposeful activity in which speakers engage as members of our culture' has been extremely influential in the work of the Sydney School of genre analysis. Martin and Rose (2007: 8), elaborating on this definition, add:

> Social because we participate in genres with other people; goal-oriented because we use genres to get things done; staged because it usually takes us a few steps to reach our goals.

Swales (2004: 61) from the field of English for specific purposes says he prefers the notion of 'metaphor' for talking about genres, rather than 'definition', saying that definitions are often not 'true in all possible worlds and all possible times' and can 'prevent us from seeing newly explored or newly emerging genres for what they really are'.

Miller's (1984) notion of 'genre as social action' has been especially important in the area known as *rhetorical genre studies* (Artemeva 2008, Schryer 2011). In this view, a genre is defined, not in terms of 'the substance or the form of discourse but on the action it is used to accomplish' (Miller 1984: 151). This action is recognized by other people and the genre is accepted, over time, as a way of doing something. Genre, thus, is a kind of 'social agreement' (Miller and Bazerman 2011) about ways of doing things with language in particular social and cultural settings. Miller also discusses the notion of *typification* in relation to genre. That is, there are typical forms a genre might take as well as typical content and typical action that the genre performs, all of which we recognize and draw on as we engage with the use of genres.

The Sydney School of genre analysis

The notion of genre is important in the teaching of writing and reading (Martin and Rose 2008, Rose 2012, Rose and Martin 2012) in the work of the Sydney School of genre studies. Here, the term *schematic structure* is often used to describe the discourse structure of texts. For Martin, the notion of genre corresponds to Malinowski's (1923, 1935) notion of *context of culture* and is responsible for the schematic structure of a text. The *register* (Halliday 1989c) of the text, on the other hand, corresponds to Malinowski's *context of situation* and is responsible for the language features of a text. Genres, thus, are culture specific and have particular purposes, stages and linguistic features associated with them, the meanings of which need to be interpreted in relation to the cultural and social contexts in which they occur.

Genre analysis and English for specific purposes

The approach to genre analysis commonly employed in the teaching of English for specific purposes is based on Swales' (1981, 1990, 2004) analyses of the discourse structure of research article introductions. Swales use the notion of *moves* to describe the discourse structure of texts. In his book *Genre analysis* Swales (1990) argued that communicative purpose was the key factor that leads a person to decide whether a text is an instance of a particular genre or not. He has since, however, revised this view, saying that it is now clear that genres may have multiple purposes and that these may be different for each of the participants involved (Askehave and Swales 2001). Also, instances of a genre which are similar linguistically and rhetorically may have 'startling differences in communicative purpose' in the words of Swales and Rogers (1995: 223). The communicative purpose of a genre, further, may evolve over time. It may change, it may expand or it may shrink (Swales 2004). Communicative purpose, further, can vary across cultures even when texts belong to the same genre category.

Rhetorical genre studies

Researchers in rhetorical genre studies describe genres as part of the social processes by which knowledge about reality and the world are made. Genres, in this view, both respond to and contribute to the constitution of social contexts, as well as the socialization of individuals. Genres, then, are more than just socially embedded; they are socially constructive. Miller (1984: 165) argues that genres 'serve as keys to understanding how to participate in the actions of a community' and that the failure to understand genre as social action turns activities such as writing instruction from 'what should be a practical art of achieving social ends into an act of making texts that fit formal requirements', a view that has important implications for genre-based teaching (for further elaboration on Miller's view of genre see Miller and Bazerman 2011, a set of *YouTube* questions and answers on genre).

Choice and constraint in the use of spoken and written genres

Drawing on the work of Devitt (1997), Swales (2004) discusses the view of genre in which there are both choices and constraints, regularity and chaos. Genres are dynamic and open to change, but it is not a case of 'free for all' or 'anything goes'. As Devitt (2004: 86) explains, conformity among genre users 'is a fact of genre, for genres provide an expected way of acting'. As she argues, there are often consequences for violating genre expectations, and these consequences cannot always be predicted. Both constraint and choice, she argues, are necessary and positive components of genres. It is not necessarily the case that choice (or creativity) is good and constraint is bad. Both need to be valued. In Bhatia's (1998: 25–6) words:

> Practicing a genre is almost like playing a game, with its own rules and conventions. Established genre participants, both writers and readers, are like skilled players, who succeed by their manipulation and exploitation of, rather than a strict compliance with, the rules of the game. It is not simply a matter of learning the language, or even learning the rules of the game, it is more like acquiring the rules of the game in order to be able to exploit and manipulate them to fulfil professional and disciplinary purposes.

Assigning a text to a genre category

A key issue underlying this discussion is how we define a text as an instance of a particular genre, or in other words, how we assign it to a 'genre category'. Cook (1989) argues that we draw on many aspects of language and context to do this. We may consider the author (or speaker) of the text and the intended audience of the text. We may also consider the purpose of text, the situation in which the text occurs, the physical form and, in the case of written texts, the title of the text. We may be influenced by a pre-sequence to the text, such as 'Once upon a time' as well as the discourse structure of the text. Other factors that might help us decide what genre the text is an instance of may include the content of the text, the level of formality of the text, the style or register of the text and whether it is a spoken or a written text. Some of these may be more important than others in helping us to decide what the genre category is that a text belongs to. Some may also be difficult to determine, such as the purpose (or purposes) of the text.

Morton's (1999) book about Monica Lewinsky, *Monica's Story*, provides an interesting example of genre classification. The following conversation between a customer and the sales assistant in a bookstore in Los Angeles tries to get at the question 'What genre is it?':

Customer:	What kind of book would you say this is? Where would you put it on your bookshelves?
Sales assistant:	Well . . . I suppose you'd call it a biography because it's got some of her earlier life in it. It's not a memoir . . . I don't know . . . It's not very interesting. She got someone else to help her write it. It should have been in the first person, I only read about half of it . . . I don't know . . . Maybe it's an exposé . . .

On the cover of the taped version of the book, *Monica's Story* is classified as 'a candid intimate biography of a young woman whose life holds some surprising secrets'. In this case, the sales assistant sees the book as an instance of a slightly different genre from that of the publisher, and perhaps even the author. In her case she draws on her expectations for different genres and what she already knows about the particular text. She draws on formal features of the genre, such as the use of the third person, the content and bias of the text, the author of the text, the purpose of the text and the physical form and situation in which the text occurs. What to one person, then, may be an instance of a particular genre may, to another person, be more like an instance of another.

Linguists such as Hasan (1989a) have suggested that the crucial properties of a genre can be expressed as a range of possible textual structures. Martin (1992), equally, puts forward the view that genres can be defined in terms of similarities and differences in the discourse structures of the texts. While discourse structure is clearly a characterizing feature of some genres, it is not always the case that every instance of a particular genre will have exactly the same discourse structure (nor indeed the same communicative purpose) (Askehave and Swales 2000). An academic essay, for example, may be an 'explanation', 'evaluation' or 'argument' type text, or a combination of these, as indeed may be a summing up in a court of law. Equally, advertisements may serve not only to inform, but also to persuade, cajole, frighten, shock, worry or arouse (Cook 1989).

Communicative purpose is an important (although complex) criterion for deciding whether a text is an instance of a particular genre. That is, a text may be presented in an unusual way (for that particular genre) but still have the same communicative aim as other instances of the particular genre. In some cases, the text might be considered a 'best example' of the particular genre, and in others, it might be so atypical as to be considered a 'problematic' example of the genre. Shopping lists, responses to letters of recommendation and company brochures, for example, may have more than a single communicative purpose (Askehave and Swales 2000). A book review may describe and evaluate a book but may also 'promote' the book. Book introductions which introduce the work may also promote it (Bhatia 1997).

The issue of genre identification is, thus, a complex one and requires a flexible rather than a static view of what it is that leads users of a language to recognize a communicative event as an instance of a particular genre. A key factor in this process lies in a perspective on genre based on the notion of prototype (Rosch 1978, 1983) rather than on sets of defining features. Genres are most helpfully seen as 'resources for meaning' rather than 'systems of rules' (Swales 2002: 25). There may be typical ways in which they are organized at the discourse level, typical situations in which they occur and typical things they 'aim to do'. It is not always the case, however, that these will necessarily be the same in every instance, even though they may be in the majority of cases.

Assigning a text to a genre category, then, does not necessarily involve an exact match in terms of characteristics or properties. Rather, it involves the notion of 'sufficient similarity'

(Swales 1990) to have a relationship with other examples of the genre in the particular genre category.

4.2 Relationships between genres

A recent development in genre theory has been the notions of *genre networks*, *genre chains*, *genre sets* and *repertoires of genres* (Tardy 2003, Devitt 2004, Swales 2004). A key issue here is the way the use of one genre may assume or depend on the use of a number of other interrelated genres. An example of this is the academic essay which may draw from and cite a number of other genres such as academic lectures, specialist academic texts and journal articles. Academic essays also interrelate closely with assignment guidelines, statements of assessment criteria, tutorial discussions and teacher–student consultations.

Uhrig (2012) carried out a study in which he examined the relationship between genres that graduate law and MBA students at a major US university engaged in as they worked towards meeting the assessment requirements for their courses. He found these genres differed for each of the students he looked at, as well as across the two areas of study. He also found the ways in which they prepared for their assessments were quite different. In law, for example, he found informal study group sessions and hornbooks (summaries of legal cases) were especially important, whereas for MBA students class discussions and oral presentations of business cases made important contributions to their assessment outcomes. Uhrig argues that in order to assist students in these situations it is not sufficient to examine just the final assessments that are required of them. We also need to find out more about the genres they take part in as they prepare for these assessments.

Cope (2009) carried out an analysis of the genres that students need to interact with in order to apply for admission to vocational colleges. She found that the application process was much more complicated than she has expected. The students had to engage in a range of spoken and written genres each of which was interconnected with the other, as well as have almost an insider's understanding of how to stand the greatest chance of being admitted to their preferred course of study. Some of the courses, she found, had 'walk-in' enrolment where students are allocated a place on a first-come, first-served basis. The students she spoke to told her that in order to get into these courses they had to be in the queue early in the morning, at 6 am or so, or they stood no chance of being admitted to the course, no matter how well they had read the course guide, how well they had sought advice from the student counsellor or how well they had completed the application form.

A further example of the interrelatedness of genres can be seen in the job interview which interacts with a number of other genres in a particular genre network which includes the job advertisement, the position description, the letter of application and the resumé. The job interview may then be followed by an offer of appointment and, perhaps, a negotiation of offer, each of which interrelate closely with the genres which precede them. The typical sequence for these genres is shown in Figure 4.2.

Job advertisement	Position description	Letter of application	Resumé	Job interview	Offer of appointment	Negotiation of offer

Figure 4.2 A genre chain: Applying for a job

At times people may draw on a repertoire of genres to carry out a particular task. A company may, for example, seek further information on a job applicant by means of a telephone call, an email, a letter, a fax or (in some circumstances) a casual conversation. Further information may also be sought by asking a question in passing at lunch or dinner, over a drink, or in a casual corridor conversation with the applicant. In some countries the genre network for job applications may be more complex than this. When applying for certain jobs in Italy, for example, it is often helpful to have someone who knows you who can 'put in a word for you' when you apply for the position; that is, what in Italian is called a 'raccomandazione'. Some public positions in Italy, including very senior ones, also require the applicant to take part in a public written examination, or 'concorso', something which occurs much less often in English-speaking job application settings.

Knowledge about genres, thus, includes an understanding of 'the totality of genres available in the particular sector' (Swales 2004: 22), how these genres interact with each other, which genres a person might choose to perform a particular task and what the typical sequence and hierarchy of these genres might be; that is, which genres might have the most value in the particular setting. In Italy, for example, a 'raccomandazione' may have higher value than a letter of recommendation, or public examination, in the job application process. In other cultures, someone 'putting in a word' for a job applicant may have much less influence or, indeed, a negative effect.

An example of a genre chain: Letters to the editor

Letters to the editor provide a useful example of genre chains in that they often refer to and assume a knowledge of other genres and other preceding events. They may refer to another instance of the same genre – that is, a previous letter to the editor – or to a range of different genres (and other knowledges). The letter to the editor from the beginning of this chapter (see Figure 4.1) is an example of this. In this letter, Sally Sartain refers to a review of a restaurant published in a previous edition of the same newspaper (Downes 1995). A subsequent newspaper article (Walker 1997) about the particular food reviewer provides more background to this particular situation. In this article, the reporter writes about an occasion where the reviewer was refused entry to a restaurant he had come to review because of his reputation for giving damning reviews. He returned a month later with his company lawyer and was again refused entry. The restaurant owner told him 'You're welcome to eat, but not to write'. The letter to the editor, then, is clearly more than just a reaction to a single text. It is a reaction to a number of previous texts and previous events. Each of these texts interacts with each other within their own particular genre network. Looking at the texts in isolation removes them from this context as well as removes much of the information needed to more fully interpret the texts and to make a judgement about them.

An example of a genre network

Figure 4.3 is an example of a genre network based on the genres research students at US universities need to be familiar with. This network shows genres outside of the typical ones research students might assume they need to be able to take part in in order to succeed in (and beyond) their university studies. The sequence in which they take part in these genres may vary, and may not be necessarily the same for every student, but they are part of a typical repertoire of genre needs for many research students. A further issue for students

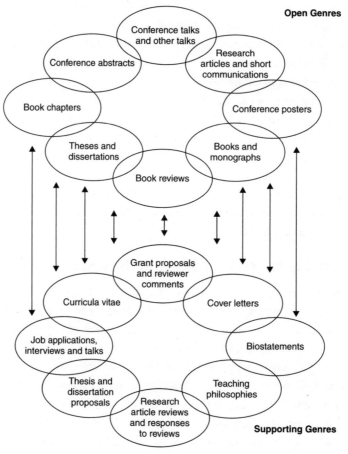

Figure 4.3 A genre network for graduate research students (Swales and Feak 2011: x)

in this kind of setting is that many of the genres they need to be able to participate in are what Swales (1996) terms occluded or supporting genres (Swales and Feak 2000, 2011), that is, genres which are 'closed', not public in nature and often difficult to access examples of. Swales and Feak contrast these with open genres, that is, genres that are public, are often published, and are easily visible or audible. As they point out supporting genres often pose particular problems for graduate students and people who are beginning to carry out research.

An example of genre sets

Figure 4.4 shows the genre chains and genre sets around the writing of Swales' (1998) book *Other Floors, Other Voices*. It shows the relationship between his original book proposal and the other genres that he was involved in, and which influenced the production of the final text of his book. Other genres not included here would no doubt include the interviews that were conducted for the study the book is based on (most by Swales, but in the case of his own case study, the interview with Swales by Tony Dudley-Evans), the other data that was

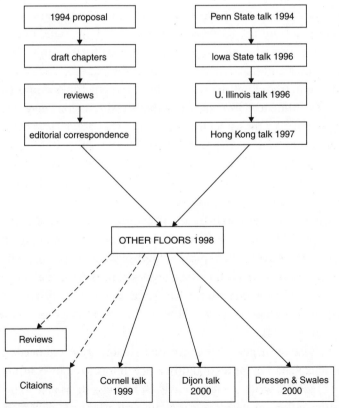

Figure 4.4 Genre chains and genre sets for the writing of Swales' (1998) *Other Floors, Other Voices* (Swales 2004: 24)

examined for the writing of the book, the publisher's contract, any permissions or ethics application that were required for carrying out the research and publication of the book and any other conversations that may have taken place between the author and the study participants in the process of carrying out the study the book is based on.

4.3 Written genres across cultures

The area of research known as contrastive rhetoric (Connor 1996) or more recently *intercultural rhetoric* (Connor 2004) which looks at the use of genres across cultures also has implications for discussions of genre. Many studies in the area of contrastive and intercultural rhetoric have focused on the discourse structure of academic writing in different languages and cultures.

Contrastive rhetoric has its origins in the work of Kaplan (1966) who examined different patterns in the academic essays of students from a number of different languages and cultures. Although Kaplan has since revised his strong claim that differences in academic writing in different languages are the result of culturally different ways of thinking, many studies have found important differences in the discourse structure of academic texts in different languages and cultures. Other studies, however, have found important similarities in the discourse structure of academic writing across cultures. Cahill (2003), for example, argues that in Chinese and Japanese essay writing, for example, the discourse structure is not always as different from English essay writing as is sometimes supposed. Some Western teachers, he argues, influenced by contrastive rhetoric discussions may expect to see 'Asian ways of writing' in their Asians students' essays 'when they are in fact not there at all' (Cahill 2003: 187). Kubota (1997) argues that just as Japanese expository writing has more than one typical discourse structure so too does English, and that it is misleading to try to reduce discourse types to the one single norm and to overgeneralize the cultural characteristics of academic writing from a few specific examples.

Leki (1997) argues that many stylistic and discourse devices that are said to be typical of Chinese, Japanese and Thai writing, for example, also occur in certain contexts in English. Equally, features that are said to be typical of English writing appear, on occasion, in other languages as well. Contrastive rhetoric, she argues, can most usefully be seen, not as the study of culture-specific thought patterns, but as the study of 'the differences or preferences in the pragmatic and strategic choices that writers make in response to external demands and cultural histories' (244).

Canagarajah (2002: 68) argues that contrastive rhetoric research needs 'to develop more complex types of explanation for textual difference' if it is to enjoy continued usefulness in the teaching of academic writing. Genre analysis, he suggests, is able to help provide some of this explanation, as long as it keeps away from normative, rule-governed and 'value-free' descriptions of genre-specific discourse patterns. This call has been taken up by Connor,

Nagelhout and Rozycki (2008) in their book *Contrastive Rhetoric: Reaching to Intercultural Rhetoric* where they draw on theories in composition studies, cultural anthropology, translation studies and text linguistics to address this issue. Pedagogical implications of this are outlined in Connor's (2011) *Intercultural Rhetoric in the Writing Classroom*. Wang (2007), in his book *Genre across Languages and Cultures*, also, makes a case for further complexifying contrastive genre studies. By drawing together research in intercultural rhetoric, rhetorical genre studies, the systemic functional view of genre and critical discourse analysis, he examines the relationship between texts and the sociocultural contexts in which they are produced in order to gain an understanding of why the texts have been written as they are (see Paltridge and Wang 2010, 2011 for further discussion of this work).

4.4 Spoken genres across cultures

Much less attention has been given, however, to differences in spoken genres across cultures. One interesting study that does do this is Nakanishi's (1998) examination of 'going on a first date' in Japanese, which in his study meant mostly having dinner with someone for the purpose of getting to know them better. Nakanishi collected data from 61 Japanese women and 67 Japanese men. He then compared his findings with similar research carried out in the United States. Nakanishi was interested in the typical sequence of events in the lead up to, the carrying out and the closing of this genre in Japanese. He was also interested in how Japanese men and women acted during, and at the end of, the first date. He found the way men and women conceptualized this genre in Japanese was very similar. He found, however, gender specific behaviour in the performance of this genre such as the Japanese women avoiding silence during the date and asking a lot of questions to find out more about their dating partner. The Japanese women were also much less hesitant in expressing their ideas and feelings on a first date than they would be in many other genres in Japanese. This was especially interesting as in other genres silence and reticence are perfectly acceptable in Japanese and, indeed, quite normal. If the Japanese women had been silent he found, they often thought the date had not been a success. What is especially interesting about this study is that the women in Nakanishi's study behaved in a way during the date that is not typical of what someone familiar with Japanese culture and communication styles might expect.

In the US study, the men took proactive roles in setting up the date and deciding where it would be, as they did in the Japanese study. The men in both sets of data were also more proactive and the women more reactive in the closing of the date. The role of conversation in the two sets of data differed remarkably however. In the US data the women saw their role as following their dating partner's lead in the conversation, and helping to keeping the conversation going, whereas the Japanese women much more often initiated the conversation and the choice of topics in the conversation. There was also an important role for non-verbal behaviour during the date in the Japanese data that was quite different from the US data. The Japanese women observed their dating partner's behaviour as a way of finding out more about them. They looked at the way the men ate (my Japanese students tell me they can tell a lot about a person's upbringing from the way they eat) and their use of eye contact. The American women commented more on what the men physically did, or did not do on the date, saying things such as 'He lost points for not opening my car door' and 'He never touched me the whole night . . . I began to wonder about him' (my Japanese female students tell me they would be horrified if a boy touched them on the first date). The role of conversation and non-verbal behaviour in the two settings, thus, was quite different. It is important to remember, then, that while there may be ways of performing the same genre across cultures that are quite similar, there may also be parts of the genre that are significantly (and importantly) quite different.

4.5 Genre and academic writing

The notion of genre is especially important for the teaching of academic writing. This has been taken up, however, in different ways in different parts of the world. In Britain and the United States, for example, English for specific purposes genre work has focused mostly on second language graduate student writing (see Paltridge 2001, forthcoming, Hyland 2004a, Bawarshi and Reiff 2010 for reviews of this work). Work in rhetorical genre studies has focused on first language academic and professional writing in North American colleges and universities (although, increasingly, beyond) (see e.g. Artemeva and Freedman 2008, Bazerman et al. 2009). Genre-based teaching in Australia, on the other hand, has had a rather different focus. This, in part, draws from the underlying concern in the Australian work with empowering underprivileged members of the community and providing them with the necessary resources for academic success. While initially focusing on writing in elementary and secondary school settings, the Australian genre work (often known as the 'Sydney School') has now moved to writing in higher education as well (Humphrey et al. 2010).

Discourse and academic writing

Many of the analyses of the discourse structure of academic texts have been based on Swales' (1981, 1990) work in this area. These studies have examined, for example, the discourse structures of research articles, master's theses and doctoral dissertations, job application and sales promotion letters, legislative documents, the graduate seminar, academic lectures, poster session discussions and the texts that students read in university courses. One model that has had a particular impact in this area is what has come to be known as the CARS (Create a research space) framework (see Feak and Swales 2011). This framework describes the typical discourse structure of the Introduction section of research articles. Swales shows how in this section of research article introductions authors establish the territory for their research by showing how it is important and relevant in some way, indicate the gap in previous research that the study aims to address and how the study being described will fill the gap that the earlier sections of the Introduction have identified. This model has since been applied to the Introduction section of other genres such as theses and dissertations (see e.g. Bunton 2002; Paltridge and Starfield 2007). Other analyses have focused on how micro-genres (Martin and Rose 2008), or *rhetorical types*, such as arguments and descriptions, etc. come together in the writing of academic genres such as student assignments and essays, etc. (see Paltridge 1996, 2002a, Paltridge et al. 2009; also Section 4.8 below on the discourse structure of genres).

Language and academic writing

There have been a number of views on the nature of genre-specific language. Hutchinson and Waters (1987), for example, made a distinction between the language of an area of specialization and the language of the genres found in these particular areas. They argued that the main way in which language varied between areas of specialization was in the use of technical and specialized vocabulary rather than in its use of genre-specific language. More recent developments in the area of corpus studies, however, have disputed this view.

Biber (1988), for example, in an important study found a wide range of linguistic variation within the particular genres that he examined, some of which he describes as surprising and contrary to popular expectation. His conclusion is that different kinds of texts are complex in different ways and that many earlier conclusions that have been reached about specific purpose language reflect our incomplete understanding of the linguistic characteristics of discourse complexity (Biber 1992). In his view, there clearly *are* language differences between genres. These differences, however, can only be revealed through the examination of actual texts rather than through any intuitions we may have about them. This is an area where genre studies have already devoted a great amount of attention, from early frequency studies through to more recent corpus-based studies of the language of academic genres. Biber's (2006) *University Language* and Hyland's (2009a) *Academic Discourse* provide reviews of much of this work.

Charles, Pecorari and Hunston (2009) in their book *Academic Writing* explore the interface between corpus studies and discourse analysis in the analysis of academic writing. They argue that these two approaches are complementary in that discourse analysis is more 'top-down' while corpus-based analyses are more 'bottom-up'. Studies, such as Koutsantoni's (2009) examination of rhetorical patterns in research funding proposals are an example of *corpus-assisted discourse studies* while studies such as Hyland's (2009b) study of the ways in which student writers establish the presence of their readers in their texts is an example of *corpus informed discourse analysis*. By using interview data to supplement the corpus component of his study, Hyland shows how each approach can 'inform and enrich each other, thereby leading to more insightful analyses of language use' (Hyland 2009b, 110).

Academic writing and metadiscourse

The term *metadiscourse* was first coined by the linguist Zellig Harris (1959) to describe the way in which a writer or speaker tries to guide their audience's perception of their text (Hyland 2005b). As Hyland points out, however, different people have defined this term differently. Williams (1981), for example, describes metadiscourse as 'writing about writing' while Crismore (1983, 1989) describes metadiscourse as 'discourse about discourse', defining the term as 'the author's intrusion into the discourse, either explicitly or inexplicitly' (Crismore 1983: 2). Hyland (1998a) describes metadiscourse as 'aspects of a text which explicitly refer to the organization of the writer's stance towards either its content or the reader' (438). This includes *interactive* rhetorical features which reflect the writer's awareness of their audience, its interests and expectations and *interactional* rhetorical features which include the ways in which authors convey judgements and align themselves with their readers (Hyland 2005b).

Interactive rhetorical resources

Interactive metadiscourse resources, then, help guide readers through a text. This includes ways of expressing relations between clauses, the stages of the text, information that is in other parts of the text, information that has been drawn from other texts and ways of elaborating on meanings in the text. These resources aim to lead readers to the author's preferred interpretation of their text. Examples of interactive rhetorical resources and their functions are shown in Table 4.1.

Table 4.1 Interactive metadiscourse resources in academic writing (Hyland 2005b: 49)

Category	Function	Examples
Interactive	**Help to guide the reader through the text**	**Resources**
Transitions	Express relations between main clauses	in addition; but; thus; and
Frame markers	Refer to discourse acts, sequences or stages	finally; to conclude; my purpose is
Endophoric markers	Refer to information in other parts of the text	noted above; see Fig; in Section 4.2
Evidentials	Refer to information from other texts	according to x; z states
Code glosses	Elaborate propositional meanings	namely; e.g.; such as; in other words

Interactional rhetorical resources

Interactional metadiscourse resources include the ways in which writers express their *stance* towards what they are saying as well as how they explicitly engage with or address their readers in their texts (Hyland 2005b). Stance is the ways in which writers present themselves and convey their judgements, opinions and commitments to their own and other people's work. In doing this a writer may either 'intrude to stamp their personal authority onto their arguments, or step back and disguise their involvement' (176). *Engagement* is the strategy writers use to acknowledge and recognize the presence of their readers, 'pulling them along with their argument, focusing their attention, acknowledging their uncertainties, including them as discourse participants and guiding them to interpretations' (Hyland 2005b: 176). The key ways in which academic writers do this are shown in Table 4.2.

Table 4.2 Interactional metadiscourse resources in academic writing (Hyland 2005b: 49)

Category	Function	Examples
Interactional	**Involve the reader in the text**	**Resources**
Hedges	withhold commitment and open dialogue	might; possibly; about
Boosters	emphasize certainty or close dialogue	in fact; definitely; it is clear that
Attitude markers	express writer's attitude to proposition	unfortunately; I agree; surprisingly
Self mentions	explicit reference to author(s)	I; we; my; me; our
Engagement markers	explicitly build relationship with reader	consider; note; you can see that

4.6 Steps in genre analysis

Bhatia (1993) and Bawarshi and Reiff (2010) present steps for carrying out the analysis of genres, in their case written genres. It is not necessary to go through all the stages that they list, nor in the order in which they are presented. For example, we may decide to take a 'text-first' or a 'context-first' approach to the analysis of a particular genre (Flowerdew 2002, 2011). That is, we may decide to start by looking at typical discourse patterns in the texts we are interested in (a text-first approach), or we may decide to start with an examination of the context of the texts we want to investigate (a context-first approach). The steps, then, should be used flexibly and selectively depending on the starting point of the analysis, the purpose of the analysis, the aspect of the genre that we want to focus on and the level of prior knowledge we already have of the particular genre.

The first step, however, is to collect samples of the genre you are interested in. Bhatia suggests taking a few randomly chosen texts for exploratory investigation, a single typical text for detailed analysis, or a larger sample of texts if we wish to investigate a few specified features. Clearly, the more samples you can collect of the genre, however, the better you will be able to identify typical features of the genre.

The next step is to consider what is already known about the particular genre. This includes knowledge of the setting in which it occurs as well as any conventions that are typically associated with the genre. For information on this, we can go to existing literature such as guide books and manuals as well as seek practitioner advice on the particular genre. It is also helpful to look at what analyses have already have been carried out of the particular genre, or other related genres, by looking at research articles or books on the topic.

We next need to refine the analysis by defining the speaker or writer of the text, the audience of the text and their relationship with each other. That is, who uses the genre, who writes in the genre, who reads the genre and what roles the readers perform as they read the text.

We also need to consider the goal, or purpose, of the texts. That is, why do writers write this genre, why do readers read it and what purpose does the genre have for the people who use it?

A further important consideration is typical discourse patterns for the genre. That is, how are the texts typically organized, how are they typically presented in terms of layout and format and what are some language features that typically re-occur in the particular genre?

Equally, what do people need to know to take part in the genre, and what view of the world does the text assume of its readers? That is, what values, beliefs and assumptions are assumed or revealed by the particular genre (Bawarshi and Reiff 2010)?

We should also think about the networks of texts that surround the genre (see Section 4.2 above) and to what extent knowledge of these is important in order be able to write or make sense of a particular genre.

4.7 The social and cultural context of genres

An important stage in genre analysis, then, is an examination of the social and cultural context in which the genre is used. In the case of a written text, factors that might be considered include:

- the setting of the text;
- the focus and perspective of the text;
- the purpose(s) of the text;
- the intended audience for the text, their role and purpose in reading the text;
- the relationship between writers and readers of the text;
- expectations, conventions and requirements for the text;
- the background knowledge, values and understandings it is assumed the writer shares with their readers, including what is important to the reader and what is not;
- the relationship the text has with other texts.

These aspects of a genre, of course, are not as distinct as they appear in this kind a listing. As Yates and Orlikowski (2007) point out, they are deeply intertwined and each, in its way, has an impact on what a writer writes, and the way they write it.

A context analysis of theses and dissertations

Figure 4.5 is an analysis of the social and cultural context of theses and dissertations. It shows the range of factors that impact on how the text is written, how it will be read and, importantly, how it will be assessed.

Setting of the text	The kind of university and level of study, the kind of degree (e.g. honours, master's or doctoral, research or professional)
	Study carried out in a 'hard' or 'soft', pure or applied, convergent or divergent area of study (Becher and Trowler 2001)
Focus and perspective of the text	Quantitative, qualitative or mixed method research
	Claims that can be made, claims that cannot be made
	Faculty views on what is 'good' research
Purpose of the text	To answer a question, to solve a problem, to prove something, to contribute to knowledge, to display knowledge and understanding, to demonstrate particular skills, to convince a reader, to gain admission to a particular area of study
Audience, role and purpose in reading the text	To judge the quality of the research
	Primary readership of one or more examiners, secondary readership of the supervisor and anyone else the student shows their work to
	How readers will react to what they read, the criteria they will use for assessing the text, who counts the most in judging the quality of the text
Relationship between writers and readers of the text	Students writing for experts, for admission to an area of study (the primary readership), students writing for peers, for advice (the secondary readership)
Expectations, conventions and requirements for the text	An understanding and critical appraisal of relevant literature
	A clearly defined and comprehensive investigation of the research topic
	Appropriate use of research methods and techniques for the research question
	Ability to interpret results, develop conclusions and link them to previous research
	Level of critical analysis, originality and contribution to knowledge expected
	Literary quality and standard of presentation expected
	Level of grammatical accuracy required
	How the text is typically organized, how the text might vary for a particular research topic, area of study, kind of study and research perspective
	What is typically contained in each chapter
	The amount of variation allowed in what should be addressed and how it should be addressed
	The university's formal submission requirements in terms of format, procedures and timing
Background knowledge, values and understandings	The background knowledge, values and understandings it is assumed students will share with their readers – what is important to their readers, what is not important to their readers
	How much knowledge students are expected to display, the extent to which students should show what they know, what issues students should address, what boundaries students can cross
Relationship the text has with other texts	How to show the relationship between the present research and other people's research on the topic, what counts as valid previous research, acceptable and unacceptable textual borrowings, differences between reporting and plagiarizing

Figure 4.5 The social and cultural context of theses and dissertations

It is crucial, then, not just to analyse the discourse structure of texts, but also to gain an understanding of the socially situated nature of texts and the role they are playing in their particular setting. Lillis (2008: 353), in her discussion of strategies for 'closing the gap between text and context' suggests ways in which researchers may contextualize their research as a way of 'adding value' to their studies. These include what she terms 'ethnography as method', 'ethnography as methodology' and ethnography as 'deep theorizing'.

An example of ethnography as method is 'talk around text'. Talk around texts aims to get writers' perspectives on texts they have produced. Often this involves carrying out text-based interviews or using survey data to supplement the textual analysis. Peng (2010) did just this when she combined text analysis with talk around text in her genre study of Chinese PhD students' acknowledgements texts. She carried out an analysis of 80 acknowledgements sections from PhDs submitted at a major Chinese university in the areas of classic Chinese, computer science, genetic engineering and world economics. She examined how the writers drew on their genre knowledge of acknowledgements texts and the disciplinary community in which they were writing to accommodate their audience's expectations. In order to find out reasons for the textual choices that the students made, she interviewed students, their supervisors, as well as the other people that were referred to in the texts.

Ethnography as methodology involves using multiple data sources as well as a period of sustained involvement in the context in which the texts are produced to try to gain an understanding of the 'dynamic and complex situated meanings and practices that are constituted in and by the writing' (Lillis 2008: 355). Curry and Lillis' (2010) book *Academic writing in a global context* where they employed text analysis, interviews, observations, document analysis, written correspondence, reviewers' and editors' comments to examine second language writers' experiences of getting published in English is an example of this. A further example of the use of multiple data sources is the study by Paltridge et al. (2011a, 2011b) into doctoral writing in the visual and performing arts. Here, text analysis was combined with surveys, text-based interviews with students and their supervisors, the examination of university prospectuses, published advice to students, previous research into visual arts PhD examination, books and journals on visual and performing arts research, analysis of in-house art school publications and attendance at students' exhibition openings.

Ethnography as deep theorizing takes these approaches a step further by considering how the use of language and orientation of the texts index and connect to certain social structures, values and relations in the same way that particular ways of speaking may point to, or index, a person's gender, social class or ethnic identity. Starfield (2002, 2011) does this, for example, in her examination of first year students' writing in a former whites-only university in South Africa, as do Lillis and Curry (2010) in their study of second language scholars negotiating the peer-review and writing for publication process.

These studies parallel what Berkenkotter (2009: 18) calls a context-based, rhetorically oriented, 'wide-angle' approach to genre analysis that moves beyond solely text-based analysis to explore factors that influence the creation and reception of genres in particular social, cultural and political settings. Indeed, as Devitt (2009) argues, the forms of genres are only meaningful within their social, cultural (and individual) contexts. That is, forms in genres 'take their meaning from who uses them, in what ways, with what motives and expectations' (35) (see Paltridge and Wang 2011 for further discussions of contextualized genre studies, Bucholtz 2011 for examples of ethnographically situated spoken discourse studies).

4.8 The discourse structure of genres

There are a number of ways in which the discourse structure of genres can be analysed. One of these is by identifying its *generic structure* based on its genre category membership such as letter to the editor, doctoral dissertation, etc. Another is to examine its *rhetorical structure* by looking at *rhetorical types* such as argument, description and problem–solution that occur within the text. The letter to the editor in Figure 4.1 for example shows the generic structure of the text as an instance of a letter to the editor, and the rhetorical type that occurs simultaneously in the text, that of an argument type text. The text shown in Figure 4.6 of the abstract section of an experimental research report is analysed in terms of both its generic structure and as an instance of a problem–solution rhetorical type text.

Generic Structure		Rhetorical structure
Title	*Composing letters with a simulated listening typewriter*	Situation
Background	With a listening typewriter, what an author says would be automatically recognized and displayed in front of him or her. However, speech recognition is not yet advanced enough to provide people with a reliable listening typewriter.	Situation
Aim of the study	An aim of our experiments was to determine if an imperfect listening typewriter would be useful for composing letters.	Problem
Methods	Participants dictated letters, either in isolated words or in consecutive word speech. They did this with simulations of listening typewriters that recognized either a limited vocabulary or an unlimited vocabulary.	Solution
Results	Results indicated that some versions, even upon first using them, were at least as good as traditional methods of handwriting and dictating.	
Conclusion	Isolated word speech with large vocabularies may provide the basis of a useful listening typewriter.	Evaluation

Figure 4.6 Abstract of an experimental research report/problem–solution text (based on Gould, Conti and Hovanyecz 1983: 295)

Two different perspectives, thus, can be offered on the structure of texts: one that identifies the text's *generic structure* based on its genre category and another that describes its *rhetorical structure* based on its patternings of rhetorical organization. These rhetorical types together make up larger, more complex texts.

An example: The discourse structure of theses and dissertations

Figure 4.7 is an analysis of the typical generic structure of theses and dissertations. This analysis comes from a study (Paltridge 2002b) that examined theses and dissertations written in a range of different study areas. The texts were collected and analysed in terms of the

Traditional: simple	Topic-based
Introduction	Introduction
Literature review	Topic 1
Materials and methods	Topic 2
Results	Topic 3, etc.
Discussion	Conclusions
Conclusions	
Traditional: complex	**Compilation of research articles**
Introduction	Introduction
Background to the study and review	Background to the study
of the literature	Research article 1
(Background theory)	Introduction
(General methods)	Literature review
Study 1	Materials and methods
Introduction	Results
Methods	Discussion
Results	Conclusions
Discussion and conclusions	Research article 2
Study 2	Introduction
Introduction	Literature review
Methods	Materials and methods
Results	Results
Discussion and conclusions	Discussion
Study 3, etc.	Conclusions
Introduction	Research article 3, etc.
Methods	Introduction
Results	Literature review
Discussion and conclusions	Materials and methods
Discussion	Results
Conclusions	Discussion
	Conclusions
	Discussion
	Conclusions

Figure 4.7 The discourse structure of theses and dissertations (Paltridge 2002b: 135)

overall organizational structure of each of the texts. A comparison was then made between the texts in order to see if there was a recurring pattern of structural organization across the set of texts. The study showed that, rather than there being just the one single type of discourse pattern that is typical for theses and dissertations, there are at least four different types of pattern that writers typically choose from depending on the focus and orientation of their thesis or dissertation. Following previous research on the topic, these four thesis and dissertation types were labelled 'simple traditional', 'complex traditional', 'topic-based' and 'compilations of research articles'. The four types are shown in Figure 4.8. The sequence of items in the chart shows the typical sequence in the sections of the texts. The sections in brackets are 'optional' in the texts. That is, they occurred in some instances of the genre, but not in all of them.

Generic Structure		Rhetorical Structure
Title of the dissertation	*Newspaper commentaries on terrorism in China and Australia: A contrastive genre study*	Situation
Sub-section of the dissertation	Abstract	
Overview of the study	This dissertation is a contrastive genre study which explores newspaper commentaries on terrorism in Chinese and Australian newspapers. The study not only examines the textual organization of the Australian and Chinese commentaries, it also explores interpersonal and intertextual features as well as considers possible contextual factors which contribute to the formation of the commentaries in the two cultures and languages.	Situation Problem
Methodology used in the study	To explore the textual, intertextual and contextual aspects of the texts, the study draws on theories from systemic functional linguistics, new rhetoric genre studies, critical discourse analysis, and other discussions of the role of the mass media.	Response
Results of the study	The study reveals that Chinese writers often use explanatory rather than argumentative expositions in their newspaper commentaries. They seem to distance themselves from outside sources and seldom indicate endorsement to these sources. Australian writers, on the other hand, predominantly use argumentative expositions to argue their points of view. They integrate and manipulate outside sources in various ways to establish and provide support for the views they express. These textual and intertextual practices are closely related to contextual factors, especially the roles of the media and opinion discourse in contemporary China and Australia.	Solution
Aims of the study	The study, thus, aims to provide both a textual and contextual view of the genre under investigation in these two cultures and languages.	Problem
Reasons for the study	In doing so, it aims to establish a framework for contrastive rhetoric research which moves beyond the text into the context of production and interpretation of the text as a way of exploring reasons for linguistic and rhetorical choices made in the two sets of texts.	Evaluation

Figure 4.8 An analysis of an abstract for a doctoral dissertation (based on Wang 2006b)

Figure 4.8 is an analysis of an abstract from a doctoral dissertation in terms of both its generic and rhetorical structures. In this example, the text follows the typical generic structure for a dissertation abstract (Paltridge and Starfield 2007, Swales and Feak 2009). It is also an example of a problem–solution text (Hoey 1983, 2001).

4.9 Applications of genre analysis

Writers such as Hammond and Macken-Horarick (1999) argue that genre-based teaching can help students gain access to texts and discourses which will, hopefully, help them participate more successfully in second language spoken and written interactions. Other writers, such as Luke (1996), argue that teaching 'genres of power' (such as academic essays or dissertations) leads to uncritical reproduction of the status quo and does not necessarily provide the kind of access we hope it might provide for our learners. Others, such as Christie (1993) and Martin (1993) argue that not teaching genres of power is socially irresponsible in that it is the already disadvantaged students who are especially disadvantaged by programmes that do not address these issues.

Other issues that have been raised include the extent to which the teaching and learning of genres might limit student expression if this is done through the use of model texts and a focus on audience expectations. This is clearly something teachers need to keep in mind in genre-based teaching. Teachers equally need to think about how they can help students bring their own individual voices into their use of particular genres (Swales 2000). Students also need to be careful not to overgeneralize what they have learnt about one genre and apply it inappropriately to their use of other genres (Hyon 2001, Johns 2008). As Devitt (2004) points out, the ways in which students draw on prior genre knowledge to create a further instance of the particular genre are not at all straightforward and may take place in a number of different ways (see Reiff and Bawarshi 2011 for further discussion of this).

Kay and Dudley-Evans (1998) discuss teachers' views on genre and its use in second language classrooms. Some of the teachers Kay and Dudley-Evans spoke to were concerned that a genre-based approach may become too prescriptive. The teachers pointed to the need to highlight the kind of variation that occurs in particular genres as well as consider why this might be. Care, then, needs to be taken to avoid a reductive view of genres and the textual information that is given to students about them.

The teachers Kay and Dudley-Evans spoke to also stressed the importance of contextualizing genres in the classroom by discussing purpose, audience and underlying beliefs and values before moving on to focus on the language features of a text. They said learners should be exposed to a wide range of sample texts and that these should be both authentic and suitable for the learners. They also felt a genre-based approach should be used in combination with other approaches, such as process and communicative approaches to language teaching and learning. They said, however, they thought a genre-based approach was especially suitable for beginner and intermediate level students in that the use of model texts gave them confidence as well as something to fall back on. They concluded that genre provided a useful framework for language teaching and learning as long as it was made clear that the examples of genres they presented with were just possible models and not rigid sets of patterns.

Scott and Groom (1999) present a similar view, saying that genres are not fixed codes but just one of the resources students need for the expression and communication of meaning. The teaching of generic forms, for Scott and Groom, does not discount the use of models, but rather sees models as part of a of wider repertoire of resources that students can draw on and adapt, as appropriate, to support their meaning making.

Tardy (2006) examines the research into genre-based teaching, in both first and second language contexts. As she points out, genre theory has gone beyond looking at genres as just 'text types' to considerations of genre as 'a more social construct which shapes and is shaped by human activity' (79). The work of Cheng (2006a, 2006b, 2007, 2008a, 2008b) is especially important in discussions of genre-based teaching and learning. Cheng (2008a) discusses how his students found genre 'a supportive, explicit tool of learning' (68) which he felt helped address other researchers' concerns about the product-oriented nature of ESP genre-based teaching. Dressen-Hammouda's (2008) study of a geology student's experiences in learning to write showed how he benefitted from a focus on genre, especially in relation to the acquisition of disciplinary identity. She argues, along with others, that the teaching of genres should include more than just linguistic and rhetorical features of genres. It should also focus on the disciplinary community's ways of perceiving, interpreting and behaving; that is, the 'ways of being, seeing and acting' (238) that are particular to the student's disciplinary community.

Other research that has examined genre-based teaching include Bax's (2006) examination of the role of genre in language syllabus design in a secondary school in Bahrain and Kongpetch's (2003, 2006) examination of genre-based writing teaching in a Thai university. Kongpetch found that the genre-based approach she employed had a significant impact on the quality of her students' writing. While she was only looking at a single case, her study does suggest that this approach can have many benefits for students. Johns (2008) points out, however, that in all this students need to develop both genre awareness and rhetorical flexibility. That is, they need to learn the expectations of particular genres in particular settings, as well as remain flexible when applying this knowledge to the requirements of the particular text they are producing.

Genres, then, provide a frame (Swales 2004) which enables people to take part in, and interpret, particular communicative events. Making this genre knowledge explicit can provide learners with the knowledge and skills they need to communicate successfully in particular situations. It can also provide learners with access to socially powerful forms of language.

4.10 Summary

This chapter has provided definitions of as well as examples of genre analysis. It has outlined features of Sydney School, English for specific purposes and rhetorical genre studies analysis. It has discussed the issue of choice and constraint in the use of spoken and written genres and the complex issue of assigning a text to a genre category. It has argued that genre identification is complex one and requires a flexible, rather than a static view of what it is that leads users of a language to recognize a text as an instance of a particular genre. The chapter has also argued that genre is an extremely useful notion of pedagogic purposes. It has cautioned, however, against using descriptions of genre in the classroom simply as rules that need to be followed; that is, being careful not to mistake the 'stabilized for now' (Schryer 1993) nature of the genre, as a template that needs to be adopted in order for a text to be considered a successful instance of a particular genre.

4.11 Discussion questions

(1) Bazerman (1988: 7) argues that 'attempts to understand genre by the texts themselves are bound to fail'. Select several examples of a genre. Consider what there is 'beyond the text' (Freedman 1999) that you need to know about in order to fully understand the texts. For example, what is it you need to know about the social and cultural setting of the text, the people involved in the text or the social expectations and values which underlie the particular text. Read Paltridge (2004) for an example of an analysis which examines some of these issues.

(2) Read Johns (1993) on genre and audience. Consider what Johns has to say about audience in relation to a genre that is important for university students. How might the notion of audience help the students with their written work? For example, how useful is it for students to think about who they are writing for, and what that person expects of them?

(3) Look at a number of newspaper reports in several different newspapers which are all on the same topic. What background knowledge do the reports assume? That is, what do they expect you already know (and don't know) about the topic of the article? Also, in what way is each of the newspaper reports different? That is, how does the intended readership of the newspaper effect how the article is written? How can you explain these differences?

(4) Find several instances of a genre which seem to you to be prototypical of the particular genre. What are some features of the genre that seem to you to be typical for the particular genre? Then find one text which is not so typical for the genre. Try to explain these differences.

4.12 Data analysis projects

(1) Look at examples of essays written in different subject areas. Have a look for similarities and differences in the way they are written. For example, are they all laid out the same way? Do they use headings or are they just continuous text? How do the writers support their arguments? Do they refer to published sources, or do they refer to their own personal experiences? Consider what the reason might be for these differences.

(2) Collect a number of examples of a genre that has developed or changed in response to changes in technology. For example, look at email messages and consider what some of the characteristics are that are particular to them. Consider why they are written this way.

(3) Do a context analysis of a spoken or written genre based on the following set of headings:

- the setting of the genre;
- the focus and perspective of the genre;
- the purpose(s) of the genre;
- the intended audience for the genre;
- the relationship between participants in the genre;
- expectations, conventions and requirements for the genre;
- the background knowledge, values and understandings it is assumed genre participants will share with each other, including what is important to them and what is not;
- the relationship the genre has with other texts and genres.

Look at a number of sample texts to help you with this. Also interview people who take part in the genre and ask them about each of these points.

(4) Collect a number of examples of a particular genre and analyse the schematic structure of each text. Look at Chapter 2 in Hyland (2004a) for suggestions on how to do this. What is common to all of the texts and what is not? Why might some of the texts be different?

4.13 Exercises

Exercise 1: Discourse structures: A student essay

Look at the following example of a student essay/problem–solution type text.

This is the typical structure of a problem–solution text:

Situation ^ Problem ^ Response/Solution ^ Evaluation (Hoey 1983, 2001)

(^ indicates 'followed by')

Identify:

- the generic structure of the text as an instance of a student essay.
- the rhetorical structure of the text as an instance of a problem–solution text.

The Kakapo, which is found in the remote and inhospitable south of Stewart Island, is one of New Zealand's most highly endangered birds.

Kakapos are flightless but good climbers, and usually live in native forests, sub-alpine zones. Leave, stems roots and fruit are their main food. They were once described as the most beautiful bird in the world. But nowadays there are only about 50 left.

Because of developments of human beings such as removing soil and grass, cutting the forest for new roads, houses, or factories, the kakapo has lost its habitat and food resources. Huge numbers of them have died from starvation or hunting.

A recovery programme has been launched to save the kakapo from extinction. In this programme, they are attempting to raise kakapos in captivity. In 1981, nests were located and several chicks were hatched.

To conclude, the kakapo is nearly extinct. We have to protect the rest of them and try our best with the recovery programme. We do not want to loose this gentle friend, which is part of New Zealand's heritage.

Exercise 2: Discourse structures: A dissertation abstract

(1) Look at the following abstract from a masters thesis and identify these stages of the text:
- Overview of the study
- Aim of the study
- Reason for the study
- Methodology used in the study
- Findings of the study

(2) Now analyse the text as an instance of a problem–solution text.

The political and educational implications of gender, class and race in Hollywood film: Holding out for a female hero.

Abstract

   This thesis examines the articulations of gender, class, and race in a specific sample of films from the 1930s to the 1990s. The tendency in these films is to depict women as passive, rather than heroic. Because this has been the common practice, I chose to outline it through fourteen films that exemplified an inherent bias when dealing with women as subject matter. Brief summaries of several recently produced progressive films are provided to show that it is possible to improve the image of women in film, hence we may finally witness justice on the big screen.

   In this discursive analysis, I trace specific themes from the feminist and film literature to provide a critical overview of the chosen films, with a view to establishing educational possibilities for the complex issues dealt with in this study. (Lewis 1998)

Exercise 3: Genre and language: Metadiscourse

Look at the dissertation abstract in Exercise 2 as well as Tables 4.1 and 4.2 in this chapter. Identify examples of interactive and interactional metadiscourse features in the text.

Exercise 4: Genre and language: Choice of verb tense

Cooley and Lewkowicz (2003) discuss the use of verb tense in dissertation abstracts. They suggest there are two ways a student may view their abstract: as a summary of their thesis or dissertation, or as a summary of the methodology and findings of the study. The first of these will typically use the *present simple* tense (This thesis *examines* . . .). The second will typically use the *past simple* tense (The study *employed* interview data. . . ., The study *revealed* that . . .) or the *present perfect* tense (The study has *revealed* that . . .).

   Look at the dissertation abstract in Exercise 2 and identify the tenses used in the abstract. Why have the different tenses been used?

Exercise 5: Genre and language: Use of the passive voice

It is a popular view that academic writing uses the passive voice more often than the active voice. Research, however, has shown this to not be the case. Look at the dissertation abstract in Exercise 2 and see to what extent the passive or the active voice predominates. What is the result of this?

Exercise 6: Genre and language: Use of personal pronouns

Hyland (2002c) points out that students are often told to write in an impersonal way and not use 'I' or 'We' in their writing. There is however an increasing shift towards more personal styles of writing in academic texts. Look at the dissertation abstract in Exercise 2 and see to what extent the writer uses personal pronouns in her text. When she does use a personal pronoun, what is the effect of this?

4.14 Directions for further reading

Bawarshi, A. and Reiff, M. J. (2010), *Genre: An Introduction to History, Theory, Research, and Pedagogy*. West Lafayette, IN: Parlor Press.

This book provides an extensive review of the history of genre-based teaching, the theories and research that underlie genre-based teaching and the ways in which these have been taken up in the classroom. Equal attention is given to the work of the Sydney School, the ESP School and rhetorical genre studies.

Martin, J. R. (2011), 'Systemic functional linguistics', in K. Hyland and B. Paltridge (eds), *Continuum Companion to Discourse Analysis*. London: Continuum, pp. 101–19.

This chapter provides a detailed account of the theoretical basis of the work of the Sydney Genre School, systemic functional linguistics. A sample study is provided which illustrates the framework for analysis outlined in the chapter.

Martin, J. R. and Rose, D. (2008), *Genre Relations: Mapping Culture*. London: Equinox.

Martin and Rose's book provides an introduction to the Sydney School work on genre analysis. Detailed accounts of narratives, historical accounts, expositions, reports, explanations and procedures are provided, as well as many analyses of sample texts. Pedagogic applications of this work are discussed further in Rose and Martin's (2012) *Learning to Write/Reading to Learn: Genre, Knowledge and Pedagogy in the Sydney School*.

Paltridge, B. (forthcoming), 'Genre and English for specific purposes', in B. Paltridge and S. Starfield (eds). *Handbook of English for Specific Purposes*. Boston: Blackwell.

This chapter focuses on the English for specific purposes perspective on genre. It describes the history of this view of genre and reviews studies that examine specific purpose genres from this perspective.

Tardy, C. M. (2011), 'The history and future of genre in second language writing', *Journal of Second Language Writing*, 20, 1–5.

In this editorial to a special issue of the *Journal of Second Language Writing* Tardy focuses on the future of genre in second language writing teaching and research in North American contexts. She outlines the papers that address this issue in the collection as well as provides a history to the development of genre-based teaching in North America.

For an extended list of references and further readings see the companion website to this book.

5
Discourse and Conversation

A major area of study in the analysis of discourse is conversation analysis. Conversation analysis looks at ordinary everyday spoken discourse and aims to understand, from a fine-grained analysis of the conversation, how people manage their interactions. It also looks at how social relations are developed through the use of spoken discourse. This chapter discusses the principles underlying conversation analysis. It then outlines procedures in transcribing and coding data. The chapter gives examples of the kinds of conversational strategies speakers use as well as providing examples of these in a number of different kinds of conversational interactions.

> *Conversation analysis* is an approach to the analysis of spoken discourse that looks at the way in which people manage their everyday conversational interactions. It examines how spoken discourse is organized and develops as speakers carry out these interactions. Conversation analysis has examined aspects of spoken discourse such as sequences of related utterances (*adjacency pairs*), preferences for particular combinations of utterances (*preference organization*), *turn taking*, *feedback*, *repair*, *conversational openings and closings*, *discourse markers* and *response tokens*. Conversation analysis works with recordings of spoken data and carries out careful and fine-grained analyses of this data.

5.1 Background to conversation analysis

Conversation analysis originated in the early 1960s at the University of California, Los Angeles. It has it origins in the ethnomethodological tradition of sociology and, in particular, the work of Garfinkel (e.g. 1967) and Goffman (e.g. 1981). Following on from this work Sacks (e.g. 1992, 2007) and his colleagues developed conversation analysis as:

> an approach to the study of social action which sought to investigate social order as it was produced through the practices of everyday talk. (Liddicoat 2011: 4)

Sacks had a particular interest in the orderly nature of talk and the ways in which there might be systematic commonalities in spoken interactions that occur across participants and contexts (Liddicoat 2011).

Conversation analysis started with the examination of telephone calls made to the Los Angeles Suicide Prevention Centre. This work then continued with the examination of more 'ordinary' telephone calls and conversations and has since been extended to include spoken interactions such as doctor–patient consultations, legal hearings, news interviews, psychiatric interviews and interactions in courtrooms and classrooms.

Conversation analysis takes less of a 'linguistics' view of spoken discourse than some other forms of discourse analysis. This draws from its interest, in particular, in how language goes about performing social action. Conversation analysts are interested, in particular, in how social worlds are jointly constructed and recognized by speakers as they take part in conversational discourse.

Issues in conversation analysis

A key issue in conversation analysis is the view of ordinary conversation as the most basic form of talk. For conversation analysts, conversation is the main way in which people come together, exchange information, negotiate and maintain social relations. All other forms of talk-in-interaction are thus derived from this basic form of talk. It is not the case that other forms of talks are the same as ordinary conversation. They do, however, exploit the same kinds of resources as 'ordinary conversation' to achieve their social and interactional goals.

A further key feature of conversation analysis is the primacy of the data as the source of information. Analyses, thus, do not incorporate speakers' reflections on their interactions, field notes or interviews as ways of gathering information about the discourse. In the view of conversation analysts, the use of this kind of data represents idealizations about how spoken discourse works and is, thus, not valid data for analysis. Conversation analysis, thus, focuses on the analysis of the text for its argumentation and explanation, rather than consideration of psychological or other factors that might be involved in the production and interpretation of the discourse.

One of the aims of conversation analysis is to avoid starting with assumptions about analytical categories in the analysis of conversational data. Conversation analysts, rather, look for phenomena which regularly occur in the data and then make that the point of further investigation. Interest is, in particular, in fine-tuned analysis of the sequence, structure and coherence of conversations.

In this view, conversation is seen as being 'context-shaped' and 'context-renewing' in the sense that 'anything anyone says in conversation both builds on what has been said or what has been going on. . . [as well as] creates the conditions for what will be said next' (Gardner 1994: 102). Conversation analysts, thus, aim to demonstrate how participants both produce and respond to evolving social contexts, using conversational, rather than contextual data, as the source for the claims it wishes to make.

Transcribing and coding conversation analysis data

In conversation analysis, the transcription of the data is also the analysis. Texts are, thus, recorded (either on tape or by video) then analysed at the same time as they are transcribed. If a particular feature such as the use of increased pitch or particular sequences of utterances becomes apparent in the analysis, this then becomes the starting point for further analysis. The analyst listens and transcribes to see how frequently this aspect of the conversation occurs and, importantly, if speakers respond to it in the same way each time it occurs. In this way, the analysis aims to understand how speakers manage their conversational interactions.

5.2 Transcription conventions

Particular transcription conventions are used in conversation analysis. The extract from *Sex and the City* that was discussed in Chapter 2 is presented here, transcribed from a conversation analysis perspective. The transcription conventions that are used in this analysis are based on the work of Jefferson (2004) and are shown as a key to the analysis at the end of the conversation:

Charlotte:	you're getting engag↑ed
Carrie:	I threw up I saw the ring and I threw up (0.5) that's not normal.
Samantha:	that's my reaction to marriage.
Miranda:	what do you think you might do if he asks.
Carrie:	I don't know.
Charlotte:	just say ye:::s::
Carrie:	well (.) it hasn't been long enough (0.5) has it?
Charlotte:	Trey and I got engaged after only a month=
Samantha:	=how long before you separated.
Charlotte:	we're together <u>NOW</u> and that's what matters. (.) when it's right you just know
Samantha:	Carrie doesn't <u>know</u>.
Carrie:	Carrie threw up=
Samantha:	=so it might not be right.

(King 2001)

<u>Key</u>

↑	shift into especially high pitch
NOW	especially loud sounds relative to the surrounding talk
::	prolongation of the immediately prior sound
(.)	a brief interval (about a tenth of a second) within or between utterances
(0.5)	the time elapsed (by tenths of seconds) between the end of the utterance or sound and the start of the next utterance or sound
<u>now</u>	stress
=	latched utterances – no break or gap between stretches of talk
?	rising intonation
.	falling intonation
,	unfinished intonational contour

The analysis, thus, shows a rising pitch in Charlotte's exclamation 'You're getting engaged!' The . at the end of this utterance indicates an ending with falling intonation, as with most of the other utterances in the conversation. There is no delay between Charlotte's statement and Carrie's response. There is, however, a .5 second pause in Carrie's response before she adds 'That's not normal'. Another speaker could have taken the conversation away from her at the point of the pause but they chose not to, allowing her to comment on what she had previously said.

Charlotte's lengthened vowel in 'Just say yes' emphasizes the point she is making before Carrie replies with 'well' followed by a microsecond pause which allows her to hold the floor in the conversation, and a further .5 second pause before she invites a response from the others with her use of rising intonation and the tag question 'has it?' The next two lines are examples of latched utterances. That is, Samantha adds her comment to Charlotte's statement without allowing anyone else to intervene.

The underlining and use of capitals in 'NOW' in Charlotte's response to Samantha indicates both loud talk and word stress. Charlotte's microsecond pause, again, enables her to hold the floor so that no one is able to intervene and she is able to complete what she wants to say. If she had not done this, one of the other speakers could have taken the turn from her as her completed syntactic unit, intonational contour and 'completed action' would have indicated a point at which another speaker could taken the turn; that is, a transition-relevance place (TRP) in the conversation. The final example of latched utterances shows that Samantha is able to project, in advance, that a TRP is approaching as Carrie is speaking and takes the floor from Carrie with her consent, and without difficulty.

This analysis, thus, shows how Carrie and her friends manage their conversation in a cooperative manner. They let each other continue with what they want to say, rather than compete for a place in the conversation. It also shows the strategies they use when they want to take a turn in the conversation, such as not letting too much time to lapse before speaking, in case another speaker should take the turn.

5.3 Sequence and structure in conversation

A particular interest of conversation analysis is the sequence and structure of spoken discourse. Aspects of conversational interactions that have been examined from this perspective include conversational openings and closings, turn taking, sequences of related utterances ('adjacency pairs'), preferences for particular combinations of utterances ('preference organization'), feedback and conversational 'repair'.

Opening conversations

One area where conversational openings have been examined in detail is in the area of telephone conversations. Schegloff analysed a large data set of telephone openings to come up with the following 'canonical opening' for American private telephone conversations:

	((ring))		summons/ answer sequence
Recipient:	Hello		
Caller:	Hi Ida?		identification/recognition sequence
Recipient:	Yeah		
Caller:	Hi, this is Carla=		greeting sequence
Recipient:	=Hi Carla.		
Caller	How are you.		how are you sequence
Recipient:	Okay:.		
Caller:	Good.=		
Recipient:	=How about you.		
Caller:	Fine. Don wants to know ..	reason for call sequence	

(Source: Schegloff 1986: 115)

A study carried out by O'Loughlin (1989) in Australia found a similar pattern for opening telephone conversations, except that in the Australian data the caller most frequently self-identified in their first turn after they had recognized their recipient rather than in the second turn, as in the American data.

In a study of telephone openings in Mandarin Chinese, Yang (1997) found the speakers in her study also began their calls with summons/answer and identification/recognition sequences. The greeting and 'how are you' sequences found in American and Australian phone calls, however, were less common or even absent in her data. The majority of the telephone openings she examined went straight from the identification/recognition sequence to the first topic of the conversation. Below is a typical example of the opening of telephone calls in Chinese. The double brackets surrounding the ring of the telephone indicates a sound that is not transcribed:

	((ring))		summons
Recipient:	Wei?	(Hello)	answer
Caller:	Jinghong	(Jinghong)	identification
Recipient:	Ei	(Yes)	recognition

(Source: Yang 1997: 25)

The following example from a radio call-in programme illustrates a further way of opening a conversation:

Announcer:	For husband Bruce of twenty-six years Carol has this dedication (.) So how are things going.
Caller:	Absolu::tely wonderful.
Announcer:	That's great to hear you're still happy.
Caller:	Oh yes (0.5) very much so.
Announcer:	And what's your dedication all about for Bruce.
Caller:	Well:: we're going away tomorrow to the Whitsundays (.) and (0.5) umm:: I'm looking forward to it very much and I know he is too:: for a break.

In this conversation the announcer opens the conversation by saying who is on the line and what the conversation will be about. That is, his utterance introduces the caller to the listening audience and readies the speaker for being on-air and for discussing the topic of the call. The middle stage of the conversation is devoted to the topic of the call, finding the dedication that the caller will make. The conversation ends when the caller has provided the dedication and all the information that was asked for, completed a syntactic unit and employs falling intonation as a signal that she has completed her turn. The announcer does not take the opportunity to take another turn but instead plays the music dedicated to the caller's husband as his way of closing the conversation. He, thus, constrains what the caller can say, excluding the possibility of her bringing up other things that would cause a delay in moving on with the programme (Thornborrow 2001).

Closing conversations

Schegloff and Sacks (1973) have also looked at conversational closings. This work has since been continued by Button (1987) who in his discussion of telephone closings points out that telephone closings usually go over four turns of talk, made up of pre-closing and closing moves. The pre-closing is often made up of two turn units consisting of items such as 'OK' and 'all right' with falling intonation. The closing is made up of two further units, such as 'bye bye' and 'goodbye.' Button (1987: 102) calls this an archetype closing. In this closing both speakers mutually negotiate the end of the conversation. Other material, however, in the form of an insertion sequence can be introduced between the two units which make up these turns, before the closing finally takes place.

The closing may also be preceded by a number of pre-sequences, such as the making of an arrangement, referring back to something previously said in the conversation, the initiation of a new topic (which may not be responded to), good wishes (such as 'give my love to Jane'), a restatement of the reason for calling and thanks for calling. Sometimes, however, the closing may be foreshortened when the archetype closing is skipped over and a foreshortened closing takes place. Equally the closing may be extended by continued repetition of pre-closing and closing items (such as 'bye', 'bye', 'love you', 'love you', 'sleep well', 'you too', etc.). Closings are, thus, complex interactional units which are sensitive to the speaker's orientation to continuing, closing (or not wanting to close) the conversation (Button 1987, Thornborrow 2001).

Turn taking

Conversation analysis has also examined how people take and manage turns in spoken interactions. The basic rule in English conversation is that one person speaks at a time, after which they may nominate another speaker, or another speaker may take up the turn without being nominated (Sacks, Schegloff and Jefferson 1974, Sacks 2004). There are a number of ways in which we can signal that we have come to the end of a turn. This may be through the completion of a syntactic unit, or it may be through the use of falling intonation, then pausing. We may also end a unit with a signal such as 'mmm' or 'anyway', etc. which signals the end of the turn. The end of a turn may also be signalled through eye contact, body position and movement and voice pitch.

By contrast, we may hold on to a turn by not pausing too long at the end of an utterance and starting straight away with saying something else. We may also hold on to a turn by pausing during an utterance rather than at the end of it. We may increase the volume of what we are saying by extending a syllable or a vowel, or we may speak over someone else's attempt to take our turn.

The previous examples of conversational openings show how speakers give up turns by the completion of syntactic units and falling intonation. The final utterance in the telephone call-in extract shows how the speaker holds on to her final turn, until she has said everything she wants to. She lengthens the syllable in 'well' and 'umm', pauses during her utterance and lengthens the vowel in 'too'. She then indicates she is ready to end her turn.

When speakers pause at the end of a turn, it is not always the case, however, that the next speaker will necessarily take it up. In this case, the pause and the length of the pause become significant (in English, at least). In the following example of a university tutorial discussion, the nominated speaker, Wong Young, does not respond so after a one second pause the lecturer asks again. Wong Young pauses again before he actually takes the turn, during and at the end of the turn. He then extends the syllable in 'uh' and the vowel in 'so', when the lecturer overlaps with 'comments?' as her way of insisting he provide a response to her question. Here the square brackets indicate the point of overlap in the utterances. The normal brackets indicate barely audible speech, and the symbol 'o' indicates speech that is noticeably quieter than the surrounding talk:

Lecturer:	<u>O</u>kay, let's move on, =Tadashi: and (.) Wong Young can you,
	(1.0)
Lecturer:	The <u>l</u>ast, (.) El<u>e</u>ven,
	(0.6)
Wong Young:	What is a profession. (0.3) What distinguishes profession from trade, (0.2) What does it mean to be a professional? (0.4) Does being a pro-professional affect the way you dress (0.2) speak behave towards others at work?
	(0.7)
Wong Young:	Uh: o [(so:)] o
Lecturer:	[Comm]ents?

(Source: Nakane 2007: 132)

A speaker may also use overlap as a strategy for taking a turn, as well as to prevent someone else from taking the turn. The following example, from the same data set, shows this. Here the lecturer has asked Tadashi a question but another student, Kylie, wants to take the turn and constantly uses overlap to do this.

```
Lecturer:    There are hundred and forty nine HSC courses, how
             many languages cour[ses].
Kylie:                          [thi]rty ei[ght]?
Tadashi:                        [uh:]
Kylie:       [thir]ty eight?
Tadashi:     [uh:]
             (0.3)
Lecturer:    no there are thirty eight langu[ages],
Tadashi:                                    [(lan]gauge)=
Lecturer:    =but each language is more than one [cour]se.
Tadashi:                                          [ye:h]
Kylie:       ah [that's right. Yeah that's right yeah]
Lecturer:       [many languages ha[ve mo]re than one]
Tadashi:                           [ uh: ]
Kylie:       [that's]
Lecturer:    [course.]
Kylie:       right.=
Tadashi:     =uh huh huh=
Lecturer:    =all right? (.) do you remember?
Tadashi:     I don't remember.= ((giggling))
Lecturer:    =no? (0.2) okay.
```

(Source: Nakane 2007: 126–7)

Turn taking, then, varies according to particular situations. In a classroom, for example, it is often the teacher who nominates who can take a turn. A student may, or may not respond, or students may compete to take the turn (as in the example above). Students may also put up their hand to ask permission to take a turn. Turn taking may also depend on factors such as the topic of the conversation, whether the interaction is relatively cooperative, how well the speakers know each other and the relationship between, and relative status of, the speakers (Burns and Joyce 1997).

A turn constructional unit, further, can be made up of a single word such as in the above example where the lecturer simply says 'Comments?', or it may be an extended multi-unit turn. The unit may, simply be a sound such as 'uh' or it may be made up of a word, a phrase, a clause or a sentence with change between speakers occurring at the end of any of these units or during them if another speaker succeeds in taking the floor (Gardner 2004).

Adjacency pairs

Adjacency pairs are a fundamental unit of conversational organization and a key way in which meanings are communicated and interpreted in conversations. Adjacency pairs are utterances produced by two successive speakers in a way that the second utterance is identified as related to the first one as an expected follow-up to that utterance. The following example, again from a radio call-in programme, illustrates speakers using adjacency pairs in a typical and expected way. In each of the pairs of utterances in this interaction the first speaker stops and allows the second speaker to produce the expected second part to the pair of utterances:

Announcer: Sharon Stone's on the phone. (.) how are yo:::u.
Caller: very good.
Announcer: I bet you get hassled about your surname.
Caller: yes I do::
Announcer: and what do you want to tell Patrick.
Caller: umm that I love him very much (0.5) and I (0.5) and I wish him a very happy birthday for today.

Arguments show a similar pattern in that once a point of view has been expressed, a possible follow-up is a 'challenge' followed by a 'response'. The following examples from an argument about the need for a bouncer at a party show this:

Ryan:	I'm gonna have to get Peter ta come over too (0.1)	Point of view
Marie:	why=	Challenge
Ryan:	=so people don't crash the pa::rdy	Response

(Source: Orr 1996: 35)

Marie:	Oh they won't crash the [pardy sweetheart]	Challenge
Ryan:	[OH YEAH (.) YEAH]	Response
	Maybe twenty years ago mmm (.) you know (.2) like today (.1) I-I- (.) th-there be ea-easy another forty people if ya didn't have a person at the gate	

(Source: Orr 1996: 36)

Adjacency pairs across cultures

It is important to point out that what is an expected follow-up to a seemingly everyday utterance in one language and culture might be quite different in another. Be'al's (1992) study of communication problems in a workplace setting between French and English speakers provides an example of this. Be'al found that the French workers often responded to the everyday greeting 'Did you have a good weekend?' by stopping and telling the English-speaking workers all about their weekend. The English-speaking workers were irritated by this and did not realize that a French speaker would not ask this question if they did not want a real (and complete) answer. They did not realize, further, that this is not a typical question French speakers would ask each other in an everyday conversational situation and, even though they sometimes responded by telling them about their weekend, they also saw the question as an invasion of their privacy. Expected follow-ups in the use of adjacency pairs, then, vary across language and cultures.

Adjacency pairs and stage of the conversation

The particular context and stage of the conversation are especially important for assigning an utterance the status of a particular pair part. For example, 'Hello' can perform many different functions in a conversation. It can be a summons in a telephone call and it can be response to a summons in a telephone call. It can also be a way of greeting someone in the street, although clearly not the only way. An utterance such as 'thanks' equally can be a response to a compliment, a congratulation or a response to an offer of service. An utterance, thus, may play more than one role in a conversation.

5.4 Preference organization

The basic rule for adjacency pairs, then, is that when a speaker produces a first pair part they should stop talking and allow the other speaker to produce a second pair part. There is, however, a certain amount of freedom in responding to some first pair parts. For example a compliment can be followed by an 'accept' or a 'reject'. Thus, some second pair parts may be preferred and others may be dispreferred. For example a question may be followed by an expected answer (the preferred second pair part) or an 'unexpected or non-answer' (the dispreferred second pair part). When this happens, the dispreferred second pair part is often preceded by a 'delay', a 'preface' and/or an 'account'. The following example illustrates this:

A: Are you going out with anyone at the moment? (Question)
B: Uhhh . . . (Delay)
   Well, kind of . . . (Preface)
   There is someone I met a while back . . . (Account) Actually, I'm getting married at the end of the year (Unexpected answer)

Table 5.1 is a summary of some common adjacency pairs, together with typical preferred and dispreferred second pair parts.

A study carried out by O'Shannessy (1995) looked at preference organization in barrister–client interactions where the barrister was collecting his clients' history in preparation for presenting their case in court. O'Shannessy found there was a preference for

Table 5.1 Common adjacency pairs and typical preferred and dispreferred second pair parts (Levinson 1983).

First pair parts	Second pair parts	
	Preferred	Dispreferred
request	acceptance	refusal
offer/invite	acceptance	refusal
assessment	agreement	disagreement
question	expected answer	unexpected answer or non-answer blame
blame	denial	admission

'other-correction' (rather than 'self-correction') in these interactions. That is, when one of the speakers said something that contained an inaccuracy, it was corrected by the other person rather than the person who had made the error. If an inaccuracy was not corrected, it formed the basis of an inference – that the information provided was correct. The following example shows 'other correction' by the client. The barrister follows the correction with a 'correction accept', then a 'correction confirm', again, preferred responses:

Barrister:	the twins Michael and Allan (.) live with the wife (1.0) Michael is employed as an apprentice butcher.=
Client:	oh not MIChael, ALLan=
Barrister:	ALLAN. Ye:s.
Solicitor:	alrigh.
Barrister:	(0.1) ALLAN is employed as an apprentice but[cher]

(Source: O'Shannessy 1995: 56)

The following example, a continuation of the above extract, shows an example of the client not providing an expected answer to the solicitor's question. The solicitor asks his question again to try to get his preferred response, his 'expected answer'. The client does not want (or is unable) to provide the detail the solicitor asks for and draws the set of pairs to a close with 'just leave it that's fine':

Solicitor:	[How] long has he been an apprentice butcher.=
Client:	not very long.
Solicitor:	o how long. o
Client:	maybe three four months I'm not sure=
Solicitor:	is now employed?
Client:	no just leave it that's fine

(Source: O'Shannessy 1995: 56)

Insertion sequences

Sometimes speakers use an insertion sequence; that is, where one adjacency pair comes between the first pair and the second pair part of another adjacency pair. In the following example Ryan asks his mother, Marie, if he can have a DJ for his party. She doesn't reply but, by means of an insertion sequence, passes the question on to her husband, John:

Ryan:	and (0.2) can I have a DJ too (0.1) is that OK (0.2)
Marie:	John
John:	what
Marie:	can he have a DJ (.) DJ=
Ryan:	=cause you won't be spending much on foo:d so I thought (0.2)
John:	well how much does a DJ cost
Ryan:	yeah I've got to find out

(Source: Orr 1996: 59)

5.5 Feedback

Another aspect of spoken interactions that has been examined by conversation analysts is the ways speakers provide each other with feedback; that is, the ways in which listeners show they are attending to what is being said. This can be done, for example, by the use of 'response tokens' such as 'mmm' and 'yeah', by paraphrasing what the other person has just said or through body position and the use of eye contact. In the following example from the tutorial discussion, the students, Tadashi and Kylie, provide feedback to each other by use of the token 'yeah', the repetition of key words, falling intonation and latched utterances:

Lecturer:	And the middle one (.) i:s:
Tadashi:	Co[mmunity ?] community.
Kylie:	[community] ?
Kylie:	Community, I think it is?
Tadashi:	o Yeah o.=
Kylie:	=Yeah,=
Tadashi:	= o Oh yeah, o
	(0.4)
Kylie:	Communi – self community. [yeah] .=
Tadashi:	o [yeah]. o =
	=Community French community

(Source: Nakane 2007: 183)

It is not always the case, however, that an item such as 'yeah' or 'mm' performs an acknowledging function in a conversation. Gardner (2001), for example, shows that the item 'mmm' can perform many other functions as well. Where it does provide an acknowledging function, it may also serve to prompt a topic change, a recycling of a topic or it may solve a dispreferred action, for example. The function response items such as 'mmm', 'yeah' and 'OK' perform are also influenced by the intonation, place and timing of the utterance.

5.6 Repair

An important strategy speakers use in spoken discourse is what is termed repair; that is, the way speakers correct things they or someone else has said, and check what they have understood in a conversation. Repair is often done through self repair and other repair. The following example from O'Shannessy's study of barrister–client interactions shows an instance of self-repair. In this case, there was no apparent error to the other speaker that needed to be corrected in what had been said:

Client:	because (1.0) he's got a girlfriend – oh (0.5) a woman and ah (0.5)

Other repair occurs where the error is apparent to the other speaker. The following example from the same data set shows this:

Barrister: Michael is employed as an apprentice butcher.=
Client: =oh not <u>MICh</u>ael, <u>ALL</u>an

(Source: O'Shannessy 1995: 14)

5.7 Discourse markers

Discourse markers (Schiffrin 1987, 2001, Fraser 1990, 1999) are items in spoken discourse which act as signposts of discourse coherence. This includes interjections such as *oh*, conjunctions such as *but*, adverbs such as *now* and lexical phrases such as *y'know* (Schiffrin 2001). They can be at the beginning, middle or end of an utterance and can serve both as anaphoric (pointing back) and cataphoric (pointing forward) reference in the discourse (Mendoza-Denton 1999).

Oh can be a marker of information management where it indicates an emotional state as in:

Jack   Was that a serious picture?
Freda   *Oh*:! Gosh yes!

(Source: Schiffrin 1987: 73)

Oh can also initiate a self-repair as in:

There was a whole bunch of oth – I was about – *oh*: younger than Robert. I was about uh . . . maybe Joe's age, sixteen.

(Source: Schiffrin 1987: 76)

and it can act as other-initiated repair:

Jack   How bout uh . . . how bout the one . . . uh . . . Death of a Salesman?
Freda   Well that was a show, sure.
Jack   *Oh* that was a movie too

(Source: Schiffrin 1987: 76)

But can be used to preface an idea unit as in:

Jack   The rabbis preach 'Don't intermarry'
Freda   *But* I did- *But* I did say those intermarriages that we have in this country are healthy

(Source: Schiffrin 2001: 57)

Now can indicate attention to an upcoming idea unit as in:

> So I em . . . I think for a woman t'work, is entirely up t'her. If, she can handle the situation. *Now* I could not now: alone.

> (Source: Schiffrin 1987: 230)

and it can be used to indicate a comparison as in:

a. It's nice there
b. *Now* our street isn't that nice

> (Source: Schiffrin 1987, 231)

Y'know can be used (among many other things) to gain hearer involvement and consensus as in:

b. I believe . . . that . . . *y'know* it's fate.
s. So eh *y'know* it just s- seems that that's how things work

> (Source: Schiffrin 1987: 54)

Fraser (1990, 1998), also, discusses discourse markers. He defines discourse markers as items which signal a relationship between the segment they introduce and a prior segment in the discourse. He argues that they have a core meaning, but that their specific interpretation is negotiated by the linguistic and conceptual context in which the item occurs.

The use of some discourse markers can also carry social stigmas such as the use of *like* being associated negatively with California 'Valley Girl' speech (Mendoza-Denton 2007, Bucholtz 2010) and *or nothing* as in 'I don't know or nothing' being stereotyped as an indicator of young working class British speech (Mendoza-Denton 2008) (for further discussion of discourse markers see Fraser 1998, Jucker 1998, Schiffrin 2001, Blakemore 2002).

Fung (2003, 2011) examined the use of discourse markers by British and Hong Kong speakers of English. She found that British speakers of English use discourse markers for a variety of pragmatic functions whereas the Hong Kong speakers in her study used a much more restricted range of discourse markers, mostly functional discourse markers such as *and, but, because, OK* and *so*, etc., and to a lesser extent markers such as *yeah, really, sort of, I see, well, right, actually* and *you know*, etc. Fung and Carter (2007) argue that discourse markers should be explicitly taught to students in order to facilitate more successful language use as well as to prepare them to become interactionally competent speakers.

5.8 Gender and conversation analysis

Conversation analysis has, in recent years, made a major contribution to discussions of language and gender. With the move from the view of language as a reflection of social reality to a view of the role of language in the construction of social reality (and in turn identity) a number of researchers have examined the social construction of gender from a conversation analysis perspective.

Conversation analysis is able to reveal a lot about how, in Butler's terms, people 'do gender', that is, the ways in which gender is constructed, as a joint activity, in interaction. Weatherall (2002: 114) discusses the concept of gender noticing for accounting for gender when 'speakers make it explicit that this is a relevant feature of the conversational interaction'.

The analysis of data from a conversation analysis perspective can help reveal aspects of gendered interactions that might, otherwise, not be considered. Stokoe (2003), for example, does this in her analysis of gender and neighbour disputes. Using membership categorization (Schegloff 2007) analysis she shows how, in the neighbourhood disputes she examined, the category woman was drawn on by people engaged in the interactions to legitimate complaints against their neighbours as well as to build defences against their complaints. The following examples from her data illustrate this. In these examples, Edgar and Vernon are talking about their neighbours for a television documentary called Neighbours at War. In their view 'bad' women are foul mouthed, argue in the street and are bullies. Edgar and Vernon, thus, engage in 'gender noticing' in their negative evaluation of their female neighbours:

Edgar: well (.) she just <u>flew</u> at me (.) <u>a</u>nd (.) the language it was and er oh it was <u>incredible</u> for a lady I mean she's only a small (.) old lady (.) I really couldn't believe what was happening (.) and then

Vernon: she's a bully (0.5) that's the best word a b<u>ull</u>y (.) and she's a foul mouthed woman (.) she's got nothing going for her as far as I'm concerned (.) she wants to get herself sorted out

(Source: Stokoe 2003: 337)

5.9 Conversation analysis and second language conversation

While most studies in the area of conversation analysis have examined native speaker talk, in recent years attention has also shifted to non-native speaker talk. Markee (2000), for example, shows how conversation analysis can be used as a tool for analysing and understanding the acquisition of a second language. He discusses the importance of looking at 'outlier' data in second language acquisition studies pointing out that, from a conversation analysis perspective, all participants' behaviour makes sense to the individuals involved and must be accounted for, rather than set aside, in the analysis.

Storch (2001a, 2001b) carried out a fine-grained analysis of second language learner talk as her students carried out pair work activities in an ESL classroom. She found this analysis allowed her to identify the characteristics of the talk, and the nature of the interactions they engaged in that contributed to or impeded their success in the acquisition of the language items they were focusing on. She also found how the grouping of pairs in the class were important for the nature of their discourse and the extent to which the discourse was collaborative, and facilitated their learning or not (see Wong and Zhang Waring 2010 for a discussion of how conversation analysis can be drawn on in second language teaching and learning).

5.10 Criticisms of conversation analysis

While conversation analysis has very many strengths, it has also attracted criticism. Baxter (2002: 853), while describing conversation analysis as an invaluable tool for the analysis of spoken discourse, also describes it as somewhat 'monolithic'. Hammersley (2003) argues that conversation analysis' view of itself as a self-sufficient research tool is problematic; that is, the view that it does not need data other than the conversation to explain and justify its claims. In Hammersley's view the rejection in conversation analysis of what people say about the world they live in and their conversational interactions as sources of insight into the data is a major weakness. He suggests that when we analyse data from a conversation analysis perspective, we are working as 'spectators' not 'participants' in the interaction. It is, thus, not really possible for us to know how the participants view the conversation unless we ask them. It is also not, in reality, possible for an analyst to start on the analysis of their text completely unmotivated; that is, just looking at the text to see 'what's there' without any preconceived notions of what this might be.

A debate (Billig 1999) that took part in the journal *Discourse & Society* on the relationship between conversation analysis and critical discourse analysis further illustrates these points. In this debate Schegloff criticizes critical discourse analysis (see Chapter 8 of this book) for relying on the analyst's view of what is happening in the text rather than looking at how the participants 'take up' what is said in a text. Schegloff also criticizes critical discourse analysts for drawing on what they know about people engaged in an interaction for their interpretation of the data. As Hammersley points out in this debate, however, even Schegloff does this to some extent in his analyses. He gives the example of a study of two parents in a strained relationship, either separated or divorced, talking about their son on the telephone. As Hammersley shows, there is no information about the relationship between the people involved in the conversation in the transcript. This information is, however, crucial to an understanding of the conversation and is, in fact, drawn on by Schegloff in his analysis and interpretation of the data. Just because something is not observable in the data, then, does not mean that it is not relevant. Hammersley's view is that conversation analysis could be more usefully combined with other qualitative, and even quantitative, approaches to discourse analysis to help us further understand how people use conversation to engage in and construct their social lives. Conversation analysis on its own, he argues, does not tell us all there is to know about human social life.

Bucholtz (2003) argues that conversation analysis severely limits what she calls 'admissible context' (52). She argues that it needs to draw on the contextual groundings that ethnography has to offer, citing the work of Goodwin (1999) and Mendoza-Denton (1999) as studies which do just this. Moerman's (1988) *Talking Culture* and Phillips' (1983) *The Invisible Culture* are also works that draw together conversation analysis and ethnography. Bucholtz's (2007) study into branding, consumption and gender in American middle-class young people's interactions is a further example of this. Here, she combines a fine-grained analysis of high school students' talk about where they shop and what they buy with observations of their interactions gained over a year long study. Mori (2002), in an example of 'applied conversation analysis', aims to expand the notion of context in her study of interactions in a Japanese language classroom by drawing on applied linguistics literature on language pedagogy and second language acquisition to help explain and draw pedagogical implications from her observations.

Wooffitt (2005) in his book Conversation Analysis and Discourse Analysis outlines further criticisms of conversation analysis. The first of these is conversation analysis' lack of attention to issues of power, inequality and social disadvantage. The second is the lack of attention in conversation analysis studies to wider historical, cultural and political issues. Wetherell (1998) argues that conversation analysis would benefit from considering post-structuralist views on discourse, such as agency and the subject positions speakers take up in the discourse, rather than just looking at the text itself. That is, the analyses would be enhanced by considering the positions speakers take and the social and cultural values that underlie how they perform in the discourse. Post-structuralist discourse analysis, equally, she adds, would be improved by greater attention to the details of conversational interaction that is typical of work in the area of conversation analysis.

Feminist researchers such as Kitzinger (2000, 2008), however, argue that conversation analysis is not incompatible with work that examines issues of power and the wider social and political implications of discourse. She argues that if researchers want to 'understand what people are saying to each other, and how they come to say it, and what it means to them' (Kitzinger 2000: 174) they have to attend to the data at the same level of detail and attention that the speakers do in their talk. She is optimistic, then, of the potential of conversation analysis for feminist and other forms of socially engaged discourse analysis research. Kitzinger (2008) argues that it is legitimate to draw on information that is 'outside the data' such as follow-up interviews and observations to inform the discussion of the analysis. Indeed, in her words, 'this is not only inevitable, but also often desirable for competent conversation analysis' (187).

5.11 A sample study: Refusals

Kitzinger and Frith (1999) provide an example of a study which draws on conversation analysis and other data sources to examine what speakers say, why they say it and how what they say is taken up by other people. Their study is about how women communicate (as well as fail to communicate) to men that they do not want to have sex with them; that is, how women refuse unwanted sex.

Their study commences with an examination of how the conversation analysis literature says that people typically refuse offers. As we have seen earlier in this chapter an offer may be followed by one of two possible second pair parts: an acceptance or a refusal. The acceptance is the preferred second pair part to an offer so is less complex than a refusal. It is usually immediate and involves the use of a direct speech act, such as 'Yes, I'd love to'. A refusal, however, is a face-threatening act and is the dispreferred second part to an offer. It is, thus, usually more complex, often indirect and less immediate. The refusal often involves the use of delays, accounts, hedges and prefaces before the speaker gets to the actual refusal of the offer. Thus, telling a woman to 'Just say no' to unwanted sex goes against how people normally carry out refusals, and may not indeed be 'read' by the other person as a refusal, for just this reason.

Kitzinger and Frith outline how conversation analysis shows how people typically accept an offer giving the following as an example of this:

A: Why don't you come up and <u>see</u> me
        some[time
B: [I would like to

(Source: Atkinson and Drew 1979: 58)

Here, there is no delay. Indeed the acceptance starts before the offer is completed. The reply also uses a direct speech act (I would like to).

The following is an example of how people typically refuse an offer. The second pair part in this example includes an outbreath as a delay (hehh), a preface (Well that's awfully sweet of you), before it gets to the refusal, which is hedged (I don't think I can make it this morning), a further delay (hh uhm) before it gets to the account, or reason, for the refusal (I'm running an ad in the paper and-and uh I have to stay near the phone):

A: Uh if you'd care to come and visit a little while this morning I'll give you a cup of <u>coffee</u>
B: hehh Well that's awfully sweet of you. I don't think I can make it this morning. . hh uhm
        I'm running an ad in the paper and-and uh I have to stay near the phone.

(Source: Atkinson and Drew 1979: 58)

Kitzinger and Frith then interviewed women who talked about having refused unwanted sex. In response to advice to 'Just say no' the women showed an awareness of how they should normally perform a face-threatening act such as a refusal in conversation and that this required much more conversational work than just a simple 'no'. One of the respondents said:

It just doesn't seem right to say no when you're up there in the situation. (Kitzinger and Frith 1999: 303)

As Kitzinger and Frith point out:

> Telling a man that you do not want to have sex by saying things like 'I really don't know if we should do this', or 'not now, can't we wait', or 'I really like you but I'm not sure' . . . can be miscon-strued that you need a little more urging to become cooperative. (Wiseman 1994: 65)

The women in their study knew that 'just saying no' was not enough for a refusal in this kind (or indeed most kinds) of situation. Kitzinger argues that men who claim, in a date rape situation, that the woman's delay in refusing them meant they really meant 'yes', are:

> claiming not to understand perfectly normal conversational interactions and laying claim to an implausible and clearly self-interested ignorance of normative conversational patterns. (Kitzinger 2000: 180)

As Kitzinger and Frith (1999: 306) argue, the women's experience tells them that 'just saying no' in refusing an offer is rude and that 'the word "no" is neither sufficient, nor necessary, for a refusal to be heard as such'. It is not, they argue, the adequacy of the women's communication in these kinds of situations that should be questioned, 'but rather their male partner's claims not to understand that these women are refusing sex' (310). Their study, then, is one that exploits the level of detail provided in conversation analytic work, as well as data from other sources for social, educational and political purposes; that is, talking to women about how they can say no to unwanted sex.

5.12 Summary

Conversation analysis, then, provides a way of carrying out fine-grained analyses of spoken discourse which can help not just describe the social word, but understand how, through the use of language, it is constructed. There are differing views, however, as to whether looking at the data alone is sufficient to explain what is going on in conversational interactions. Many conversation analysts would argue that it is. Others, however, suggest combining conversation analysis with more ethnographic descriptions in a kind of 'multi-method/multi- level' analysis which combines the strengths of the insights that can be provided by conversation analysis with data that can be gathered using procedures such as interviews, questionnaires and participant observations (Wodak 1996). Cicourel (1992) supports this view, arguing that what is most important is for researchers to justify explicitly what has been included and what has been excluded in an analysis and how this relates to their particular theoretical and analytical goals.

5.13 Discussion questions

(1) Read Schegloff (2004) on answering the telephone in English. How do you typically answer a telephone call in English? How similar or different is this to Schegloff's 'canonical opening' for telephone conversations? Why do you think this might be the case?

(2) Think of ways in which you signal that it is someone else's turn to speak in a conversation. Do you finish a syntactic unit and pause? Do you use falling intonation to show you are coming to the end of what you are saying? Do you look at the person you want to take up the turn? What do you do if the other person does not take up the turn?

(3) If you have learnt a second language, think of an example of the kinds of things that conversational analysis looks at that you have found difficult in your second language. For example, have you found refusing an offer of food difficult in your second language? Have you sometimes not been sure how to participate in a conversation? Why do you think this might be the case?

5.14 Data analysis project

Collect an example of naturally occurring spoken data and carry out a conversation analysis of it. Look at Jefferson (2004) for guidance on how to write up your transcription. The main categories you could explore in your analysis, depending on your interests and the texts are adjacency pairs, sequence organization, turn taking, feedback, repair organization, openings, pre-closings and closings. Look for regular patterns in what you observe in your analysis. What could your analysis explain about the particular interaction?

5.15 Exercises

Exercise 1: Keeping the floor, giving up the floor and claiming the floor

Analyse the following conversational extracts and indicate how the speakers keep the floor, give up the floor, claim the floor and signal the end of a turn. (In this extract = indicates a 'latched' utterance. That is, there is no gap between the end of one utterance and the start of another. A full stop at the end of the first utterance indicates falling intonation, and a ? at the end of the second utterance indicates rising intonation.)

A: Twelve pounds I think wasn't it. =
B: =//Can you bel*ie*ve it?
C: Twelve pounds on the Weight Watchers' scale.

(Source: Sacks, Schegloff and Jefferson 1978: 16)

Exercise 2: Turn taking

How is turn taking managed in the following extract? (In this extract the number in brackets indicates the length of a pause in seconds. Brackets around text indicate the analyst was unsure of what was said).

A: Well no I'll drive (I don't mi//nd)
B: hhh
    (1.0)
B: I meant to *offer*:
    (16.0)
B: Those shoes look nice . . .

(Source: Sacks, Schegloff and Jefferson 1978: 25)

Exercise 3: Self-repair and other-repair

Find examples of self-repair and other-repair in the following extracts:

(1)

A: I'm going to the movies tomorrow . . . I mean, the opera.

(2)

A: I'm going to that restaurant we went to last week. You know, the Italian one in Brunswick St.
B: You mean Lygon St, don't you?
A: Yeah. That's right. Lygon St.

(3)

A: What would happen if you went back home and didn't get your diploma?
B: If I didn't get my <u>degree</u>?
A: Yeah.
B: Well . . . it wouldn't be too serious really . . . No . . . actually . . . I'd get into a lot of trouble . . . I don't know what I'd do.

(Source: Hatch 1992, modified)

Exercise 4: Preferred and dispreferred responses

Identify preferred and dispreferred responses in the following extracts:

(i) A: That's a nice shirt
     B: Oh thanks
(ii) A: Would you like to come to the movies on Friday?
     B: Uhhh . . . I don't know for sure. I think I might have something on that night. Can we make it another time?

Exercise 5: Closing a conversation

How do the speakers in the following extract indicate they are about to close the conversation?

A: Why don't we all have lunch?
B: Okay so that would be in St Jude's would it?
A: Yes
   (0.7)
B: Okay so:::
A: One o'clock in the bar
B: Okay
A: Okay?
B: Okay then thanks very much indeed George =
A: = All right
B: //See you there
A: See you there
B: Okay
A: Okay // bye
A: Bye

(Source: Levinson 1983, 316–17, modified)

5.16 Directions for further reading

Heritage, J. and Cayman, S. (2010), *Talk in Action: Interactions, Identities, and Institutions.* Oxford: Wiley Blackwell.
  This book looks at a four key area of research: calls to 911 emergency numbers, doctor–patient interactions, court-room trials and mass communications. There is a particular emphasis on institutional practices, tasks and social identities. The book also contains a methodological and theoretical review of conversation analysis as well as a review of the historical development of conversation analysis.

Liddicoat, A. J. (2011), *An Introduction to Conversation Analysis* (2nd edn). London: Continuum.
  This second edition of Liddicoat's book is a thorough review of conversational analytic research, its history and its areas of interest. It provides advice on collecting, transcribing and analysing conversational data as well as suggestions for using conversation analysis to study second language acquisition.

Richards, K. and Seedhouse, P. (eds) (2005), *Applying Conversation Analysis.* Basingstoke, England: Palgrave Macmillan.
  In this book, Richards and Seedhouse provide many examples of studies that draw on conversation analysis as their analytical tool. This includes research into speech therapy, professional discourse, native and non-native speaker interactions and interactions in language learning classrooms. The book concludes with a chapter on conversation analysis as research methodology, addressing such issues as reliability, validity, quantification and triangulation in conversation analytic research.

Wilkinson, S. and Kitzinger, C. (2011), 'Conversation analysis', in K. Hyland and B. Paltridge (eds), *Continuum Companion to Discourse Analysis.* London: Continuum, pp. 22–37.

Wilkinson and Kitzinger's chapter provides an accessible review of the development of conversation analysis as well a summary of key analytic work in the area. This includes research into turn-taking, sequence organization, repair, word selection, overall structural organization and collaborative completion. Critiques and future directions for conversation analysis are also discussed.

Wong, J. and Zhang Waring, H. (2010), *Conversation Analysis and Second Language Pedagogy.* New York: Routledge.
Wong and Zhang Waring's book is an excellent discussion of how the results of conversation analysis can be drawn on in second language teaching and learning. The book contains a review of key concepts and findings of conversation analysis, transcriptions of actual talk, and many suggestions for practical teaching activities.

For an extended list of references and further readings see the companion website to this book.

6

Discourse Grammar

In recent years discussions of grammar have moved from sentence-based perspectives to more of a discourse-based perspective. Hughes and McCarthy (1998), for example, have argued that traditional explanations of grammar do not adequately capture grammatical selection in longer, real-world texts. As they have shown, a number of linguistic items show quite different patterns of use when looked at from a discourse perspective. Linguists such as Halliday and Hasan have also done work in the area of discourse grammar, although from rather a different perspective. Their interest has been in patterns of grammar and vocabulary that combine to tie meanings in the text together as well as connect the text to the social context in which it occurs; that is, items that combine together to make the text cohesive and give it unity of texture. This chapter discusses both these views of discourse grammar, starting with the first of these perspectives.

6.1 Grammar from a discourse perspective

A number of linguistic items such as *it*, *this* and *that* have been shown to have quite different patterns of use when looked at from a discourse, rather than a sentence perspective. McCarthy (1994) found that *it* often signals reference to a continuing or ongoing topic in a text, rather than just something inside or outside the text, as more traditional explanations might suggest. *This* often indicates the raising of a new topic or a new focus in the current topic, and *that* has a distancing or marginalizing function in a text, rather than just demonstrative functions. McCarthy (1998) has also found similar differences in relation to the use of tenses such as the past perfect, the use of *be to* with future meaning, and other language items such as *wh*-cleft constructions (as in 'What you need is . . .').

Celce-Murcia (1997) has, for some time, argued for contextual analyses that look at grammatical form in relation to where, why and how frequently it is used in written and spoken discourse rather than in isolated sentences. She makes a similar argument to McCarthy about *this* and *that* showing how, in extended texts, *this* and *that* function in ways other than just pointing to something. She also shows how tense and aspect choices differ in extended discourse. Celce-Murcia and Olshtain (2000) discuss how *be going to* and *will*, when looked at from a discourse perspective, show different functions other than just the expression of future time. They found 'be going to' is typically used when English speakers narrate future scenarios, which they then follow with a contracted form of 'will', for example. They also found the present simple is often used alongside 'will' to add descriptive details to the future event being recounted.

Hughes and McCarthy (1998) make a helpful comparison between discourse and sentence-based grammars. A discourse-based grammar, they argue, makes a strong connection between form, function and context and aims to place appropriateness and use at the centre of its descriptions. Larsen-Freeman (2003) makes a similar argument in her view that form, meaning and use need to be at the basis of all grammatical descriptions. A discourse-based grammar, Hughes and McCarthy continue, acknowledges language choice, promotes awareness of interpersonal factors in grammatical choice and can provide insights into areas of grammar that, previously, lacked a satisfactory explanation. Aspects of language they feel are especially suitable to this view include ellipsis and tense-function correlations. Discourse-based analyses are also useful for looking at the relationship between vocabulary items in texts, the relationship between items such as 'it' and 'others' and the items they are referring to inside or outside of the text, and conjunction.

6.2 The texture of a text

Hasan (1989a, 1989b) discusses two crucial attributes of texts and which are important for the analysis of discourse. These are *unity of structure* and *unity of texture*. Unity of structure refers to patterns which combine together to create information structure, focus and flow in a text, including the schematic structure of the text. The notion of schematic structure was presented in Chapter 4 of this book. This chapter will introduce the notions of *theme*, *rheme* and *thematic progression*, another way in which information flow and focus take place in texts. It will also discuss *patterns of cohesion*, a further way in which unity of texture is achieved in a text.

Unity of texture

Unity of texture refers to the way in which resources such as patterns of *cohesion* create both cohesive and coherent texts. Texture results where there are language items that tie meanings together in the text as well as tie meanings in the text to the social context in which the text occurs. An example of this is where the meaning of items that refer outside of the text, such as 'it' and 'that', can be derived from the social context in which the text is located.

Texture, then, is a result of the interaction of these kinds of features (Halliday 2009b). In her chapter 'The texture of a text', Hasan (1989b: 71) describes texture as being 'a matter of meaning relations'. A crucial notion in this discussion is that of a *tie* which connects the meanings of words to each other as well as to the world outside the text. The basis for cohesion, and in turn texture, thus, is semantic. It is both explicit and implicit and is based in the ways in which the meanings of items are tied in a semantic relationship to each other. The interpretation of these items is found by reference to some other item, or source, within or outside the text. In the following sentence, for example, I use my knowledge of the text and the context in which it is located to work out what 'it' (in this case, gravy) is referring to in the text:

Waiter: Where would you like *it* sir?
Customer: Just a little on the meat thanks.

6.3 Cohesion and discourse

An area of language in which grammar and discourse are highly integrated is in *patterns of cohesion* in texts. The main patterns of cohesion are *reference, lexical cohesion, conjunction, substitution* and *ellipsis*. These are discussed in the sections which follow.

> *Cohesion* refers to the relationship between items in a text such as words, phrases and clauses and other items such as pronouns, nouns and conjunctions. This includes the relationship between words and pronouns that refer to that word (*reference* items). It also includes words that commonly co-occur in texts (*collocation*) and the relationship between words with similar, related and different meanings (*lexical cohesion*). Cohesion also considers semantic relationships between clauses and the ways this is expressed through the use of *conjunctions*. A further aspect of cohesion is the way in which words such as 'one' and 'do' are used to substitute for other words in a text (*substitution*) and the ways in which words or phrases are left out, or ellipsed, from a text (*ellipsis*). All of this contributes to the *unity of texture* of a text and helps to make the text cohesive.

6.4 Reference

Reference refers to the situation where the identity of an item can be retrieved from either within or outside the text. The main reference patterns are *anaphoric, cataphoric, exophoric* and *homophoric* reference.

Anaphoric reference

Anaphoric reference is where a word or phrase refers back to another word or phrase used earlier in a text. In the following example, from a review of the book *He's Just Not That Into You: The No-excuses Truth to Understanding Guys* (Behrendt and Tuccillo 2004), examples of anaphoric reference are shown in italics in the text. The identity of the and it are retrieved by reference to an earlier mentioned item (the name of the book) in the text:

> It seems everyone's read that self-help book: Greg Behrendt and Liz Tuccillo's He's Just Not That Into You . . . First in the US, then all over the world, women became converts to *the* book's tough-love message. When *it* was published late last year, Oprah sang *its* praises, tearful women called *it* 'the Bible', and others declared *it* had changed their lives forever. (Cooper 2005: S38)

Once the title of the book has been mentioned, the author assumes that the reader will be able to work out what she is referring to in her use of 'it' further on in the text. Equally, she assumes the reader will know 'which book' she is referring to when she says 'the book's tough-love message'. If a reader is not sure what is being referred to, they will typically read back in the text to find the answer.

Cataphoric reference

Cataphoric reference describes an item which refers forward to another word or phrase which is used later in the text. In the following example, from the same extract, the identity of the italicized item follows, rather than precedes, the reference item. It is thus an example of cataphoric, rather than anaphoric, reference:

> It seems everyone's read *that* self-help book: Greg Behrendt and Liz Tuccillo's He's Just Not That Into You. (ibid.)

In this case, the reader knows the item being referred to is yet to come in the text and reads forward to find the meaning of 'that'.

Exophoric reference

Exophoric reference looks outside the text to the situation in which the text occurs for the identity of the item being referred to. The following example from Chapter 3 illustrates this. Both speakers clearly know what book is being referred to in this conversation (*Monica's Story*). 'You' and 'your' are also examples of exophoric reference. Both speakers know, from outside the text, who these items are referring to:

> Customer: What kind of book would *you* say *this* is? Where would you put *it* on *your* bookshelves?

Homophoric reference

Homophoric reference is where the identity of the item can be retrieved by reference to cultural knowledge, in general, rather than the specific context of the text. An example of this, again from the review of *He's Just Not That Into You*, follows:

> First in *the* US, then all over *the* world, women became converts to the book's tough-love message. (ibid.)

This is different from the final use of 'the' in this sentence. To answer 'which book' we know it is the one being discussed in the text. We know, however, from our cultural knowledge 'which' United States and 'which' world are being referred to in the text.

Comparative and bridging reference

Further types of reference include *comparative* and *bridging* reference. With *comparative reference*, 'the identity of the presumed item is retrieved not because it has already been mentioned or will be mentioned in the text, but because an item with which it is being compared has been mentioned' (Eggins 2004: 35). 'Others' and 'opposite' in the following extracts are examples of this:

> When it was published late last year, Oprah sang its praises, tearful women called it 'the Bible', and *others* declared it had changed their lives forever.

> The book assumes all men are confident, or that if they really like a girl, they'll overcome their shyness. The *opposite* is true. (Cooper 2005: S38)

These are a little more complex than the other kinds of reference just described. The author proceeds, however, on the assumption that we will know 'which' people and that we will know 'which' opposite she is referring to.

A *bridging reference* (Martin 1992, Martin and Rose 2007) is where an item refers to something that has to be inferentially derived from the text or situation; that is, something that has to be presumed indirectly. In the following example we are not told which 'blokes' Stuart is referring to. The author presumes that we can indirectly derive this:

> Stuart agrees. 'I was hopeless', he says with a laugh. 'I'm just not one of *those* blokes that finds approaching women easy.' (Cooper 2005: S38)

Each of these forms of reference makes a contribution to the texture of a text and the ways in which we interpret the text as we read it. The same is true of the relationship between vocabulary items in the text; that is, lexical cohesion, the subject of the next section of this chapter.

6.5 Lexical cohesion

Lexical cohesion refers to relationships in meaning between lexical items in a text and, in particular, content words and the relationship between them. The main kinds of lexical cohesion are *repetition, synonymy, antonymy, hyponymy, meronomy* and *collocation*.

Repetition

Repetition refers to words that are repeated in a text. This includes words which are inflected for tense or number and words which are derived from particular items such as 'Stuart' and 'Stu' in the following example. Although the form of these two items is (slightly) different, the author is certain that it will be clear that she is still referring to the same person:

> Jen Abydeera, 27, and *Stuart* Gilby, 22, . . . are convinced they wouldn't be a couple if Jen had done things the [He's Just Not That Into You] way when they first met. '*Stu* was quiet and shy, while I was more confident and forward,' says Jen. 'He was more reluctant than I was to ask questions or to initiate a date. I would be the one to say to him: "When do you want to go out, then?"' (ibid.)

Thus, as she writes, Cooper (the author) exploits the readers' understanding of patterns of cohesion in her text.

Synonymy

Synonymy refers to words which are similar in meaning such as 'date' and 'go out' in the above example and 'blokes' and 'men' in the following example:

> 'I'm just not one of those *blokes* that finds approaching women easy. The book assumes all *men* are confident, or that if they really like a girl, they'll overcome their shyness. The opposite is true.' (ibid.)

In English it is not good style to continuously repeat the same word in a text. Both 'blokes' and 'men' are referring to the same concept but in a different way.

Antonymy

Antonymy describes opposite or contrastive meanings such as 'shy' and 'forward' in the earlier text and 'women' and 'men', 'real players' and 'boofheads' in the following text:

> Andy Stern, 28, a builder, says he's worried the book will drive *women* towards dodgy *men*. 'Only *real players* do full-on charm,' he says. 'The rest of us are *boofheads*. We often do nothing at all, and just hope girls notice that we like them.' (ibid.)

We know as we read the text which meanings contrast with each other. Part of their meaning, indeed, derives from this contrast.

Hyponymy and meronymy

Halliday (1990) describes two kinds of *lexical taxonomies* that typically occur in texts: *superordination* and *composition*. These are words which are in a 'kind of' relationship with each other (superordination) and words that are in a 'whole-part' relationship with each other (composition). In the previous texts, Jen and Stuart are 'part of' the lexical item 'couple' whereas *He's Just Not That Into You* is a 'kind of' self-help book. The relationship between

'Jen' and 'couple' is an example of *meronymy*. The relationship between 'self-help book' and *He's Just Not That Into You* is one of *hyponymy*.

Hyponymy

Hyponymy, then, refers to classes of lexical items where the relationship between them is one of 'general-specific', 'an example of' or in a 'class to member' type relationship. This relationship could be represented diagrammatically as shown below in Figure 6.1. In this example, *He's Just Not That Into You, I'm Okay, You're Okay, You Can Let Go Now: It's Okay to Be Who You Are, Ready or Not, Here Life Comes* and *Be Honest: Your Not That Into Him Either* can also be described as *co-hyponyms* of the *superordinate* term 'self-help books'.

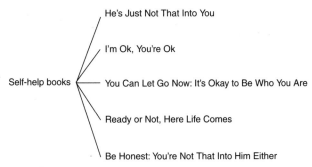

He's Just Not That Into You

I'm Ok, You're Ok

Self-help books — You Can Let Go Now: It's Okay to Be Who You Are

Ready or Not, Here Life Comes

Be Honest: You're Not That Into Him Either

Figure 6.1 Hyponymy

Meronymy

Meronymy is where lexical items are in a 'whole to part' relationship with each other, such as the relationship between 'Jen' and 'Stuart' in relation to the item 'couple'. 'Jen' and 'Stuart' are *co-meronyms* of the superordinate item 'couple'. These relationships could be represented diagrammatically as follows:

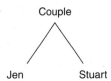

Couple

Jen   Stuart

Figure 6.2 Meronymy

Further examples of these kinds of relationships, drawn from research reports in the area of environmental studies, are shown in Figures 6.3 and 6.4.

Hyponomy

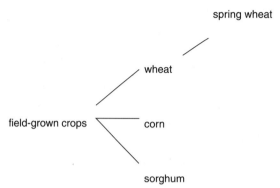

Figure 6.3 Further example of hyponymy (Paltridge 1998: 265)

Meronomy

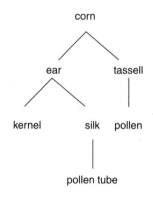

Figure 6.4 Further example of meronymy (ibid.)

In each kind of relationship, an understanding of one item in the taxonomy may depend on an understanding of other items and on the organization and relationship between the items in the taxonomy. As Halliday (1990: 19) points out, these taxonomies 'can become very complicated, with many layers of organisation built into them'. There is also the problem that these relationships are usually not made explicit, with the result that if someone does not already know the relationship between the items they are left to work it out from the text. An example of such a taxonomy is shown in Figure 6.5, again from the field of environmental studies. The relationship between some of these items is extremely complex and depends on a specialized knowledge of the subject being discussed, without which it could be hard to make complete sense of the text this analysis is drawn from.

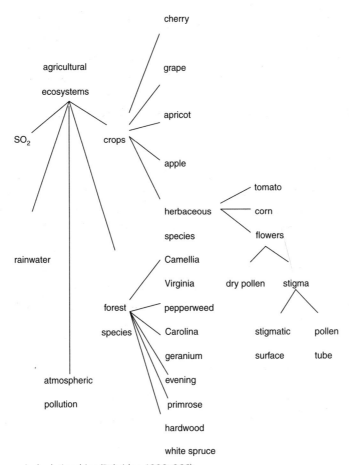

Figure 6.5 Taxonomical relationships (Paltridge 1998: 266)

6.6 Collocation

Collocation describes associations between vocabulary items which have a tendency to co-occur such as combinations of adjectives and nouns, as in 'real-estate agent', the 'right direction' and 'Aussie men' in the following example. Collocation includes the relationship between verbs and nouns such as 'love' and 'book' and 'waste' and 'time' also in the following example. It also includes items which typically co-occur such as 'men' and 'women' and 'love' and 'hate':

> Sarah Hughes, 21, a *real-estate agent*, agrees that *Aussie men* need more help than most when it comes to romance. 'They're useless! They need a good push in the *right direction*. I *loved* the *book* and its message about not *wasting* your *time* – but if a man's shy there's no way it'll happen unless you do the asking.' (Cooper 2005: S38)

Collocation is not something that is restricted to a single text but is part of textual knowledge in general. A writer and speaker of a language draws on this knowledge of collocations as he/she writes and speaks. Expert writers (and readers) know that only certain items collocate with each other. That is, we know we can say 'real-estate agent' but not 'real-estate fruit and vegetables'. Or that we can say 'fresh fruit and vegetables' but not (with the same meaning) 'fresh real-estate agents'. This knowledge of collocation is another way in which a text has the property of texture.

Expectancy relations

A further kind of relationship, related to collocation, is *expectancy relations*. This occurs where there is a predictable relationship between a verb and either the subject or the object of the verb. These relations link nominal elements with verbal elements (e.g. love/book, waste/time) as in the previous example. They can also link an action with a participant (e.g. ask/guy) or an event with its location (e.g. dating/sites) as in the following examples. Expectancy can also refer to the relationship between individual lexical items and the composite nominal group that they form (e.g. art/classes, life/drawing, online/dating):

> *Art classes*
> You can do just about anything in the name of art. Try *asking* a *cute guy* to sit as your model, and if he still doesn't take the hint, you can literally draw him a picture. Take a free *life-drawing* class at the ArtHouse Hotel.
>
> *Online dating*
> Hand out as many kisses as you like – virtual ones, that is. *Dating sites* are all about being proactive and choosing your best match.
>
> (Sun-Herald, 6 February 2005, p. S38)

Lexical bundles

Lexical bundles are multi-word combinations such as *as a result of, on the other hand, if you look at* and *as can be seen* that occur in genres such as university textbooks (Biber, Conrad and Cortes 2004, Biber 2006), academic essays (Byrd and Coxhead 2010, Chen and Baker 2010) theses and dissertations (Hyland 2008a) and research articles (Hyland 2008a, 2011b) as well as spoken genres such as academic lectures and conversation (Biber 2006, Biber and Barbieri 2007).

Byrd and Coxhead (2010) define lexical bundles as three or more words that occur in fixed or semi-fixed combinations 'that are repeated without change for a set number of times in a particular corpus' (32). They need to occur widely in the texts that make up the corpus, rather than just be characteristic of a particular speaker or writer. Byrd and Coxhead also describe the process for identifying lexical bundles in a corpus. This involves using a software program that will find all of the set phrases of a certain length, such as three or four words, in the particular texts in the corpus. The frequency of occurrence of these items can be from ten times per million words (Biber et al. 1999), 20 times per million words (Hyland 2008a) through to 40 times per million words (Biber and Barbieri 2007).

The study by Biber and his colleagues into the use of lexical bundles in university teaching and textbooks found that these items can serve a range of functions in the discourse. For example, they can express stance such as certainty, possibility and probability as in *I don't know if* and *I don't think so*. They can express speaker attitude towards actions as in *I want you to* and *I'm not going to*. They can express desire (*I don't want to*), obligation (*you have to do*) and intention (*what we're going to*). Lexical bundles can also have a discourse organizing focus as in *What I want to do* and *If we look at*. They can be used to single out something as especially important as in *something like that* and *As shown in Figure 4.4*. Lexical bundles can also be multi-functional in that they can be both directives and topic introducers (as in *take a look at*) and a time, place and textual reference, as in *the beginning of the* and *at the end of* (Biber 2006). Lexical bundles are most often not complete grammatical structures, nor are they idiomatic; yet they function as basic building blocks of discourse (Biber, Conrad and Cortex 2004). The use of lexical bundles varies, further, across genres and disciplines. Their use, Hyland (2011a) argues, 'helps to identify competent language ability among individuals and to signal membership of a particular academic community' (12).

6.7 Conjunction

A further way in which language contributes to the texture of a text is through the use of *conjunction*. Conjunction refers to words, such as 'and', 'however', 'finally' and 'in conclusion' that join phrases, clauses or sections of a text in such a way that they express the 'logical-semantic' relationship between them. They are a further important part of discourse knowledge that both speakers and writers, and readers and listeners, draw on as they both produce and interpret spoken and written discourse.

Conjunctions are described by Halliday and Hasan (1976) under the groupings of additive, adversative, causal and temporal conjunctions. Martin (1992) and Martin and Rose (2007) discuss conjunctions under the categories of *additive*, *comparative*, *temporal* and *consequential* conjunctions, extending Halliday and Hasan's work in this area. Martin and Rose's work on conjunction is summarized in Table 6.1.

Additive conjunctions include 'and', 'or', 'moreover', 'in addition' and 'alternatively'. That is, they draw on the notion of 'addition' in both a positive and a contrastive sense.

Comparative conjunctions include 'whereas', 'but', 'on the other hand', 'likewise' and 'equally', drawing on the notion of comparison in both a positive and negative sense. Temporal conjunctions include items such as 'while', 'when', 'after', 'meanwhile', then', 'finally' and 'at the same time'. Consequential conjunctions include items such as 'so that', 'because', 'since', 'thus', 'if', 'therefore', 'in conclusion' and 'in this way'.

Table 6.1 Basic options for conjunction (Martin and Rose 2007)

Logical relation	Meaning	Examples
addition	addition	and, besides, in addition
comparison	similarity	like, as if, similarly
	contrast	but, whereas, on the other hand
time	successive	then, after, subsequently, before
consequence	cause	so, because, since, therefore
	means	by, thus, by this means
	condition	if, provided that, unless

The following extracts, from the review of *He's Just Not That Into You*, show 'but' being used to express a comparative point of view, 'because' to express a consequential relationship between clauses and 'and' to express addition:

> When it was published late last year, Oprah sang its praises, tearful women called it 'the Bible', and others declared it had changed their lives forever. *But* now the initial fuss has subsided, women are examining the book's philosophy a little more closely – *and* many don't like what they see.
>
> 'When a guy is really into you' says Behrendt . . . 'he lets you know it. He calls, he shows up, he wants to meet your friends. Why would you think we would be as incapable as something as simple as picking up the phone and asking you out?' *Because*, of course, the dating game is a clumsy dance of blunders and misunderstandings. *And* sometimes, romantically challenged men really do need a helping hand from women. (Cooper 2005: S38)

Not all authors, however, see conjunction in this way. Vande Kopple (1985), for example, talks about *text connectives*, rather than conjunctions, which are used to indicate how parts of the text are connected to each other. Crismore, Markkanen and Steffensen (1993) discuss *textual markers* which help to organize discourse. Hyland (2005b) adds the category of *frame markers* to the discussion. Frame markers are items which sequence the material in a text (such as 'first' and 'next'), items which label the stages of text (such as 'in conclusion' and 'finally'), items which announce the goal of the discourse (such as 'my aim here is to . . .') and items which announce a change in topic (such as 'well' and 'now'). Frame markers, along with conjunction and other markers of this kind, lead the reader of a text to 'preferred interpretations' of the text as well as help form convincing and coherent texts 'by relating individual propositions to each other and to other texts' (Hyland 1998a: 442).

6.8 Substitution and ellipsis

A further way in which texture is achieved in a text is through the use of substitution and ellipsis.

Substitution

With *substitution*, a substitute form is used for another language item, phrase or group. It can involve substituting an item for a noun. In the following example, 'one' substitutes for the noun 'book':

Try reading this book. That *one*'s not very good.

It can involve substituting an item for a verb. In this example 'done' substitutes for 'had dinner':

A: Has he had dinner yet?
B: He must have *done*. There's no food in the fridge.

An item may also substitute for a clause. In the following example, 'so' substitutes for the clause 'you're still happy':

A: That's great to hear you're still happy.
B: Oh yes very much *so*.

Ellipsis

With *ellipsis* some essential element is omitted from the text and can be recovered by referring to a preceding element in the text. Ellipsis may involve the omission of a noun or noun group, a verb or verbal group or a clause. In the following extract, from a radio call-in show, there are examples of ellipsis in each of the caller's responses. In the caller's first response the main clause 'I want to say' is ellipsed. In the second response 'It was over' is ellipsed. In the final response a whole clause is omitted ('they usually are silly') and the main clause of the next two dependent clauses ('I want to say') are omitted. These are ellipsed as the caller's responses build on the content of what has been said before and are, thus, not necessary for an understanding of what the caller wants to say. Indeed, including these items would be unnatural in this kind of interaction:

Announcer: Gary, what did you want to say to Allison tonight?
Caller: [I want to say] that I'm very sorry for the fight we had the other night.
Announcer: What was that over?
Caller: [It was over] something rather silly actually
Announcer: They usually are, aren't they?
Caller: Yeah [they usually are silly] and [I want to say] that I love her very much and [I want to say that] we'll have to stick it through, you know?

Differences between reference, ellipsis and substitution

It is important to point out differences between reference and ellipsis-substitution. One difference is that reference can reach a long way back in the text whereas ellipsis and substitution are largely limited to the immediately preceding clause. Another key difference is that with reference there is a typical meaning of co-reference. That is, both items typically refer to the same thing. With ellipsis and substitution, this is not the case. There is always some difference between the second instance and the first. If a speaker or writer wants to refer to the same thing they use reference. If they want to refer to something different they use ellipsis-substitution (Halliday 1985).

6.9 Patterns of cohesion: A sample analysis

Figures 6.6 and 6.7 are an analysis of the following two paragraphs of A. A. Milne's *Winnie-the-Pooh* (1988) in terms of lexical cohesion and the main reference chains in this section of the text. These two paragraphs open A. A. Milne's book:

> Here is Edward Bear, coming downstairs now, bump, bump, bump, on the back of his head, behind Christopher Robin. It is, as far as he knows, the only way of coming downstairs, but sometimes he feels that there really is another way, if only he could stop bumping for a moment and think of it. And then he feels perhaps there isn't. Anyhow, here he is at the bottom, and ready to be introduced to you. Winnie-the-Pooh.
>
> When I first heard his name, I said, just as you are going to say, 'But I thought he was a boy?' (Milne 1988: 1)
>
> From *Winnie the Pooh* by A. A. Milne. Text © The Trustees of the Pooh Properties 1926. Published by Egmont UK Ltd London and used with permission.

As can be seen in Figure 6.6, there are three main lexical chains in this section of the text. The first is the subject of the text, Winnie-the-Pooh. The second is the staircase and the third is the way in which Winnie-the-Pooh comes down the stairs. Winnie-the-Pooh's formal name is Edward Bear. This is what he is called the first time he is mentioned in the text. The next item (*head*) is in a part–whole relationship with *Edward Bear*. That is, a head is part of a bear, in this case Edward Bear. The relationship between these two items, thus, is one of meronymy. The relationship between *Winnie-the-Pooh* and *head* is exactly the same, meronymy. In order to understand this relationship it is essential for the reader to realize that Edward Bear and Winnie-the-Pooh are the same person. This relationship is made clear at the end of the first paragraph where Edward Bear's informal name is presented to the reader: Winnie-the-Pooh. The relationship between *his name* and *Winnie-the-Pooh* is one of *naming*.

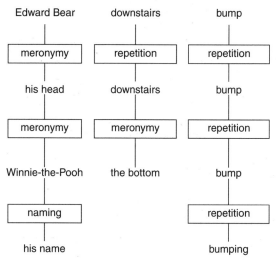

Figure 6.6 Lexical chains: *Winnie-the-Pooh*

The second lexical chain in the text contains an example of repetition and meronymy. The *bottom* (of the stairs) is in a whole–part relationship with the general area *downstairs*. All of the items in the third chain are an example of the same item *bump*, or the final case – a grammatical variation on *bump* (*bumping*).

There are four main reference chains in this section of the text (see Figure 6.7). In the first chain, once the item *Edward Bear* is presented, all the other reference items in this chain (his and he) are examples of anaphoric reference. That is, they all refer back to Edward Bear. In the second chain, the first *it* refers to *coming downstairs on the back of his head*. This is an example of *whole text referencing*. *It* is referring to a section of the text up to this point. *Another way* makes a comparison with *coming downstairs on the back of his head* so is an example of comparative reference. The next item in the chain, *it*, refers to *another way* (of coming downstairs). In *the back of his head, the* is an example of *esphoric* reference. That is, the item *it* refers to immediately follows in the same nominal group.

The third and fourth reference chains in this text are a little more complex for readers to follow. The reader needs to know who the you being referred to in the text is. The first *you* is the reader of the text so is thus exophoric. *You*, here, refers to someone outside the text (the reader). The following *you* and *I* refer to the same person, the reader, so are both anaphoric. They refer back to the first mention of the reader and now go back in the text, not outside it. The two instances of *I* at the beginning of the second paragraph, however, refer to someone completely different – the author of the text, A. A. Milne. The final *I* in this extract takes the reader back to the previous chain. That is, *I* refers once more to the reader of the text. In this way the author of the text involves the reader right from the beginning, by addressing them directly. This, together with the subject matter of the text, accounts for our feeling that

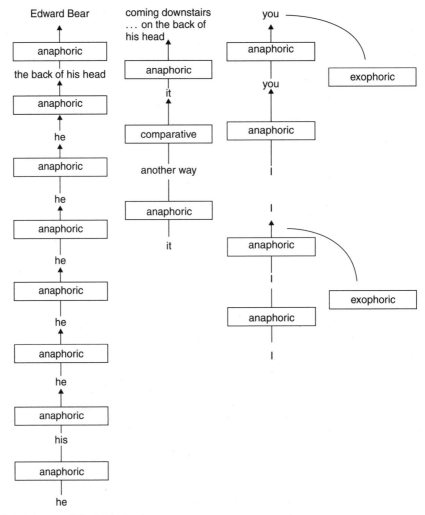

Figure 6.7 Reference: *Winnie-the-Pooh*

the story is being read aloud to someone, most likely a child, the 'you' in the text. As Cook explains, referring expressions thus:

> fulfil a dual purpose of unifying the text (they depend on some of the subject matter remaining the same), and of economy because they save us from having to repeat the identity of what we are talking about again and again. (Cook 1989: 18)

6.10 Theme and rheme

Two further elements that contribute to the texture of a text is the relationship between *theme* and *rheme* in a clause and its contribution to the *focus* and *flow of information* in a text. An understanding of this is important, especially for the writing of successful student texts.

> *Theme* is the starting point of a clause; that is, what the clause is 'about'. The remainder of the clause is the *rheme*. Thus, in the sentence 'Hiragana represents the 46 basic sounds of the Japanese language', the theme is 'Hiragana'. The rest of the sentence is the rheme; that is, what the sentence has to say about Hiragana. In this instance 'Hiragana' is a *topical theme*. Conjunctions such as *and* or *but* when they occur at the beginning of a clause are an example of *textual theme*. An item that expresses a point of view on the content of the clause such as *of course* is an *interpersonal theme*.

Theme

Theme is 'the element which serves as the point of departure of the message' (Halliday 1985: 38). It also introduces 'information prominence' into the clause. For example, in the sentence in Table 6.2 from *A Dictionary of Sociolinguistics* (Swann et al. 2004: 123), 'genre' is the theme of the clause and the rest of the sentence is its *rheme*. The rheme is what the clause has to say about the theme – what it has to say about genre. The theme in this sentence is a *topical theme*, in contrast with a structural element such as a conjunction (such as 'and' or 'but'), which is a *textual theme*.

Table 6.2 Theme and rheme

Theme	Rheme
Genre	is a term in widespread use to indicate an approach to communication which emphasizes social function and purpose.

An example of a textual theme can be seen in the final sentence of the text, shown in Table 6.3, where 'but' joins two clauses together. The rest of the themes in this extract are topical themes.

Table 6.3 Examples of theme and rheme

Topical theme	Textual theme	Topical theme	Rheme
Genre			is a term in widespread use to indicate an approach to communication which emphasizes social function and purpose.
Significant debate			surrounds the definition of genre, particularly the extent to which it refers to texts or activities in which texts are embedded.
It			is often vaguely defined
	but	several uses of the term	can be identified which are illustrated in different types of genre analysis.

Interpersonal theme

Interpersonal theme refers to an item that comes before the rheme which indicates the relationship between participants in the text, or the position or point of view that is being taken in the clause. The example in Table 6.4 from a student essay (North 2005) shows an example of a textual theme, an interpersonal theme and a topical theme. Here the interpersonal theme expresses uncertainty about the proposition that follows:

Table 6.4 Examples of textual theme

Textual theme	Interpersonal theme	Topical theme	Rheme
However …	it seems unlikely that	Descartes	would deliberately challenge the church

An interpersonal theme can express probability (e.g. perhaps), usuality (e.g. sometimes), typicality (e.g. generally) or obviousness (e.g. surely). It can also express opinion (e.g. to my mind), admission (e.g. frankly), persuasion (e.g. believe me), entreaty (e.g. kindly), presumption (e.g. no doubt), desirability (e.g. hopefully) or prediction (e.g. as expected) (Halliday and Matthiessen 2004).

> Patterns of theme and rheme combine in a text to give it a sense of *thematic development*. The theme of a clause, for example, may pick up, or repeat, the meaning from a preceding theme. This leads to a pattern of *theme reiteration*, where the theme of each clause is the same. Zigzag or *linear theme* is where the rheme of one clause is picked up in the theme of the next clause. These patterns may also be combined into *multiple/split rheme* patterns.

Multiple theme

The extract in Table 6.5 from the review of *He's Just Not That Into You* shows a further example of textual, interpersonal and topical themes. It is an example of *multiple theme*. That is, there is more than a single thematic element in the Theme component of the clause.

Table 6.5 Multiple themes

Textual theme	Interpersonal theme	Topical theme	Rheme
Because,	of course,	the dating game	is a clumsy dance of blunders and misunderstandings.

6.11 Thematic progression

The notions of theme and rheme are also employed in the examination of *thematic progression* (Eggins 2004), or *method of development* of texts (Fries 2002). Thematic progression refers to the way in which the theme of a clause may pick up, or repeat, a meaning from a preceding theme or rheme. This is a key way in which *information flow* is created in a text. There a number of ways in which this may be done. These are discussed below.

Constant theme

One example of thematic progression is *theme reiteration* or *constant theme*. In this pattern, 'Theme 1' is picked up and repeated at the beginning of the next clause, signalling that each clause will have something to say about the theme. In Table 6.6, there are two sets of constant themes. The thematic progression of this text is shown in Figure 6.8.

Table 6.6 Theme reiteration/constant theme (based on Cornbleet and Carter 2001: 3)

Theme	Rheme
Text	can be used for both spoken and written language.
It	usually refers to a stretch, an extract or complete piece of writing or speech
Discourse	is a much wider term.
It	can be used to refer to language in action, such as legal discourse, which has characteristic patterns of language.

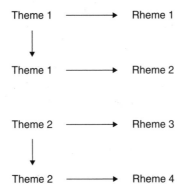

Figure 6.8 Thematic progression: Theme reiteration/constant theme (based on Table 6.6)

Linear theme

Another common pattern of thematic progression is when the subject matter in the rheme of one clause is taken up in the theme of a following clause. The text analysed in Table 6.7 shows an example of this kind of progression. This is referred to as a *zigzag* or *linear pattern* theme. This pattern is illustrated in Figure 6.9.

Table 6.7 Theme and rheme: A zigzag/linear theme pattern (based on Knapp and Watkins 2005: 55)

Theme	Rheme
The term 'modality'	describes a range of grammatical resources used to express probability or obligation
Generally, obligation	is used in speech, speech, especially when wanting to get things done such as 'You should keep your room tidy'.

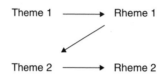

Figure 6.9 Thematic progression: Zigzag/linear theme (based on Table 6.7)

Multiple theme/split rheme

Texts may, equally, include other kinds of progression such as a 'multiple-theme' or 'split rheme' patterns. In 'multiple-theme'/'split rheme' progression, a rheme may include a number of different pieces of information, each of which may be taken up as the theme in a number of subsequent clauses.

The analysis of the text in Table 6.8 and the illustration of its thematic progression in Figure 6.10 include an example of 'multiple theme'/'split rheme' progression. In this text, the two pieces of information in Rheme 2 ('two alphabets' and 'Chinese ideograms') are picked up in Themes 3 and 4 respectively. Also 'Hiragana' and 'Katakana' in Rheme 3 are picked up in Themes 5 (Hiragana), 6 and 7 (Katakana) respectively (although in the case of Theme 7 'Katakana' is ellipsed). This text also incudes examples of 'theme reiteration'/'constant theme' between the first two clauses and the sixth and seventh clauses and a zigzag/linear theme pattern between a number of rhemes and subsequent rhemes.

Table 6.8 Theme and rheme: A multiple theme/split rheme pattern (based on Nesbitt, Nesbitt and Uchimaru 1990: 21)

Theme	Rheme
When Japanese people	write their language
they	use a combination of two separate alphabets as well as ideograms borrowed from Chinese
The two alphabets	are called hiragana and katakana.
The Chinese ideograms	are called Kanji.
Hiragana	represents the 46 basic sounds that are made in the Japanese language
Katakana	represents the same sounds as hiragana
but (Katakana)	is used mainly for words borrowed from foreign languages and for sound effects.
Kanji	are used to communicate an idea rather than a sound.

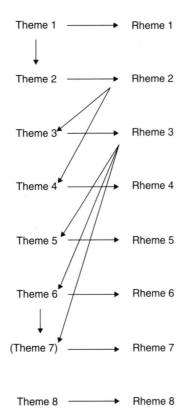

Figure 6.10 Thematic progression: Multiple theme/split rheme (based on Table 6.8)

6.12 Attitude and grammar

Relations between participants influence a number of key pragmatic, and in turn, language choices in a text. In particular, we use the resources of *appraisal* (Martin 2002, Hood 2004, 2010, Martin and White 2005, Martin and Rose 2007) to negotiate relationships, to tell people how we feel about things and how we feel about other people; that is, to tell people what our attitudes are to people, their feelings and things. *Attitude*, as Droga and Humphrey (2002: 75) explain, 'refers to resources used to make either a positive or negative evaluation of phenomena'; that is, the ways in which writers and speakers evaluatively position themselves in relation to others, what they believe, how they feel, and what they believe that they know (Hood, 2004).

Appraisal theory divides Attitude into three main categories: *affect*, *judgement* and *appreciation* (White 1998). These categories are interconnected in that 'they are all motivated at some level with affectual response' (White 1998: 108). Affect, judgement and appreciation may be expressed either explicitly through the use of individual lexical items or implicitly through the process of implicature (see Chapter 3). It, thus, may not always be clear what attitude is being expressed as it may not be directly expressed in the text and may need to be inferred from the context in which the text occurs. It may also be the case that an item may be evaluated differently by different people. Some items, then, may have a *double coding*. They may be read differently by different people depending on factors such as their socio-cultural background, their age or gender. It may also be the case that an item may have more than the one coding for the same person. That is, an item may have a *double layered inter-pretation*, drawing on more than one subsystem of the appraisal network at the same time (Rothery and Stenglin 2000). The division between each of these categories may, at times, be fuzzy and not always be clearcut. One appraisal value may, however, be more dominant in a text than another and be a characteristic of a particular genre. Hard news stories, in English for example, may typically have a high level of intensity in the ways in which interpersonal values are expressed (White 1998).

In the extract below from a newspaper commentary on Afghan boatpeople going to Australia written days after the events of September 11, the author's attitude is expressed through the use of positive appreciation (*smart*) and negative appreciation (*appalling, fool-ish, terrible, mysterious*) resources.

> Australia's reaction to the Afghan boatpeople, in the wake of the *appalling* terrorist attacks in the US, will serve as a metaphor for the US – and general Western – response to the terrorist acts themselves. Nothing would be more *foolish* than to think it's *smart* to keep out the Afghans because they are in some *mysterious* way linked to Islamic politics which, in its terrorist manifes-tation, produced Tuesday's *terrible* tragedy. That would be to blame the victims, par excellence (Wang 2007: 87).

Attitude can also be graduated in terms of *force*. This can be done in two ways; meanings can be graded in terms of intensity (*intensification*) and they can be quantified (*quantification*). For example, in the above extract 'terrorist attacks' is intensified by the use of 'appalling' and 'tragedy' is intensified by 'terrible'. Later in the text, the author writes 'There will likely be a big increase in the US military budget'. Here, 'big' quantifies the 'increase in the US military budget' (see Martin and White 2005 for further discussion of appraisal analysis).

6.13 Grammar and engagement

Grammatical resources are also drawn on to express *engagement*. Engagement 'is concerned with the sourcing of attitude and acknowledgement of alternative voices' (Martin 2002: 58) in a text. It is the way in which people intertexually position what they say; that is, the lin-guistic resources they draw on to include and adopt a stance towards the words, observa-tions, beliefs and viewpoints of others. Speakers (and writers) may endorse what another person says, or they may distance themselves from what other people say. They may take responsibility for what they say, they may take no responsibility for what they say, or they may share some responsibility with the words or views of the person or source they are quoting. There may be a clear separation between the source they are quoting or the source may be assimilated into what they are saying (White 2005). Meanings, thus, may be expressed as contentious or problematic, unproblematic and taken for granted, or somewhere in between (White 1998). The main ways in which engagement is expressed is through *attribution*, *modality* and *disclaimers* and *proclaimers*.

Attribution is where someone refers to the words, views or thoughts of another source, or person. By doing this they are evaluating (although not necessarily endorsing) the material as being relevant. They may indicate support for the material (*endorsement*). They may not support the material (*dis-endorsement*). Or they may be neutral about the material (*non-endorsement*). Speakers and writers use a number of different resources for evaluating sources. They may use a reporting verb such as 'demonstrate' (endorsement), 'claim' (dis-endorsement) or 'say' (non-endorsement). They may nominalize reporting verbs by using items such as 'statement', 'demonstration' and 'suggestion'. They may also qualify a statement with an evaluative item such as 'controversial', 'unbiased' or 'questionable'. They may use *modal items* such as 'always', 'normally' and 'possibly' to express certainty, usuality or probability, for example, and to convey their position on the attributed material. The material may be directly quoted or it may be paraphrased; that is, it may be *textually integrated* or not. A speaker or writer may also *disclaim* or *proclaim* the source material. That is, they may reject the outside source (that is, disclaim it) in order to replace it with something else, or they may present the material in such as way that it is difficult for someone else to challenge it (that is, proclaim it) (Droga and Humphrey 2002).

The following example from the review of *He's Just Not That into You* contains an example of non-endorsement ('pointed out') and endorsement ('agree'). 'Old-fashioned' is an example of dis-endorsement where the writer evaluates the source material and separates herself from its view. The source material here is textually integrated, that is, *assimilated*, rather than directly quoted, or *inserted* into the text. The source material is *identified, singular* and *specific*, rather than *unidentified, generalized* or *plural* (see White 2005 for further discussion of source types). The text expresses high *affect* in its reference to *The Rules* and in Jen Abydeera's response to the book. The text also, simultaneously, expresses high negative judgement. Jen Abydeera's response to the views of the book shows high intensity, or *force*, which is explicitly, rather than implicitly graded. Her response also shows sharpened *focus*.

> Some critics have *pointed out* that He's Just Not That into You's advice to women to let men do all the running is similar to The Rules, which infuriated women with its *old-fashioned* insistence on passive, compliant, female behaviour. Jen Abydeera *agrees*. 'It takes your power away and puts it all on the men's' side. And it reinforces old gender stereotypes. It's OK for women to be proactive now, and I think that not only do men like it – they expect it.' (Cooper 2005: S38)

6.14 Grammatical differences between spoken and written discourse

There are a number of grammatical differences between spoken and written language which have implications for discourse analysis. These are not, however, simple, clearcut boundaries but, rather, represent a continuum of differences between spoken and written discourse. A number of these differences are discussed below.

Grammatical intricacy and spoken and written discourse

A commonly held view is that writing is more structurally complex and elaborate than speech. Halliday (1989b, 2009c), however, argues that speech is no less highly organized than writing. Spoken discourse, he argues, has its own kind of complexity. He presents the notion of *grammatical intricacy* (Halliday and Matthiessen 2004) to account for the way in which the relationship between clauses in spoken discourse can be much more spread out and with more complex relations between them than in writing, yet we still manage to keep track of these relations. The following extract by a judge on a television song competition contains sets of clauses that are long and spread out in the way that Halliday describes. The judge is talking about the winner of the show who came to the auditions dressed in a grunge outfit and who transformed herself throughout the show:

> You are fabulous, truly, truly fabulous. And you know what's fabulous about you? I believe that the real, true artists, the people that are around for a long time, who touch people's lives, are those artists that have lots of contradictions within them, and you had many contradictions within you when you first rocked up. You looked like a skate punk and you had this aura of 'Don't mess with me' about you, and, but every time you step in front of us you take another step towards being what we wanna create here, which is a superstar artist. That was a fantastic song for you. You just rocked the house and I can't believe they have got you in heels! Absolute class act, darling. (Australian Idol Blog 2004)

Lexical density in spoken and written discourse

Written discourse, however, according to Halliday tends to be more *lexically dense* (Halliday and Matthiessen 2004) than spoken discourse. Lexical density refers to the ratio of content words to grammatical or function words within a clause. Content words include nouns and verbs while grammatical words include items such as prepositions, pronouns and articles. In spoken discourse content words tend to be spread out over a number of clauses rather than being tightly packed into individual clauses which is more typical of written discourse. The following extract from Brown's (1992: 9) foreword to the book *Casablanca: Script and Legend* illustrates the higher lexical density that is typical of many written texts. In this extract, there are seven content words in each of the clauses. The content words in this extract are in italics. There are many more content words than grammatical words in this extract:

> If *Casablanca defined true love* for a *generation* of *incurable romantics,* it also *defined* the *aesthetic possibilities* of *cinema* for a generation of *film lovers.*

In the following extract from the script of *Casablanca* (Koch 1996: 56) a woman who had a brief affair with the star of the film, Rick, is speaking. The content words in the text are italicized. Here, there is a lexical density of 2.5 (the number of content words divided by the number of clauses), lower than the written text which has a lexical density of 7.

> Yvonne: Who do you *think* you are, *pushing* me around? What a *fool* I was to *fall* for a *man* like you.
>
> > > (TM & © Turner Entertainment Co. (s06))

Nominalization and grammatical metaphor in written and spoken discourse

There is also a high level of *nominalization* in written texts; that is, where actions and events are presented as nouns rather than as verbs. Halliday (1989b) calls this phenomenon *grammatical metaphor*; that is, where a language item is transferred from a more expected grammatical class to another. Written texts also typically include longer noun groups than spoken texts. This leads to a situation where the information in the text is more tightly packed into fewer words and less spread out than in spoken texts. The following extract from an analysis of *Casablanca* by Corliss (1992: 233) illustrates this. The first two examples highlighted in the text show long noun groups which are typical of much written discourse. The third example includes an example of grammatical metaphor. Here, the adjective 'turgid' (its more 'expected' grammatical class) is changed into the noun 'turgidity', an example of nominalization:

> Although Casablanca defines Bogey for all time as *the existential-hero-in-spite-of-himself, several of his roles just preceding this one (notably High Sierra and The Maltese Falcon)* had prepared his fans for *the misanthropy and climatic selflessness* he would embody as Rick Blaine. Bergman (as Ilsa Lund) and Henreid (as Victor Laszlo) are hardly incandescent lovers – neither are Bergman and Bogart, for that matter – but their *turgidity as sexual partners* works, intentionally or not, to the film's advantage.

This extract also includes two examples of *qualifiers* (Halliday 1985) following a noun which are also typical of much written discourse. In the following illustration of this extract, the first highlighted section of the text qualifies the noun group 'several of his roles'. The second highlighted section qualifies the noun group 'their turgidity'. This use of qualifiers is also typical of much written scientific discourse (Conduit and Modesto 1990) and adds to the length of noun groups in written discourse.

> Although Casablanca defines Bogey for all time as the existential-hero-in-spite-of-himself, several of his roles *just preceding this one (notably High Sierra and The Maltese Falcon)* had prepared his fans for the misanthropy and climatic selflessness he would embody as Rick Blaine . . . their turgidity *as sexual partners* works, intentionally or not, to the film's advantage.

The next extract, also from *Casablanca* (Koch 1996: 127), is an example of the typically low level of nominalization and shorter noun groups in spoken discourse. The noun groups, shown in italics in this extract, are simpler and less dense than in the previous example.

Ilsa: Can I tell you *a story*, Rick?
Rick: Has it got *a wow finish*?
Ilsa: I don't know *the finish* yet.
Rick: Well, go on, tell it. Maybe one will come to you as you go along.

                                        (TM & © Turner Entertainment Co. (s06))

In the above extract, *finish* is an example of *grammatical metaphor*. It is an event that would be normally expressed as a verb but, here, is expressed as a noun. Thompson (2004) describes grammatical metaphor as:

> the expression of a meaning through a lexico-grammatical form which originally evolved to express a different kind of meaning. The expression of the meaning is metaphorical in relation to a different ways of expressing the 'same' meaning which would be more congruent (223)

These include *experiential* and *interpersonal* metaphors. An example of an experiential metaphor is where something that would normally (or congruently) be expressed by a verb such as *criticize* is expressed by a noun, as in *criticism*. An interpersonal metaphor arises when an item such as *perhaps* that would congruently be expressed by a modal item is 'regrammaticised' (Halliday 1998) as a noun, as in *possibility* (Thompson 2004). In the example from *Casablanca* shown above, *Has it got a wow finish? – finish* is an example of experiential metaphor. In the example *Casablanca . . . defined the aesthetic possibilities of cinema for a generation of film lovers, possibilities* is an example of interpersonal metaphor.

A continuum of differences between spoken and written discourse

As McCarthy (2001) argues, there is no simple, one-dimensional difference between spoken and written discourse. These differences are most usefully seen as being on a scale, or continuum; for example, from texts which are more involved interpersonally such as some casual conversations, to texts which are more detached such as some written public notices.

Some spoken texts may be more implicit and leave a lot of what is to be understood unsaid whereas written texts (in English at least) may often be more explicit. There is also a scale of real time to lapsed time for spoken and (most) written discourse. Some texts are also more fragmented than others in their performance such as casual conversations and online chat room discussions. Other texts, such as prepared academic lectures and published academic writing may be more tightly organized and integrated. This idea of a spoken to written scale, or continuum, 'avoids over-simplified distinctions between speech and writing but still brings out keys areas in which spoken and written discourse may be differentiated' (McCarthy 2001: 94).

Written discourse, then, is not just speaking written down. Speaking and writing draw on the same underlying grammatical system but in general they encode meanings in different ways depending on what they wish to represent. Biber's (1988, 1992) corpus-based analyses of differences between spoken and written texts have found that there is no single absolute difference between speech and writing in English, but rather dimensions of variation where linguistic features tend to cluster, all of which varies for different kinds of texts, or genres.

Biber's work supports this notion of a spoken–written continuum. He has shown that there are no absolute differences between spoken and written language in terms of the predominance of certain linguistic features, but that spoken and written language are, rather, 'multidimensional constructs' with some spoken and written genres having a number of features in common with other spoken and written genres and a number of characteristics which show them to be quite different. Biber points out how certain linguistic features may cluster in texts that share a similar communicative function. These clusters, however, are often distributed differently in different types of spoken and written texts. Spoken and written styles, further, may intermingle with each other in that forms that are typically associated with spoken language may also occur in written language, such as in informal letters, email, text messages and advertising (McCarthy 2001).

6.15 Summary

This chapter has discussed grammar from a discourse perspective. It has shown how individual linguistic features work together in whole texts. This includes how interpersonal factors result in the use of certain grammatical choices as well as ways in which the use of particular items provide texture to texts. The repetition and collocation of lexical items has been discussed, as has patterns of progression in texts. The ways in which attitude is expressed through grammar has been given particular attention, as have grammatical differences between spoken and written discourse. The chapter has argued that there is no simple, one-dimensional difference between spoken and written discourse but, rather, these differences are most usefully seen as being on a scale, or continuum.

6.16 Discussion questions

(1) Think of an example of a grammatical feature that people use differently in conversation from the way grammar books suggest people use it. What reasons can you give for this difference?

(2) Think of an experience you have had reading or listening to someone speak where you haven't understood a vocabulary or a reference item. How can the theory of cohesion help explain how you resolved this situation?

(3) This chapter has discussed the topic of thematic progression. What kind of thematic progression is typical of the way you write?

(4) Hasan says that unity of structure and unity of texture are two crucial attributes of texts. Think of a text you have just written. In what way does it have unity of structure and unity of texture?

6.17 Data analysis projects

(1) Read Hilles (2005) and carry out a contextual analysis of a language feature you think may be useful to consider from a discourse perspective. Compare what you have found to a description of this language feature in a grammar book you are familiar with. In what way(s) is it similar and in what way(s) is it different?

(2) Choose a text you have written and analyse it in terms of patterns of cohesion. Refer to Section 5.4 in Bloor and Bloor (2004) for help with your analysis. How do you think your text could be improved from the point of view of cohesion?

(3) Choose a text you have written and analyse it in terms of conjunction. Read pages 47–51 from Chapter 2 in Eggins (2004) for help with your analysis. Are there any ways in which you could improve the use of conjunction in your text?

(4) Read Section 5.3 in Bloor and Bloor (2004) for a discussion of thematic progression. Then do a thematic progression analysis of a text you have written. How do you think your text could be improved from this point of view?

6.18 Exercises

Exercise 1: Lexical chains

Analyse the following text in terms of *reference* and *lexical chains*:

FLAN (Caramel coated custard)

Ingredients

Caramel   *Custard*

1/2 cup sugar   2 cups milk
2 tablespoons water   1/2 cup sugar
                                                  4 eggs
                                                  1 teaspoon vanilla
                                                  Pinch of salt

---

Method

1. Choose a four cup mould with a smooth inside surface, or use 6 individual moulds.
2. To caramelize mould: In a small saucepan, over high heat, boil 1/2 cup sugar with 2 tablespoons of water. When golden, pour into mould, turning quickly in all directions to coat bottom and sides.
3. Custard: In a blender, put milk, sugar, eggs, vanilla, and salt. Blend for 3 minutes on a medium speed.
4. Pour into mould. Place the mould in a larger pan. Pour warm water into the larger pan halfway up to the sides of the mould. (In Spanish this is a *Bano de Maria*, Mary's bath).
5. Bake at 325 degrees Farenheit (160 degrees Celcius) in a pre-heated oven for about 1 hour. Check occasionally during the baking to be sure the Bano de Maria does not boil. If it should, reduce oven heat slightly; however, do not reduce below 300/150 degrees.
6. Test for doneness by inserting a kitchen knife only halfway into the custard. (Do not pierce bottom.) If the knife comes out clean, it's done. Cool for 1 hour and refrigerate for 3 hours.
7. Unmould by running a kitchen knife around the edge. Place a serving dish over the mould and flip.

Exercise 2: Conjunction

Analyse the extract from *Winnie-the-Pooh* below in terms of conjunction:

Here is Edward Bear, coming downstairs now, bump, bump, bump, on the back of his head, behind Christopher Robin. It is, as far as he knows, the only way of coming downstairs, but sometimes he feels that there really is another way, if only he could stop bumping for a moment to think of it . . . And then he feels perhaps there isn't.

Anyhow, here he is at the bottom, and ready to be introduced to you, Winnie-the-Pooh.

When I first heard his name, I said, just as you are going to say, 'But I thought he was a boy?'

Exercise 3: Theme and rheme

Identify the *theme and rheme* in each clause in the text below.

The day I was lost

I went over to my friend's house and I said 'We'll go for a walk'. And we went far away and I said 'I don't know our way home'. And we kept on walking and we were hungry. And we saw a village and we went to talk to them and we said 'We are hungry'. And they gave us some food. And we thanked them and we went walking off and then we stopped and sat down. And then we saw a giant and I screamed 'Cooee'.

(Butt et al. 2000: 138; Reproduced by permission of Macmillan Education Australia)

Exercise 4: Thematic progression

Break each clause in the following texts into *Theme* and *Rheme*, then identify patterns of *thematic progression* in each of the texts.

Putonghua and pinyin

Putonghua is the Chinese expression for Mandarin Chinese. It means 'common language'. Pinyin is a phonetic spelling system for Chinese characters, which uses the Roman alphabet. Pinyin is not just useful to teach the standard pronunciation of Putonghua; we also use pinyin to teach the standard pronunciation of Putonghua, or mandarin Chinese, to Chinese people wwho speak other dialects.

Chinese pronunciation

Chinese pronunciation is not difficult for English speakers because most of the sounds are quite similar in English. These sounds are Romanized by using the Roman alphabet. This makes learning Chinese easier for English-speaking learners. Although there are 21 initials and 30 finals in Chinese, there are only a few sounds that are tricky for English speakers.

Extract from: 'Discover China, Student's Book One' by Angi Ding. © *2010* Macmillan Publishers Limited. Used by Permission. All Rights Reserved.

Exercise 5: Grammatical metaphor

Grammatical metaphor is where a language item is transferred from a more 'expected' grammatical class to another, such as the verb 'entertain' (the expected class) being transferred to the grammatical class of noun, as in 'entertainment' (the unexpected class). Below is an extract from the book *Mad Men and Philosophy* (Carveth and South 2010), a collection of chapters about the US television show *Mad Men*. List the words in the text that seem to you to be examples of grammatical metaphor.

> Authenticity is a word frequently heard in connection with Mad Men, a show lauded for the detailed accuracy of it portrayal of the fashion, hairdos, furnishings, office furniture, and social mores of Madison Avenue in the 1960s. Cigarettes everywhere, martini lunches, sexual harassment as an office norm. (Dunn 2010: 20) (Reprinted with permission of John Wiley & Sons, Inc.)

Exercise 6: Lexical density

Below are a spoken and a written text. The spoken text is from an interview with John Hamm who plays the character Don Draper in the US television show *Mad Men* (amctv.com 2011). The written text is from *The Ultimate Guide to Mad Men* (Dean 2010), a collection of notes on the show. Calculate the lexical density of each text by dividing the lexical items by the number of clauses in each text. Lexical items include nouns, verbs, adjectives and adverbs. Grammatical items include prepositions, conjunctions, auxiliary verbs, modal verbs, pronouns and articles (Droga and Humphrey 2002).

A spoken text:

> The closest thing I have in common with Don is that I'm looking for something. If you look at the literature of the early sixties, it's existentialist. People sitting around smoking, thinking 'what am I doing with my life?' (Iley 2010: 28) (Extracted from *The Ultimate Guide to Mad Men* by Will Dean, Guardian Books, 2010)

A written text:

> My own personal satisfaction while watching the show was helped enormously by being asked to write a series of episode by episode blogs for guardian.co.uk in which I would share a brief recap and a few talking points with readers. It quickly became a part of the routine of watching the series for many viewers eager to share their thoughts. (Dean 2010: viii) (Extracted from *The Ultimate Guide to Mad Men* by Will Dean, Guardian Books, 2010)

6.19 Directions for further reading

Bloor, T. and Bloor, M. (2004), *The Functional Analysis of English: A Hallidayan Approach* (2nd edn). London: Arnold. Chapter 4. Information structure and thematic structure. Chapter 5. Grammar and text.

This book is a very accessible introduction to functional grammar. Chapter 4 provides a clear outline of theme and rheme. Chapter 5 discusses patterns of cohesion and thematic progression. There are examples and practice exercises in both chapters.

Eggins, S. (2004), *An Introduction to Systemic Functional Linguistics* (2nd edn). London: Continuum. Chapter 2. What is (a) text?

Eggin's book is a comprehensive overview of systemic functional grammar. Chapter 2 discusses patterns of cohesion in texts and gives examples from both spoken and written texts.

Liu, D. (2000), 'Writing cohesion: Using content lexical ties in ESOL', *English Teaching Forum*, 38(1), 28–35.

Liu's article gives examples of student writing that are problematic in terms of their use of patterns of cohesion. Liu analyses their texts and suggests ways in which they could be improved. He then gives suggestions for focusing on patterns of cohesion in language learning classrooms.

Martin, J. R. and Rose, D. (2007), *Working with Discourse: Meaning Beyond the Clause* (2nd edn). London: Continuum.

This book contains sections on taxonomic relations, logical connections, reference and more. There are sample analyses which illustrate each of the points being made.

McCarter, S. and Jakes, P. (2009), *Uncovering EAP: How to Teach Academic Writing and Reading*. Oxford: Macmillan. Chapter 6. Academic vocabulary.

This chapter of McCarter and Jakes's book has practical suggestions for dealing with lexical sets, lexical relations and collocation in the teaching of academic writing.

For an extended list of references and further readings see the companion website to this book.

7

Corpus Approaches to
Discourse Analysis

There are a number of advantages in using corpora to look at the use of language from a discourse perspective. As Biber, Conrad and Reppen (1998) point out, until recently many discourse studies have been based on comparatively small sets of textual data and have not typically been corpus-based. As a result it is often hard to generalize from these analyses. Larger sets of data analysed from a corpus perspective can make these findings of discourse studies more generalizable. Corpus studies can make an important contribution to our understanding of the characteristics of spoken and written discourse.

7.1 What is a corpus?

Before discussing corpus-based approaches to discourse analysis it is necessary to define what a corpus actually is. It is generally assumed that a corpus is a collection of spoken or written authentic texts that is representative of a particular area of language use, by virtue of its size and composition. It is not always the case, however, that the corpus is representative of language use in general, or even of a specific language variety, as the data set may be very specialized (such as material collected from the internet) and it may not always be based on samples of complete texts. The data may also be only of the spoken or written discourse of a single person, such as a single author's written work. It is important, then, to be aware of the specific nature and source of corpus data so that appropriate claims can be made from the analyses that are based on it (Kennedy 1998, Tognini-Bonelli 2004).

A corpus is usually computer-readable and able to be accessed with tools such as concordances which are able to find and sort out language patterns. The corpus has usually (although not always) been designed for the purpose of the analysis, and the texts have been selected to provide a sample of specific text-types, or genres, or a broad and balanced sample of spoken and/or written discourse (Stubbs 2004).

Corpus studies draw on collections of texts that are usually stored and analysed electronically. They look at the occurrence and re-occurrence of particular linguistic features to see how and where they occur in the discourse. They may look at words that typically occur together (*collocations*) or they may look at the frequency of particular items. Corpus studies may look at language use in general, or they may look at the use of a particular linguistic feature in a particular domain, such as spoken academic discourse, or use of the item in a particular genre, such as university tutorial discussions.

7.2 Kinds of corpora

General corpora

Corpora may be general or they may be specialized. A *general corpus*, also known as a *reference corpus*:

> aims to represent language in its broadest sense and to serve as a widely available resource for baseline or comparative studies of general linguistic features. (Reppen and Simpson 2004: 95)

One use of a general corpus, for example, might be to examine words that collocate with *girl* and *lady* in English in general (Sigley and Holmes 2002) as opposed to words they collocate in particular domains of use, such as online personal ads. A further use of a general corpus might be to see to what extent hedges such as *sort of* and *kind of* are typical of English, in general, compared with what words these hedges typically collocate with in spoken academic discourse (Poos and Simpson 2002).

A general corpus, thus, provides sample data from which we can make generalizations about spoken and written discourse as a whole, and frequencies of occurrence and co-occurrence of particular aspects of language in the discourse. It will not, however, tell us about the language and discourse of particular genres or domain of use (unless the corpus can be broken down into separate genres or areas of use in some way). For this, we need a *specialized corpus*.

Specialized corpora

A *specialized corpus*, as Hunston (2002: 14) explains is:

> a corpus of texts of a particular type, such as newspaper editorials, geography textbooks, academic articles in a particular subject, lectures, casual conversations, essays written by students etc. It aims to be representative of a given type of text. It is used to investigate a particular type of language.

Specialized corpora are required when the research question relates to the use of spoken or written discourse in particular kinds of texts or in particular situations. A specialized corpus might be used, for example, to examine the use of hedges in casual conversation or the ways in which people signal a change in topic in an academic presentation. It might look at an aspect of students' academic written discourse and compare this with use of the same features in published academic writing, or it may look at discourse features of a particular academic genre such as theses and dissertations, or a discourse level aspect of dissertation defences.

The Michigan Corpus of Academic Spoken English

In contrast to a general corpus, then, a specialized corpus is usually designed with a particular research project in mind. An example of this is the Michigan Corpus of Academic Spoken English (MICASE) which has data from a wide range of spoken academic genres as well as information on speaker attributes and characteristics of the speech events contained in the data. This is an open access corpus and is available without charge to people who wish to use it (http://quod.lib.umich.edu/m/micase/).

One study carried out using the MICASE corpus was an investigation of the uses of hedges such as *sort of/sorta* and *kind of/kinda* in spoken academic discourse. These were found to be more common in some disciplines such as the humanities, than in others such as science (Poos and Simpson 2002). Other MICASE studies have examined the ways in which new episodes are flagged in academic lectures and group discussions by the use of frame markers such as *OK*, *so* and *now* (Swales and Malczewski 2001) as well as other aspects of spoken academic discourse such as hedging in the discourse of academic lectures (Mauranen 2001). In the following example from Mauranen's study the hedging is in italics:

> okay. okay, um, let me get into *sort of* the more serious stuff, and, um, what i'm hoping to do with the remainder of of this first hour, is *just* give you *some uh* bit of perspective, show where biology fits into, *sort of* the rest of your education, and *hopefully* i can, um begin this framework that we're gonna fill in in the rest of the term. so i i have entitled this lecture, philosophy of science . . . or *at least* that's the point i'm talking about now. (Mauranen 2001: 174)

Findings from MICASE projects have been integrated into training courses for international teaching assistants and for the teaching of oral presentations (Reinhart 2002). The MICASE data has also been used in the development of English language tests (MICASE online).

The British Academic Spoken English corpus

A similar spoken corpus to the Michigan corpus, the British Academic Spoken English (BASE) corpus (www2.warwick.ac.uk/fac/soc/al/research/collect/base/) was developed at the University of Warwick and the University of Reading in the United Kingdom. One study based on the British corpus looked at the relationship between lexical density and speed in academic lectures (Nesi 2001). This study drew on data from 30 undergraduate lectures and found there was a range of speeds in the spoken discourse of the people delivering academic lectures. The lectures that were faster tended to be less lexically dense and the lectures that were slower tended to be more lexically dense. Lecturers spoke more quickly or were more lexically dense if they did not expect students to take notes, or if they were not presenting new content in their lecture. They also spoke more quickly if they were telling an anecdote which was an aside to the main content of the lecture. Nesi found, in looking at published coursebooks on listening to lectures that this range of speeds and ways of talking were not included in the books that she examined. Observations of this kind then have important implications for the development of English for academic purposes courses which aim to prepare students to study in English medium universities.

The British Academic Written English corpus

Specialized corpora may also be based on written discourse alone. An example of this is the British Academic Written English (BAWE) corpus (Nesi 2011) developed at the University of Warwick, the University of Reading and Oxford Brookes University in the United Kingdom (www2.warwick.ac.uk/fac/soc/al/research/collect/bawe). This corpus examines students' written assignments at different levels of study and in a range of disciplines with the goal of providing a database for use by researchers and teachers to enable them to identify and describe academic writing requirements in British university settings. The BAWE corpus includes contextual information on the students' writing such as the gender and year of study of the student, details of the course the assignment was set for and the grade that was awarded to the piece of work so as to be able to consider the relationship between these variables and the nature of the students' written academic discourse (see wwwm.coventry.ac.uk/researchnet/elc/Pages/corpora.aspx for information on other spoken academic English corpora).

The TOEFL Spoken and Written Academic Language Corpus

A specialized corpus may include both spoken and written discourse. An example of a corpus which does this is the *TOEFL 2000 Spoken and Written Academic Language Corpus* (a specialized corpus). This corpus aimed to provide a comprehensive linguistic description of spoken and written registers in US universities, although not, in this case, examples of student writing. The TOEFL corpus was made up of 2.7 million words and aimed to represent the spoken and academic genres that university students in the United States have to participate in, or read, such as class sessions, office hour conversations, study group discussions, on-campus service encounters, text books, reading packs, university catalogues and brochures. The corpus data was collected across four academic sites, each representing a different type of university: a teacher's college, a midsize regional university, an urban research university and a rural research university. The spoken data was mostly recorded by students, although academic and other staff recorded office hours material and service encounters. The spoken and written classroom material focused on the disciplines of business, education, engineering, humanities, natural and social science, at lower and upper undergraduate and graduate levels of study (Biber et al. 2002).

A key observation of the TOEFL study was that spoken genres in US university settings are fundamentally different from written genres. The study found, however, that classroom teaching in the United States was similar in many ways to conversational genres. It found that language use varied in the textbooks of different disciplines, but not in classroom teaching in different disciplines.

7.3 Design and construction of corpora

There are, thus, a number of already established corpora that can be used for doing corpus-based discourse studies. These contain data that can be used for asking very many questions about the use of spoken and written discourse both in general and in specific areas of use, such as academic writing or speaking. If, however, your interest is in what happens in a particular genre, or in a particular genre in a setting for which there is no available data, then you will have to make up your own corpus for your study.

Hyland's (2002a) study of the use of personal pronouns such as *I*, *me*, *we* and *us* in Hong Kong student's academic writing is an example of a corpus that was designed to answer a question about the use of discourse in a particular genre, in a particular setting. The specific aim of his study was to examine the extent to which student writers use self-mention in their texts 'to strengthen their arguments and gain personal recognition for their claims' in their written discourse, as expert writers do (Hyland 2005a: 178). His question was related to issues of discourse and identity, and the place of this writing practice in a particular academic and social community. A corpus collected at another institution or in another country would not have told him what students at his institution did. He was, however, able to use an existing corpus to compare his findings with how published academic writers use personal pronouns in their writing as a reference point for his study. Thus, by using his own custom-made corpus and an existing corpus, he was able to compare the findings of his study with the practices of the broader academic community and make observations about the way the students position themselves in the discourse, in particular, on the basis of this.

Harwood (2005) also compiled his own corpus for his study of the use of the personal pronouns *I* and *we* in journal research articles. For his study, Harwood selected research articles from electronic versions of journals as well as manually scanned articles and converted them to text format. His analysis of his data was both quantitative and qualitative. The quantitative analysis examined the frequency of writers' use of *I* and *we* in the texts and the disciplines in which this occurred. The qualitative analysis examined the use of *I* and *we* from a functional perspective; that is, what the function was of these items in the texts, as well as possible explanations for their use. He then compared his findings with explanations of the use of *I* and *we* in published academic writing textbooks.

A further example of a researcher-compiled corpus is Ooi's (2001) study of the language of personal ads on the world wide web (discussed later in this chapter). Ooi had to make up his own corpus to see how people use language in this particular genre. A large-scale corpus of language use on the world wide web, in general, would not have told him this. 'Off the shelf' corpora and custom-made corpora, then, each have their strengths, and their limitations. The choice of which to use is, in part, a matter of the research question, as well as the availability, or not, of a suitable corpus to help with answering the question.

It is not necessarily the case, however, that a custom-made corpus needs to be especially large. It depends on what the purpose of collecting the corpus is. As Sinclair (2001) has argued, small manageable corpora can be put together relatively quickly and can be honed to very specific genres and very specific areas of discourse use. They can also be extremely useful for the teaching of particular genres and for investigating learner needs.

7.4 Issues to consider in constructing a corpus

There are a number of issues that need to be considered when constructing a corpus. The first of these is what to include in the corpus; that is, the variety or dialect of the language, the genre(s) to be included, whether the texts should be spoken, written or both and whether the texts should be monologic, dialogic or multi-party. The next issue is the size of the corpus and of the individual texts, as well as the number of texts to include in each category. The issue is not, however, just corpus size, but also the way in which the data will be collected and the kinds of questions that will be examined using the data (McCarthy and Carter 2001). Even a small corpus can be useful for investigating certain discourse features. The sources and subject matter of the texts may also be an issue that needs to be considered. Other issues include sociolinguistic and demographic considerations such as the nationality, gender, age, occupation, education level, native language or dialect and the relationship between participants in the texts.

Authenticity, representativeness and validity of the corpus

Authenticity, representativeness and validity are also issues in corpus construction, as well as whether the corpus should present a static or a dynamic picture of the discourse under examination; that is, whether it should be a sample of discourse use at one particular point in time (a static, or sample corpus) or whether it should give more of a 'moving picture' view of the discourse that shows change in language use over a period of time (a dynamic, or monitor corpus) (Kennedy 1998; Reppen and Simpson 2002).

Kinds of texts to include in the corpus

A key issue is what kind of texts the corpus should contain. This decision may be based on what the corpus is designed for, but it may also be constrained by what texts are available. Another issue is the permanence of the corpus; that is, whether it will be regularly updated so that it does not become unrepresentative, or whether it will remain as an example of the use of discourse at a particular point in time (Hunston 2002).

Size of the texts in the corpus

The size of texts in the corpus is also a consideration. Some corpora aim for an even sample size of individual texts. If, for example, the corpus aims to represent a particular genre, and instances of the genre are typically long, or short, this needs to be reflected in the collection of texts that make up the corpus.

Sampling and representativeness of the corpus

Sampling is also an issue in corpus design. The key issue here is defining the target population that the corpus is wishing to represent. Biber (1994: 378) points out that while any selection of texts is a sample:

> Whether or not a sample is 'representative', however, depends first of all on the extent to which it is selected from the range of text types in the target population; an assessment of this representativeness thus depends on a prior full definition of the 'population' that the sample is intended to represent, and the techniques used to select the sample from that population.

The representativeness of the corpus further:

> depends on the extent to which it includes the range of linguistic distribution in the population. That is, different linguistic features are differently distributed (within texts, across texts, across text types), and a representative corpus must enable analysis of these various distributions. (ibid.)

A corpus, then, needs to aim for both representativeness and balance, both of which, as Kennedy (1998) points out, are in the end matters of judgement and approximation.

All of this cannot be done at the outset, however. The compilation of the corpus needs to take place in a cyclical fashion with the original design being based on theoretical and pilot study analyses, followed by the collection of the texts, investigation of the discourse features under investigation, then, in turn, revision of the design (Biber 1994). As Reppen and Simpson (2002: 97) explain 'no corpus can be everything to everyone'. Any corpus in the end 'is a compromise between the desirable and the feasible' (Stubbs 2004: 113).

7.5 The Longman Spoken and Written English Corpus

The *Longman Spoken and Written English (LSWE)* Corpus is an important example of a corpus study. The LSWE was used as the basis for the *Longman Grammar of Spoken and Written English*. The LSWE corpus is made up of 40 million words, representing four major discourse types: conversation, fiction, news and academic prose, with two additional categories: non-conversational speech (such as lectures and public meetings) and general written non-fiction prose.

The main source of the conversational data in the corpus was British English, although a smaller sample of conversational American English data was added for comparison. The news data contained an almost equivalent amount of British English and American English data. The fiction sample drew on British English and American English, as did the academic prose. The non-conversational speech was all British English data and the general prose contained both British English and American English data.

The study was designed to contain about five million words of text in each discourse category. Most of the texts in the corpus were produced after 1980 so the sample is mostly of contemporary British and American English usage. The corpus was made up of 37,244 texts and approximately 40,026,000 words. The texts in the corpus varied, however, in length. The newspaper texts tended to be the shortest while fiction and academic prose were the longest.

The LSWE corpus aimed to provide a representative sampling of texts across the discourse types it contained. The conversational data in the corpus was collected in real-life settings and is many times larger than most other collections of conversational data. Both the British and American conversational data were collected from representative samples of the British and US populations. The conversational data in the corpus aimed to represent a range of English speakers in terms of age, sex, social and regional groupings (Biber et al. 1999).

7.6 Discourse characteristics of conversational English

The major aim of the *Longman Grammar of Spoken and Written English*, which was derived from the LSWE corpus, was to provide a grammar of English based on an analysis of actual language use. The project has also made important observations about discourse characteristics of conversational English. Some of these characteristics are described below in the sections which follow. The data used to illustrate these features is a family argument from a reality television show.

Non-clausal units in conversational discourse

A key observation made in the Longman grammar is that conversational discourse makes wide use of *non-clausal units*; that is, utterances which do not contain an explicit subject or verb. These units are independent or self-standing in that they have no grammatical connection with what immediately precedes or follows them. The use of these units in conversational discourse is very different from written discourse where they rarely occur. Conversation, as Biber et al. (1999) point out, is highly interactive and often avoids elaboration, or specification of meaning. The use of non-clausal units is, in part, a result of this. The non-clausal units in the following extract are in italics:

Ryan: And . . . can I have a DJ too, is that OK?
Marie: *John?*
John: *What?*
Marie: Can he have a DJ . . . *a DJ?*
Ryan: Cause you won't be spending much on food so I thought . . .
John: Well, how much does a DJ cost?
Ryan: *Yeah*, I've gotta find out.
Marie: [to Ryan] *The DJ*, why d'you have to have a DJ? What does he do? *Just plays records all night?*
Marie: [to John] What d'you think about the DJ, is that OK with you?
John: I just wanna know how much it is, first.
Marie: [to Ryan] *Right*, that's what you've gotta do first, *right?*
Ryan: I'm gonna have to get Paul to come over, too.
Marie: *Why?*
Ryan: So people don't crash the party.
Marie: They won't crash the party, sweetheart, you can easily put them off.
Ryan: *Oh yeah, yeah*, maybe twenty years ago, Mum, you know. Today . . . if . . . there'd be easy another forty people if you didn't have a person at the gate.
John: [Quietly] *Bullshit*.

Personal pronouns and ellipsis in conversation

Conversational discourse also makes wide use of personal pronouns and ellipsis. This is largely because of the shared context in which conversation occurs. The meaning of these items and what has been left out of the conversation can usually be derived from the context in which the conversation is taking place. In the following example, which continues on from the previous extract, the identity of *I* (John) and *you* (Ryan) are clear from the situation in which the people are speaking and cannot be derived from the text alone:

John: Look, *I* don't want [to be embarrassed . . .
Marie: [But . . . Don't *you* think it's a little dramatic saying you've gotta have a bouncer at a private [person's party?
Ryan: [OK . . . Fine . . .

Later in the conversation Marie and John are alone. There is an ellipsis in John's reply to Marie as they both know what he is referring to in his reply. There is no need for him to repeat this. The ellipsis is in italics, in brackets:

Marie: I hope you're gonna put that magazine down and give me a bit of hand in a minute.
John: (*You want me to give you a*) Bit of a hand with what?

Situational ellipsis in conversation

Some of what speakers say in conversational discourse, thus, is predictable and does not need to be fully spelled out. Speakers often use *situational ellipsis* in conversation, leaving out words of low information value where the meaning of the missing item or items can be derived from the immediate context, rather than from elsewhere in the text. For example, John leaves out the subject and the verb in the following utterance when he sums up what he thinks about the number of people that might come to the party:

John: We've only got room for thirty people here, maximum, so if you've invited thirty-seven and they're all going to bring friends, we haven't got enough room, have we? *Common sense.*

He does this again, later in the conversation:

John: If you wanna have a party here, forty people is the limit. *Simple as that.*

Non-clausal units as elliptic replies in conversation

Non-clausal units as elliptic replies often occur in conversational discourse, as in the example below where Marie simply says 'Why (do you have to get Paul to come over)?' In the shared social situation in which the conversation is taking place both speakers know what she is asking about:

Ryan: I'm gonna have to get Paul to come over, too.
Marie: *Why?*

Repetition in conversation

Conversation also uses repetition much more than written discourse. This might be done, for example, to give added emphasis to a point being made in a conversation. One way speakers may do this is by echoing each other. An example from further in the conversation illustrates this. Marie's loud repetition of John's *I don't know why* emphasizes the point she wants to make:

Marie: It's more drama living in this house than out of it
John: (Quietly) *I don't know why.*
Marie: (Loudly) *I don't know why.*

Later in the conversation Marie and John both make repeated use of parallel structures which is also typical of conversational discourse. In this case, their use of repeated structures gives emphasis to their disagreement with what Ryan has just said:

Ryan:	*You guys are livin' in the past*, I think.
John:	No we're not. No we're not.
Marie:	*We're living in our home.*
John:	*We're living in our time*, right here and now.
Marie:	*We're living in our home. We're living in our home*, Ryan
John:	*We're not living in the past.*

Lexical bundles in conversational discourse

Conversational discourse also makes frequent use of lexical bundles; that is, formulaic multiword sequences such as *It's going to be, If you want to* and or *something like that* (Biber, Conrad and Cortes 2004). Research has shown that lexical bundles occur much more frequently in spoken discourse than they do in written discourse. Speakers may, for example, use them to give themselves time to think what they will say next. They do this as conversation occurs in real time and speakers often take and hold on to the floor at the same time as they are planning what to say next. Ryan uses the lexical bundle *I'm just saying*, then the utterance launcher *well* to take and hold on to his turn while he plans what to say to Marie:

Marie:	Why do you need a bouncer at the gate? Come on.
Ryan:	*I'm just saying, well* say I invite three guys, they bring a friend along. He's . . . a guy that I don't like . . .

John gives himself thinking time with *All I'm saying is* in the following example:

John:	*All I'm saying is* if you've invited thirty-seven people and . . . they're all going to bring friends, you can't bring friends

A speaker may also use lexical bundles to give the person they are speaking to time to process what they have just said. Ryan does this with his use of *you know* when he says:

Ryan:	Maybe twenty years ago, Mum, *you know*. Today . . . if . . .

As does John in:

John:	I don't want to be embarrassed, *you know*

Lexical bundles can also function as *discourse organizers* in conversation. Ryan uses the lexical bundle *Here we go again* to show the conversation has gone back to the original topic in:

John:	Well, if you've got any idea that there's gonna be trouble here . . . then we don't want trouble.
Ryan:	Ah, *here we go again*. I didn't . . .

7.7 Performance phenomena of conversational discourse

The Longman grammar discusses performance phenomena that are characteristic of conversational discourse. Speakers need to both plan what they are going to say and speak at the same time as they are doing this, meaning that their speech contains pauses, hesitations and repetitions while this happens.

Silent and filled pauses in conversation

Performance phenomena that are characteristic of conversational discourse include silent and filled pauses, in the middle of a turn or a grammatical unit. In the following example Marie uses a silent pause to hold on to her turn. As she has not completed a syntactic unit, she is less in danger of losing the turn than if she were to pause at the end of the unit:

> Marie: You are being . . . a sixteen-year-old twit. Sit down and write down your guests.

Utterance launchers and filled pauses

Filled pauses at transition points in conversational discourse typically use *utterance launchers* such as 'well', 'and' and 'right' as the speaker prepares what they will say. At the beginning of the conversation Ryan uses 'and' as an utterance launcher:

> Ryan: *And* . . . can I have a DJ too, is that OK?

John and Marie both use *Well* as utterance launchers to take follow-up turns and fill potential pauses as they discuss how many people are coming to the party:

> John: How many people's coming?
> Marie: *Well*, he wrote the invitations yesterday
> John: *Well*, how many's he invited?
> Marie: I don't know.
> John: *Well*, find out how many he's invited!
> Marie: Will we need a bouncer?
> John: *Well*, we'll have to find out how many's comin'

Later, Marie uses *Right* as an utterance launcher to both take the turn, to fill a pause and to affirm the point she is about to make:

> Marie: *Right*, so we get out there and we do the twist and the bop and the shimmy shimmy and whatever, do we?

Attention signals in conversation

Speakers often use another person's name as an *attention signal* to make it clear who they are speaking to as in:

Marie: *John?*
John: What?

Response elicitors in conversation

There are a number of typical ways of eliciting a response in conversational discourse. A question tag, for example, can function as a response elicitor as in:

Marie: We'll keep an orderly party for Saturday night . . . *All right?*

as can a single item as in the example below:

Marie: We had your damn party over at the park. We didn't have any gatecrashers.
Ryan: Party over at the park. How old was I Mum? *Eight?*
Marie: Six.

Non-clausal items as response forms

Non-clausal items such as *uh huh*, *mm*, *yeah* and *OK* often operate as response forms in conversation as in:

Marie: The DJ, why d'you have to have a DJ? What does he do? Just plays records all night?
Ryan: *Yeah.*

Extended coordination of clauses

Conversational discourse often includes long extended turns. These turns may be extended by coordination where one clausal unit is added to another and then another with items such as *and* and *but*, or by the direct juxtaposition of clauses as in:

Ryan: We'll leave the gate open. We'll leave the pontoon there, *and* you'll see just see. You . . . you think I'm so stupid. *But* if you . . . you look around and open your eyes, you'll see.

7.8 Constructional principles of conversational discourse

The Longman grammar discusses three key principles which underlie the production of conversational discourse. The principle of *keep talking* refers to the need to keep a conversation going while planning for the conversation is going on. The principle of *limited planning ahead* refers to human memory limitations on planning ahead; that is, restrictions on the amount of syntactic information that can be stored in memory while the planning is taking place. The principle of *qualification of what has been said* refers to the need to qualify what has been said 'after the event' and to add things which otherwise would have already been said in the conversation. This may be done by the use of digressions inserted in the middle of something else, or by the use of 'add-ons' to what has been said.

In the following example, a main clause is added on, retrospectively, to make the first part of the sentence a dependent clause:

> Ryan: You guys are livin' in the past, *I think.*

Prefaces in conversation

In conversation, the main part of a speaker's message is often preceded by a preface which connects what they have to say to the previous utterance as well as giving the speaker time to plan what they will say next. Prefaces may include fronting of clausal units, noun phrase discourse markers and other expressions such as interjections, response forms, stance adverbs, linking adverbs, overtures, utterance launchers and the non-initial use of discourse markers. Below is an example of a noun phrase, the object of the sentence, used as a preface:

> Marie: *The DJ*, why d'you have to have a DJ?

In the next example Marie uses a single word (*Truly*) as a preface to orient John to what she is about to say:

> Marie: *Truly*, it's more drama living in this house than out of it.

The following is an example of a lexical bundle (*All I'm saying is*) being used as an overture to preface what John wants to say:

> John: *All I'm saying is*, if you've invited thirty-seven people . . . and they're all going to bring friends, you can't bring friends.

Tags in conversation

Speakers add tags in many ways as an afterthought to a grammatical unit in conversational discourse. They can do this by use of a question tag at the end of a sentence. The effect of this is to turn a statement into a question. Ryan does this in his reply to John and Marie:

> Marie: Well, there's not going to be any trouble.
> John: Well, Ryan seems to think there is.
> Ryan: Oh yeah, there's gonna be gang warfare in my backyard, *is there*?

A tag can also be added to the end of a statement to reinforce what has just been said. This can be done by repeating a noun phrase, by paraphrasing what has been said or by adding a clausal or non-clausal unit retrospectively to what has just been said. In the following example Marie paraphrases *now* as *right this minute*:

> Marie: You can cut it out now, *right this minute*.

Conversational discourse, then, has many features which are not typical of more formal kinds of spoken discourse, or of written discourse. Because conversation takes place in a shared context, and in real time, there is often less specification of meaning than there is in other spoken and written genres. Also, because conversations take place between people who usually know each other it is less influenced by traditional views of accuracy and correctness that is associated with more publicly available texts. The need to keep talking while planning what to say next also has an influence on the nature of conversational discourse.

7.9 Corpus studies of the social nature of discourse

Corpus studies have also considered what the use of the discourse means in wider social terms. Using the MICASE corpus, Swales (2003), for example, asks whether the use of spoken language in academic settings can help us understand whether the university is a single community of practice or a set of 'tribalized coteries' of communities of practice. He found (as did Biber et al. 2002 in the TOEFL study, although the framework for their analysis was quite different) that, in the area of academic speaking (in contrast to academic writing), there were fewer differences between disciplines than he had expected and that many spoken academic interactions had a lot in common with general conversational English. He found academic speaking across the university tended to be informal and conversational, guarded rather than evaluative and deferential rather than confrontational. He found spoken discourse to be unpretentious in terms of vocabulary choice. It also generally avoided name-dropping and the use of obscure references. He concludes as a result of his analysis that from a language point of view there are fewer barriers to cross-disciplinary oral communication than there perhaps might be in written academic communication because of the convergence of spoken discourse styles. Swales found, for example, the same use of non-clausal units such as *um* and *uh* being used as fillers in spoken academic discourse as did Biber et al. (1999) in their study of conversational discourse. The following example from a research talk illustrates this:

> You remember I mentioned *um*, that *uh* Sir William B. Hardy, in nineteen twenty-five or thereabout, *uh* did an experiment dropping fatty acid in water . . . (Swales 2003: 208)

Swales also found the same level of informality and casualness in academic speech as in conversational discourse. The following example from the opening of an ecology colloquium is an example of this. This example shows the extended coordination of clausal units by the use of *and* referred to above. The hedge *sort of* at the beginning is also typical of conversational discourse, as well as spoken academic discourse:

> what we plan to here is uh i'll talk for a little bit, um, about *sort of* the underlying theoretical framework that we think we are operating under here *and* then when I finish that, there'll be just five minutes or so *and* then i'll talk about the work that we're doing in Nicaragua *and* when I finish talking about the work that we're doing in Nicaragua, why Ivette will talk about the work that we're doing in Mexico, *and* then finally when fe- she finished why i'll come back up here to talk uh, um a little bit s- more reflective about how the, uh theoretical framework fits into the work that we're doing *and* what we plan to do in the future *and* how people might be, might b- uh be wanting to join us, okay? (209)

Hyland's (2004b) study of the generic structure of second language students' dissertation acknowledgements is a further example of a corpus study which examines the discourse structure of part of a genre, as well as the social role of this part of the discourse. His analysis shows not only the typical ways in which these texts are organized but also how students use their texts to display their disciplinary membership and networks at the same time as they express gratitude to the people that have helped them in their academic undertaking. As Hyland (2004b: 323) points out, these short and seemingly simple texts 'bridge the personal and the public, the social and the professional, and the academic and the moral'. Through these texts, students balance debts and responsibilities at the same time as give their readers 'a glimpse of a writer enmeshed in a network of personal and academic relationships'. The following is an example of how one of the students in Hyland's study expressed gratitude in their dissertation acknowledgements section:

> *The writing of an MA thesis is not an easy task*. During the time of writing I received support and help from many people. In particular, *I am profoundly indebted to* my supervisor, Dr James Fung, who was very generous with his time and knowledge and assisted me in each step to complete the thesis. *I am grateful to* The School of Humanities and Social Sciences of HKUST whose research travel grant made the field work possible. *Many thanks* also *to* those who helped arrange the field work for me. And finally, but not least, *thanks* go *to* my whole family who have been an important and indispensable source of spiritual support. However, *I am the only person responsible for errors in the thesis*. (Hyland 2004b: 309)

In this acknowledgements section, the student shows disciplinary membership and allegiances at the same time as thanking people for their support. The acknowledgement observes appropriate academic values of modesty (*The writing of an MA thesis is not an easy task*), gratitude (*I am profoundly indebted to, I am grateful to, Many thanks to*, etc.) and self-effacement (*I am the only person responsible for errors in the thesis*). This study then, as with the Swales study, reveals not only important characteristics of academic discourse, but also what the use of this discourse means in social and interpersonal terms (see Hyland 2012 for further discussion of this).

7.10 Collocation and corpus studies

Corpus studies have also been used to examine collocations in spoken and written discourse. Hyland and Tse's (2004) study of dissertation acknowledgements, for example, found the collocation 'special thanks' was the most common way in which dissertation writers expressed gratitude in the acknowledgements section of their dissertations. This was followed by 'sincere thanks' and 'deep thanks'. They found this by searching their corpus to see how the writers typically expressed gratitude, and then what items typically occur to the left of the item 'thanks'. Through their use of language, Hyland and Tse (2004: 273) argue, dissertation students 'display their immersion in scholarly networks, their active disciplinary membership, and their observance of the valued academic norms of modesty, gratitude and appropriate self-effacement', as the example in the previous section shows.

Ooi (2001) carried out a corpus-based study of the language of personal ads on internet sites in the United States and in Singapore, while Bruhiaux (1994) carried out a corpus-based study of the language of ads in personal columns in *LA Weekly*. Ooi used the concordance program *WordSmith Tools* to examine word frequency and lexical and grammatical collocations in his sample texts. His interest was in how people in different cultures communicate on the internet on the same topic and in the same genre, as well as what gender differences there might be in the ways that they do this. He found, for example, that many US writers used the terms 'attractive' and 'great' as descriptive devices whereas the Singaporean writers largely did not. When writers used the item 'old' many more men preceded this with a specification of age (as in '39 years old') than did women. The verb 'looking for' predominated the data and commonly collocated with an item which represented the writer's 'hope or dream', as in 'someone special', 'that special woman', 'a discreet relationship', etc. Ooi then goes on to suggest ways in which students can carry out studies of this kind, looking for features of the language of romance, dating, intimacy and desire.

Bruthiaux (1994) found in his study that writers frequently used *personal chaining* and *hyphenated items* in personal advertisements; that is, strings of adjectives and nouns such as *artistic, athletic, adorable 18–32 year old* (personal chaining) and hyphenated items such as *good-looking* (hyphenated items) that collocate with nouns such as *man* and *woman* and synonyms of these items. There was also a high use of conventionalized abbreviations for collocations such as *SAM* for single Asian male and *SWF* for single white female. The following contains an example of the use of a conventionalized abbreviation (*SWF*) and examples of personal chaining (in italics):

> Serene, cerebral beauty, SWF, 34 journalist, wants to turn new page with sage, intrepid, winsome, commitment-minded professional. (149)

The genre of personal ads, further, commonly uses *linguistic simplification* and an economy of language that is characteristic of other discourse types, such as newspaper headlines, academic note taking and conversational discourse. The following example has an abbreviated 'heading' (*SWF*), personal chaining (*attractive, young 40, cool, off-beat guy 30–45*) and a non-clausal unit (*Secure and laid back*) as an add-on, a feature which is also characteristic of conversational discourse:

> SWF, attractive, young 40, seeks cool, off-beat guy 30–45 who likes film, literature, music, outdoors. Secure and laid back. (ibid.)

7.11 Corpus studies and academic writing

Corpora have been extremely useful for academic writing teachers in that they are able to show how language is used in particular academic genres. Hyland's (2002a) study of the use of personal pronouns in Hong Kong student's academic writing is an example of this kind, as are his (2008a, 2008b) analyses of word clusters in published research articles and graduate student writing. Hirsh's (2010) *Academic Vocabulary in Context* examines recurring patterns of vocabulary in academic texts in terms of both frequency and function. Thurstun and Candlin's (1997) *Exploring Academic English* is an example of a book that has been developed based on computer generated concordancing of language items. Bennett (2010), Lynne Flowerdew (2011a), Lee and Swales (2006) and Reppen (2010) provide examples of the use of corpus studies in the teaching of academic writing.

Biber's (2006) book *University Language* examines linguistic features of written (and spoken) academic genres as well as describes methodological tools for carrying out this kind of analysis. The Appendix by Federica Barbieri in Biber and Conrad's (2009) *Register, Genre, and Style* provides an extensive summary of major corpus-based genre studies, approaches and methods of analysis used in the studies, and the findings of each of the studies, many of which are relevant to the teaching of academic writing.

Biber, Connor and Upton's (2007) *Discourse on the Move* describes studies that use corpus techniques to carry out discourse-oriented analyses of academic writing. They do this by employing both *top-down* and *bottom-up* approaches in their analyses. A top-down approach identifies the discourse structures first, then examines lexical/grammatical characteristics of the units that make up the discourse structures. A bottom-up approach identifies discourse structures based on shifts in the repetition of vocabulary items and other linguistic features as indicators of the start of discourse unit boundaries in the texts. Organizational tendencies in the texts are then identified on the basis of this analysis. One way in which this can be done is through using a program such as AntMover (Anthony 2003, Anthony and Lashkia 2003) (www.antlab.sci.waseda.ac.jp/) a tool that that can be used to identify the text structure of particular genres.

Flowerdew (2011b), drawing on Hyland (2009a), describes three main approaches to corpus-based discourse analysis that have been used in the study of academic writing. These are *textual*, *critical* and *contextual* approaches. Textual approaches include Biber, Connor and Upton's (2007) top-down and bottom-up approaches to corpus-based discourse analysis. These sorts of studies focus on, for example, language patterns in texts, often, although not necessarily, in relation to the discourse structures of texts (see Glendhill 2000, Flowerdew and Forest 2010, for examples of this). Critical approaches aim to draw together insights from critical discourse analysis (see Chapter 9) and the tools of corpus-based analyses (see Baker et al. 2008, Kandil and Belcher 2011 for examples of this). Contextual approaches take situational factors into account using, for example, interview data and other ethnographic techniques to try to gain an 'insider's view' of the worlds in which the texts are written. Hyland's (2002a) study of Hong Kong student's academic writing and Harwood's (2005) examination of personal pronouns in published research articles are examples of this.

A sample study: Academic writing and identity

Hyland (2008c, 2010, 2012) employed corpus techniques in his analysis of the writing of the applied linguist John Swales. Swales is a researcher who has been extremely influential in the area of teaching English for specific purposes and research related to that area. His research into genre analysis (e.g. Swales 1981, 1990, 2004) has been the basis for much research into the analysis of academic genres which is aimed at providing a research base for the teaching of academic writing. Swales has been described as having a distinctive prose style (Hyland 2008c) but until recently there had been little analysis of this aspect of his work. Hyland (2008c, 2010, 2012) studied Swales' writing using a corpus of 342,000 words made up of 14 single authored papers and most of the chapters from his books *Genre Analysis: English in Academic and Research Settings* (Swales 1990), *Other Floors, Other Voices: A Textography of a Small University Building* (Swales 1998) and *Research Genres: Explorations and Applications* (Swales 2004). He then compared the Swales corpus with a larger reference corpus of 750,000 words made up of 75 research articles and 25 chapters from books in the area of applied linguistics. Hyland used *Wordsmith Tools Version 4* (Scott 2004) to search for the most frequent single words and multi-word clusters in Swales' writing. He then concordanced the more frequent items into categories to try to capture the central aspects of Swales' writing. In doing this Hyland aimed to explore not only typical features of Swales' writing but also what these revealed about Swales the person in terms of his identity as an academic writer; that is, how, through his use of language Swales both constructed and performed a particular academic identity.

Hyland found, beyond key content words such as *research*, *genre*, *English*, *discourse*, *language*, *academic* and *writing*, an extremely high level of *self-mention* (Hyland 2001), in particular *I* and *my*, in Swales' texts. Swales used these items at nearly double the level of that found in the reference corpus, 9.1 times per 1000 words in Swales' work compared to

5.2 times per 1000 words in the reference corpus, suggesting a very high level of personal investment, personal conviction and human voice in Swales' writing (Hyland 2008c). This is in marked contrast with the common view that academic writers should not (or rather do not) use personal pronouns in their writing.

Hyland also found a respect for opposing views in Swales' writing by his use of *hedges* (Hyland 1998a) such as *suggest, probably* and *perhaps*. When Swales wants to make a claim, however, he does this unambiguously by using items such as *certainly* and multi-word groups such as *The key point I want to make*. Swales tends to evaluate issues positively using items such as *remarkable, proficient* and *dedicated*. He also engages his readers and draws them into his texts by addressing them as *the reader*, four times as often as in the reference corpus. Swales also commonly uses *we* to engage his readers as in *As we have seen* and *I think we know*. There is also a high level of *interactive metadiscourse* (Hyland 2005b) features in Swales' texts such as *in the next section* and *as we have seen* which aim to help readers follows his texts and the arguments he is making. What we see, then, in Swales' writing is a gentle, self-deprecating author (Hyland 2008c) who is aware, and considerate of, his readers, who considers others' points of view and, at times, understates his position and contribution to the field.

What Hyland's study shows is how authorial identity is accomplished through sets of repeated acts (Butler 1993) on repeated rhetorical occasions (Hyland 2010), and that this is achieved through the use of discourse. As Hyland (2011) argues, every text projects an identity claim. We do not do this in a vacuum, however. We do this by drawing on the resources available to us on the particular occasion, in the particular setting and within the particular community of practice. Corpus techniques, then, are able to help us understand what those resources are and how expert writers draw on them to construct representations of who they are and how they wish to be seen.

7.12 Criticisms of corpus studies

There have, however, been criticisms of corpus studies. Flowerdew (2005) and Handford (2010) provide a summary of, and response to some of these criticisms. One criticism is that the computer-based orientation of corpus studies are a bottom-up investigation of language use. A further criticism is that corpora are so large they do not allow for a consideration of contextual aspects of texts (Widdowson 1995, 2000, Virtanen 2009). Tribble (2002) counters this view by providing a detailed discussion of contextual features, such as the social context of the text, communicative purpose of the text, roles of readers and writers of the text, shared cultural values required of readers and writers of the text and knowledge of other texts that can be considered in corpus studies to help address this issue. Each of these features, he argues, can be drawn on to locate the analysis and to give the findings a strong contextual dimension. As he argues, understanding language use includes understanding social and

Table 7.1 Contextual and linguistic framework for analysis (adapted from Tribble 2002)

Contextual analysis	
Name	What is the name of the genre of which the text is an example?
Social context	In what social setting is this kind of text typically produced?
	What constraints and obligations does this impose on the text?
Communicative purpose	What is the communicative purpose of the text?
Role	What roles may be required of writers and readers/ speakers and their audience in the use of this genre?
Cultural values	What cultural values are shared by writers and readers/ speakers and their audience in the performance of this genre?
Text context	What knowledge of other texts may be required by writers and readers/speakers and their audience in this example of the genre?
Formal text features	What shared knowledge of written or spoken conventions are required to effectively use this genre?
Linguistic analysis	
Lexico-grammatical features	What lexico-grammatical features of the text are statistically prominent and stylistically salient?
Text relations/ textual patterning	Can textual patterns be identified in the text? What is the reason for such textual patterning?
Text structure	How is the text organized as a series of units of meaning?

From Corpora and corpus analysis: New windows on academic writing, Christopher Tribble, © Pearson Education Limited 2002.

contextual knowledge, not just knowledge of the language system. Table 7.1 presents the contextual and linguistic components of Tribble's framework. This kind of analysis is especially suited to smaller, specialized corpora which have a genre focus (e.g. academic essays) rather than a register focus (e.g. academic discourse) (Handford 2010). Tribble suggests three stages for this kind of analysis: (i) chose a text which is considered an expert example of the particular genre, (ii) compile contextual information about how the text was created, (iii) carry out a corpus-assisted analysis of linguistic features of the texts that can then be integrated with the contextual analysis.

One way of gaining contextual information for an analysis is by the use of interviews and focus group discussions with users of the genre and consideration of the textual information revealed in the corpus study in relation to this information, as Hyland (2004c) did in his *Disciplinary Discourses*. The analysis can also be combined with other contextual information available on the data such as information on the speech event and speaker attributes and other information that is available on the data, such as the information that accompanies the MICASE and BAWE corpora. Each of these strategies can help offset the argument that corpus studies are, necessarily, decontextualized and only of interest at the item, rather than the discourse level (see Handford 2010 for further discussion of this).

7.13 Summary

This chapter has outlined key issues in corpus-based approaches to discourse analysis. It has described different kinds of corpora as well as the role they play in corpus studies. It has given examples of both written and spoken corpora and provided details of how they can be accessed. The chapter has also discussed issues in the design and construction of corpora. It has then discussed the *Longman Grammar of Spoken and Written English*, using data for a reality television show to illustrate the observations it makes about conversational discourse. Corpus studies of the social nature of discourse have also been discussed as well as the ways in which corpus studies have contributed to our understanding of academic writing. The chapter has concluded with a review of criticisms of corpus studies as well as suggestions for how these criticisms might be addressed.

7.14 Discussion questions

(1) Make a note of how people around you speak. To what extent is how they speak typical of the characteristics of conversational discourse described in this chapter?

(2) Choose a sample of a written text you often read. What are some discourse features that are typical of this kind of text? How could a corpus study help you examine this?

(3) Have a look at the findings of a discourse-oriented corpus study. How do you think an ethnographic examination of the texts that were examined would help explain its findings? Read Tribble (2002) for suggestions on this.

7.15 Data analysis projects

(1) Look at Bruthiaux's (1994) corpus-based study of personal advertisements in *LA Weekly*. Collect a similar set of data from a newspaper, magazine or internet site. Carry out a similar kind of analysis of one or more of the features that Bruthiaux examined. In what ways are your results similar to his and in what ways are they different? Why do you think this might be the case?

(2) Read Ooi's (2001) chapter on investigating genres using the world wide web. Think of a genre you would like to investigate and carry out a similar investigation. Use Tribble's (2002) framework for considering the contextual aspects of your analysis. Develop a set of interview questions from Tribble's framework, then interview people who you think could help explain the findings of your analysis.

(3) Record, then analyse a conversation between yourself and a friend for features which are characteristic of it being an example of conversational discourse in the terms outlined in the *Longman Grammar of Spoken and Written English* (Biber et al. 1999).

7.16 Exercises

Exercise 1: Spoken discourse

The *Longman Grammar of Spoken and Written English* describes discourse characteristics of conversational English. Below are extracts from the BBC (1995) Panorama interview with Diana, Princess of Wales that was presented earlier in this book.

Look for examples in these texts of non-clausal units, personal pronouns and ellipsis, situational ellipsis, repetition of utterances and utterance launchers.

(1)

Diana:	People's agendas changed overnight. I was now separated from the Prince of Wales, I was a problem, I was a liability (seen as), and how are we going to deal with her? This hasn't happened before.
Bashir:	Who was asking those questions?
Diana:	People around me, people in this environment, and
Bashir:	The royal household?
Diana:	People in my environment, yes, yes.
Bashir:	And they began to see you as a problem?
Diana:	Yes, very much so, uh uh

(2)

Diana:	And so it was, it was so isolating, but it was also a situation in which you couldn't indulge in feeling sorry for yourself: you had to either sink or swim. And you had to learn that very fast.
Bashir:	And what did you do?
Diana:	I swam.

(3)

Bashir:	Did you have the alleged telephone conversation?
Diana:	Yes we did (have the telephone conversation), absolutely we did (have the telephone conversation). Yup, we did (have the telephone conversation)

(4)

Bashir:	Did you allow your friends, your close friends, to speak to Andrew Morton?
Diana;	Yes, I did. Yes, I did.
Bashir:	Why?

(5)

Bashir:	Do you really think that a campaign was being waged against you?
Diana:	Yes I did, absolutely, yeah.
Bashir:	Why?

Diana: I was the separated wife of the Prince of Wales, I was a problem, full stop. Never happened before. What do we do with her?

(6)

Bashir: Did you make what were described as nuisance phone calls?

Diana: I was reputed to have made 300 telephone calls in a very short space of time which, bearing in mind my life style at that time, made me a very busy lady. No, I didn't, I didn't.

(7)

Bashir: Explain what you mean when you say that.

Diana: Well, er . . .

Bashir: When you say, when you say you were never given any credit, what do you mean?

Diana: Well anything good I ever did nobody ever said a thing, never said, 'well done'

Exercise 2: Written discourse

Hyland (2010, 2012) also analysed the writing of the linguist Deborah Cameron with the goal of exploring the ways in which her academic identity is revealed through her writing. Look at the following extracts from Hyland's data. Features that Hyland found salient in her writing are in italics. To what extent do these features reveal a particular academic identity?

(1)

. . . *gender is regulated* and policed by rather rigid social norms.

. . . *language is actually* the symbolic arena in which some other ideological contest is being fought out.

(2)

It is important to distinguish between the ideological representations of gender found in texts like conduct books and the actual practice of real historical gendered subjects.

It is difficult to think of any human occupation whose performance does not depend on some kind of knowledge.

(3)

It is my own view that generalization remains a legitimate goal for social science . . .

What has not changed is my conviction that theoretical arguments about meaning are not just a side issue in debates on sexism in language.

In this context *it is problematic that* unmarked or generic occupational terms are also often masculine.

(4)

The specification just quoted attracted criticism in the mid-1990s as an instance of the 'politically correct' impulse to dignify even the most menial positions by describing them in absurdly elevated terms. In my view, *however*, what it really illustrates is a more general discursive and rhetorical shift in the way experts think and talk about all kinds of work.

(5)

In most cases the styles of speech women are urged to adopt are presented as gender neutral; they are simply the most effective ways of using language in a particular domain, regardless of the speaker's sex. *Arguably however,* this is only a subtler form of androcentrism. *Undoubtedly,* the call centre industry is a hi-tech service industry which deals in symbols (words and bits); but as I will shortly seek to demonstrate by describing their work regime, the suggestion that operators have to deploy high levels of knowledge or skill in order to perform their functions is extremely misleading.

7.17 Directions for further reading

Baker, P. (2006), *Using Corpora in Discourse Analysis*. London: Continuum.

> Baker's book provides a very clear overview of discourse analysis from a corpus perspective. Topics covered include corpus building, frequency and dispersion, concordances and collocation. Step-by-step guidelines are provided for the analysis of concordances and collocation from a corpus perspective.

Biber, D., Conrad, S. and Reppen, R. (1998), *Corpus Linguistics: Investigating Language Structure and Use*. Cambridge: Cambridge University Press.

> This text provides a discussion of corpus research in areas such as lexicography, grammar, discourse, register variation, language acquisition and historical linguistics. Issues in corpus design are discussed and advice is given on tagging, norming frequency counts and statistical measures used in corpus studies.

Flowerdew, L. (2011), 'ESP and corpus studies', in D. Belcher, A. M. Johns and B. Paltridge (eds), *New Directions in English for Specific Purposes Research*. Ann Arbor: University of Michigan Press, pp. 222–51.

> Flowerdew's chapter discussed the use of corpus studies in the area of English for specific purposes. She discusses the compilation of specific purposes corpora and what this involves. She then discusses possible foci of analysis such as frequency, keywords and lexical bundles.

 Gray, B. and Biber, D. (2011), 'Corpus approaches to the study of discourse', in K. Hyland and B. Paltridge (eds), *Continuum Companion to Discourse Analysis*. London: Continuum, pp. 138–54.

> In this chapter Gray and Biber describe how corpus tools can be used to examine variation in linguistic forms across language varieties and discourse contexts. The nature and strengths of corpus-based studies are discussed. A sample study is then provided which compares structural complexity and elaboration in conversation and academic writing as an illustration of this kind of research.

Kandil, M. and Belcher, D. (2011), 'ESP and corpus-informed critical discourse analysis: Understanding the power of genres of power', in D. Belcher, A. M. Johns and B. Paltridge (eds), *New Directions in English for Specific Purposes Research*. Ann Arbor: University of Michigan Press, pp. 252–70.

> In this chapter, Kandil and Belcher show how corpus studies can be combined with other views on the nature of discourse, in this case critical discourse analysis. A sample study which examines news reporting on the Israeli–Palestinian conflict on CNN, the BBC and Al-Jazeera is provided as an illustration of this.

For an extended list of references and further readings see the companion website to this book.

8

Multimodal Discourse Analysis

Many readings of texts are constructed not just by the use of words but by the combination of words with other modalities, such as pictures, film, video images and sound. The ways in which people reacted to the events of 11 September, for example, were very much affected by the images they saw on television as they were by verbal reports of the events. This use of *multimodal discourse* (Machin 2007, Kress 2010) both established a 'proximity' to the events and engaged people in the events. Street shots from Manhattan helped to create proximity and involvement with the events. They compressed distance and brought images and experiences into people's homes that would otherwise have been unavailable to them. This moved the viewer from a position of 'spectator' to a position of 'witness' of the events. The use of video footage to accompany the reports put the viewer 'right there' in the scene of suffering, as the events were unfolding. The viewers were 'both there' yet powerless to act (Chouliaraki 2004).

The multimodal use of discourse is as much a feature of print genres as it is of television genres. The presentation of women in magazines, for example, relies not just on words on the page but as much on the images that are used to accompany the words. These representations are not necessarily just local and in the case of magazines with a worldwide network of distribution and publication are just as much global. The magazine *Cosmopolitan* is a case in point. *Cosmopolitan* is published in 44 different versions across the world in countries such as the United Kingdom, the Netherlands, Germany, Spain, Greece, Finland, India, Taiwan, the United States, Brazil and others. While there are local differences in these editions of the magazine, there is also a global brand to the magazine and presentation of women in the magazine (Machin and Thornborrow 2003). Indeed, local editors of *Cosmopolitan* go to New York to learn about *Cosmo* so they can each adopt an identical focus and format in the local editions of the magazine (Machin and van Leeuwen 2007).

Cosmopolitan, Machin and Thornborrow argue, is not just about selling magazines to its readers. It is also about selling values of independence, power and fun. The multimodal use of discourse in the magazine highlights this. Women appear in the magazine as playful fantasies. Images of the café's they go to and the clothes they wear are presented and discussed in the pages of the magazine. *Cosmopolitan*, thus, has a 'brand', which it promotes via the magazine, as well as through other products such as television programmes, clothes and fashion and Cosmo café's. Central to this branding are the discourses it draws on, and the strategies it employs for the presentation of its view of women and its underlying values of independence, power and entertainment. It does this through the background, setting, use of colour and lighting in the images it displays. It also does this through the agency it gives to women in their pursuit of men and sex.

Women are presented in *Cosmopolitan* as fun and fearless with 'a take charge attitude that's totally you' (Machin and Thornborrow 2003: 462). Terms such as 'powerful' and 'go-getting' are used to describe women in bed. Sex in the office is described as 'exciting and fun', and as a way in which a woman can achieve or maintain power. Women in the magazine, Machin and Thornborrow argue, 'rely on acts of seduction and social manoeuvring, rather than on intellect, to act in and on the world' (453). The power they have, however, 'is always connected to their body, rather than their professional competence' (466.)

Cosmopolitan, thus, presents women as advancing themselves through the use of particular social and discourse strategies, rather than through technical or intellectual skills. Women are aligned with the values and views of the magazine as well as with the other products that it sells. These values are expressed not just in words, but through the clothes that Cosmo women wear, the lipstick they use, the way they do their hair, the places they shop and the places they go to for lunch (Machin and Thornborrow 2003). These are all presented to readers of the magazine through a range of multimodal discourse practices, each of which contributes to a particular reading of the text.

8.1 Background to multimodal discourse analysis

Much of the work in multimodal discourse analysis draws from Halliday's (1978, 1989a) social semiotic approach to language, a view that considers language as one among a number of semiotic resources (such as gesture, images and music) that people use to communicate, or make meaning, with each other. Language, in this view, cannot be considered in isolation from meaning but needs to be considered within the sociocultural context in which it occurs. Multimodal discourse analysis, thus, aims to describe the socially situated semiotic resources that we draw on for communication.

> *Multimodal discourse analysis* considers how texts draw on modes of communication such as pictures, film, video, images and sound in combination with words to make meaning. It has examined print genres as well as genres such as web pages, film and television programmes. It considers how multimodal texts are designed and how semiotic tools such as colour, framing, focus and positioning of elements contribute to the making of meaning in these texts.

Halliday (2009a) describes three types of social meanings, or functions that are drawn on simultaneously in the use of language. These are *ideational* (what the text is about), *interpersonal* (relations between participants) and *textual* meanings (how the message is organized). In multimodal texts these meanings are realized visually in how the image conveys aspects of the real world (the ideational, or representational meaning of the image), how the images engage with the viewer (the interpersonal, or modal meaning of the image) and how the elements in an image are arranged to archive its intention or effect (the textual, or compositional meaning of the image) (de Silva Joyce and Gaudin 2007). Examples of multimodal discourse analysis that are influenced by this view include Kress and van Leeuwen's (2006) *Reading images: The grammar of visual design*, Kress' (2010) *Multimodality: A social semiotic approach to contemporary communication*, van Leeuwen's (2005a) *Introducing social semiotics* and O'Halloran's (2004a) *Multimodal discourse analysis* and Painter, Martin and Unsworth's (2012) *Reading visual narratives*. Machin and van Leeuwen (2007) discuss multimodality in relation to global media discourse, Bednarek and Martin (2010) discuss systemic functional perspectives on multimodality and Bednarek and Caple (2012) examine multimodality and news discourse.

Jewitt (2009a) describes four theoretical assumptions that underlie multimodal discourse analysis. The first is that language is part of an *ensemble* of modes, each of which has equal potential to contribute to meaning. Images, gaze and posture, thus, do not just support meaning, they each contribute to meaning. The second is that each mode of communication realizes different meanings and that looking at language as the principal (or sole) medium of communication only reveals a partial view of what is being communicated. The third assumption is that people select from and configure these various modes in order to make meaning and that the interaction between these modes and the distribution of meanings between them are part of the production of meaning. The fourth assumption is that meanings that are made by the use of multimodal resources are, like language, social. These meanings, further, are shaped by the norms, rules and social conventions for the genre that are current at the particular time, in the particular context.

8.2 Examples of multimodal discourse analysis

When people communicate with each other, thus, it is seldom done by one means of communication alone, that is, language. They most typically draw on a number of modes simultaneously, such as images, gesture, gaze and posture – as well as language (Machin 2007, Jewitt 2009a). Each of these modes has particular *affordances* (Gibson 1977) within the particular context; that is, what it is possible to represent and express through a particular mode (Kress 1993). This *meaning potential* (van Leeuwen (2005a)) of the particular mode is 'shaped by how mode has been used, what it has been repeatedly used to mean and do, and the social conventions that informs its use in context' (Jewitt 2009a: 24).

Images have been given special attention in much of the work in multimodal discourse analysis. These images may include photographs, diagrams, maps or cartoons. Images, further, can be seen as having a grammar of their own. For example, the social relationship between an image and its viewer is strongly influenced by whether the subject in the image establishes eye contact with the viewer or does not. Each of these possibilities could be seen as an example of *mood*, where eye contact could perhaps suggests a demand, whereas no eye contact might suggest an offer. The *point of view*, or perspective, of the image is also relevant. For example, a horizontal image suggests involvement as the viewer is on the same level as the subject of the image. A high angle shot might suggest superiority and a low angle shot may suggest respect. Other meanings are conveyed through the distance of a shot (close vs. medium vs. long), the lighting, colour and focus of the shot and the extent to which the image in the shot aims to reflect reality, or not (Feez, Iedema and White 2010).

The 1 June 2009 issue of *Time Magazine* carried a picture of Michelle Obama with the accompanying text 'The Meaning of Michelle' (www.time.com/time/covers/0,16641,20090601,00.html). In the image, Michelle Obama looks straight at the camera, establishing eye contact with the reader. Her face occupies the whole page providing a closeness which also involves the reader. The image is well lit and is in focus. The shot is horizontal suggesting the reader is on the same level as the subject of the image. The image, thus, aims to be read as true and real, and one that connects with its readers. The layout of the page and the placement of the image on it are also significant in that they each convey a certain *information value* as well as communicate the *salience* of the message to the readers (Kress and van Leeuwen 2006). The Michelle Obama image is centrally placed on the page so as to be most eye-catching. It, further, occupies the whole page, dominating it in a way that gives a particular weight to the image. The image is centrally *framed* within the borders of the magazine cover and supported by the text 'The Meaning of Michelle', showing how these two elements (the words and the image) clearly belong together, providing a strong *intermodal complementarity* (Painter and Martin forthcoming) to the elements on the page. The image, further, makes a strong interpersonal connection with readers by its use of front-on angle (showing *involvement*), extreme close-up (creating close *social distance*) and her eyes making direct contact with the readers (showing *visual focalisation*). Each of the aspects of the *composition* of the page, *information value*, *salience* and *framing*, together with the *interpersonal* connection the image makes with its readers, thus, come together to encourage a certain reading of the page.

Kress (2010) in *Multimodality: A social semiotic approach to contemporary communication* provides a social-semiotic theory of multimodality. Among other things, a social-semiotic theory of multimodality asks:

- *What meaning* is being made in a text?
- *How* is meaning being made in the text?
- What *resources* have been drawn on to make the meaning in the text?
- In what *social environment* is the meaning being made?
- *Whose interest* and *agency* is at work in the making of the meaning?

It does this by considering modes such as writing, images, colour and facial expressions and the relation between them. It considers which mode is foregounded, which mode carries major informational weight and which mode has what function in the text (Kress 2010).

In the case of the cover of *Time*, the image of Michelle Obama is foregrounded and carries the major informational load in the text. It aims to attract readers to buy the magazine and read the article on Michelle Obama within it pages. The text is written within the early days of Barrack Obama's time as president of the United States and in its image, and text, describes a Michelle Obama who is both casual and in charge. The image that is chosen for the cover and its presentation conveys exactly this message. It is an orderly yet inviting image that parallels the way she is described in the text inside the pages of the magazine. The authors of the text (Gibbs and Scherer 2009) clearly have an interest in presenting this image to their readers and give agency to their subject by presenting, with sympathy, her personal views on life in the White House, as the First Lady, and the way she conducts herself in this role.

8.3 Genre, speech acts and multimodality

Van Leeuwen (2005a, 2005b) discusses speech acts and genre in relation to multimodality, using these two notions to capture the 'how' (vs. the 'what') of multimodal communication. A key point he draws from speech act theory is how a speech act is both an *illocutionary act* (what the speech act is aiming to do) and a *perlocutionary act* (the effect it has on the thoughts and actions of people). An advertisement, thus, may aim to persuade a person to buy a particular product (the illocutionary act). If the person is convinced by the advertisement and buys the product, this is the effect, or *perlocutionary force*, of the advertisement. Texts, thus, draw on a range of modalities to create a perlocutionary effect. It is not just the words of the advertisement that persuade a person to buy the product. It is through the use of linguistic *and* visual resources in combination with other non-linguistic and contextual factors that this occurs (van Leeuwen 2005a).

Van Leeuwen discusses how genres provide resources, or templates, for doing things. The genre of service encounters, for example, and its accompanying 'stages' provide a conventionalized way of getting things done (in this case buying something) in a particular culture. Part of this will (or may) be done through language, as well as through actions such as handing goods and a credit card to a sales person. With the case of other genres, such as taking money from an automatic teller machine, the verbal components of the interaction may be written and accompanied by visual components such as an image of how to insert the card and which buttons to press to complete the event. In some cases, both of these may be combined as in any of many IKEA stores where customers are able to complete a purchase themselves by using a machine and without interacting with a salesperson at all.

Throughout all of this, however, there will be routine ways in which the genre is performed and often typical stages through which it moves, many of which may be multimodal, in order to successfully complete the transaction.

Multimodality and global media discourse

Machin and van Leeuwen (2007) discuss genre and multimodality in relation to global media discourse. Taking the example of advertisements in *Cosmopolitan* magazine, they show how their representations aim to create a certain perlocutionary effect on readers; that is, to use or purchase a particular service, or product. Using the example of an advertisement for a Health Diet Clinic, they show how the advertisement employs a 'problem-solution' rhetorical structure to do this. The problem presented in the advertisement is skin problems. The solutions are in the Diet Clinic's guidance and advice and the purchasing of a particular product, the Diet Clinic's Skin Care System. The problems are expressed by use of strategies such as an image of blemished skin with accompanying texts such as 'Do you suffer from skin problems?' The solution is a picture of the product for sale. The 'result' is a picture of unblemished skin. Both words and images, thus, interact in the advertisements to construct their particular message.

A genre and multimodality framework

Bateman (2008) discusses genre in relation to written genres saying that nowadays:

> Text is just one strand in a complex presentational form that seamlessly incorporates visual aspects 'around', and sometimes even instead of, the text itself. (1.)

Genre, he argues, plays a central role in all of this in that it is able to account for the range of possibilities for how multimodal texts are realized and the ways in which we can interact with them. He proposes a *genre and multimodality framework* that provides several layers of description for multimodal texts. These are the *content structure*, the *genre structure*, the *rhetorical structure*, the *linguistic structure*, the *layout structure* and the *navigation structure* of the text. Each of these operates within the constraints of the physical nature of the text being produced (e.g. paper or screen size), constraints arising from production technologies (e.g. page limits, colour, size of graphics, deadlines) and consumption constraints (e.g. time, place, and manner of obtaining and consuming the document, the ease with which the text can be read). A summary of Bateman's framework can be seen in Table 8.1.

The cover of *Time* magazine referred to earlier, thus, was constrained by the size of the page of the magazine, the one page limit for the cover and the need to produce a text that would be easily recognized and read. It was not limited, however, by the use of colour, even though colour is used simply (largely red and black), yet effectively, in the text. The colour is intense and intensely saturated. It is also maximally dark and pure, giving high value to

Table 8.1 Areas of analysis in Bateman's Genre and Multimodality framework (Bateman 2008: 19)

Content structure	The content-related structure of the information to be communicated – including propositional content
Genre structure	The individual stages or phases defined for a given genre: i.e., how the delivery of the content proceeds through particular stages of activity
Rhetorical structure	The rhetorical relationships between the content elements: i.e., how the content is 'argued', divided into main material and supporting material and structured rhetorically
Linguistic structure	The linguistic details of any verbal elements that are used to realize the layout elements of the page/ document
Layout structure	The nature, appearance and position of communicative elements on the page, and their hierarchical inter-relationships
Navigation structure	The ways in which the intended mode(s) of consumption of the document is/are supported: This includes all elements on a page that serve to direct or assist the reader's consumption of the document

the colour. The red background of the page suggests warmth, energy and salience (see Kress and van Leuuwen 2007 for further discussion of colour in multimodal discourse). In terms of content structure, the text is equally simple. There is just the single image of Michelle Obama and a brief title that gives a clue to the content of the article inside the journal. In terms of genre structure, the image and the text appear simultaneously making up just a single 'move', a lead-in to the main text. The rhetorical structure is equally simple, made up of 'background' (the image) and 'elaboration' (the title of the article) which adds extra information to the image.

There is also a *Given-New* (Halliday 1985) arrangement to the *Time* magazine cover where the image is the information that is already known to the readers and the text is what is not yet known by the them. This New element then becomes the Given component of a new Given-New relationship when the reader turns to the text inside the magazine. Similarly, the image might be called the Theme (see Chapter 6), or 'point of departure' of the message, while the text is the Rheme, that is, what will be said 'about' the Theme, Michelle Obama. The linguistic structures of the key verbal components of the text are a single noun (*Time*), and a noun group (*The Meaning of Michelle*). The layout structure follows expected conventions for covers of *Time* magazine with the image being given central place and the title of the magazine, the article and other articles in the issue placed above and below the main image, in what Kress and van Leeuwen (2007) term a *vertical triptych* arrangement of the page. The navigation structure for the written text requires the reader to consume the image and its caption before reading the full text of the article by opening the pages of the magazine. The online version of the article, interestingly, has a different and less dramatic image of Michele Obama at the top of the page (www.time.com/time/magazine/article/0,9171,1900228,00.html). This image, as with the paper version of the magazine, also sets the scene for article. Readers then scroll down the page to read the full article, or hit the print option to create a paper copy of the article.

Multimodality and newspaper genres

Caple (2009, 2010) and Knox (2007, 2010) discuss newspaper genres from a multimodal per-spective and how new technologies are leading to evolutions in these genres. Caple gives the example of *image-nuclear news stories*; that is, stories which comprise just a photograph and a heading, and/or a short caption (see Figure 8.1 at the end of this chapter for an example of an image-nuclear news story). Knox discusses *newsbites*, online newspaper texts which comprise a headline and an image with a hyperlink to a full story. Image-nuclear news sto-ries, in contrast with newsbites, are independent texts in themselves and do not point to a fuller story elsewhere in the newspaper.

Newspapers often draw on the strength of visual images in image-nuclear news stories to capture and retain the interest of their readers (Caple 2009). In the majority of the texts Caple collected she found the headings that accompanied the images were an idiomatic expression that fitted with the subject matter of the photograph. For example, in an image-nuclear news story about drought in China there was an image of dry, cracked earth which had central prominence in the photo with a row of people in the background carrying work tools. The heading that accompanied the image 'Dry hard with a vengeance' was a play on the 1995 American movie title *Die Hard: With a Vengeance,* the third in the *Die Hard* film series. In doing this, Caple argues, 'the newspaper is assuming knowledge on the part of the reader of the cultural allusions of the idioms, which in turn, enables the newspaper to express cultural and social solidarity with the readers' (250). The three components of this text are the *Heading* which appears above the text, the *Image* which has central place and the *Caption* which appears in a smaller font beside the image. The image orients the reader to the event being reported on and, together with the Heading, provides an intertextual reference to the reader's knowledge of idioms as well as the cultural and world knowledge required for the particular reading of the text. This kind of *allusion* to films (as well as tel-evision, songs, literary works and sporting events etc.), she found, is common in these kinds of texts and often requires very specialized knowledge for the text–image relation to work (Caple 2010).

Online newspapers, Knox (2007) points out, are much more fluid and dynamic than print-based newspapers in that they can be, and often are, updated continuously. The entry point to online newspapers is their *home page* which provides information and links to other parts of the newspaper. The home page provides an overview of news of the day and, in particular, the news that the editors (or owners) of the newspaper consider most impor-tant. Within the home page are *section pages* which orient the readers to news in particular areas of interest such as domestic news, international news, sports and entertainment. The newsbite is one of the central elements on these pages. Newsbites are often single-sentence news stories with a link to a fuller story. The function of newsbites is to highlight the most important stories of the day (in the newspaper's view) and to indicate the level of importance of the stories as illustrated by the size of the text, its positioning on the page, the font and size of the headline and the colour and size of an image, if there is one on the page.

Knox (2007) identifies three key elements to the genre of newsbites: The *Headline*, the *Lead* (typically the first sentence of the fuller text) and the *Link* to the complete text. Sometimes the Link is indicated by the words 'Full report'. Often, also, the Link is a hyperlink from the headline or an *illustration* that accompanies the text. The stance of the newspaper and its relationship with its readers are reflected in the presentation of the home page and the newsbites that are placed on it. These pages, thus, have a strong interpersonal value and create an environment in which the texts are read (Knox 2010) (see Bednarek and Caple 2010, 2012, Knox 2008, 2009 for further discussion of online news genres).

Multimodality in film and television genres

Multimodality has also been discussed in relation to film and television genres. Iedema (2001) provides a framework for the analysis of films and television by drawing on work in film theory and genre theory. The levels of analysis he proposes are *frame, shot, scene, sequence* (from film theory), *generic stage* and *work as a whole* (from genre theory). These levels are summarized in Table 8.2.

Table 8.2 Iedema's (2001: 189) levels of analysis for television and film genres

Level	Description
1 Frame	A frame is a salient or representative still of a shot
2 Shot	In a shot the camera movement is unedited (uncut); if the camera's position changes this may be due to panning, tracking, zooming and so on, but not editing cuts
3 Scene	In a scene the camera remains in one time-space, but is at the same time made up of more than one shot (otherwise it would be a shot)
4 Sequence	In a sequence the camera moves with specific character(s) or subtopic across time-spaces; when it is hard to decide whether you're dealing with a scene (1 time space) or a sequence (multiple time-spaces), this is because editors may render time-space breaks as either more obvious (-> sequence boundary) or less obvious (-> scene boundary)
5 Generic stage	Roughly, stages are beginnings, middles and endings; each genre has a specific set of stages: narratives tend to have an orientation, a complication, a resolution and maybe a coda; factual or expository genres maybe have an introduction, a set of arguments or facts and conclusion or an introduction and a series of facts or procedures
6 Work as a whole	Depending on lower levels, the work will be more or less classifiable as a particular genre; the primary distinction is between 'narrative' (fictional, dramatic genres) and 'factual' (expository, thematic, issue-oriented genres); genres are predictable relations between social–cultural, industrial–economic and symbolic–mythic orders

Key:
-> : more obvious sequence boundary
-> : less obvious scene boundary

To take the opening section of Barrack Obama's 2008 victory speech (http://edition.cnn.com/2008/POLITICS/11/04/obama.transcript/#cnnSTCVideo), we may choose to look at a single *frame* from the event such as when he delivers his opening lines:

> If there is anyone out there who still doubts that America is a place where all things are possible, who still wonders if the dream of our founders is alive in our time, who still questions the power of our democracy, tonight is your answer. (Williams 2009: 207)

At this moment, Obama is alone on the stage, looking at his audience and with a flag of the United States in the background. The composition of the frame and the shot come together to provide both the orientation and the point of departure for the rest of the speech. In terms of distance, the *shot* is close, just his head and shoulders, suggesting close social distance between him and his viewers. The flag in the background of the shot reminds us of the context of the speech. In terms of perspective, the shot is horizontal with Obama at the centre of the frame. This, plus his manner, gaze and use of language aim to connect with his audience. This moment (and, in turn, the shot) is part of a larger *scene* which takes place at a very particular time (the evening of election day 4 November 2008) and place (the victory rally in Grant Park in Chicago, Illinois, where Obama was a junior senator). In terms of *sequence*, the camera has moved from a shot of a waving US flag held by someone in the crowd and continues with Obama in centre frame until 'tonight is your answer'. The camera then moves to a shot of Obama at the podium with a row of US flags in the background. The first rows of the crowd are in front of him, many of whom are taking photos of Obama on their cell phones. The *generic stage* is the Introduction to the speech and the *work as a whole* is very early classified as an expository genre, a victory speech, due to its rhetorical character, the place and occasion on which it occurs, as well as it intertextual relationship with previous victory speeches delivered by former presidents-elect.

Baldry and Thibault (2005) and O'Halloran (2004b, 2011) also discuss multimodal analyses of television and film genres. Baldry and Thibault relate the analysis of television genres to the notions of *context of culture* and *context of situation* (see Chapter 1, also Halliday 2009a), highlighting the importance of relating the analysis to specific social and historical events, the time of day of the broadcast, and the specific viewers the program is aimed at. O'Halloran (2011) makes a similar point about context arguing that contextual considerations are an essential part of a multimodal analysis (see Bateman and Schmidt 2011 for further discussion of the multimodal analysis of film).

Multimodality and film trailers

Maier (2011) discusses multimodality in relation to film trailers. She describes trailers for comedies as typically having the stages shown in Table 8.3. The first stages she lists are *implicitly promotional*. These relate to information that is part of the story of the film (*diegetic* information). The next set of stages is explicitly promotional. They often mix together information about the story of the film and information that is not part of the story of the film (*non-diegetic information*) such as voiceover commentaries, evaluations and recommendations. Not all film trailers have all of these stages but most seem to contain a combination of them. Maier shows how the modes of voice, music, images and text all contribute to the goal, or *function*, of each section of the trailer. The fragments of the film that are presented in the trailer and the voiceover's commentaries on them, thus, combine to create the overall goal of the trailer, to promote the film.

Table 8.3 Stages of comedy film trailers and their functions (Maier 2011: 147)

Types	Stages	Functions
Implicit promotional (diegetic information)	Prologue	Appetiser
	Orientation	Contextualization
	Complication	Introduction of disruptive action
	Evaluation	Interpretations of events/outcomes
Explicit promotional (non-diegetic and diegetic information)	Promotional identification	Foregrounds meaning of film company, directors and actors
	Promotional recapitulation	Introduces new orientative information from an evaluative point of view
	Promotional interpretation	Explains possible impacts of film upon viewers
	Promotional recommendation	Advises the viewers
	Promotional information	Introduces extra non-diegetic information about Internet address, release dates, etc.

From 'Structure and function in the generic staging of film trailers'. In R. Piazza, F. Rossi and M. Bednarek (eds), *Telecinematic Discourse: Approaches to the Language of Films and Television Series*, 2011, pp. 141–58. Reprinted with kind permission from John Benjamins Publishing Company, Amsterdam/Philadelphia. [www.benjamins.com].

8.4 Carrying out multimodal discourse analysis

The steps involved in carrying out multimodal discourse analysis are similar to those of any discourse analysis project (see Chapter 10). A difference does lie, however, in how the data is analysed and what aspects of the data are seen to contribute to the meaning of the text. Whether it is spoken or written data, it first of all needs to collected. The data then needs to be logged; that is, the data needs to be summarized in some way, with accompanying notes that will help to give a contextual understanding of the data. Additional commentary can be added here where first thoughts, or ideas, about the data can be recorded that can be pursued in greater depth in the analysis.

It is then necessary to repeatedly view the data (if it is in video format) focusing on both the sound and vision of the data, the vision only and the sound only. If the data is print- or web-based text you should take a similar approach, considering what each mode that has been used (e.g. words, font, format, images) contributes to the overall meaning of the text and the ways in which they each are doing this. These features can then be considered in relation to the contextual notes that were made when the data was first collected. From this data, the extract(s) need to be chosen that will be the focus of the analysis. In most cases there will be far too much data for analysis so there is a need to be selective in terms of what will be examined. The focus could be on some aspect of the data that seems to stand out. You can then go back to the larger data set to see to what extent this is typical of the particular data set you have collected. You should then proceed to the more detailed analysis of the data which, as we have seen in this chapter, may be quite different in some ways from how you might analyse other data from a discourse analytic perspective (Bezner and Jewitt 2010).

Baldry and Thibault (2005) provide detailed guidelines for how to transcribe and analyse data from a multimodal perspective. They discuss printed texts such as advertisements and cartoons, web pages, as well as film and television genres. Baldry and Thibault use the idea of *cluster* to refer to groupings of items on print or web pages and *cluster analysis* to capture how these parts of texts are connected to other items, rather than separate from each other. These connections are important as, in the words of Baldry and Thibault (2005: 27),

> It is the cluster and the relationship between clusters, rather than the individual parts of the individual clusters, that make meaning in a specific context.

In terms of film and television genres Baldry and Thibault's discussion includes *shots*, *phases* and *transitions* between phases in these genres. They also discuss the relation between the soundtrack and images on the screen and the ways in which features of the soundtrack, such as music, provide *contextual ground* to the image. In all of this, their aim is to show the relationships between *context of situation*, *genre* and *context of culture* in multimodal genres.

Prior (2013) and Street, Pahl and Rowsell (2009) highlight the value of employing ethnographic research techniques as a way of helping us better understand the production and consumption of multimodal genres. Molle and Prior (2008), for example, collected book reports, posters, term papers and reaction papers written in graduate courses in the areas of Architecture, Music and Civil and Environmental Engineering at a large US university. They interviewed students and teachers and collected course documents such as syllabi, handouts and course evaluations. They analysed the students' texts as well as observed classes. They found that many of the texts the students were producing were multimodal and could not be neatly divided into verbal and non-verbal sections. The visual elements in the students' texts, they found, often occurred within and were integral to the verbal texts and were not separate from them. The interviews and other data they obtained gave them important insights into how the students' texts were evaluated and the relations between the students' texts and other texts that they drew on. Molle and Prior conclude by arguing for the importance of examining multimodal texts in ways that help us understand not just what the final products look like, but also the processes through which they are produced and, in turn, read by their intended audience.

8.5 Limitations of multimodal discourse analysis

Iedema (2001) discusses limitations of multimodal discourse analysis. Among these is the amount of time it takes to do this kind of analysis. Also, he points out, while the analysis may at some stages be quite technical, it can also, like all discourse analysis, be very interpretative. Multimodal analyses also, less often, looks at readers' or viewers' readings of texts. McHoul (1991), for example, has pointed out that analysts' readings are not always the same as actual readings of text. Multimodal texts, further, are often examined on the basis of the final product alone and are not considered in relation to the people who were involved in its creation.

Further limitations are tied up in the aims and scope of multimodal discourse analysis. While multimodal analyses pay attention to features of communication that are often left out of other approaches to discourse analysis, there is sometimes less attention given to aspects of language that approaches to discourse analysis might consider. There is also the issue of how the analyses can be linked to wider social issues (Jewitt 2009a). This can, however, be dealt with by linking the analyses to wider social theories, such as in the work of Machin and van Leuuwen (2007) who connect multimodal analyses to discussions of global media communication and the theories that inform that work. The use of ethnographic data to provide insights into the context of production and consumption of the texts can also be extremely useful for linking multimodal discourse analyses to broader social and contextual issues.

8.6 Summary

This chapter has provided an overview of multimodal discourse analysis, an approach which considers how texts that employ more than one mode of presentation, such as words and graphics, make meaning. It has provided the theoretical background to multimodal discourse analysis as well as given examples of analyses that have been carried out from this perspective. It has also discussed relations between genre, speech acts and multimodality. A genre and multimodality framework has then been presented as a proposal for examining layers of meaning in multimodal texts. A number or suggestions have been made for steps involved in carrying out multimodal discourse analysis. Limitations of multimodal discourse analysis have also been discussed.

8.7 Discussion questions

(1) Think of the front page of a newspaper you are familiar with. In what ways does the composition of the page – use of images, colour, font and text size – contribute to how you respond to the text?

(2) Think of the cover of a magazine you have recently read. What strategies are used to give the images on the cover particular salience?

(3) Think of a scene in a film that is particularly memorable to you. How does the use of colour, sound, costuming and setting contribute to the impact this scene has had on you?

8.8 Data analysis projects

(1) Collect a set of covers of a magazine that regularly contain photos of people. Analyse the covers in terms of Kress' (2010) questions:

- What meanings are being made in the texts?
- How are meaning being made in the texts?
- What resources have been drawn on to make the meanings in the texts?
- In what social environment are the meanings being made?
- Whose interest and agency is at work in the making of the meanings?

(2) Collect a set of image-nuclear news stories from the online version of a newspaper you are familiar with. Analyse the stories in terms of headings, images and captions. What is the relationship between the headings, images and captions in each of the texts? To what extent do the headings draw on the kinds of allusions Caple (2009) refers to in her discussion of image-nuclear news stories?

(3) Collect examples of web pages from an Internet site that you regularly visit. Analyse the pages using Bateman's (2008) Genre and Multimodality framework presented in this chapter.

(4) Record a short television programme you watch regularly. Choose an extract from the programme and analyse it using Iedema's (2001) framework for analysis presented in this chapter.

8.9 Exercises

Exercise 1: An image-nuclear news story

The art work in the image-nuclear news story in Figure 8.1 is by the Chinese artist Sui Jianguo. It is a sculpture of the right hand of Mao Zedong. Sui Jianguo, a professor of sculpture at the Central Academy of Fine Arts in Beijing, creates (often very large) sculptures that reinterpret China's cultural symbols (Zhang 2008).

Identify the components of the text which are typical of image-nuclear news stories. What is the relationship between the text and the image in this story?

Give the Ladies a Big Hand

Two women walk past a sculpture of the hand of Mao Zedong at the entrance to a gallery at the former No.798 factory in Beijing (Press Association Images)

Figure 8.1 An image-nuclear news story

Exercise 2: A book cover

Look at the cover to the first edition of this book (reproduced in black and white in Figure 8.2). How would you describe the layout of the cover? Is it a horizontal triptych or a vertical triptych (Kress and van Leeuwen 2006: 201)? What is the relationship between the words and the image on the cover? What is the information value of the different parts of the text on the cover? What prominence does the size and choice of fonts give to the various components of the cover?

Figure 8.2 Cover of the first edition of *Discourse Analysis* (Paltridge 2006)

Exercise 3: A film trailer

Look at *YouTube* for the trailer to the movie *Bridget Jones's Diary* (www.youtube.com/watch?v=vp08csjN_xI) and Maier's (2011) description of the structure of movie trailers in Table 8.3. Analyse the Orientation in the trailer using Maier's framework; that is, the section of the trailer which contextualizes the story by introducing elements such as the opening situation, the main characters, and the relationship between them. What modes are used to suggest that this is the Orientation for the trailer?

8.10 Directions for further reading

Bezemer, J. and Jewitt, C. (2010), 'Multimodal analysis: Key issues', in L. Litosseliti (ed.), *Research Methods in Linguistics*. London: Continuum, pp. 180–97.

>   This chapter is a very accessible summary of key issues in multimodal analysis. Background theories are discussed, and advice is given on collecting and analyzing multimodal data. A study of classroom interaction which drew on video data, observations and interviews is provided as an example of multimodal analysis.

Jewitt, C. (ed.) (2009), *The Routledge Handbook of Multimodal Analysis*. London: Routledge.

>   Chapter 1 of Jewitt's book provides a background to multimodal analysis while Chapter 2 outlines different approaches to multimodal analysis, specifically the social semiotic approach to multimodal discourse analysis (as in the work of Kress and van Leeuwen) and the systemic functional view of multimodal discourse analysis

(as in the work of O'Halloran etc.). Subsequent chapters provide examples of each of these approaches to multimodal discourse analysis. There is a glossary of key terms used in multimodal discourse studies at the end of the book.

Kress, G. and van Leeuwen, T. (2006), *Reading Images: The Grammar of Visual Design* (2nd edn). London: Routledge.

In this second edition of their book *Reading Images*, Kress and van Leeuwen present a grammar of visual design. Using examples such as children's drawings, textbook illustrations, photo-journalism, fine art and web pages, they examine the ways in which images communicate meaning.

Machin, D. (2007), *Introduction to Multimodal Analysis*. London: Hodder Arnold.

Machin's book is a clear and thorough introduction to multimodal analysis. Tools for analysis are explained and illustrated, often with reference to media texts.

van Leeuwen, T. (2005), *Introducing Social Semiotics*. London: Routledge.

In this book van Leeuwen uses elements such as photographs, advertisements, magazine pages and film stills to examine how different semiotic resources are drawn on to communicate meaning. The book contains a glossary of terms, exercises and suggestions for further reading.

For an extended list of references and further readings see the companion website to this book.

9
Critical Discourse Analysis

The norms and values which underlie texts are often 'out of sight' rather than overtly stated. As Hyland (2005b: 4) observes, acts of meaning making (and in turn discourse) are 'always engaged in that they realize the interests, the positions, the perspectives and the values of those who enact them'. The aim of a critical approach to discourse analysis is to help reveal some of these hidden and 'often out of sight' values, positions and perspectives. As Rogers (2004: 6) puts it, discourses 'are always socially, politically, racially and economically loaded'. Critical discourse analysis examines the use of discourse in relation to social and cultural issues such as race, politics, gender and identity and asks why the discourse is used in a particular way and what the implications are of this kind of use.

> *Critical discourse analysis* explores the connections between the use of language and the social and political contexts in which it occurs. It explores issues such as gender, ethnicity, cultural difference, ideology and identity and how these are both constructed and reflected in texts. It also investigates ways in which language constructs and is constructed by social relationships. A critical analysis may include a detailed textual analysis and move from there to an explanation and interpretation of the analysis. It might proceed from there to deconstruct and challenge the text(s) being examined. This may include tracing underlying ideologies from the linguistic features of a text, unpacking particular biases and ideological presuppositions underlying the text, and relating the text to other texts and to people's experiences and beliefs.

Critical discourse analysis starts with the assumption that language use is always social and that discourse both 'reflects and constructs the social world' (Rogers 2011: 1). A critical analysis might explore issues such as gender, ideology and identity and how these are reflected in particular texts. This might commence with an analysis of the use of discourse and move from there to an explanation and interpretation of the discourse. From here, the analysis might proceed to deconstruct and challenge the texts, tracing ideologies and assumptions underlying the use of discourse, and relating these to different views of the world, experiences and beliefs (Clark 1995).

9.1 Principles of critical discourse analysis

There is no single view of what critical discourse analysis actually is, so it is difficult to present a complete, unified view on this. Fairclough and Wodak (1997), however, describe a number of principles for critical discourse analysis which underlie many of the studies done in this area. These include

- social and political issues are constructed and reflected in discourse;
- power relations are negotiated and performed through discourse;
- discourse both reflects and reproduces social relations;
- ideologies are produced and reflected in the use of discourse.

Each of these is discussed in the sections which follow.

Social and political issues are constructed and reflected in discourse

The first of Fairclough and Wodak's principles is that critical discourse analysis addresses social and political issues and examines ways in which these are constructed and reflected in the use of certain discourse strategies and choices.

Recently, I received mail in my letter box about a proposal to build 125 apartments on top of a shopping mall which is very near where I live. There was a letter from the local council and a pamphlet from a local protest group, each of which expressed very different views on the development. One was very factual (the letter from the council) which aimed to remain 'neutral' on the topic in that it did not express a particular point of view on the project. It just outlined the procedures for the development, and how the public would be consulted about it, largely through written submissions and a public meeting that would be held in the near future. The pamphlet from the protest group, by contrast, outlined the problems the development would create for the neighbourhood such as overshadowing of properties, increased demand for on-street parking and lack of privacy from windows in the apartments that would overlook people's back gardens. Both texts, then, referred to the same event but chose very different ways of approaching it which were, in turn, reflected in their discourse. One gave the impression it was neutral on the topic whereas the other had a very particular take on the new development and what it would mean for people living in the area.

A further example of this is Teo's (2005) study of slogans for Singapore's 'Speak Mandarin' campaign. In this campaign there is clearly a view that Singaporeans of Chinese decent should speak Mandarin despite the fact that at the time of the launch of the campaign only a small percentage of them actually spoke Mandarin as their first language. The aim of the campaign was to connect Chinese Singaporeans with Chinese cultural traditions as well as help counter 'negative effects of westernisation' (123). The campaign was also motivated by an economic policy which aimed at attracting foreign investment, especially from China. These arguments were captured in slogans such as *Mandarin: Window to Chinese Culture, Speak Mandarin, It's an Asset* and *Speak Mandarin: Your Children's Future Depends on Your Effort*. Mandarin was also presented as cool and of contemporary relevance, as well as a 'stepping-stone to greater business opportunities' with the Chairman of the Promote Mandarin Council saying that Mandarin is '"cool" in more ways than one', 'Mandarin is definitely "in"' and Mandarin is 'a store of linguistic and cultural treasure waiting to be explored' (134). The discourse of the campaign, thus, constructs the view of Mandarin as a language that has both cultural, social and, in particular, economic value for the people of Singapore.

Power relations are negotiated and performed through discourse

The next principle of critical discourse analysis is that power relations are both negotiated and performed through discourse. One way in which this can be looked at is through an analysis of who controls conversational interactions, who allows a person to speak and how they do this.

In the case of the building of the apartments near my house the two different texts I received gave very different impressions of how people were encouraged to speak on the topic and negotiate different points of view on the development. The letter from the Council said that people would be free to speak at the public meeting, but that they would be required to register their intention to speak at the start of the meeting. The letter did not mention that the full Council plus representatives of the developers who had put forward the proposal would be at the meeting. The pamphlet encouraged residents to write to their local councillors about the issue and gave the names and address of each of the members of the local council. The area in which I live however is very multicultural. I am not certain the elderly Vietnamese couple who live next door to me would have written to the councillors, or would have felt their voices would have been heard had they gone to the meeting. They would most likely not have felt they had the power to change things, nor were they in a position to influence the outcomes of this discussion. The 90-year old woman who lives by herself on the other side of my property may also not have felt comfortable going to the meeting and standing up in front of everyone to have her say, as unhappy as she was about the development.

Hutchby (1996) examined issues of power in his study of arguments in British radio talk shows. As Hutchby and Wooffitt (2008) point out, the person who speaks first in an argument is often in a weaker position than the person who speaks next. The first person has to set their opinion on the line whereas the second speaker merely has to challenge the opponent to expand on, or account for the claims. In a radio talk-back programme it is normally the host that comes in the second position and has the power to challenge the caller's claim, or to ask them to justify what they have just said. The following example shows how a talk-back show host does this simply by saying *Yes* and *So?*:

Caller: I: have got three appeals letters here this week. (0.4) All a:skin' for donations. (0.2). hh
       Two: from tho:se that I: always contribute to anywa:y,
Host: *Yes?*
Caller: .hh But I expect to get a lot mo:re.
Host: So?
Caller: .h Now the point is there is a limi[t to . . .
Host: [What's that got to do – what's that got to do with
       telethons though.
Caller: hh Because telethons. . . .

                                          (Hutchby 1996: 489)

The host does this again in the next example where *What's that got to do with it?* challenges the caller and requires them to account for what they just said:

Caller: When you look at e:r the childcare facilities in this country, hh we're very very low, (.)
       i-on the league table in Europe of (.) you know of you try to get a child into a nursery it's
       very difficult in this country . . . hh An' in fa:ct it's getting wor::se.
Host: *What's that got to do with it.*
Caller: .phh Well I think whu- what 'at's gotta d-do with it is. . . .

                                          (Hutchby 1996: 490)

The caller can take the second speaking part in this kind of interaction only when the host has moved, or been manoeuvred, into first position by giving an opinion of their own. If this does not happen, it is hard for the caller to take control of the conversation and challenge the control of the host. This kind of analysis, then, shows how power is brought into play, and performed, through discourse (Hutchby 1996).

Discourse both reflects and reproduces social relations

A further principle of critical discourse analysis is that discourse not only reflects social relations but is also part of, and reproduces, social relations. That is, social relations are both established and maintained through the use of discourse.

    The letter from my Council that I referred to earlier was written with authority and contained a lot of technical detail, setting up a very clear power imbalance between the writer and readers of the text. It was signed 'Director – Planning and Development' – and gave no actual name for people to call to speak to. The pamphlet from the protest group, however, was much more informal and gave an email address to write to for further information and advice on what to do to change the situation. The social relations produced (and reproduced) through the two texts were, thus, quite different.

    Page's (2003) study of representations in the media of Cherie Blair, wife of the former British Prime Minister Tony Blair, illustrates this further. Page shows how representations of Cherie Blair in the media as a lawyer, a wife and, especially, a working mother aim to establish a certain relationship between her and the public and, in particular, other working mothers. While Cherie Blair is largely presented by the media as a success story for managing her role as a working mother, as Page points out, working mothers are more typically presented in negative terms in everyday discourse in a way that produces quite different readings of the term and, in turn, different views of working women who have children. Stokoe's (2003) study of neighbourhood disputes shows, equally, how terms such as *mother* and *single women* can be used to make moral assessments about women as well as perpetuate 'taken-for-granted "facts" about women's appropriate behaviour' (339) and social relations with other people. The use of language in this way both reflects and reproduces certain social views and relations. It, equally, reinforces social and gendered stereotypes and inequalities (Page 2003).

Ideologies are produced and reflected in the use of discourse

Another key principle of critical discourse analysis is that ideologies are produced and reflected in the use of discourse. This includes ways of representing and constructing society such as relations of power, and relations based on gender, class and ethnicity.

Each of the pieces of mail I received on the development project near my house was quite different. The letter from the Council presented the addition of 125 new apartments (plus additional retail and commercial floor space and three eight-storey residential towers on top of the already five-storey mall) at the end of my street as a neutral event that would have no consequences for me or for where I am living. The pamphlet from the protest group made it clear what the consequences of this would be, outlining them in detail and strongly voicing its opposition to the project.

Mallinson and Brewster's (2005) study of how stereotypes are formed in everyday spoken discourse is a further illustration of the ways in which ideologies are produced and reflected in the use of discourse. As Mallinson and Brewster point out, negative attitudes towards non-standard social dialects of English are often transferred to negative views of the people who speak these dialects. A job applicant who speaks a non-standard dialect, for example, may not be hired when an employer sees this use of discourse as a way of predicting the applicant's future occupational performance; that is, the view that 'good workers' speak standard English and 'bad workers' do not.

In their study of US restaurant workers' views of their customers, Mallinson and Brewster found that the (white) workers viewed all black customers as the same, in negative terms, and using stereotypes to form their expectations about future interactions with black customers, and the broader social group of African Americans. This was clear in the 'discourse of difference' (Wodak 1997) that they used as they spoke about their black customers and distanced themselves from them. The workers' views of rural white Southerner customers were similarly stereotyped, although they talked about this group in somewhat different ways, referring to where they lived, the ways they dressed and their food and drink preferences as a way of justifying their claims about them. In both cases, the workers' use of discourse privileged their own race and social class, reflecting their ideological, stereotyped views of both groups of customers.

Fairclough and Wodak also argue that all texts need to be considered in relation to the texts that have preceded them and those that will follow them. They also need to be understood by taking sociocultural knowledges of the texts and the matter at hand more broadly into consideration. In the letter from my Council, there was no mention that this was the third time the development company was attempting to have their proposal approved, and that there had been two previous public meetings on the topic where the application had been rejected. The pamphlet from the protest group, however, made this very clear. A critical analysis of these communications then, is a form of social action in that it attempts to intervene and bring about change in both communicative and sociopolitical practices (Fairclough and Wodak 1997).

Critical discourse studies, then, aim to make connections between social and cultural practices and the values and assumptions that underlie the discourse. That is, it aims to unpack what people say and do in their use of discourse in relation to their views of the world, themselves and their relationships with each other. Critical discourse analysis takes the view that the relationship between language and meaning is never arbitrary in that the choice of a particular genre or rhetorical strategy brings with it particular presuppositions, meanings, ideologies and intentions (Kress 1991). As Eggins (1994: 10) argues:

> Whatever genre we are involved in, and whatever the register of the situation, our use of language will also be influenced by our ideological positions: the values we hold (consciously or unconsciously), the biases and perspectives we adopt.

Thus, if we wish to complain about a neighbour we may chose a genre such as a neighbour mediation session, or we may decide to air our complaint in a television chat show, as some of the speakers did in Stokoe's (2003) study of neighbour complaints. We may also do this by complaining to another neighbour about them. Our intention in speaking to the other neighbour may be to build up a 'neighbourhood case' against the person we are unhappy with. If the neighbour we are complaining about is a single mother we may draw on other people's prejudices against single mothers, and our own biases and moral judgements about them as an added rationale for complaining about the neighbour. The woman being complained about may pick up on this, as did one of Stokoe's subjects, Macy, in a neighbour mediation session where she says 'if I had a big bloke living with me . . . none of this would happen' (Stokoe 2003: 329). Macy does not allow her single status to be used as a reason to complain about her.

In a further extract Stokoe shows how speakers may draw on the fact that their neighbour has boyfriends (more than one) as added ammunition against her; that is, the view that women should be monogamous (but not men) and if a woman breaches this rule, they should be held morally accountable for their behaviour. The following example illustrates this. In this example Terry (T) is the chat show host and Margaret (M) is a member of the audience who is complaining about her neighbour:

T: I want to know (.) what happened to you
(0.5)
M: after living very happily (.) in my (.) one bedroom flat for thirteen years (.) it was a *three* storey block of flats and I was on the top floor (.) and the young woman was put in the flat below me (0.5) I them had (.) seven and a half *ye:ars* (.) of sheer hell
T: *what* sort of hell?
M: loud music (.) night *and* day (.) it just depended=
T: =well that wasn't the worst was it?
M: = (0.5) it was boyfriends (.) and lovemaking that . . . (333)

The rhetorical strategy here, then, is to draw on a moralizing discourse about women (and especially, single women who have sex) as a way of legitimating complaints about female neighbours, as well as building a defence for making the complaint (Stokoe 2003).

Resende (2009) provides a similar example of how, through the use of discourse, groups of people are framed in particular ways. She examines a report of a meeting on homeless people which was sent, as a circular, to residents of a middle-class apartment building in Brazil. The circular reported on a meeting that had been convened by a local restaurant owner who was concerned about homeless people living in the area and the financial impact it was having on his business. What she found was the genre of 'apartment circulars' which normally addresses issues such as building maintenance had been appropriated to make a case for the removal of people from the area. It used terms such as 'government authorities' and 'public security representative' to give it authority so that the views expressed in the circular would be taken as given and not open for discussion. Views were expressed categorically and disguised the main issue, the problem of living on the streets. The issue was reframed in terms of individual and community comfort and avoided the underlying social cause of the problem.

Meadows (2009) employed *ethnographically-sensitive critical discourse analysis* to examine the relationship between nationalism and language learning in an English language classroom on the Mexico/US border. The students in the classes he examined were all Mexican management-level employees who held positions of economic and social privilege in their particular community. The data he collected included participant observations, interviews, questionnaires, classroom activities and emails. The data collected was then examined from a critical discourse perspective with the aim of exploring how the relationship between nationalism and language learning played out in the classroom. Meadows found that the classroom provided a site for the reproduction of nationalist border practices as well as a place in which hierarchies of privilege were reinforced. This was revealed

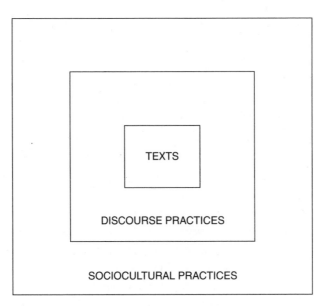

Figure 9.1 The relationship between texts, discourse practices and sociocultural practices in a critical perspective (adapted from Fairclough 1992: 73)

through the ways in which the students discussed border categories using, for example, polar categories such as *americano* and *mexicano,* and negative attitudes to categories which blurred these boundaries such as *Spanglish, Mexican-American* and *paisano.* The teacher, further, often used nationalist categories in the classroom which the students positively responded to. His study shows how language classrooms are not only about developing language proficiency. They are also often closely linked to students' investment in their worlds outside the classroom.

A key focus, then, of critical discourse studies is the uniting of texts with the discourse and sociocultural practices that the text reflects, reinforces and produces (Fairclough 1995). The chart in Figure 9.1 summarizes this. Discourse, in this view, simultaneously involves each of these dimensions.

9.2 Doing critical discourse analysis

Critical discourse analysis 'includes not only a description and interpretation of discourse in context, but also offers an explanation of why and how discourses work' (Rogers 2004: 2). Researchers working within this perspective

> are concerned with a critical theory of the social world, the relationship of language and discourse in the construction and representation of the social world, and a methodology that allows them to describe, interpret and explain such relationships. (Rogers 2011: 3)

A critical analysis, then, might commence by deciding what discourse type, or genre, the text represents and to what extent and in what way the text conforms to it (or not). It may also consider to what extent the producer of the text has gone beyond the normal boundaries for the genre to create a particular effect.

The analysis may consider the *framing* of the text; that is, how the content of the text is presented, and the sort of angle or perspective the writer or speaker is taking. Closely related to framing is the notion of *foregrounding*; that is, what concepts and issues are emphasized, as well as what concepts and issues are played down or *backgrounded* in the text. Equally important to the analysis are the background knowledge, assumptions, attitudes and points of view that the text presupposes (Huckin 1997).

At the sentence level, the analyst might consider what has been *topicalized* in each of the sentences in the text; that is, what has been put at the front of each sentence to indicate what it is 'about'. The analysis may also consider who is doing what to whom; that is, *agent-patient relations* in the discourse, and who has the most authority and power in the discourse. It may also consider what agents have been left out of sentences such as when the passive voice is used, and why this has been done (ibid.).

At the word and phrase level, connotations of particular words and phrases might be considered as well as the text's degree of formality or informality, degree of technicality and what this means for other participants in the text. The choice of words which express degrees of certainty and attitude may also be considered and whether the intended audience of the text might be expected to share the views expressed in the text, or not (ibid.).

The procedure an analyst follows in this kind of analysis depends on the research situation, the research question and the texts that are being studied. What is essential, however, is that there is some attention to the *critical, discourse* and *analysis* in whatever focus is taken up in the analysis (Rogers 2011).

Critical discourse analysis, then, takes us beyond the level of description to a deeper understanding of texts and provides, as far as might be possible, some kind of explanation of why a text is as it is and what it is aiming to do. It looks at the relationship between discourse and society and aims to describe, interpret and explain this relationship (ibid.). As van Dijk (1998) has argued, it is through discourse that many ideologies are formulated, reinforced and reproduced. Critical discourse analysis aims to provide a way of exploring this and, in turn, challenging some of the hidden and 'out of sight' social, cultural and political ideologies and values that underlie texts.

9.3 Critical discourse analysis and genre

One way in which a question might be approached from a critical perspective is by considering the genres that have been chosen for achieving a particular discourse goal. Flowerdew (2004) did this in his study of the Hong Kong government's promotion campaign of Hong Kong as a 'world-class city'. He discusses the various genres that were involved in constructing this view of Hong Kong. These included committee meetings, policy speeches, commission reports, an inception report, public fora, exhibitions, focus group discussions, presentations, a website, consultation documents, information leaflets, consultation digests and videos. He discusses how each of these genres played a role in the construction of this particular view of Hong Kong. He then carries out an analysis of three different genres which made this claim: a public consultation document, the Hong Kong annual yearbook and a video that was produced to promote Hong Kong as 'Asia's World City'.

Flowerdew shows how the Hong Kong bureaucracy developed and constructed this particular view, from the generation of an initial idea through to the public presentation of this view. He also shows that while the official aim of the consultation process was to gain feedback on the proposal, it was as much designed to win over the public to this view. The public consultation document, Flowerdew shows, used a language of 'telling' rather than a language of 'asking' (or indeed consulting). The tone of the text was prescriptive in its use of the modal verb will, for example, as in *every Hong Kong resident will, HK 2030 will involve* and *This will ensure*. The voice of authority, thus, was dominant in the use of the genre and discouraged dissent from the view that it promoted.

The yearbook that Flowerdew examined extolled the virtues of Hong Kong and was overtly promotional in nature. Other voices were brought in to give authority to this view such as 'perceptions of Hong Kong internationally' and 'our review on international perspectives of Hong Kong'. Who these views actually belonged to was not stated. This text, interestingly, was produced before the actual public consultation process commenced and suggests the government had already decided on the outcome of its consultation, before it had actually commenced.

The voice on the video that was examined, as with the yearbook, was overwhelmingly promotional. The difference between this and the yearbook was that the video used the discourse of advertising and public relations to make its point, rather than the discourse of bureaucracy. The video used short sharp pieces of text such as *The pace quickens* and *Horizons expand*. These statements were accompanied by a series of images of technology, architecture and nightlife that presented Hong Kong as a vibrant and fast-paced, modern city. The mix of traditional Chinese and Western music on the soundtrack of the video gave both an Asian and an international feel to the video. The video was also produced before the public consultation actually took place. As Flowerdew points out, this is consistent with branding theory which emphasizes the importance of gaining support and the belief of the public in the promotion of a brand, or product. It is not, however, the sequence of genres that might be expected to conform with a public consultation process. Flowerdew, then, shows how the voices of three very different genres come together to impose, rather than negotiate, a certain point of view on the readers and viewers of the texts, which formed part of the campaign.

9.4 Critical discourse analysis and framing

A further way of doing a critical analysis is to examine the way in which the content of a text is used; that is, the way in which the content of the text is presented to its audience, and the sort of perspective, angle and slant the writer or speaker is taking. Related to this is what is foregrounded and what is backgrounded in the text; that is, what the author has chosen to emphasize, de-emphasize or, indeed, leave out of the text (Huckin 1997).

Huckin (1997) looks at a newspaper report on a demonstration at a nuclear test site in the United States in just this way. Figure 9.2 is the opening section of the text he examined.

The demonstration described in this report is framed as a confrontation between the group of protesters and law-officials. The report does not discuss the issue that motivated the protest. The protesters and how many were arrested is presented to the readers. The protesters are presented negatively, as trespassers, rather than as people with a concern for the environmental future of their country. A 'police versus protesters' frame is foregrounded, and also presented, rather than the social, public health or environmental issues they are protesting about. There is much that is backgrounded, or omitted from the text. Information on nuclear testing planned for the site is left out, nor is anything mentioned of the health issues faced by people living near the site. The role of the government is also omitted from the text. The story, thus, presupposes that the most interesting and important aspect of the story is the number of protesters that were arrested, not the issues they were protesting about (ibid.).

Huckin goes on to examine topicalization in the text. As he shows, the topic of the sentences support his claim that the text is 'about' protesters versus officials, not the issues

---

Nevada Officials Arrest 700 At Test-Site Gulf Protest

MERCURY, NV (AP) – More than 700 people were arrested Saturday during an anti-nuclear, anti-Persian Gulf buildup protest at the Nevada Test Site, an official said.

Thousands turned out for the demonstration. Those arrested on misdemeanour trespass charges were taken to holding pens, then transported by bus to Beatty, 54 miles north of the remote nuclear proving ground.

An Energy Department spokesman estimated the crowd at 2,200 to 2,500 people. A sponsor of the protest, American Peace Test, said the crowd was 3,000 to 4,000 strong.

The turnout was one of the largest since anti-nuclear demonstrations began at the test site nearly a decade ago, but it failed to match a turnout of 5,000 demonstrators in 1987, when 2,000 people were arrested on trespass charges.

The DOE spokesman, Darwin Morgan, said more than 700 people were arrested and would be released in their own recognizance. 'Some of the demonstrators were a bit more aggressive, kicking at the guards when they were brought out of the pens' Morgan said....

Figure 9.2 A newspaper report on an anti-nuclear demonstration (Huckin 1997: 85) Used with permission of The Associated Press © 2011.

that prompted the demonstration. In the following examples the topic of each sentence is in italics:

> *More than 700 people* were arrested Saturday during an anti-nuclear, anti-Persian Gulf buildup protest at the Nevada Test Site.
>
> *Thousands* turned out for the demonstration.
>
> *A sponsor of the protest, American Peace Test,* said the crowd was 3,000 to 4,000 strong.

Throughout the text, it is the officials that largely have the agency; that is, it is they who initiate the action. They do the arresting and decide if the protestors will be released. The protesters only have agency when they are engaged in antisocial behaviour, such as kicking the guards.

The text is mostly written in the semi-formal register of 'objective' news reporting. Events are presented as factual, 'without the slightest trace of uncertainty'. This has the effect of making the issues that underlie the protest 'completely closed to discussion and negotiation' (89–90). As Huckin shows, the tactics used by the writer put a particular slant on the text and encourage the reading of the text in a particular way. Analyses of this kind, thus, aim to bring hidden meanings to the surface by unpacking the assumptions, priorities and values that underlie texts.

9.5 Critical discourse analysis and larger data sets

Much of the work in critical discourse analysis often draws its discussion from the analysis of only a few texts which have sometimes been criticized for being overly selective and lacking in objectivity. One way in which the scale of texts used for a critical analysis can be expanded is through the use of texts that are available on the world wide web. Using material from the world wide web is not without its problems, however. It is not always possible to identify the source of texts on the web. It is also not always possible to determine which texts have more authority on a topic than others on the web. It is also difficult to see sometimes who in fact is writing on the web. Texts on the web, further, also often rely on more than just words to get their message across. The multimodal nature, thus, needs to be taken account of in any analysis of material from the web. Texts on the web are also more subject to change than many other pieces of writing. Each of these issues needs to be considered when using data from the world wide web for a critical (or indeed any kind of) discourse study (Mautner 2005a).

The world wide web has, however, been used productively to carry out critical discourse studies which draw on the strengths of the web's capacity to collect a lot of relevant data. Mautner's (2005b) study of 'the entrepreneurial university' is an example of this. Mautner did a search of the web for the term 'entrepreneurial university' to see who was using this term, what genres it typically occurs in and how it is typically used. She used a search engine to do this as well as carried out a trawl through the websites of 30 of the top UK universities to find further uses of the term. She also used a reference corpus to see what words 'entrepreneurial' typically collocated with, outside of her particular area of interest.

Mautner observes that the use of the term entrepreneurial university brings together the discourses of business and economics with the discourse of the university. It is not just the newer, seemingly more commercially driven universities, however, that are doing this. The following example from the Oxford University website illustrates this:

> Oxford is one of Europe's most innovative and *entrepreneurial universities*. Drawing on an 800-year tradition of discovery and invention, modern Oxford leads the way in creating jobs, skills and innovation for the 21st century. (109)

The term 'entrepreneurial university' was not, however, used positively in all the texts that Mautner examined. On occasions writers purposely distanced themselves from the term by putting scare quotes around these words. Even those who were advocates of the entrepreneurial university also showed they were aware of the potentially contentious nature of the term by adding qualifying statements to their use of the term, such as 'we still care about education and society' and 'it isn't about commercialisation' (111). Studies such as this, then, show the enormous potential of using the world wide web for the critical study of the use of discourse.

9.6 Criticisms of critical discourse analysis

Critical discourse analysis has not been without its critics, however. One argument against critical discourse analysis has been that it is very similar to earlier stylistic analyses that took place in the area of literary criticism. Widdowson (1998, 2004) for example, argues that a critical analysis should include discussions with the producers and consumers of texts, and not just rest on the analyst's view of what a text might mean alone. Others have suggested that critical discourse analysis does not always consider the role of the reader in the consumption and interpretation of a text, sometimes mistaking themselves for a member of the audience the text is aimed at (van Noppen 2004). Critical discourse analysis has also been criticized for not always providing sufficiently detailed, and systematic, analyses of the texts that it examines (Schegloff 1997).

There have been calls for critical discourse analysts to be more critical and demanding of their tools of analysis, as well as aim for more thoroughness and strength of evidence for the claims that they make (Toolan 1997). Others, however, have come to the defence of critical discourse analysis arguing that its agenda is important and of considerable social significance but that there are important details and arguments that still need to be carefully worked out (Stubbs 1997).

Writers such as Cameron (2001) discuss textual interpretation in critical discourse analysis saying it is an exaggeration to say that any reading of a text is a possible or valid one. She does, however, agree with the view that a weakness in critical discourse analysis is its reliance on just the analyst's interpretation of the texts. She suggests drawing more on recipients' interpretations in the analysis and interpretation of the discourse as a way of countering this. As Cameron (140) suggests, a critical discourse analysis

> is enriched, and the risk of making overly subjective or sweeping claims reduced, by going beyond the single text to examine other related texts and to explore the actual interpretations recipients make of them.

As she points out, all discourse and all communication is interactive, and this needs to be accounted for in the analysis.

Benwell (2005) aimed to deal with this in her study of the ways in which men respond to the discourse of men's lifestyle magazines. Drawing on a textual *culture* approach, two groups of readers were interviewed about their reading habits, practices and dispositions with reference to issues such as gender, sexism, humour and irony in articles and images in the magazines. Conversation analysis and *membership categorization analysis* (Schegloff 2007) were used for the analysis of the data. One of the interviewees said, laughing, *Lucky this is anonymous!* when admitting that he had responded to the influence of an advertisement in a magazine and had gone and bought a skin care product, more commonly associated with women. In his hesitation in revealing this, he also showed his alignment with the constructions of masculinity promoted by the magazine as well as his affiliation with the view that '"real" men do not use grooming products' (164). The combination, thus, of Benwell's reading of the texts, with readers' views in relation to the texts tells us more about the texts themselves, as well as about how many men may read them.

A further way in which critical discourse studies could be enhanced is through a more detailed linguistic analysis of its texts than sometimes occurs. Systemic functional linguistics has been proposed as a tool for one way in which this could be done (Fairclough 2003, Martin 2000). Corpus approaches have also been proposed as a way of increasing the quantitative dimension of critical discourse analyses (Mautner 2005a). Others have proposed expanding critical discourse studies by drawing on work such as schema theory and work in the area of language and cognition (McKenna 2004).

Threadgold (2003) proposes a greater bringing together of work in the area of cultural studies with work in the area of critical discourse analysis, suggesting the issue of *performativity* (see Chapters 1 and 2 of this book) be given greater prominence in this work to give a better explanation and understanding of what people 'do' in their use of spoken and written discourse. Trautner (2005) did this in her examination of how exotic dancers do gender and social class in their presentations of themselves to their clients. She found that gender and social class are a central feature of the interactions that take place in dance clubs. They are reflected, she found, 'in very concrete ways: in the appearance of dancers and other staff, dancing and performance styles, and the interactions that take place between dancers and customers' (786). The notion of performativity, thus, provides an important way for thinking about language, identity, class, social memberships and, in turn, the critical analysis of discourse.

9.7 Summary

This chapter has discussed key issues and principles in critical discourse analysis. It has given examples of studies that have been carried out from this perspective, all of which have aimed to uncover out-of-sight norms and values which underlie texts which are key to understanding the roles that texts play in particular social, cultural and political contexts. Suggestions have then been made for ways of doing critical discourse analysis. Criticisms of critical discourse analysis have also been discussed and ways of responding to these criticisms have been suggested.

9.8 Discussion questions

(1) To what extent do you think texts reflect hidden and 'often out-of-sight' values? Choose a text which you think illustrates this and explain in what way you think this is done through the use of the discourse.

(2) To what extent do you think that the way a text is 'framed' encourages a certain reading of it. Choose a text which you think illustrates this. Discuss framing, foregrounding, backgrounding and the presuppositions that underlie the way the text is presented to its audience.

(3) Choose a text which you feel encourages a certain reading from its use of illustrations, pictures, layout and design, etc. How do you feel each of these resources aim to 'position' the reader in a particular way?

9.9 Data analysis projects

(1) Choose a text which you feel would be useful to examine from a critical perspective. Analyse it from the point of view of genre and framing. Link your analysis to a discussion of how you feel the text aims to 'position' its readers. Read Huckin (1997) on critical discourse analysis to help with this.

(2) Choose a text which you feel uses multimodal discourse such as layout, design and images to communicate its message to its audience. Analyse your text highlighting the ways in which it does this. Look at Van Leeuwen's (2005) *Introducing Social Semiotics* for suggestions on how to do this.

9.10 Exercises

Exercise 1: Textual silences

Huckin (2002), in his article 'Textual silence and the discourse of homelessness' examines newspaper reporting on homelessness in the United States. He defines textual silence as 'the omission of some piece of information that is pertinent to the topic at hand' (348). One of the silences he discusses is *manipulative silence*, a strategy of deliberately concealing relevant information from readers to the advantage of the writer. The writer, thus, decides 'what to say and what not to say about the topic' (356). In his study of 163 newspaper articles and editorials on this topic he found the most common themes were *causes* of homelessness, *effects* of homelessness, *public responses* to homelessness and *demographics* such as number and types of homelessness. That is, these were the topics that were foregrounded (Huckin 1997) in the texts. Topics such as treatment of the causes of homelessness, for example, were omitted, or generally 'textually silent'.

Look at the following extracts from one of the editorials Huckin analyses in his article. Which of the themes Huckin lists are represented on this text? What are some of the issues that are not mentioned, but could have been featured in this text?

Sunday, 3 January 1999 – Final edition Editorial – page B6 (Editorial)

Off-Ramp Etiquette

YOU see them at the highway on- and off-ramps. These freeway destitutes, with their imploring eyes and scribbled signs of woe, make passers-by uncomfortable. 'Homeless single mom', waits at one exit. 'Need gas money' and 'Will work for food' huddle in the rain and wind at other locations. Where to stop the car, especially if you don't plan to give?

Due to a combination of necessity, pluck and success, an increasing number of panhandlers place themselves prominently in your daily path: freeway exits, the grocery store, the post office. Cruel as it sounds, don't roll down the window, salve your conscience and offer a five-spot. Give the time or money to recognized organizations catering to the homeless. . . .

Saying no to the guy on the off-ramp holding a hard-luck sign and leaning on a pair of crutches may seem cold, mean-spirited. But good citizens can still give generously to a recognized shelter or food bank. Give the panhandler a coupon to a fast-food restaurant. Buy the Real Change newspaper. Some proceeds go to the sellers. That at least shows some initiative and dignity. Volunteer time at a food bank or shelter.

Give gifts that feed, clothe and attempt to break the cycle of chronic homelessness. In the long run, such acts of kindness are far more helpful and meaningful.

© 1999 The Seattle Times, All Rights Reserved. (2936473)

Exercise 2: Migration and identity

Krzyzanowski and Wodak (2008), in a chapter titled 'Multiple identities, migration and belonging' discuss ways in which belonging in relation to migration is constructed through discourse. The data they analyse is based on focus group discussions held in eight European countries (Austria, Cyprus, France, Germany, Italy, Sweden, Poland and the United Kingdom). Look at the following extracts from their data. In what way is belonging (and not belonging) constructed in their discourse? What is the point of difference between where the speaker is living and their home country in each of these extracts?

(1) And since 7 years (.) I've been standing astride, one leg here and another there. We want to be at home because we have nothing to live on, no work and here we are fine (1.0) but it is not our home, I mean, not fully ours. Not because we are not fine here but because our roots are there (.) in the Ukraine. We have friends there, a family. . . . (female speaker living in Poland)

(2) I know my religion keeps me apart from the English people because nearly every English person was a protestant. (female speaker living in the United Kingdom)

(3) Having another culture is useful [. . .] it is important to know where one is from [. . .] many don't know. I like to talk about it, because if you don't know your origins and your roots, it has no sense. (female speaker living in Italy)

(4) Because you see other people with other ideas different from you (female speaker living in Italy)

Exercise 3: Gender, identity and online chat rooms

In their paper 'Constructing sexuality and identity in an online teen chat room' Subrahmanyam, Greenfield and Tynes (2004) discuss ways in which gender roles and expectations can become blurred, and indeed resisted, in online chat rooms. The following data is an example of what they term 'cyber-pickup', where one of the participants identifies a potential partner with whom they will 'pair off'. They will then go off with that person into a private instant message space.

In what ways do these extracts show resistance of traditional gendered expectations? (The numbers refer to lines from the data set. FoxyR and Breethebrat are teenage girls. DEREKH101 is a teenage boy).

210.	FoxyR:	wassssssssssup yallllllllllll
212.	FoxyR:	anybody here like 50 cent press 1234
214.	FoxyR:	1234
221.	FoxyR:	wassssssssssssup
222.	FoxyR:	wanna chat
262.	FoxyR:	any body wanna chat with a hot chick
264.	FoxyR:	press 1234
265.	Breethebrat:	if there r any m/13/Tx in here if so im me
266.	DEREKH01:	1234
304.	FoxyR:	any body wa nna chat

9.11 Directions for further reading

Bloor, M. and Bloor, T. (2007), *The Practice of Critical Discourse Analysis*. London: Hodder Arnold.

Bloor and Bloor's book contains many useful exercises and activities. Sample texts are drawn from history, advertising, literature, newspapers and television. Specialized terminology is explained and there is a glossary and grammar appendix which outlines systemic functional terms used in the text.

Flowerdew, J. (2008), 'Critical discourse analysis and strategies for resistance', in V. K. Bhatia, J. Flowerdew and R. Jones (eds), *Advances in Discourse Analysis*. London: Routledge, pp. 195–210.

This chapter gives details of linguistic features that critical discourse analysis might examine as part of its overall project. Future directions of critical discourse analysis are also discussed.

Rogers, R. (ed.) (2011), *An Introduction to Critical Discourse Analysis in Education* (2nd edn). London: Routledge.

This second edition of Rogers' book contains a wide range of chapters that are useful for understanding what critical discourse analysis is and how to do it. The book explains key concepts and issues in critical discourse analysis and provides many examples of critically oriented discourse studies.

van Leeuwen, T. (2008), *Discourse and Practice: New Tools for Critical Discourse Analysis*. Oxford: Oxford University Press.

This book brings together van Leeuwen's work in the area of critical discourse analysis, drawing on the work of Foucault, Bernstein and Halliday. There are examples and sample analyses in each of the chapters.

Wodak, R. (2011), 'Critical discourse analysis', in K. Hyland and B. Paltridge (eds), *Continuum Companion to Discourse Analysis*. London: Continuum, pp. 38–53.

Wodak's chapter reviews current approaches and developments in critical discourse analysis. She also provides a sample study as an example of how to do critical discourse analysis.

For an extended list of references and further readings see the companion website to this book.

10
Doing Discourse Analysis

The previous chapters in this book have outlined a number of different perspectives on discourse analysis as well as described a range of approaches to the analysis of discourse data. This chapter discusses issues that need to be considered when planning and carrying out a discourse analysis project. A number of sample studies are discussed to give you an idea of how previous students have gone about answering discourse analysis questions that have interested them. The chapter concludes with a discussion of issues to consider in evaluating the quality of a discourse analysis project.

10.1 Developing a discourse analysis project

There are a number of issues that need to be considered when planning a discourse analysis project. The first of these is the actual research question. The key to any good research project is a well-focused research question. It can, however, take longer than expected to find this question. Cameron (2001) has suggested that one important characteristic of a good research project is that it contains a 'good idea'; that is, the project is on something that is worth finding out about. As Cameron and others have pointed out, deciding on and refining the research question is often the hardest part of the project. It is, thus, worth spending as much time as necessary to get it right.

Criteria for developing a discourse analysis project

In her book *Qualitative Methods in Sociolinguistics*, Johnstone (2000) lists a number of criteria that contribute to the development of a good and workable research topic. In her case, she is talking about research in the area of sociolinguistics. What she says, however, applies equally to discourse analysis projects. These criteria include

- a well-focused idea about spoken or written discourse that is phrased as a question or a set of closely related questions;
- an understanding of how discourse analytic techniques can be used to answer the research question(s) you are asking;

- an understanding of why your question(s) about spoken or written discourse are important in a wider context; that is, why answering the question(s) will have practical value and/or be of interest to the world at large;
- familiarity with and access to the location where your discourse analysis project will be carried out;
- ability to get the discourse data that is needed for the research project;
- the time it will realistically take to carry out the discourse analysis project, analyse the results and write up the results of the project;
- being comfortable with and competent in the ways of collecting the discourse data required by the project;
- being competent in the method(s) of analysis required for the project.

10.2 Choosing a research question

A good place to start in choosing a research question is by drawing up a shortlist of topics that interest you. You can do this by speaking to other students, by asking colleagues, by asking teachers and by asking potential supervisors, as well as by looking up related research in the library. As Cameron (2001: 183) points out, good ideas for research do not 'just spring from the researcher's imagination, they are suggested by previous research'.

It is important, then, to read widely to see what previous research has said about the topic you are interested in, including what questions can be asked and answered from a discourse perspective. This reading will also give a view of what the current issues and debates are in the approach to discourse analysis you are interested in, as well as how other researchers have gone about answering the question you are interested in from a discourse perspective. It is important to remember, however, that a research question and a research topic are not the same thing. A research topic is your general area of interest, whereas the research question is the particular thing you want to find out and which grows out of your research topic (Sunderland 2010).

Choosing and refining a research question is not, however, a linear process. As one of my students explained,

> It is, rather, a process of going back-and-forth between the research questions, the analytical framework, and the data until a balance has been struck between each of these. A high level of consistency needs to be achieved between the research questions, the analytical framework, the analysis of the data and the conclusions reached in the study. The research question, thus, can be refined [and often is] at any stage of the research. This may be the result of further reading of the literature, the analysis of the data, or simply getting some new ideas from somewhere else.

A good example of this can be seen in how this student chose and refined his research questions. His point of departure was his interest in intercultural rhetoric and second language writing. He had first met intercultural rhetoric in a course he had done on literacy and language education. As a Chinese writer of English he had often been surprised, in his first English academic writing, by some of the different conventions and expectations between Chinese and English academic writing. He wondered if intercultural rhetoric could help him understand these differences. He was also interested in discourse analysis having done a course on this as well; so some sort of discourse analysis of Chinese and English writing seemed to him to be a useful, as well as an interesting topic to investigate. As he read on this topic he saw that Chinese and English writing had indeed been investigated from an intercultural rhetoric perspective. He also saw that there were differing views on whether Chinese writing has an influence on Chinese students' second language writing in English. So he had an area of interest, but not yet a topic. And he had an area of interest that, at this point, was still very wide and not yet focused.

10.3 Focusing a research topic

My student, then, needed to focus his research topic. Often aspiring researchers start off with a project that is overly large and ambitious. Stevens and Asmar (1999: 15) suggest that 'wiser heads' know that a good research project is 'narrow and deep'. In their words, 'even the simplest idea can mushroom into an uncontrollably large project'. They highlight how important it is for students to listen to more experienced researchers in their field and to be guided by their advice in the early stages of the research. They suggest starting off by getting immersed in the literature and reading broadly and widely to find a number of potential research topics. This can be done by making heavy use of the library as well as by reading the abstracts of recent theses and dissertations, some of which are available on the world wide web (see *Directions for further reading* at the end of this chapter for some of these URLs).

Once the reading has been done, it is useful to write a few lines on each topic and use this as the basis to talk to other people about the research. Often one topic may emerge as the strongest contender from these conversations, not only because it is the most original or interesting but also because it is the most doable in terms of access to data and resource facilities, your expertise in the use of discourse analysis techniques, as well as supervision support.

Here are some of the ideas my student interested in comparing Chinese and English writing started off with.

Topic 1: A comparison of Chinese students' essay writing in Chinese and English written in their first year of undergraduate studies

Topic 2: A comparison of students' Master's theses in Chinese and English

Topic 3: An examination of newspaper articles in Chinese and English from an intercultural rhetoric perspective

Each of these questions is influenced by previous research on the topic. Each of them, however, has its problems. The first question is an interesting one. It would be difficult, however, to get texts written by the same students in their first year of undergraduate studies in the two different settings. It is also not certain (or perhaps not even likely) that they will be asked to do the same or even comparable pieces of writing in the two sets of first-year undergraduate study. It is also not likely that a Chinese student who has completed an undergraduate degree in a Chinese university would then do the same undergraduate degree in an English medium university. There is also no suggestion in the first topic as to how the pieces of writing would be analysed.

The second question is more possible as some Chinese students do go on to do a degree that includes a thesis in English after having done a degree with a thesis component in Chinese. There would, however, be many more students writing coursework essays and assignments in English who had done something similar in Chinese. So there is a problem of gaining sufficient pieces of writing for the study. There is also the problem of gaining access to the students, and hoping the students will still have the pieces of writing that they did when they were students in China. It is, of course, possible to do both of these first two studies with writing done by different students, as most studies of this kind have done. There is still, however, the problem of getting comparable pieces of writing so that the same, or at least similar things, can be compared.

The third topic, in some ways, solves the data collection issue as newspaper texts are publicly available as long as you have access to a library, or an electronic database where previous copies of newspapers are held. The theoretical framework in this topic, intercultural rhetoric, however, in the sense of cultural influences of ways of writing in one language on another, has not been used to examine newspaper articles as it is probably not very common that Chinese writers of newspaper articles are required to write a newspaper article in English. So while the third topic is practical in many ways, the theoretical framework had not been used to approach it at this stage. My student who was working on this topic decided the notion of genre, rather than intercultural rhetoric, might be a better place to start. He still retained an interest in intercultural rhetoric, however, and wanted to include this in some way in his study. His refocused topic, then, became:

> A contrastive study of letters to the editor in Chinese and English.

10.4 Turning the topic into a research question

My student had settled on his topic, but it still needed to be turned into a research question. A possible first attempt at this question might be,

> What are the differences between letters to the editor in Chinese and English?

This question however presupposes an outcome before the study has been carried out; that is, that there would indeed be differences between the two sets of writings.

The question also does not capture anything of the theoretical models that might be used to answer this question. The refocused set of questions that my student ended up with was:

(1) In what ways are Chinese and English letters to the editor similar or different?
(2) Can we use genre theory and intercultural rhetoric to understand these similarities and differences?

His question, thus, became more focused. It did not yet state exactly what aspects of genre theory he would draw on for his analysis, however. These became clearer as he read further on his topic and carried out trial analyses. He then decided to look at the *generic structures* in the two sets of texts and the typical *rhetorical types* (such as problem–solution, compare and contrast, etc.) present in the texts. He also decided to look at the use of *logico-semantic relations* (Martin 1992) between clauses in the two sets of texts as his reading had told him this was an aspect of writing, in some genres at least, that differs in Chinese and English writing. His plan was then to see to what extent previous research in the area of intercultural rhetoric into other genres might help him explain whatever similarities and differences he might observe in his two sets of data.

His questions, thus, were now *worth asking* and *capable of being answered* from a discourse analysis perspective. As he argued, most studies of Chinese and English writing either looked at Chinese, or English writing, but not at both. Also few studies used the same textual criteria for the two sets of analyses. Many previous studies of this kind, further, focused on 'direct' or 'indirect' aspects of Chinese and English writing and did not go beyond this to explore how the various parts of the texts combine together to create coherent texts. So what he was doing was theoretically useful, it was possible to collect the texts and he was capable of analysing the data in the way that he proposed.

It is important, then, as my student did, to strike a balance between the value of the question and your ability to develop a discourse analysis project you are capable of carrying out; that is, a project for which you have the background, expertise, resources and access to data needed. It is also important to spend as much time as is needed to get the research question(s) right as research questions that are well-designed and well-worded are key to a good research project (Sunderland 2010).

10.5 Connecting data collection, analysis and research questions

Sunderland (2010) provides helpful advice on how to connect data collection and analysis with your research question(s). She suggests completing a table such as the one shown in Table 10.1 to do this.

Table 10.1 Connecting data collection, analysis and research questions (Sunderland 2010: 25)

	Research question	Data needed	Data collection	Data analysis
1.				
2.				
3.				

She points out, however, that things are not always as neat as Table 10.1 might suggest. Sometimes one research question might require more than one set of data or you might be able to use one set of data to address more than one research question. What you will see, however, from your chart is whether there are any gaps that still need to be filled or data that still needs to be collected to address each of your questions (Sunderland 2010).

10.6 Kinds of discourse analysis projects

There are a number of different kinds of projects that can be carried out from a discourse analysis perspective. A number of these are described below, together with examples of previous discourse projects and details of the data that were collected for each of these projects.

Replication of previous discourse studies

One kind of study to consider is a replication study. Indeed, there has been a resurgence of interest in these kinds of studies in recent years. The editor of the journal *Language Teaching*, for example, argues that

> such research should play a more significant role in the field than it has up to now and that it is both useful and necessary. (Language Teaching review panel 2008: 1)

As Santos (1989) points out, the findings of many studies are often not tested by further studies which follow the same methodology and a similar data set either at the same point in time or at some stage later when the findings may be different. Santos describes this lack of replication studies as a serious weakness in applied linguistics research. Such studies provide both the accumulation and consolidation of knowledge over time. They can confirm or call into question previous findings in the research literature (see Language Teaching review panel (2008) for a discussion of the advantages and difficulties of replication studies; also Language Teaching (2007) for a call for replication studies).

Samraj's (2005) study of research article abstracts and introductions is an example of a replication study. Her aim was to test the results of previous research into the discourse structure of research article introductions to see whether they apply to articles written in the area of conservation biology and wildlife behaviour. She also wished to look at whether the discourse structure of the research article abstracts was as different from the discourse structure of research article introductions as previous research had claimed them to be. To carry out her study, she randomly selected 12 research article abstracts and 12 research article introductions from two key journals in the area of conservation biology and wildlife behaviour. She analysed her data using models that had been used in previous research on this topic, namely Swales' (1990) research into research article introductions and Bhatia's (1993) and Hyland's (2004c) research on research article abstracts. Once she had compared her findings with the results of previous research, she then compared her two data sets with each other to examine the extent to which they were similar in terms of discourse organization and function, also the focus of previous research.

Using different discourse data but the same methodology

A further way of using previous research is to carry out a study which uses different discourse data from a previous study, but the same methodology so as to be able to compare and contrast your findings with those of the original study. Yang's (1997) study of the opening sequences in Chinese telephone calls did this. She collected 80 Chinese telephone conversations made by three Chinese families living in Beijing. She analysed the opening sequences of these conversations, then compared her findings with the findings of previous research into opening sequences in telephone calls in the United States and a number of other countries and, in particular, published claims about 'canonical' openings of telephone conversations in English.

Analysing existing data from a discourse analysis perspective

Channell's (1997) study of telephone conversations took already published data, a conversation purported to be between the Prince of Wales and Camilla Parker-Bowles, and analysed it to see in what way the speakers expressed love and desire, what the effect of the telephone was on their talk and what features of the conversation mark it as being the talk of two people who are in a close and intimate relationship. She looked at topic choice and topic management, ways of expressing love and caring, the language of desire and the way in which the speakers said goodbye to each other. Her study confirmed previous work on telephone closings in that both speakers employed an elaborate set of pre-closings and continued repetitions (such as 'love you', 'love you forever' and 'love you too') before concluding their conversation. She did not follow the conversation analysis procedure of transcribing the data herself as the data had already been published (and was not, in any case, available in audio form). It had also been tidied up to some extent when it was originally published. Notwithstanding, her study does show the value of taking already existing data to see how discourse analytic techniques can help to further understand already published data.

Analysing discourse data from a different perspective

Another possibility is to take data that has already been analysed from one discourse perspective and analyse it from another. Orr (1996) did this in her study of arguments in a reality TV show. Her particular interest was in using conversation analysis as an alternate way of looking at data that had already been examined from a frame semantics perspective (Lee 1997) to see what this other perspective might reveal about the nature of the interactions. Her study followed the philosophy of conversation analytic studies in that she started with the data and allowed the details of the analysis to emerge from her transcriptions. Through repeated listenings to the data she saw how the speakers challenged and countered each other's points of view in a series of cyclical moves until one or the other speaker accepted the point of the argument. She then compared her findings with the findings of the study that had used frame semantics as its framework for analysis.

Considering the validity of a previous claim

A further possibility is to design a project which considers the validity of a previous claim in the research. Liu's (2004, 2008) study of Chinese ethnic minorities' and Han Chinese students' expository writing in English aimed to examine an existing claim in his particular setting. He examined, in particular, the claim that the typical Chinese rhetorical structure of *Qi-cheng-zhuan-he* would influence his students' expository writing in English. He collected texts from a preparation test in which the students were asked to produce a piece of expository writing in English. The data was made up of English texts written by Tibetan students, Mongolian students and Han Chinese students. He examined both the schematic structure and thematic structure of the students' texts. He then examined these structures to see to what extent they were influenced by the Chinese rhetorical structure he was interested in. Finally, he made a comparison of the three student groups' writing to see if there were any differences in the discourse structures of their writing.

Focusing on unanalysed genres

Another possibility is to focus on data that has not been analysed before and describe characteristic features of the particular discourse. This could, for example, be an analysis of one of the many new genres that are emerging through the use of new technologies, or it may be examples of a genre that has not been analysed before from a discourse perspective. Ooi (2001) looked at a new and emerging genre in his study of personal advertisements on the internet. His study was based on data collected from internet dating sites in the United States and Singapore. He broke his data up into three groupings based on three types of 'sought after relationship': 'romance', 'dating' and 'intimacy'. He found his data by doing an internet search, typing in the keywords 'personal ads', 'personal advertisements' and 'personal classifieds'. He collected 12 files of texts, with ten texts in each file, for his study based on further subcategories of his groupings. He then carried out a lexical analysis of the texts, looking at word frequency and collocations by gender and country of origin to see to what extent males and females differ in their expectations of each other in writing this kind of advertisement, and the kinds of words and expressions they use to express these expectations.

Shalom (1997) carried out a similar study in her examination of personal advertisements in London's *Time Out* entertainment guide. She collected 766 ads from the *Lonely Hearts* section of *Time Out* over a period of 4 months. Her interest was in the attributes of the person the writers were seeking to meet. She broke up her corpus of texts into four groupings for her analysis: straight men (367 texts), straight women (186 texts), gay men (155 texts) and lesbian women (58 texts) to see in what ways each of these groups typically described the person of their desire.

Combining research techniques

Mixed-methods studies (Cresswell 2003, Cresswell and Plano Clark 2007, Ivankova and Cresswell 2009) which combine quantitative and qualitative research techniques have become increasingly popular in recent years. This combining of research techniques can increase the validity as well as help gain greater insights into the topic under investigation. Ivankova and Cresswell describe a number of ways in which these sorts of studies might be carried out. These are *explanatory design*, *exploratory design*, *triangulation design* and *embedded design*. *Explanatory design* is where qualitative findings are used to help explain or expand on quantitative findings. *Exploratory design* is where a researcher examines something qualitatively, before measuring it quantitatively. *Triangulation design* is where a researcher collects multiple perspectives on something in order to gain a more complete understanding of the topic they are investigating. This might involve using multiple data sources (e.g. surveys and interviews), multiple groups of participants (e.g. writers and readers) or multiple research techniques (e.g. observations and interviews) in addition to linguistic analysis to examine the topic under investigation. *Embedded design* is where one research approach is embedded within another, with the data collected either concurrently or sequentially. An example of this a large-scale quantitative design such as a corpus study which embeds interviews within it to help understand the results of the corpus study. In this case one of the designs (e.g. the corpus study) would take on more emphasis than the other (i.e. the interviews).

Eckert's (2000) *Linguistic Variation as Social Practice* is an example of a study which combines both quantitative and qualitative analyses for the analysis of spoken discourse. She carried out a study of phonemic variation in the speech of two polarized groups of students in a Midwestern high school in the United States: 'jocks' (students with a high level of participation in athletics or other school activities and generally from the upper half of the local socioeconomic continuum) and 'burnouts' (students who are generally from the lower half of the local socioeconomic continuum and who are more likely to go into the workforce than to university at the end of high school).

Eckert looked not just at language variation, but also at the way the identity of the speakers was constructed in their use of language. Her data included interviews in which she collected speech samples that she then analysed for the particular linguistic features she was interested in. She also carried out day-to-day observations in and around the school where she carried out her study. She walked around and took notes on who was where, what they were doing and who they were doing it with. She took notes from extracurricular activities, in the park, in the neighbourhood and at McDonalds. She interviewed people separately and in groups, both in and out of school hours. She kept notes on how the students dressed, how they did their hair and makeup, as well as where they hung out, who they hung out with and when. Working with *social network theory*, the notion of *communities of practice* and *friendship clusters*, she discusses her observations about stylistic variation, the social meaning of that variation and the social and linguistic construction of identity through the use of spoken discourse.

Ohashi's (2000, 2008) study of the speech act of thanking in Japanese is a further example of a discourse study which combines a number of different research techniques. He combined elicited data in the form of discourse completion tasks, role plays and letter writing tasks with actual examples of language use. He looked at his data from both cross-cultural pragmatic and interlanguage pragmatic perspectives. His interest was in the notion of a debt–credit equilibrium in thanking as an expression of politeness in Japanese. He carried out four data-based studies, each of which examined this issue. The real-life data was drawn from telephone conversations recorded at the time of the *seibo* season, one of two major gift-giving seasons in Japan. This was then contrasted with the findings of the other data: discourse completion tasks completed by native speakers of Japanese, native speakers of English and adult learners of Japanese; role-plays performed by native speakers of Japanese; and letters of request and letters of thanks written by native and non-native speakers of Japanese. By comparing both elicited and real-life data he contributes to cross-cultural discussions of politeness as well as shows the strength of *methodological triangulation* in this sort of investigation (see Mason 2006, Morse 2010 for further discussion of studies which draw on combinations of qualitative research techniques).

Mixed methods studies, then, clearly have a lot to offer discourse studies. As Angouri (2010) argues, they can help overcome the limitations posed by relying on just the one single research method or approach to answer to our research questions. Mixed methods can also give us greater insights into the use of spoken and written discourse as well as the settings in which it occurs.

10.7 Two sample discourse studies

The two projects which follow are both examples of studies which combine approaches to research in the analysis of discourse. Both studies draw on discourse and non-discourse analysis perspectives on their particular topic. This use of *methodological triangulation* (Denzin 1970) is a particular strength of these two studies, as is the detail of analysis that each of the students carried out in their discourse analysis projects.

10.8 A spoken discourse project

Silence in Japanese students' tutorial interactions in English.

Summary of the study

Nakane's (2005, 2007) examination of silence in Japanese students' interactions in university tutorials in English looked at the students' actual performance in the university classrooms as well as the students', other students' and lecturer's perceptions of the Japanese students' performance. She combined the techniques of conversation analysis with ethnographic data in order to get multiple perspectives on the question she was investigating.

Aim of the study

The aim of Nakane's study was to examine the communication problems faced by Japanese students in mainstream English medium university classrooms. She also wanted to see whether there were characteristic discourse patterns of Japanese students which could be sources of their communication problems. This question drew from her own experience as an English teacher in Japan, where she had begun to wonder how Japanese students would cope with academic interactions in an English-speaking country. She discovered, from her research, that we know very little about what happens to these students in mainstream university classrooms. Her study looked at the actual performance of these students in mainstream university classes, as well as exploring other people's perceptions of these students' performances in these classes.

Methodology

Nakane carried out a conversation analysis of the students' classroom interactions. She also conducted individual interviews, focus group discussions and administered questionnaires. She combined this data with three case studies which drew on video and audio recordings, field notes and artefacts from her classroom observations. The case studies used stimulated recall interviews and follow-up interviews with the Japanese students, fellow English-speaking students and their teachers. A large-scale survey that had been independently carried out at another university was also used as a data source for the study. Nakane also collected data from classrooms in Japan in order to make a comparison between her observations of the English medium classrooms and how Japanese students might typically behave in a similar kind of setting in Japan. The Japanese data consisted of video recordings, field notes and artefacts from the Japanese classrooms.

Apart from the conversation analyses of the English classroom data, a content analysis was carried out of the interview and stimulated recall data where Nakane allowed categories and sub-categories to emerge from the data, rather than using a set of predetermined categories as the starting point for her analysis. The video and audio material were coded following patterns that had emerged from the students' and staff's self reports in the stimulated recall interviews and the follow-up interviews. The conversation analysis component of the data was counter-checked by another analyst, a native speaker of English.

Results of the study

Nakane's study showed that silence was one of the major problems for the Japanese students in the English medium classrooms, both for themselves and for their lecturers. She found, however, that the degree and type of silence varied among the students. She found that gaps in assumptions about classroom communication between the Japanese students, fellow English-speaking students and their lecturers contributed to the students' silence in each of her three cases. She also considered the results of her study in relation to other issues such as teacher–student interactional modes, teacher control of classroom discourse, timing in the taking of turns and the Japanese students' perceptions of politeness and, in particular, the hierarchy-oriented politeness system they were used to in their interactions with teachers in Japan. She also considered her findings in relation to the issue of the Japanese students' language proficiency and their different schema, or interpretive frames, for classroom interactions.

Nakane found that the Japanese students' silence in class seemed to prevent the establishment of rapport between them and their lecturers. She found there was a conflict between the lecturers' view of the Japanese students' personalities (for example, as being shy) when this was not the case for the students outside of the classroom. She also found that the students' silence in class was interpreted as a negative attitude and lack of commitment to their studies, where in fact, for one of the students she examined, this was not at all the case.

Commentary

A particular strength of Nakane's study was the multiple perspectives she took on her research question in order to provide both validity and depth to her research findings. These multiple data sources provided for a detailed and fine-grained analysis of the research questions. The project showed a good understanding of the importance of triangulation in this sort of study by combining different perspectives on the research questions that were examined. Her ethnographic data provided insights into her findings that would not have been possible by looking at the spoken interactions alone. It is an example of a project that was well-conceived, well-designed and well carried out. Further, it provided answers to questions that are of value to both university teaching staff and to students that may help, in the future, to provide solutions to the kinds of communication problems the students in her study were experiencing.

Further research

Nakane is well aware of the limits to the claims that can be made on the basis of her study and argues for the accumulation of further data and analyses of the kind that she had carried out. In particular she points to the need to further explore the types and aspects of silence that she observed. She argues that these analyses need to be at both the micro and the macro levels; that is, by a detailed analysis of the actual interactions, as well as a broader analysis of the situation and circumstances that surround the interactions. She also suggests the examination of student interactions in different types of study situations to see to what extent students' interactions in these situations are similar to, or different from, the interactions that she observed. She suggests looking at the reverse kind of situation as well; that is, looking at the interactions of English-speaking students in Japanese university settings to see to what extent the English-speaking students' experiences in a Japanese university classroom are similar to, or different from, the Japanese students' interactions that she examined in her study.

10.9 A written discourse project

A contrastive analysis of letters to the editor in Chinese and English.

Summary of the study

Wang's (2002, 2004) contrastive study of letters to the editor in English and Chinese is an example of a written discourse project that drew on different, yet complementary, theoretical frameworks for his study: intercultural rhetoric and the systemic functional view of genre. He also read outside of these two areas to try to find sociocultural explanations for the similarities and differences that he observed in his study.

Aim of the study

Wang's study had several research questions: in what ways are Chinese and English letters to the editor similar or different in terms of their rhetorical structures, to what extent can systemic functional genre theory and intercultural rhetoric be used to explore and understand these similarities and differences and what are the reasons for the similarities and differences in the performance of this genre in the two different linguistic and cultural settings.

Methodology

The data Wang collected for this study consisted of ten letters to the editor in Chinese and ten letters to the editor in English published in two sets of widely read Chinese and English newspapers. He looked at the *generic structure* of each of the two sets of data, the *rhetorical types* (such as 'problem/solution', 'evaluation' and 'exposition') represented in the two data sets and *logico–semantic relationships* between the clauses and clause complexes in the two sets of texts. He then read the research literature on differences in collectivism and individualism in Chinese and Western cultures in order to try to understand the findings of his study.

Results of the study

Wang found that the Chinese and English letters to the editor shared some similarities at the level of generic structures. Notwithstanding, he found that there was often an editor's preview to the Chinese letters to the editor that was absent in the English letters. He found that appeals to values and needs were used to support claims in the Chinese letters whereas the English letters used evidence to do this. He also found that while consequential and additive logico–semantic relations were used in both the Chinese and English texts, consequential relations occurred more frequently in the Chinese texts than in the English texts.

Wang argues that the notion of evidence is deeply rooted in Western culture and therefore finds its way into English texts, whereas appeals to values and needs is especially important in Chinese culture and so is strongly present in the Chinese letters to the editor. He also argues that the editor's preview in the Chinese letters plays the role of presenting a societal norm, or point of view, that individuals in Chinese society are expected to follow. He suggests that the greater use of consequential relations in the Chinese texts is a reflection of the commonly used inductive style of Chinese writing as well as the typical subordinate–main sequences that often occur.

Commentary

By employing approaches to analysis from systemic functional genre studies and intercultural rhetoric, Wang was able to able to carry out a detailed examination of the similarities and differences between letters to editors in English and Chinese at different levels of analysis. He also looked outside of the texts to try to gain an understanding of why they had been written the way they were. There were, however, aspects in which the project could have been strengthened. The process of text sampling could have been wider and the number of texts could have been larger. He saw from his study, however, the value of combining linguistic and non-linguistic analyses in order to understand not just what occurs when the same genre is written in different linguistic and cultural contexts, but also why this occurs. This is something he decided to explore in more detail in his subsequent contrastive genre study of newspaper commentaries in Chinese and English on the events of September 11 (Wang 2007) (see also below).

Further research

Wang was aware of the limitations of the claims he could make from the size and particular geographical location of his data set and suggests further data be collected from a wider range of Chinese and English language newspapers than he did in his original study. He tried to address this issue in his subsequent contrastive genre study of newspaper commentaries in Chinese and English on the events of September 11. This study was based on an examination of 50 Chinese newspaper commentaries and 50 English language newspaper commentaries. The data he chose for his study of newspaper commentaries were drawn from national general, national specialist and regional newspapers in both Chinese and English (Wang 2006a, 2006b, 2007).

His study in his further (2006b, 2007) project drew on the strengths of two different perspectives on genre analysis: the view of genre based in systemic functional linguistics and the view of genre represented by researchers in *rhetorical genre studies* (Artemeva and Freedman 2008, Freedman and Medway 1994). His study incorporated textual, intertextual and contextual analyses of the two sets of texts. At the *textual* level, he examined the generic structure of the two sets of texts, the rhetorical types they typically represent and the ways in which key participants are introduced into and kept track of in the texts. At the *intertextual* level he explored the ways in which the texts drew on other sources, and other voices, in the production of the texts. He then combined this analysis with a discussion of the notion of intertextuality across communities of practice as a way of both broadening and giving greater depth to his analysis. His *contextual* analysis considered the textual and intertextual findings of the study in relation to their respective sociocultural and sociopolitical contexts, and, in particular, the role of the media and discourses of terrorism in each of the particular settings. Wang's second study showed how the results and insights that have been gained in one discourse analysis project can be drawn for the development of a further, more substantial, discourse analysis project. In his particular case, he learnt how much a contextual analysis has to contribute to genre analysis projects, making this a critical focus of his second project on the topic of Chinese/English writing (see Paltridge and Wang 2010, 2011 for further discussion of this study).

10.10 Combining discourse and other research perspectives

Both the Nakane and the Wang studies that have just been described drew on a number of different discourse analysis and other research perspectives to work towards answers to their research questions. When combining perspectives in this way, it is important to understand the basis of the perspectives being drawn on to appreciate what this placing together implies and, indeed, if it is possible to do this. People working in the area of conversation analysis, for example, would consider Nakane's combination of conversation analytic techniques and ethnography impossible as for a conversation analyst the evidence is in the data, and the closest an analyst is able to get to understanding an event is in the transcription and analysis of the data. For them, insiders' views are only intuitions and not, in their view, admissible in the analysis and interpretation of the data. My view, however, is that Nakane strengthened rather than weakened her study by combining perspectives in the way that she did.

Cameron (2005b: 125) discusses the problems associated with what she calls 'theoretical and methodological eclecticism'. She points out that sometimes this carries a high risk of superficiality as the researcher may be trying to do too many things at once and not end up doing any of them properly (which is not the case in either the Nakane or the Wang studies). It is not impossible to mix discourse analysis and other methods. What this requires, however, is 'a clear rationale for putting approaches together, a sophisticated understanding of each approach, and an account of how the tensions between approaches will be handled in [the] study' (127).

A researcher can, then, combine an approach to discourse analysis with a non-discourse analytic perspective on the research, as both Nakane and Wang have done in their studies. Both Nakane and Wang have shown how doing this can provide more of an account of the issue they are examining than might have been possible with just the one, single discourse analysis (or other research) perspective. It is crucial, however, in the planning of this kind of project that each of the approaches are weighed up against each other, identifying what kind of information each approach can (and cannot) supply. By doing this the use of one approach to discourse analysis in combination with another approach to discourse analysis or other approaches to research can be justified. Indeed, often an approach of this kind can provide a fuller and more explanatory perspective on the question under investigation than might be provided with just the one single perspective.

10.11 Evaluating a discourse analysis project

Each of the studies described in this chapter suggest ways in which discourse analysis can provide insights into social, pedagogic and linguistic questions. Taylor (2001) suggests a number of criteria by which discourse studies can be evaluated. These criteria, she argues, should be an integral part of any discourse analysis project and should guide readers of the project in their evaluation of it. Three key issues to consider in this are the *reliability*, *validity* and *replicability* of the project that has been carried out.

Reliability

Reliability refers to the consistency of the results obtained in the project. This is comprised of two kinds of reliability, *internal reliability* and *external reliability*. Internal reliability refers to the consistency of the data collection, analysis of the data and interpretation of the results; that is, the extent to which the researchers were consistent in what they did and whether someone else would get the same results if they carried out the same analysis of the data.

In his study of Chinese and English letters to the editor referred to earlier in this chapter, Wang decided which newspapers would best represent the genre he wanted to investigate in terms of their circulation and which of them were the most widely read in the particular social and cultural setting. To do this, he drew on the notion a *tertium comparationis* (a comparable platform) (Connor and Moreno 2005, Moreno 2008) for the two sets of newspaper to be examined. Texts were chosen from Chinese and Australian newspapers by considering geographic and demographic features that seemed to be comparable between the two countries.

Once he had decided which newspapers to select his texts from he chose his texts from only these two sets of newspapers. He then analysed each of his texts in the same way. That is, he looked at the schematic structure, rhetorical types and logico–semantic relations in each of the 20 texts in his study. He then analysed and interpreted the results of his analyses in the same way for each of the texts he examined. He looked for typical patterns in each of the sets of texts and considered the extent to which the use of the patterns he observed reflected particular sociocultural views of the relationship between the writers and their audience in the particular settings in which the texts were produced.

External reliability (or *replicability*) refers to the extent to which another researcher could reproduce the study, using the same discourse analysis procedures, and obtain the same or similar results to those obtained in the study. In order to ensure the replicability (and thereby external reliability) of his study, Wang provided his sample texts and detailed analyses of each of the aspects he examined in the appendix to his study. In the methodology section of his study he both explained and gave details of each of his categories of analysis so that readers of his study could then take these categories and re-analyse his data in the same way, if they so wished to. In the presentation of his Chinese data he provided English translations for each of his texts and glossed each of his Chinese examples in English so that a reader who cannot read Chinese would be able to follow his analysis and the arguments and claims he was making. That is, he provided sufficient information about the approach he used and his categories of analysis so that someone else approaching his data in the same way would come up with the same findings.

Validity

Validity (or *trustworthiness* in qualitative research) refers to the extent to which a piece of research actually investigates what it says it will investigate, and 'the truth or the accuracy of the generalizations being made by the researcher'. *Internal validity* refers to 'how far claims about cause are "true" in the situation being studied' (Taylor 2001: 318). *External validity* refers to the extent to which the results of the study can be generalized from the sample used in the study to a broader population.

In Wang's case he was careful to caution that his observations were limited to the set of texts that he had chosen for his study. Even though his texts were chosen at random, he was well aware that another set of 20 texts may reveal something different from what he observed, as indeed may an analysis of a larger set of texts. In terms of generalizability, then, he was well aware that this is not possible from the size of his sample. He did, however, provide sufficient details on the nature and source of his texts and his analyses of the texts so that a reader could consider the extent to which his findings could be transferred or compared to what might be found in another, similar set of texts. By doing this, he aimed to provide *credibility*, *dependability* and *transferability* (Lincoln and Guba 1985) to his study. He, thus, left an *audit trail* that other people reading his research could follow by making as clear as possible what he did, how he did it and how he reached the conclusions that he did.

10.12 Summary

This final chapter of the book has made suggestions for planning and carrying out a discourse analysis project. A number of sample studies have been discussed, as have issues to consider in evaluating the quality of a discourse analysis project. A number of websites and journals are suggested at the end of the chapter where you will find further examples of discourse analysis projects and advice on submitting discourse-oriented articles to academic journals in the area.

10.13 Planning a discourse analysis project

The final task in this book asks you to draw on the issues presented in this and previous chapters to develop a proposal for a discourse analysis project. The readings, websites and journals that follow are suggestions for places to look to read further and to help you choose a topic that you would like to investigate.

Task

Draw up a shortlist of possible research topics, writing a sentence or two about each topic. Discuss this list with an academic, considering issues which might arise with each of the topics, such as practicality, originality, focus and scale of the project. Once you have selected a topic from your list, consider the advice presented in this chapter on developing a research project. Start writing a proposal for your project, then take it to the person you spoke with for further discussion. Once you have had this discussion, read further on your topic. Now write a research proposal using the following set of headings.

- Title of the discourse analysis project;
- Purpose of the discourse analysis project;
- Research question(s) the discourse analysis project will aim to answer;
- Background literature relevant to the discourse analysis project;

- Research method(s) and discourse analysis techniques that will be used for the project;
- Significance of the discourse analysis project;
- Resources that will be required for the discourse analysis project.

10.14 Directions for further reading

Heigham, J. and Croker, R. A. (eds) (2009), *Qualitative Research in Applied Linguistics*. Basingstoke, England: Palgrave Macmillan.

Heigham and Croker's book contains many chapters that are relevant to carrying out discourse studies. These include chapters on case studies, ethnographies, mixed methods, ethics and writing up research.

Litosseliti, L. (ed.) (2010), *Research Methods in Linguistics*. London: Continuum.

Litosseliti's book includes chapters on quantitative and qualitative methods, corpus-based studies, the use of interviews and focus groups and multimodal analysis. Each chapter reviews basic concepts in the particular area and gives examples of published studies to illustrate the methodology that is discussed.

Paltridge, B. and Phakiti, A. (eds) (2010), *Companion to Research Methods in Applied Linguistics*. London: Continuum

This book contains chapters on research methods and approaches such as case studies, ethnographies and critical research as well as provides guidance on how to analyse quantitative and qualitative data. In the second half of the book there are chapters on researching areas such as speaking, writing, pragmatics, discourse, language and gender and language and identity.

Paltridge, B. and Wang, W. (2010), 'Researching discourse', in B. Paltridge and A. Phakiti (eds), *Continuum Companion to Research Methods in Applied Linguistics*. London: Continuum, pp. 256–73.

This chapter presents an overview of key approaches and areas of influence in discourse analysis. A sample study of newspaper commentaries in Chinese and English on the events of September 11 is provided. The study examines not only discourse features of the texts but also considers reasons why the texts have been written as they have.

Roever, C. (2010), 'Researching pragmatics', in B. Paltridge and A. Phakiti (eds), *Companion to Research Methods in Applied Linguistics*. London: Continuum, pp. 240–54.

In this chapter Roever outlines key issues in pragmatics research and typical stages in carrying out this kind of research. He provides a sample study which illustrates the points he raises in the chapter.

Wray, A. and Bloomer, A. (2006), *Projects in Linguistics: A Practical Guide to Researching Language* (2nd edn). London: Hodder Arnold.

This book provides advice on how to choose a research topic, how to collect data, how to analyse data and how to write up the results. Many ideas are given for possible research projects and lists of key references are provided for following up on each of the topics discussed.

10.15 Useful websites

For recommendations on good practice in research see

www.baal.org.uk/dox/goodpractice_full.pdf

www.alaa.org.au/files/alaas_statement_of_good_practice.pdf

Websites for looking for theses and dissertations which take a discourse perspective:

The Networked Digital Library of Theses and Dissertations

(www.ndltd.org/)

UMI Pro Quest Digital Dissertations

(http://search.proquest.com/)

Websites with advice on submitting discourse-oriented articles to *Discourse & Society*, *Discourse Studies* and *Discourse & Communication*

www.discourses.org/journals/das/

www.discourses.org/journals/dis/

www.discourses.org/journals/dac/

Emanuel Schegloff's webpage has a transcription module which is designed to provide practice in transcribing spoken data using conversation analytic conventions.

www.sscnet.ucla.edu/soc/faculty/schegloff/

10.16 Journals

Journals for looking for examples of studies which take a discourse perspective,

Annual Review of Applied Linguistics

Applied Linguistics

Australian Review of Applied Linguistics

Critical Discourse Studies

Critical Inquiry in Language Studies

Discourse and Communication

Discourse and Society

Discourse Processes

Discourse Studies

Discourse, Context and Media

Educational Linguistics

English for Specific Purposes

Functions of Language

International Journal of Applied Linguistics

International Journal of Corpus Linguistics

Journal of English for Academic Purposes

Journal of Gender Studies

Journal of Multicultural Discourses

Journal of Politeness Research

Journal of Pragmatics

Journal of Second Language Writing

Journal of Sociolinguistics

Language and Communication

Language and Education

Language in Society
Language Teaching
Language, Identity and Education
Pragmatics
Research on Language and Social Interaction
TESOL Quarterly
Text and Talk
Written Communication

 For an extended list of references and further readings see the companion website to this book.

Appendix: Answers to the Exercises

A1.1 Chapter 1

Exercise 1: Definitions of discourse analysis

These definitions, across them, cover many of the features of discourse analysis that will be discussed in this book. This includes the examination of spoken and written texts, and the relationship between language and the social and cultural contexts in which it is used. They also include a focus on actual language in use, and social, cultural and political implications of this use. Some of the books these definitions draw from take more of a textually oriented view of discourse analysis while others take a more socially oriented view. Many of the more recent books on discourse analysis aim to draw these two orientations together, looking not only at how people use language to do things in the world but also what this use of language means in social, cultural and political terms.

A1.2 Chapter 2

Exercise 1: Discourse and gender

Holmes (2006) discusses this extract on pages 196–7 of her book *Gendered Talk at Work*. She points out that the identity that Eric presents here as someone who enjoys 'playing the fool' is quite different from his professional identity of someone who is an expert in the field of information technology. In this extract he participates in the exchange in a way that makes him 'one of the boys'. The story is told collaboratively among the men which involves a certain kind of humorous repartee, through which the men 'do' a certain kind of masculinity; that is, someone who is a bit of a joker in social situations, and who drinks too much, both of which are approved of by the group. The interaction shows a high level of familiarity among members of the group and a shared history and approval of similar behaviour by Eric at company functions. The ways in which the members of the group laugh during the interaction and finish each other's turns shows their approval of Eric's behaviour and help create solidarity for the group.

Exercise 2: Second language identities

In this extract Wez uses a strategy called 'self repair' where he explains what he means by 'dream' and 'after your life'. That is, he clarifies what he was saying so that the other speaker can understand him better. He also pays a lot of attention to the feedback given to him by the other speaker such as, in this extract, 'whaddya mean' which indicates a request for clarification. This sort of repair strategy is what Canale (1983) calls *strategic competence*; that is, the ability to use strategies that will prevent breakdowns in communication. So while Wes' *grammatical competence* (Canale 1983; Canale and Swain 1980) marks him as a second language speaker, his levels of *sociolinguistic competence*, *discourse competence* and *strategic competence* make up for this. Wes is able to draw on these in a way that compensates for his grammatical shortcomings and makes him a very good communicator, in spite of this (Nunan 1992).

Exercise 3: Identity online

In this extract Violetta employs the symbols * * to indicate the expression of grinning. She uses abbreviations such as irl (I realise), *ppl* (people), and *thnk* (think) which would not be acceptable in more traditional types of writing. *Hehehe* represents laughing and *wayyyyyy* an extended vowel sound. She, thus, uses these features to give her written text a kind of oral quality that make it characteristic of online written 'chat'.

Exercise 4: Academic writing and identity

Below are examples of stance features in the text extracts shown in this exercise (see Hyland 2009a: 74–6 for further discussion of this data; also Hyland 2005c where stance and engagement are discussed in detail).

1. We propose several *possible* reasons of this (Hedge)
2. On this point, we must *definitely* stop following Hegel's intuitions (Booster)
3. Still, *I believe* that Dworkin's investment model has *remarkable* resonance and *extraordinary* potential power (Attitude markers)
4. What *we* found interesting about this context, however, is the degree of uniformity of their norms and attitudes (Self-mention)
5. There is *a strong tendency* for the bubbles to redissolve at the time of thaw (Hedge)
6. *Of course*, I do not contend that there are no historical contingencies (Booster)

A1.3 Chapter 3

Exercise 1: Sentence types and speech acts

This is 9457 1769	a statement	a direct speech act
I can't answer the phone right now	an apology	an indirect speech act (It is not just a statement of ability, it is also an apology)
Please leave a message after the tone	a request	an indirect speech act
It's me again	a statement or an apology	a direct speech act (if it is a statement) or an indirect speech act (if it is an apology)
I'm trying to organise the barbeque for John's birthday on Saturday	an explanation for the call	an indirect speech act
Can you give me a call	a request	an indirect speech act (It is not asking about ability)
Let me know if you'll be coming	a directive	a direct speech act

Exercise 2: Different meanings of the same utterance

Grundy (2008) gives the example of 'sorry' which can mean different things in different contexts. For example, 'sorry' can act as an apology, it can, with rising intonation, be used to ask someone to repeat what they have just said, or with a scowl, it can be daring someone to repeat what they have just said. Similarly, 'I'm tired' can be an explanation for why you are not looking well, or it can be a refusal to a request or an invitation. In Italian 'Ciao' can be both a greeting and a farewell. In Korean 'Annyung' can be a greeting and a farewell.

Exercise 3: Speech acts across cultures

Wierzbicka (2003) suggests that in English we thank someone to say we feel something good towards them because of something good they have done. That is:

(1) You did something good for me
(2) I feel something good towards you because of this
(3) I say 'thank you' because I want you to feel something good.

She argues, however, that in Japanese culture, for example, with its stress on the obligatory repayment of favours this response is generally less applicable. This is discussed in detail in Ohashi (2008a, 2008b, 2010).

Exercise 4: Indirect speech acts and Grice's maxims

There are examples of indirect speech acts in lines 1, 2, 3, 8 and 9. In line 1 'can' is not about asking ability, it is an offer of service. In line 2 'can' is not about ability, it is a request. In lines 3 and 9 'did' does not refer to past time, it is asking about the present. In line 8 'sorry' is not an apology. It is a request for clarification.

The maxim of quality (be true) is observed throughout the conversation, except in the case of the indirect speech acts where both speakers are aware of the difference between what they say and what they mean (see above).

The maxim of quantity (be brief) is also observed in this conversation. For example, in line 5 the sales person assumes the customer knows '2%' refers to milk with a '2%' fat content so there is no need to say this. Equally the sales person assumes the customer will know that 'skimmed' refers to skimmed milk so there is no need to add 'milk'. The use of ellipsis in this conversation, as in 'Anything else?' instead of 'Do you want anything else?' shows the speaker is observing the maxim of quantity. There is no need for the full sentence. Equally, the use of 'that' in line 3 and 9 (instead of 'your coffee') assumes the customer knows the sales person is referring to the coffee that has just been ordered, not something else.

The maxim of relation (be relevant) is observed throughout the conversation and works because of this. For example, the customer knows 'on the rocks' is referring to the coffee that has been ordered, not a whisky and ice which cannot be ordered in most coffee shops. Both speakers also know what a grande frappe is and that various kinds of milk are available in this coffee shop.

The speakers observe the maxim of manner (be clear) by checking throughout the conversation what kind of coffee is required ('blended or on the rocks' and '2% or skimmed'). When things are not clear the customer asks 'Sorry?' to show they are observing the maxim of manner and need clarification on what the sales person has just said.

Exercise 5: Flouting maxims

There are many examples of the flouting of maxims in Grice's article 'Logic and conversation' (1975), and in Chapter 3 of Jenny Thomas' book *Meaning in Interaction*. For example, a person may purposely give more or less information than a situation requires – flouting the maxim of Quantity. A person may say something they know is untrue, or for which they do not have evidence – flouting the maxim of Quality. Someone might flout the maxim of Relation by saying something that is irrelevant within the context of the present conversation (for example, to change the topic of the conversation). They might flout the maxim of Manner by being purposely long-winded and convoluted in a response, to avoid answering a question directly (Thomas 1995).

Exercise 6: Conversational implicature

You will find examples of exchanges which work because of conversational implicature in Grice's (1975) article 'Logic and conversation', as well as in Chapter 5 of Yule's (1996) book

Pragmatics. For example, in the following exchange you derive that Dexter did not bring the bread rather than he was violating the requirements of the maxim of Quantity:

Charlene: I hope you brought the bread and the cheese.
Dexter: Ah, I brought the cheese.

(Yule 1996: 40)

Equally, in this next example you derive 'No', rather than think that Tom is not observing the maxim of Manner:

Rick: Hey, coming to the wild party tonight?
Tom: My parents are visiting.

(Yule 1996: 41)

A1.4 Chapter 4

Exercise 1: Discourse structures: A student essay

Introduction	The Kakapo, which is found in the remote and inhospitable south of Stewart Island, is one of New Zealand's most highly endangered birds.	Situation
Body of the essay	Kakapos are flightless but good climbers, and usually live in native forests, sub-alpine zones. Leaves, stems roots and fruit are their main food. They were once described as the most beautiful bird in the world.	
	But nowadays there are only about 50 left. Because of developments of human beings such as removing soil and grass, cutting the forest for new roads, houses, or factories, the kakapo has lost its habitat and food resources. Huge numbers of them have died from starvation or hunting.	Problem
	A recovery programme has been launched to save the kakapo from extinction. In this programme, they are attempting to raise kakapos in captivity. In 1981, nests were located and several chicks were hatched.	Response/ Solution
Conclusion	To conclude, the kakapo is nearly extinct.	Problem
	We have to protect the rest of them and try our best with the recovery programme.	Response
	We do not want to loose this gentle friend, which is part of New Zealand's heritage.	Evaluation

Exercise 2: Discourse structures: A dissertation abstract

The political and educational implications of gender, class and race in Hollywood film: Holding out for a female hero

Abstract

Overview of the study	This thesis examines the articulations of gender, class, and race in a specific sample of films from the 1930s to the 1990s.	Problem
Reason for the study	The tendency in these films is to depict women as passive, rather than heroic.	Situation
	Because this has been the common practice,	Response
Methodology used in the study	I chose to outline it through fourteen films that exemplified an inherent bias when dealing with women as subject matter. Brief summaries of several recently produced progressive films are provided	
Findings of the study	to show that it is possible to improve the image of women in film, hence we may finally witness justice on the big screen.	
Methodology used in the study	In this discursive analysis, I trace specific themes from the feminist and film literature to provide a critical overview of the chosen films,	
Aim of the study	with a view to establishing educational possibilities for the complex issues dealt with in this study.	Evaluation

Exercise 3: Metadiscourse and academic writing

Interactive resources in the dissertation abstract

Category	Examples
Transitions	because this; hence
Frame markers	This thesis examines In this discursive analysis
Endophoric markers	Brief summaries . . . are provided
Evidentials	specific themes from the feminist and film literature

Interactional resources in the dissertation abstract

Category	Examples
Hedges	possible may
Boosters	establishing
Self mentions	I

Exercise 4: Choice of verb tense

Tense	Example	Focus
Present simple	This thesis examines the articulations of gender, class, and race . . . I trace specific themes from the feminist and film literature	Summary of the thesis
Past simple (active)	I chose to outline it through fourteen films . . .	Methodology of the study
Present simple (passive)	Brief summaries of several recently produced progressive films are provided . . .	Findings of the study

Exercise 5: Use of the passive voice

Both the active and the passive voice are used in this text. The active voice however predominates. Examples of the active and the passive voice are:

Voice	Example
Active	This thesis *examines* the articulations of gender, class, and race . . . I *trace* specific themes from the feminist and film literature . . . . I *chose* to outline it through fourteen films . . . I *trace* specific themes from the feminist and film literature
Passive	Brief summaries of several recently produced progressive films *are provided* . . .

In this text the passive voice is used as the student summarizes her project making the focus of this part of the text what the thesis aims to do. She moves to the active voice in the section that follows to highlight her role in initiating and selecting the topic, and carrying it out. The use of *I* or *we* (and the active voice that follows), as Hyland's (2004d) argues, is an important way in which academic writers make themselves visible in their texts and highlights their individual contribution to their project. There is, of course, a lot of disciplinary variation in this. Cultural or gender studies students might be encouraged to write in this way whereas science students, for example, may not.

Exercise 6: Use of personal pronouns

The personal pronoun 'I' is used twice in the text as in:

I chose to outline it through fourteen films that exemplified an inherent bias when dealing with women as subject matter.

I trace specific themes from the feminist and film literature. . . . . . .

To avoid using 'I' in the text the writer would have rewritten these two sentences using the passive voice thus:

> Fourteen films that exemplified an inherent bias when dealing with women as subject matter *were chosen* . . . . . .
>
> Specific themes from the feminist and film literature *were traced* . . . . . .

This would have resulted in shifting the focus from the student as the researcher to the research itself and have 'hidden' the student from the text, something the author of this abstract clearly did not want to do.

A1.5 Chapter 5

Exercise 1: Keeping the floor, giving up the floor and claiming the floor

In this extract, A gives up the floor through falling intonation and a completed syntactic unit which indicate a transition boundary. At the end of A's utterance, both B and C compete for the floor. B speaks first so has the right to continue but C does not give up the floor to B because she/he is providing the second pair part of the adjacency pair started by A. The falling intonation at the end of the first utterance indicates a 'tag question' which seeks confirmation rather than asks a real question. If A had ended with rising intonation, this would have signalled a 'real question' to which a more appropriate answer would have been something like 'yes, it was'. Notwithstanding, B still tries to keep the floor by stressing the second syllable in 'believe' and completing the syntactic unit.

Exercise 2: Turn taking

When speakers pause at the end of a turn, it is not always the case that the next speaker will necessarily take it up. In this case, the pause and its length become significant. For example, in this extract B self-selects after a one second pause because A fails to take the turn after B's 'hhh'. The same happens again where A fails to take a turn so B self-selects once more, this time by changing the topic.

Exercise 3: Self-repair and other-repair

(i)	Self-repair:	I mean, the opera.
(ii)	Other repair:	You mean Lygon St, don't you?
(iii)	Other repair:	If I didn't get my degree?
	Self repair:	actually . . . I'd get into a lot of trouble

Exercise 4: Preferred and dispreferred responses

An invitation may be followed by an 'accept' (the preferred second pair part) or a 'reject' (the dispreferred second pair part). When this happens, the dispreferred second pair part is often preceded by a 'delay' (Uhhh), a 'preface' (I don't know for sure) and/or an 'account' (I think I might have something on that night) as shown below.

A:	That's a nice shirt	(Compliment)
B:	Oh thanks	Preferred response (Accept compliment)
A:	Would you like to come to the movies on Friday?	(Invitation)
B:	Uhhh ... I don't know for sure. I think I might have something on that night. Can we make it another time?	Dispreferred response (Reject)

Exercise 5: Closing a conversation

'Why don't we all have lunch?' is the start of a pre-closing. The pre-closing is continued by the series of *Okays* which firm up the arrangements for lunch. The ? in the fourth *Okay* indicates rising intonation which seeks confirmation of the arrangements, another pre-closing strategy. The simultaneous *See you there* is another pre-closing strategy, followed by a further *Okay* to move closer the closing of the conversation. The conversation is finally closed with the simultaneous *Bye* by both speakers. That is, both speakers have mutually agreed to talk no more and the conversation is closed (Levinson 1983).

A1.6 Chapter 6

Exercise 1: Reference

There are five main reference chains in the text: *four cup mould, custard, larger pan, Bagno di Maria* and *knife*. The relations between them and the head item in each chain are *anaphoric*. The main reference chains are:

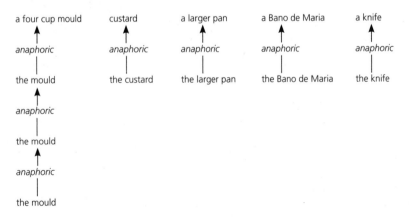

A in *a four cup mould, a larger pan* and *a Bano de Maria* are each *presenting* references. They are introducing new items in the text. *The* in 'the sides of the mould' is an example of *esphoric* reference. That is, the item it refers to immediately follows the referent item in the same nominal group. *The* in 'the side' is *presuming* reference. It is presumed we know or can infer that the author is referring to the side of the mould (rather than the side of the larger pan). There is also an example of *whole text referencing* (during *the* baking) where the referent item is referring to a section of the text up to this point.

Exercise 2: Lexical chains

There are three main lexical chains in the text: *Flan, Caramel* and *mould*. In many cases the relationship between items is *co-meronymy*; that is, the items are related by both being parts of a common whole, as in *sugar* and *water* in relation to *Caramel*.

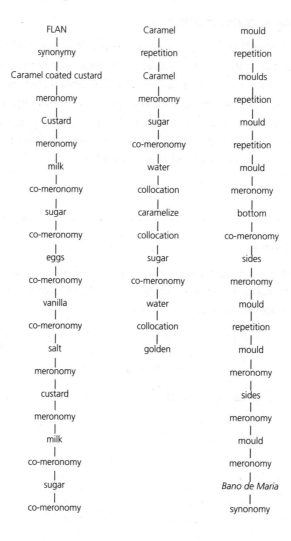

FLAN	Caramel	mould
synonymy	repetition	repetition
Caramel coated custard	Caramel	moulds
meronomy	meronomy	repetition
Custard	sugar	mould
meronomy	co-meronomy	repetition
milk	water	mould
co-meronomy	collocation	meronomy
sugar	caramelize	bottom
co-meronomy	collocation	co-meronomy
eggs	sugar	sides
co-meronomy	co-meronomy	meronomy
vanilla	water	mould
co-meronomy	collocation	repetition
salt	golden	mould
meronomy		meronomy
custard		sides
meronomy		meronomy
milk		mould
co-meronomy		meronomy
sugar		Bano de Maria
co-meronomy		synonymy

Exercise 3: Conjunction

but sometimes he feels . . .	comparison
if only he could stop	consequence
And then he feels . . .	addition
and ready to be introduced . . . (ellipsed 'He is')	addition

Exercise 4: Theme and rheme

Clause	Textual Theme	Topical Theme	Rheme
1.		I	went over to my friend's house
2.	and	I	said
3.		We'	ll go for a walk
4.	And	we	went far away
5.	and	I	said
6.		I	don't know our way home
7.	And	we	kept on walking
8.	and	we	were hungry
9.	And	we	saw a village
10.	and	we	went to talk to them
11.	and	we	said
12.		We	are hungry
13.	And	they	gave us some food
14.	and	we	thanked them
15.	and	we	went walking off
16.	and then	we	stopped and sat down
17.	And then	we	saw a giant
18.	and	I	screamed Cooee

Exercise 5: Thematic progression

Putonghua and pinyin

Theme	Rheme
Putonghua	is the Chinese expression for Mandarin Chinese.
It	means 'common language'.
Pinyin	is a phonetic spelling system for Chinese characters, which uses the Roman alphabet
Pinyin	is not just useful to teach the standard pronunciation of Putonghua;
we	also use pinyin to teach the standard pronunciation of Putonghua, or mandarin Chinese, to Chinese people who speak other dialects.

The progression in this text is thematic reiteration/constant theme

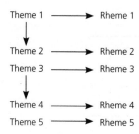

Chinese pronunciation

Theme	Rheme
Chinese pronunciation	is not difficult for English speakers because most of the sounds are quite similar in English.
These sounds	are Romanized by using the Roman alphabet.
This	makes learning Chinese easier for English-speaking learners.
Although there	are 21 initials and 30 finals in Chinese,
there	are only a few sounds that are tricky for English speakers.

The progression in this text is zigzag/linear theme

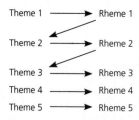

Exercise 6: Grammatical metaphor

Examples of grammatical metaphor are italicized in the text below:

> *Authenticity* is a word frequently heard in *connection* with Mad Men, a show lauded for the detailed *accuracy* of it *portrayal* of the fashion, hairdos, furnishings, office furniture, and social mores of Madison Avenue in the 1960s. Cigarettes everywhere, martini lunches, sexual *harassment* as an office *norm*.

'Authenticity' is a case of an adjective ('authentic') being transferred to the grammatical class of noun. 'Accuracy' is the same in that the expected grammatical class is the adjective, 'accurate'. This is also the case with 'norm' and 'normal'. 'Connection', 'portrayal' and 'harassment' are examples of the expected grammatical class of a verb ('connect', 'portray' and 'harass') being transferred to the class of noun (i.e. 'connection', 'portrayal' and 'harassment').

Exercise 7: Lexical density

The content words are italicized in the texts below. There are 17 lexical items and 4 clauses in the spoken (the first) text. The lexical density is, thus, 4.25 for this text. There are 30 lexical items across 3 clauses in written (the second) text. The lexical density is 10, more than double that of the spoken text.

> The *closest thing* I have in *common* with *Don* is that I'm *looking* for *something*. If you *look* at the *literature* of the *early sixties*, it's *existentialist*. *People sitting* around *smoking*, *thinking* 'what am I *doing* with my *life*?' (Iley 2010: 28)

> My own *personal satisfaction* while *watching* the *show* was *helped enormously* by being *asked* to *write* a *series* of *episode* by *episode blogs* for *guardian.co.uk* in which I would *share* a *brief recap* and a *few talking points* with *readers*. It *quickly became* a *part* of the *routine* of *watching* the *series* for many *viewers eager* to *share* their *thoughts*. (Dean 2010: viii)

A1.7 Chapter 7

Exercise 1: Spoken Discourse

Non-clausal units
The non-clausal units in the following extract are italicized.

Diana:	People's agendas changed overnight. I was now separated from the Prince of Wales, I was a problem, I was a liability (seen as), and how are we going to deal with her? This hasn't happened before.
Bashir:	Who was asking those questions?
Diana:	*People around me, people in this environment,* and
Bashir:	*The royal household*?
Diana:	*People in my environment, yes, yes.*
Bashir:	And they began to see you as a problem?
Diana:	*Yes, very much so, uh uh*

Personal pronouns and ellipsis

In the following example the identity of *you* is clear from the situation in which the people are speaking. In each case, *you* is referring to Princess Diana.

Diana: And so it was, it was so isolating, but it was also a situation in which *you* couldn't indulge in feeling sorry for yourself: *you* had to either sink or swim. And *you* had to learn that very fast.

Bashir: And what did *you* do?

Diana: I swam.

Ellipsis in the following example is italicized, in brackets.

Bashir: Did you have the alleged telephone conversation?

Diana: Yes we did (*have the telephone conversation*), absolutely we did (*have the telephone conversation*). Yup, we did (*have the telephone conversation*)

A non-clausal unit as an elliptic reply is italicized in the following extract.

Bashir: Did you allow your friends, your close friends, to speak to Andrew Morton?

Diana;   Yes, I did. Yes, I did.

Bashir: *Why?*

Situational ellipsis

Examples of situational ellipsis are italicized in the following extract.

Bashir: Do you really think that a campaign was being waged against you?

Diana: Yes I did, absolutely, yeah.

Bashir: Why?

Diana: I was the separated wife of the Prince of Wales, I was a problem, *full stop. Never happened before.* What do we do with her?

Repetition

Examples of repetition are italicized in the following extract.

Bashir: Did you make what were described as nuisance phone calls?

Diana: I was reputed to have made 300 telephone calls in a very short space of time which, bearing in mind my life style at that time, made me a very busy lady.
No, *I didn't, I didn't.*

Utterance launchers

Diana frequently uses *Well* as an utterance launcher in the interview, as italicized below.

Bashir: Explain what you mean when you say that.

Diana: *Well*, er . . .

Bashir: When you say, when you say you were never given any credit, what do you mean?

Diana: *Well* anything good I ever did nobody ever said a thing, never said, 'well done'

Exercise 2: Written Discourse

Hyland (2010) discussed this data in detail. Below is a summary of what he has to say about Cameron's academic identity as revealed through her discourse.

> In Cameron's discourse then, we see a range of rhetorical features used to confidently and force-fully advocate particular realities, often arguing for a way of seeing the world in contradiction to others. Her preferred argument strategies actively construct a heteroglossic backdrop for the text by explicitly grounding propositions in her individual subjectivity, recognizing that her view is one among others and taking on alternatives through a combative and confident dialogue. One consequence of this is the emergence of a distinctive identity as a steadfast and committed academic, a disciplinary expert confident in her beliefs and determined in her assurance. (Hyland 2010: 174)

A1.8 Chapter 8

Exercise 1: An image-nuclear news story

This story has the three functional components that are typical of image-nuclear news stories: the Heading (Give the ladies a big hand), the Image, and the Caption. The text below the Image (the Caption) contextualizes both the Image and the Heading, giving both the occasion (the women walking past the gallery) and location of the event (a former factory in Beijing that has been turned into an art gallery).

The relationship between the text and the image in this story is typical of many image-nuclear news stories in that the Heading is a play on the expression 'to give someone a hand'. Here, the hand is enormous and the ladies, by comparison, are small creating a contrast between the two key components of the image. The aim is to create a humorous relationship between the words and the text. It does, of course, rely on the reader being familiar with both the literal and figurative meaning of the expression 'to give someone a hand' (in the singular, meaning to help someone and in the plural, meaning to applaud someone). The hand is, literally, very big and is reaching out to the two women. The text also relies on the reader knowing who Chairman Mao is and his place in Chinese life. A reader in China, for example, may respond to this story quite differently to a reader in an English-speaking country.

Exercise 2: A book cover

The layout of the cover is a *vertical triptych*. The main Image is central with key text placed above and below the Image. The cover, thus, has a symmetrical and balanced arrangement. Kress and van Leeuwen (2006: 196) describe the Image in this kind of layout as the *Centre* and the elements that are placed around it as the *Margins*. In this cover, the key informational content is in the Margins, above and below the Image. The textual extracts that are part of the Image in the Centre are examples of spoken and written discourse. The Image, thus, is a visual representation of the theme of the book, discourse analysis. The key items in the Margins are the title of the book, the name of author, the name of the series the book belongs to, the name of the editor of the series and the name and logo of the publisher. Most prominence is given to the title and author of the book. The text at the bottom of the page is given less prominence by the use of a smaller font and colours that have less salience than the text at the top of the page. The textual extracts that are part of the central Image are in smaller and less prominent fonts than the text at the top and bottom of the page and so have less salience than the text in the Margins. Most information value in this cover, thus, is given to the title of the book and the name of the author.

Exercise 3: A film trailer: Bridget Jones's Diary

The lead character in the film is introduced by the words of the song 'Have you met Miss Jones' that plays while the names of production companies of the film are presented on the screen. A voiceover then continues 'In every life there comes a time to turn the page to a new beginning'. The lead character, Bridget (played by Renée Zellweger), has made a New Year's resolution to start a diary in which she will write about major changes she wants to make in her life, such as stopping smoking, losing weight and finding Mr Right. The voiceover is followed by a scene in which Bridget is introduced to one of the other lead characters in the film, a good-looking human rights lawyer called Mark (played by Colin Firth). The relationship between them is made somewhat embarrassing by her mother saying 'Mark, you remember Bridget. She used to run around your lawn with no clothes on. Remember?' We then see a scene of Bridget falling out a taxi being sick in the street – one of the things she wants to change. The voices of the actors, song, image, movement (Mark turning around looking embarrassed, Bridget falling out of the car) and voiceover are all used to set the scene. The start of the Complication comes when the other lead character in the film, Bridget's boss Daniel (played by Hugh Grant), appears and we learn that Bridget is attracted to him despite him being the wrong person for her.

A1.9 Chapter 9

Exercise 1: Textual silences

Huckin (2002) provides a detailed analysis of this text on pages 360–3 of his article. Some the themes that are present in this text are:

Causes	poverty	destitute
	transportation problems	need gas money
	bad luck	hard luck sign
Effects	exposure to severe weather	huddle in the rain and wind
		panhandlers
Demographics	types of homeless people	single mom
Public responses	donations	give time or money
		Give the panhandler a coupon to a fast-food restaurant

Issues that are not mentioned include reasons for homelessness such as lack of affordable housing, low wages, welfare cuts, racism and the failure of the health care system to deal with homelessness. Also omitted are references to transitional housing for homeless people, medical care and substance abuse treatment programmes, as well as public responses such as education, job training and child care (Huckin 2002).

Exercise 2: Migration and identity

Krzyzanowski and Wodak (2008) discuss this data on page 109 of their chapter. They show, in extract (1), how multiple attachments are constructed through expressions such as *standing astride* and *one leg here and another there. Here* is juxtaposed with *there* to give a sense of contrast in location. Attachment to the home country is shown in *our roots are there.* In extract (2) religion is the point of difference in belonging. Cultural difference is the focus of extract (3) and different ways of thinking are pointed to in extract (4).

Exercise 3: Gender, identity and online chat rooms

Subrahmanyam, Greenfield and Tynes (2004) discuss these extracts on page 662 of their article. In each of these instances it is the young female who initiates the 'cyber pickup'. Subrahmanyam, Greenfield and Tynes argue that the online space makes it easier for young girls to initiate intimate relationships than it might be in their offline worlds. They also argue that the relative anonymity and absence of actual physical bodies on the internet makes it easier for them to do this. They are able to do this, they argue, without the weight of traditional gender roles and without the possible stigmatization that might come from being 'too forward'.

Glossary of Key Terms

These definitions are in addition to the text boxes in the book where key terms in the area of discourse analysis are defined. They are, however, brief. For further explanations and definitions you should refer to works such as:

Baker, P. and Ellece, S. (2011), *Key Terms in Discourse Analysis*. London: Continuum.

Halliday, M. A. K. and Webster, J. J. (eds), (2009), *Continuum Companion to Systemic Functional Linguistics*. London: Continuum.

Hyland, K. and Paltridge, B. (eds), (2011), *Continuum Companion to Discourse Analysis*. London: Continuum.

Co-construction: A term which denotes the fact that meaning does not reside in language but is arrived at through the negotiation of the individuals participating in the exchange.

Coherence: The ways a text makes sense to readers through the relevance and accessibility of its concepts, ideas and theories.

Cohesion: Grammatical and lexical relationships which tie a text together.

Collocation: The regular occurrence of a word with one or more other words in a text. The term can also refer to the meanings associated with a word as a result of this association.

Community of practice: A term coined by Lave and Wenger (1991) to describe a group of people who share an interest, a craft or a profession. The term draws attention to the fact that it is through the process of sharing information and experiences with the group that the members learn from each other, and have an opportunity to develop themselves personally and professionally.

Concordance: A list of unconnected lines of text called up by a concordance program with the search word at the centre of each line. This list allows patterns of use to be seen and explored.

Context: The relationship between linguistic and non-linguistic dimensions of communicative events. These dimensions are seen to stand in a mutually influential relationship, with text and the interpretive work it creates helping to shape context and context influencing the conventions, values and knowledge a text appeals to.

Corpus: A collection of texts usually stored electronically, seen as representative of some subset of language and used for linguistic analysis.

Critical discourse analysis (CDA): An approach which seeks to reveal the interests, values and power relations in any institutional and sociohistorical context through the ways that people use and interpret language.

Culture: An historically transmitted and systematic network of meanings that allow us to understand, develop and communicate our knowledge and beliefs about the world.

Discourse: Language produced as an act of communication. This language use implies the constraints and choices which operate on writers or speakers in particular contexts and reflects their purposes, intentions, ideas and relationships with readers and hearers.

Discourse analysis: (i) The study of how stretches of language in context are seen as meaningful and unified by users or (ii) how different uses of language express the values of people and institutions.

Discourse community: A rather fuzzy concept used in genre studies to refer to a group of writers (or speakers) who share a communicative purpose and use commonly agreed texts to achieve these purposes. The term carries a core meaning of like-mindedness of membership which is widely used in research on writing to help explain discourse coherence.

Discursive practices: A CDA term which refers to the acts of production, distribution and interpretation which surround a text and which must be taken into account in text analysis. These practices are themselves embedded in wider social practices of power and authority.

Ethnography: A research approach that seeks to gather a variety of naturally occurring data to provide a highly situated, minutely detailed and holistic account of actors' behaviours through a period of prolonged engagement with the research site.

Generic structure: The discourse structure of a particular genre such as an essay or a research report in terms of its genre category (as opposed to *rhetorical types* – such as description, argument and problem–solution – that combine together to make up a text).

Genre: Broadly, a set of texts that share the same socially recognized purpose and which, as a result, often share similar rhetorical and structural elements to achieve this purpose.

Genre analysis: A branch of discourse analysis which seeks to understand the communicative character of discourse by looking at how individuals use language to engage in particular communicative events.

Identity: Now widely seen as the ways that people display who they are to each other; a social performance achieved by drawing on appropriate linguistic and other semiotic resources.

Ideology: A body of ideas that reflects the beliefs and interests of an individual; a group or a social institution which finds expression in language.

Intercultural communication: The study of distinct cultural or other groups in interaction with each other so that analysis provides an account of how participants negotiate their cultural and other differences.

Interdiscursivity: Wider rhetorical and generic factors which make use of one text dependent on knowledge of other texts through borrowing conventions and forms to create new texts.

Intertextuality: An element of one text that takes its meaning from a reference to another text, for instance by quoting, echoing or linking.

Lexico-grammar: A term used in systemic functional linguistics to stress that no categorical distinction can be made between grammar and lexis. Meaning is conveyed by words working in grammatical parameters, rather than separately from them.

Membership: An ability to display credibility and competence through familiarity or exploitation of discourse conventions typically used in a community. This can identify one as an 'insider', belonging to that community and possessing the legitimacy to address it.

Mixed-methods research: A mixed methods design involves the collection or analysis of both quantitative and qualitative data in a single study. The purpose of mixed methods research is to achieve a fuller understanding of a complex issue and to verify one set of findings against the other.

Move: A rhetorical or discoursal unit in a text that performs a coherent and distinctive communicative function.

Multimodal discourse: Discourse that employs and integrates more than one mode of presentation, such as words and graphics.

Narrative: Along with exposition, argumentation and description, narration is one of four Classical rhetorical modes of discourse. In Systemic Functional Linguistics it is an elemental or micro-genre which can contribute to macro-genres such as newspaper stories and novels. It is often described as having a structure of Orientation – Complication – Evaluation – Resolution.

Poststructuralism: A philosophy represented by Derrida, Foucault and Barthes which emerged in France in the 1960s as a critique to Western culture and philosophy. At root, poststructuralism rejects essentialism and argues that even gender and sexual orientation are contrived, cultural formations.

Power: The ability to impose one's will on others. In discourse studies it refers to the fact that this ability to influence and control is, at any given time, expressed through discourse and is unevenly distributed and exercised.

Qualitative research: An approach that seeks to make sense of social phenomena as they occur in natural settings. Rather than setting up a controlled environment, qualitative researchers are more interested in understanding contexts as they actually are. Qualitative researchers do not aim for quantification or standardization in the data collection and analysis of the data.

Quantitative research: A research approach that draws on numeric data. Variables are clearly defined, measurement is standardized and data generally analysed using statistical methods.

Register: A term from systemic functional linguistics which explains the relationship between texts and their contexts in terms of field (what), tenor (who) and mode (how). Register also refers to broad fields of language use such as legal, scientific or promotional discourse.

Reliability: This term relates to the quality of instruments/measures and results of a study. The reliability of an instrument or measure is concerned with the degree to which a research instrument or measure produces consistent information (e.g. whether the data would be the same if the instrument were administered repeatedly). The reliability of a result of a study is concerned with whether the result would be likely to reappear if the study were replicated under the same conditions.

Replicability: A requirement that researchers provide enough information about a study to allow other researchers to replicate or repeat the study exactly as it was originally conducted. This includes information about the participants involved in the study, how they were selected, the instruments that were used and the data collection and analysis procedures that were employed.

Rhetorical structure: The typical organizational patterning of rhetorical types such as argument, description and problem–solution type texts.

Rhetorical types: Rhetorical types are sometimes referred to as micro-genres in systemic functional discussions of genre. Rhetorical types (such as arguments, descriptions and problem–solution) combine to make up larger, more complex texts (such as essays and research reports), or in SFL (discussed below) terms, macro-genres.

Schematic structure: Also referred to as 'generic structure', the typical organizational patterning of a genre in terms of a sequence of moves or discoursal acts. This can be seen as a system of conventions or resources of meaning for generating expected texts.

Sociolinguistics: The study of how social features such as cultural norms, expectations, contexts and so on affect the way language is used. How language use differs by ethnicity, religion, status, gender, age, social class and so on and the impact of this on identity and categorization has been of particular importance.

Speech act: An act performed as an utterance with a certain intention of the speaker and effect on the hearer, for example, promising, ordering, greeting, warning, inviting and congratulating. Their study helps explain the indirect relationship between form and function – how we move from what is said to what is meant by what we say.

Speech event: Activities which can only occur through language, for example, interviews, seminars, lectures, lessons, meetings and so on.

Systemic functional linguistics (SFL): A theory of language developed by Michael Halliday based on the idea that language is a system of choices used to express meanings in context.

Text: A piece of spoken or written language.

Transcription: A written representation of spoken data based on the researcher's decisions about what types of information to preserve, which descriptive categories to use, and how to display the information.

Transferability: A qualitative trustworthiness criterion which requires researchers to describe the research design, context and conditions so that other researchers can decide for themselves if the interpretations apply to another context with which they are familiar. Transferability is analogous to the concept of generalizability in quantitative research.

Triangulation: Triangulation aims to collect multiple perspectives on an event such as the use of multiple data sources and multiple research techniques so that the researcher can gain a more complete understanding of the topic under examination.

Trustworthiness: The term for validity in qualitative research. Trustworthiness is often a preferred term in qualitative research because it takes account of the different nature of the research methods and epistemological assumptions made in qualitative research compared to those used in quantitative research.

Validity: Validity is the extent to which the research actually studies what it claims to study. The *validity of an instrument* refers to whether the instrument actually measures what it claims to measure. The *validity of the research* refers to the accuracy of the inferences, interpretations or actions made on the basis of the data.

Bibliography

Abell, J. and Stokoe, E. (1999), "'I take full responsibility, I take some responsibility, I'll take half of it but no more than that": Princess Diana and the negation of blame in the Panorama interview', *Discourse Studies*, 1, 297–310.

amctv.com (2011), *Mad Men*. Available at www.amctv.com/shows/mad-men, accessed 10 May 2011.

Anderson, B. (1991), *Imagined Communities: Reflections on the Origin and Spread of Nationalism* (Rev. edn). London: Verso.

Angouri, J. (2010), 'Quantitative or qualitative or both? Combining method in linguistic research', in L. Litosseliti (ed.), *Research Methods in Linguistics*. London: Continuum, pp. 29–45.

Anqi, D., Xin, C. and Lili, J. (2010), *Discover China 1. Student's Book One*. Oxford, UK: Macmillan.

Anthony, L. (2003), AntMover (Version 1.0) [Computer Software]. Tokyo, Japan: Waseda University. Available at www.antlab.sci.waseda.ac.jp/software.html, accessed 3 April 2012.

Anthony, L. and Lashkia, G. V. (2003), 'Mover: A machine learning tool to assist in the reading and writing of technical papers', *IEEE Transactions on Professional Communication*, 46(3), 185–93.

Artemeva, N. (2008), 'Toward a unified theory of genre learning', *Journal of Business and Technical Communication*, 22, 160–85.

Artemeva, N. and Freedman, A. (eds) (2008), *Rhetorical Genre Studies and Beyond*. Winnipeg: Inkshed Publications. Available at http://server.carleton.ca/.../Artemeva%20&%20Freedman%20Rhetorical%20Genre%20Studies%20and%20beyond.pdf, accessed 26 March 2011.

Asahi Newspaper (1993), 'Crown Prince and Masako's engagement press conference', 20 January 1993, p. 1.

Askehave, I. and Swales, J. M. (2000), 'Genre identification and communicative purpose: A problem and possible solution, *Applied Linguistics*, 22, 195–212.

Atkinson, J. M. and Drew, P. (eds) (1979), *Order in Court: The Organisation of Verbal Interaction in Judicial Settings*. London: Social Sciences Research Council.

Austin, J. L. (1962), *How to Do Things With Words*. Oxford: Clarendon Press.

Austin, T. (1998), 'Cross-cultural pragmatics. Building in analysis of communication across cultures and languages: Examples from Japanese', *Foreign Language Annals*, 31(3), 326–41.

Australian.idolblog.com (2004), Casey Donovan. Australian Idol Blog. Available at www.australian.idolblog.com/contestant/casey_donovan.php, accessed 30 November 2004.

Baker, P. (2008), *Sexed Texts: Language, Gender and Sexuality*. London: Equinox.

Baker, P. and Ellece, S. (2011), *Key Terms in Discourse Analysis*. London: Continuum.

Baker, P., Gabrielatos, C., Khosravinik, M., Krzyzanowski, M., McEnery, T. and Wodak, R. (2008) 'A useful methodological synergy? Combining critical discourse analysis and corpus linguistics to examine discourses of refugees and asylum seekers in the UK press', *Discourse and Society*, 19, 273–306.

Baldry, A. and Thibault, P. J. (2005), *Multimodal Transcription and Text Analysis*. London: Equinox.

Bargiela-Chiappini, F. and Harris, S. (2006), 'Politeness at work: Issues and challenges', *Journal of Politeness Research*, 2, 7–33.

Bartlett, N. (2006), 'A double shot 2% mocha latté, please, with whip: Service encounters in two coffee shops and at a coffee cart', in M. Long (ed.), *Second Language Needs Analysis*. Cambridge: Cambridge University Press, pp. 305–43.

Barton, D. and Tusting, K. (eds) (2005), *Beyond Communities of Practice: Language, Power and Social Context.* Cambridge: Cambridge University Press.

Barton, D., Hamilton, M. and Ivanic, R. (eds) (2000), *Situated Literacies: Reading and Writing in Context.* London: Routledge.

Basturkman, H. (2002), 'Clause relations and macro patterns: Cohesion, coherence and the writing of advanced ESOL students', *English Teaching Forum*, 38, 50–6.

Bateman, J. A. (2008), *Genre and Multimodality: A Foundation for the Systematic Analysis of Multimodal Documents.* Basingstoke, England: Palgrave Macmillan.

Bateman, J. A. and Schmidt, K. H. (2011), *Multimodal Film Analysis.* London: Routledge.

Bawarshi, A. and Reiff, M. J. (2010), *Genre: An Introduction to History, Theory, Research, and Pedagogy.* West Lafayette, IN: Parlor Press.

Bax, S. (2006), 'The role of genre in language syllabus design: The case of Bahrain', *International Journal of Educational Development*, 26, 315–28.

Baxter, J. (2002), 'Is PDA really an alternative? A reply to West', *Discourse & Society*, 13, 853–9.

Bazerman, C. (1988), *Shaping Written Knowledge.* Madison, WI: University of Wisconsin Press.

— (2004), 'Intertextuality: How texts rely on other texts', in C. Bazerman and P. Prior (eds), *What Writing Does and How it does it: An Introduction to Analyzing Texts and Textual Practices.* Mahwah, NJ: Lawrence Erlbaum, pp. 83–96.

Bazerman, C., Bonini, A. and Figueiredo, D. (eds) (2009), *Genre in a Changing World.* West Lafayette, IN: Parlor Press.

BBC (1995), 'The BBC Panorama interview'. Available at www.bbc.co.uk/politics97/diana/panorama.html, accessed 1 February 2011.

Be´al, C. (1992), '"Did you have a good weekend?" or why there is no such thing as a simple question', *Australian Review of Applied Linguistics,* 15, 23–52.

Bednarek, M. and Caple, H. (2010), 'Playing with environmental stories in the news – good or bad practice?' *Discourse and Communication*, 4, 5–31.

— (2012), *News Discourse.* London: Continuum.

Bednarek, M. and Martin, J. R. (eds) (2010), *New Discourse on Language: Functional Perspectives on Multimodality, Identity, and Affiliation.* London: Continuum.

Behrendt, G. and Tuccillo, L. (2004), *He's Just Not That into You: The No-excuses Truth to Understanding Guys.* London: Element.

Bennett, G. (2010), *Using Corpora in the Language Learning Classroom.* Ann Arbor: University of Michigan Press.

Benwell, B. (2005), '"Lucky this is anonymous!" Ethnographies of reception in men's magazines: A "textual culture" approach', *Discourse & Society*, 16, 147–72.

Berkenkotter, C. (2009), 'A case for historical 'wide-angle' genre analysis: A personal retrospective', *Ibérica: Journal of the European Association of Language for Specific Purposes*, 18, 9–21.

Bezemer, J. and Jewitt, C. (2010), 'Multimodal analysis: Key issues', in L. Litosseliti (ed.), *Research Methods in Linguistics.* London: Continuum, pp. 180–97.

Bhatia, V. K. (1993), *Analysing Genre: Language Use in Professional Settings.* London: Longman.

— (1997), 'Genre-mixing in academic introductions', *English for Specific Purposes*, 16, 181–95.

— (1998), 'Integrating products, processes, purposes and participants in professional writing', in C. N. Candlin and K. Hyland (eds), *Writing: Texts, Processes and Practices.* London: Longman, pp. 21–39.

Biber, D. (1992), 'On the complexity of discourse complexity: A multidimensional analysis', *Discourse Processes*, 15, 133–63.

— (1994), 'Representativeness in corpus design', in A. Zampolli, N. Calzolari, N. Palmer and M. Palmer (eds), *Current Issues in Computational Linguistics: In Honour of Don Walker*. Pisa: Giardini/Norwell, MA: Kluwer, pp. 377–407.

— (1998), *Variation across Speech and Writing*. Cambridge: Cambridge University Press.

— (2006), *University Language: A Corpus-based Study of Spoken and Written Registers*. Amsterdam: John Benjamins.

— (2009), 'A corpus-driven approach to formulaic language in English: Multi-word patterns in speech and writing', *International Journal of Corpus Linguistics*, 14, 275–311.

Biber, D. and Barbieri, F. (2007), 'Lexical bundles in university spoken and written registers', *English for Specific Purposes*, 26, 263–86.

Biber, D. and Conrad, S. (2009). *Register, Genre, and Style*. Cambridge: Cambridge University Press.

Biber, D., Connor, U. and Upton, T. A. (eds), (2007), *Discourse on the Move*. Amsterdam: John Benjamins.

Biber, D., Conrad, S. and Cortes, V. (2004), 'If you look at . . .: Lexical bundles in university teaching and textbooks', *Applied Linguistics*, 25, 371–405.

Biber, D., Conrad, S. and Reppen, R. (1998), *Corpus Linguistics: Investigating Language Structure and Use*. Cambridge: Cambridge University Press.

Biber, D., Conrad, S., Reppen, R., Byrd, P. and Helt, M. (2002), 'Speaking and writing in the University: A multidimensional comparison', *TESOL Quarterly*, 36, 9–48.

Biber, D., Johansson, S., Leech, G., Conrad, S. and Finegan, E. (1999), *Longman Grammar of Spoken and Written English*. London: Longman.

Billig, M. (1999), 'Critical discourse analysis and conversation analysis: An exchange between Michael Billig and Emanuel A. Schegloff', *Discourse & Society*, 10, 543–82.

Blakemore, D. (2002), *Relevance and Linguistic Meaning: The Semantics and Pragmatics of Discourse Markers*. Cambridge: Cambridge University Press.

Block, D. (2007), *Second Language Identities*. London: Continuum.

Blommaert, J. (2005), *Discourse: A Critical Introduction*. Cambridge: Cambridge University Press.

Blommaert, J., Street, B. and Turner, J. (2008), 'Academic literacies – what have we achieved and where to from here?' *Journal of Applied Linguistics*, 4, 137–48.

Bloor, T. and Bloor, M. (2004), *The Functional Analysis of English: A Hallidayan Approach* (2nd edn). London: Arnold.

Brown, G. and Levinson, S. (1987), *Politeness. Some Universals in Language Usage*. Cambridge: Cambridge University Press.

Brown, R. (1992), 'Foreword', in H. Koch (ed.), *Casablanca: Script and Legend*. Woodstock, NY: Overlook Press, pp. 7–10.

Bruthiaux, P. (1994), 'Me Tarzan, you Jane: Linguistic simplification in "personal ads" register', in D. Biber and E. Finegan (eds), *Sociolinguistic Perspectives on Register*. Oxford: Oxford University Press, pp. 136–54.

Bucholtz, M. (1999), '"Why be normal?" Language and identity practices in a community of nerd girls', *Language in Society*, 28, 203–23.

— (2003), 'Theories of discourse as theories of gender: Discourse analysis in language and gender studies', in J. Holmes and M. Meyerhoff (eds), *The Handbook of Language and Gender*. Malden, MA: Blackwell, pp. 43–68.

— (2007), 'Shop talk: Branding, consumption, and gender in American middle-class youth interaction', in B. S. McElhinny (ed.), *Word, World, and Material Girls. Language, Gender, Globalization*. Berlin: Mouton de Gruyter, pp. 371–401.

— (2009), 'From stance to style: Gender, interaction, and indexicality in Mexican youth slang', in A. Jaffe (ed.), *Stance: Sociolinguistic Perspectives*. Oxford: Oxford University Press, pp. 146–70.

— (2011), *White Kids: Language, Race, and Styles of Youth Identity*. Cambridge: Cambridge University Press.

Bucholtz, M. and Hall, K. (2003), 'Language and identity', in A. Duranti (ed.), *A Companion to Linguistic Anthropology*. Oxford: Blackwell, pp. 368–94.

— (2004), 'Theorizing identity in language and sexuality research', *Language in Society*, 33, 469–515.

— (2005), 'Identity and interaction: A sociocultural linguistic approach', *Discourse Studies*, 7, 585–614.

Bunton, D. (2002), 'Generic moves in PhD thesis Introductions', in J. Flowerdew (ed.), *Academic Discourse*. London: Longman, pp. 57–75.

Burns, A. and Joyce, H. (1997), *Focus on Speaking*. Sydney: National Centre for English Language Teaching and Research, Macquarie University.

Butler, J. (1990a), *Gender Trouble: Feminism and the Subversion of Identity*. New York: Routledge.

— (1990b), 'Imitation and gender insubordination', in D. Fuss (ed.), *Inside/Out: Lesbian Theories, Gay Theories*. New York: Routledge, pp. 13–31.

— (1993), *Bodies that Matter: On the Discursive Limits of 'Sex'*. New York: Routledge.

— (1997), *Excitable Speech: A Politics of the Performative*. London: Routledge.

— (1999), 'Performativity's social magic', in R. Shusterman (ed.), *Bourdieu: A Critical Reader*. Oxford: Blackwell, pp. 113–28.

— (2004), *Undoing Gender*. London: Routledge.

Butt, D., Fahey, R., Feez, S., Spinks, S. and Yallop, C. (2000), *Using Functional Grammar: An Explorer's Guide* (2nd edn). Sydney: National Centre for English Language Teaching and Research, Macquarie University.

Button, G. (1987), 'Moving out of closings', in G. Button and J. R. E. Lee (eds), *Talk and Social Organization*. Clevedon: Multilingual Matters, pp. 101–51.

Byrd, P. and Coxhead, A. (2010), 'On the other hand: Lexical bundles in academic writing and in the teaching of EAP', *University of Sydney Papers in TESOL*, 5, 31–64. Available at www.faculty.edfac.usyd.edu.au/projects/usp_in_tesol/currentissue.htm, accessed 18 April 2011.

Cahill, D. (2003), 'The myth of the "turn" in contrastive rhetoric', *Written Communication*, 20, 170–94.

Cameron, D. (1998), '"Is there any ketchup, Vera?": Gender, power and pragmatics', *Discourse & Society*, 9, 437–55.

— (1999), 'Performing gender identity: Young men's talk and the construction of heterosexual masculinity', in A. Jaworski and N. Coupland (eds), *The Discourse Reader*. London: Routledge, pp. 442–58.

— (2000), 'Styling the worker: Gender and the commodification of language in the globalized service economy', *Journal of Sociolinguistics*, 4, 323–47.

— (2001), *Working with Spoken Discourse*. London: Sage.

— (2005a), 'Language, gender, and sexuality: Current issues and new directions', *Applied Linguistics*, 26, 482–502.

— (2005b), 'Review of Allyson Jule: Gender, participation and silence in the language classroom: Sh-shusing the girls', *Applied Linguistics*, 26, 125–38.

— (2007), *The Myth of Mars and Venus. Do Men and Women Really Speak Different Languages?* Cambridge: Cambridge University Press.

— (2010), 'Sex/gender, language and the new biologism', *Applied Linguistics*, 32, 173–92.

Cameron, D. and Kulick, D. (2003), *Language and Sexuality*. Cambridge: Cambridge University Press.

Canagarajah, A. S. (2002), *Critical Academic Writing and Multilingual Students*. Ann Arbor: University of Michigan Press.

Canale, M. (1983), 'From communicative competence to communicative language pedagogy', in J. C. Richards and R. W. Schmidt (eds), *Language and Communication*. London: Longman, pp. 2–27.

Canale, M. and Swain, M. (1980), 'Theoretical bases of communicative approaches to second language teaching and testing', *Applied Linguistics*, 1, 1–47.

Caple, H. (2009), 'Multisemiotic communication in an Australian broadsheet: A new news story genre', in C. Bazerman, A. Bonini and D. Figueiredo (eds), *Genre in A Changing World, Perspectives on Writing*. Fort Collins, CO: The WAC Clearinghouse and Parlor Press, pp. 243–54.

— (2010), 'Doubling-up: Allusion and bonding in multi-semiotic news stories', in M. Bednarek and J. R. Martin (eds), *New Discourse on Language: Functional Perspectives on Multimodality, Identity, and Affiliation*. London: Continuum, pp. 111–33.

Carter, R. (2004), 'Introduction', in J. Sinclair, *Trust the Text: Language, Corpus and Discourse*. London: Routledge, pp. 1–6.

Carveth, R. and South, J. B. (eds) (2010), *Mad Men and Philosophy: Nothing is as it Seems*. Hoboken, NJ: John Wiley & Sons.

Casanave, C. P. (2002), *Writing Games: Multicultural Case Studies of Academic Literacy Practices in Higher Education*. Mahwah, NJ: Laurence Erlbaum.

CBS (2011), *The Good Wife*. Available at www.cbs.com/primetime/the_good_wife, accessed 11 March 2011.

Celce-Murcia, M. (1997), 'Describing and teaching English grammar with reference to written discourse', in T. Miller (ed.), *Functional Approaches to Written Text: Classroom Applications*. Washington, DC: United States Information Agency, pp. 174–85.

Celce-Murcia, M. and Olshtain, E. (2000), *Discourse and Context in Language Teaching. A Guide for Language Teachers*. Cambridge: Cambridge University Press.

Channell, J. (1997), 'I just called to say I love you: Love and desire on the telephone', in K. Harvey and C. Shalom (eds), *Language and Desire: Encoding Sex, Romance and Intimacy*. London: Routledge, pp. 143–69.

Charles, M., Pecorari, D. and Hunston, S. (2009), 'Introduction: Exploring the interface between corpus linguistics and discourse analysis', in M. Charles, D. Pecorari and S. Hunston (eds), *Academic Writing: At the Interface of Corpus and Discourse*. London: Continuum, pp. 1–10.

Chen, Y.-H. and Baker, P. (2010), 'Lexical bundles in L1 and L2 academic writing', *Language Learning and Technology*, 14(2), 30–49.

Cheng, A. (2006a), 'Analyzing and enacting academic criticism: The case of an L2 graduate learner of academic writing', *Journal of Second Language Writing*, 15, 279–306.

— (2006b), 'Understanding learners and learning in ESP genre-based writing instruction', *English for Specific Purposes*, 25, 76–89.

— (2007), 'Transferring generic features and recontextualizing genre awareness: Understanding writing performance in the ESP genre-based literacy framework', *English for Specific Purposes*, 26, 287–307.

— (2008a), 'Analyzing genre exemplars in preparation for writing: The case of an L2 graduate student in the ESP genre-based instructional framework of academic literacy', *Applied Linguistics*, 29, 50–71.

— (2008b), 'Individualized engagement with genre in literacy tasks', *English for Specific Purposes*, 27, 387–411.

Chimombo, M. and Roseberry, R. L. (1998), *The Power of Discourse: An Introduction to Discourse Analysis*. Mahwah, NJ: Lawrence Erlbaum.

Cho, H. (executive producer) (1992), 'The last appeal: The murder case of a Korean immigrant', Seoul: Seoul Broadcasting System, broadcast 13 September 1992.

Choi, J. (2010), 'Living on the hyphen', in D. Nunan and J. Choi (eds), *Language and Culture: Reflective Narratives and the Emergence of Identity*. London: Routledge, pp. 66–73.

Chouliaraki, L. (2004), 'Watching 11 September: The politics of pity', *Discourse & Society*, 15, 185–98.

Chowdhury, N. (2011), 'The China effect', *TIME online*, 25 April 2011. Available at www.time.com/time/magazine/article/0,9171,2065153,00.html, accessed 27 April 2011.

Christie, C. (2002), 'Politeness and the linguistic construction of gender in parliament: An analysis of transgressions and apology behaviour', Working Papers on the Web, 3. Available at http://extra.shu.ac.uk/wpw/politeness/christie.htm, accessed 1 February 2011.

Christie, F. (1993), 'The "received" tradition of literacy teaching: The decline of rhetoric and the corruption of grammar', in B. Green (ed.), *The Insistence of the Letter: Literacy Studies and Curriculum Theorizing*. London: Falmer Press, pp. 75–106.

Cicourel, A. V. (1992), 'The interpenetration of communicative context: Examples from medical encounters', in A. Duranti and C. Goodwin (eds), *Rethinking Context: Language as an Interactive Phenomenon*. Cambridge: Cambridge University Press, pp. 1–42.

Clark, R. J. (1995), 'Developing critical reading practices', *Prospect*, 10, 65–80.

CNNPolitics.com (2008), Transcript: 'This is your victory', says Obama. Available at http://edition.cnn.com/2008/POLITICS/11/04/obama.transcript, accessed 7 February 2011.

Conduit, A. M. and Modesto, D. V. (1990), 'An investigation of the generic structure of the materials/methods section of scientific reports', *Australian Review of Applied Linguistics*, S(6), 109–34.

Connor, U. (1996), *Contrastive Rhetoric: Cross-cultural Aspects of Second Language Writing*. Cambridge: Cambridge University Press.

— (2004), 'Intercultural rhetoric research: Beyond texts', *Journal of English for Academic Purposes*, 3, 291–304.

— (2011), *Intercultural Rhetoric in the Writing Classroom*. Ann Arbor: University of Michigan Press.

Connor, Ulla M. and Moreno, Ana I. (2005), 'Tertium comparationis: A vital component in contrastive research methodology', in P. Bruthiaux, D. Atkinson, W. G. Eggington, W. Grabe, and V. Ramanathan (eds), *Directions in Applied Linguistics: Essays in Honor of Robert B. Kaplan*. Clevedon, England: Multilingual Matters, pp. 153–64.

Connor, U., Nagelhout, E. and Rozycki, W. V. (eds), (2008), *Contrastive Rhetoric: Reaching to Intercultural Rhetoric*. Amsterdam: John Benjamins.

Cook, G. (1989), *Discourse*. Oxford: Oxford University Press.

Cooley, L. and Lewkowicz, J. (2003), *Dissertation Writing in Practice: Turning Ideas into Text*. Hong Kong: Hong Kong University Press.

Cooper, A. (2005), 'Make the first move', *The Sun-Herald*, 6 February 2005, p. S38.

Cope, J. (2009), 'Accessing the vocational college from an ESL perspective: A systems of genres analysis', *University of Sydney Papers in TESOL*, 4, 21–57. Available at www.faculty.edfac.usyd.edu.au/projects/usp_in_tesol/volume04.htm, accessed 11 April 2011.

Corliss, R. (1992), 'Casablanca: An analysis of the film', in H. Koch (ed.), *Casablanca: Script and Legend*. Woodstock: Overlook Press, pp. 233–47.

Cornbleet, S. and Carter, R. (2001), *The Language of Speech and Writing*. London: Routledge.

Cresswell, J. W. (2003), *Research Design: Qualitative, Quantitative, and Mixed Method Approaches*. Thousand Oaks, CA: Sage.

Cresswell, J. W. and Plano Clark, V. L. (2007), *Designing and Conducting Mixed Methods Research*. Thousand Oaks, CA: Sage.

Crismore, A. (1983), *Metadiscourse: What is it and How it is Used in School and Non-school Social Science Texts*. Urbana-Champaign, IL: Centre for Reading, University of Illinois.

— (1989), *Talking with Readers: Metadiscourse as Rhetorical Act*. New York: Peter Lang.

Crismore, A., Markkanen, R. and Steffensen, R. (1993), 'Metadiscourse in persuasive writing: A study of texts written by American and Finnish university students', *Written Communication*, 5, 184–202.

Crytstal, D. (2008), 'On Obama's victory style'. Available at http://david-crystal.blogspot.com/2008/11/on-obamas-victory-style.html, accessed 7 February 2011.

Cutting, J. (2008), *Pragmatics and Discourse. A Resource Book for Students* (2nd edn). London: Routledge.

Davies, R. and Ikeno, O. (2002), *The Japanese Mind: Understanding Contemporary Japanese Culture.* Boston and Tokyo: Tuttle Publishing.

de Silva Joyce, H. and Gaudin, J. (2007), *Interpreting the Visual: A Resource Book for Teachers.* Putney, NSW, Australia: Phoenix Books.

Dean, W. (ed.) (2010), *The Ultimate Guide to Mad Men.* London: Guardian Books.

Deckert, S. and Vickers, C. H. (2011), *An Introduction to Sociolinguistics: Society and Identity.* London: Continuum.

Denzin, N. K. (1970), *The Research Act in Sociology.* Chicago: Aldine.

Devitt, A. (1997), 'Genre as a language standard', in W. Bishop and H. Ostrum (eds), *Genre and Writing.* Portsmouth, NH: Boynton/Cook, pp. 45–55.

— (2004), *Writing Genres.* Carbondale, IL: Southern Illinois University Press.

— (2009), 'Re-fusing form in genre study', in J, Giltrow and D. Stein (eds), *Genres in the Internet: Issues in the Theory of Genre.* Amsterdam: John Benjamins, pp. 27–47.

Downes, S. (1995), 'Eating Out', *The Sunday Age*, 23 April 1995, Life, p. 4.

Dressen-Hammouda, D. (2008), 'From novice to disciplinary expert: Disciplinary identity and genre mastery', *English for Specific Purposes*, 27, 233–52.

Droga, L. and Humphrey, S. (2002), *Getting Started with Functional Grammar.* Berry, NSW, Australia: Target Texts.

Dunn, G. A. (2010), '"People want to be told what to do so badly that they'll listen to anyone"', in R. Carveth and J. B. South (eds), *Mad Men and Philosophy: Nothing is at it Seems.* Hoboken, NJ: John Wiley & Sons, pp. 20–33.

Eckert, P. (2000), *Linguistic Variation as Social Practice*, Oxford: Blackwell.

— (2002), 'Demystifying sexuality and desire', in K. Campbell-Kibler, R. J. Podesva, S. J. Roberts and A. Wong (eds), *Language and Sexuality: Contesting Meaning in Theory and Practice.* Stanford, CA: CSLI Publications, pp. 99–110.

— (2008), 'Variation and the indexical field', *Journal of Sociolinguistics*, 12, 453–76.

— (2011), 'Gender and sociolinguistic variation', in J. Coates and P. Pichler (eds), *Language and Gender: A Reader* (2nd edn). Boston: Wiley-Blackwell, pp. 57–70.

Eckert, P. and McConnell-Ginet, S. (2003), *Language and Gender.* Cambridge: Cambridge University Press.

— (2007), 'Putting communities of practice in their place', *Gender and Language*, 1, 27–37.

Eco, U. (1987), *Travels in Hyperreality.* London: Picador.

Eelen, G. (2001), *A Critique of Politeness Theories.* Manchester, UK/Northampton, MA: St Jerome Publishing.

Eggins, S. (1994), *An Introduction to Systemic Functional Linguistics.* London: Pinter.

— (2004), *An Introduction to Systemic Functional Linguistics* (2nd edn). London: Continuum.

Eggins, S. and Slade, D. (1997), *Analysing Casual Conversation.* London: Cassell (Republished 2005, London: Equinox Publishers).

Engardio, P. and Roberts, D. (2004), 'Special report: The China price', *Business Week*, Asian edn, 6 December 2004, pp. 48–58.

Eslami-Rasekh, Z. (2005), 'Raising the pragmatic awareness of language learners', *ELT Journal*, 59, 199–208.

Fairclough, N. (1992), *Discourse and Social Change.* Cambridge: Polity Press.

— (1995), *Critical Discourse Analysis.* London: Longman.

— (2003), *Analyzing Discourse: Textual Analysis for Social Research.* London: Routledge.

Fairclough, N. and Wodak, R. (1997), 'Critical discourse analysis: An Overview', in T. A. van Dijk (ed.), *Discourse as Social Interaction.* London: Sage, pp. 258–84.

Farrer, J. (2002), *Opening Up: Youth Sex Culture and Market Reform in Shanghai*. Chicago: University of Chicago Press.

Feak, C. B. and Swales, J. M. (2011), *Creating Contexts: Writing Introductions across Genres*. Ann Arbor: University of Michigan Press.

Feez, S., Iedema, R. and White, P. (2010), *Media Literacy*. Surry Hills, NSW, Australia: NSW Adult Migrant Education Service.

Firth, J. R. (1935), 'The technique of semantics', *Transactions of the Philological Society*, 34, 36–72. Available at http://onlinelibrary.wiley.com/doi/10.1111/j.1467-968X.1935.tb01254.x/abstract, accessed 4 February 2011.

— (1957a), 'Ethnographic analysis and language with reference to Malinowski's views', in R. W. Firth (ed.), *Man and Culture: An Evaluation of the Work of Bronislaw Malinowski*. London: Routledge, pp. 93–118.

— (1957b), 'A synopsis of linguistics theory, 1930–55', in *Studies in Linguistics Analysis*, Special Volume of the Philological Society. Oxford: The Philological Society, pp. 1–31. Reprinted in F. R. Palmer (ed.), *Selected Papers of J. R. Firth 1952–59*. London: Longman, pp. 168–205.

Flowerdew, J. (2002), 'Genre in the classroom: A linguistic approach', in A. Johns (ed.), *Genre in the Classroom: Multiple Perspectives*. Mahwah, NJ: Lawrence Erlbaum Publishers, pp. 91–102.

— (2004), 'The discursive construction of a world-class city', *Discourse & Society*, 15, 579–605.

— (2011), 'Reconciling contrasting approaches to genre analysis: The whole can equal more than the sum of the parts', in D. Belcher, A. M. Johns and B. Paltridge (eds), *New Directions in English for Specific Purposes Research*. Ann Arbor: University of Michigan Press, pp. 119–44.

Flowerdew, J. and Forest, R. (2010), 'Schematic structure and lexico-grammatical realization in corpus-based genre analysis: The case of research in the PhD literature review', in M. Charles, D. Pecorari and S. Hunston (eds), *Academic Writing. At the Interface of Corpus and Discourse*. London: Continuum, pp. 15–36.

Flowerdew, L. (2005), 'An integration of corpus-based and genre-based approaches to text analysis in EAP/ESP: Countering criticisms against corpus-based methodologies', *English for Specific Purposes*, 24, 321–32.

— (2011a), *Corpora and Language Education*. Basingstoke, England: Palgrave Macmillan.

— (2011b), 'Corpus-based discourse analysis', in J. P. Gee and M. Handford (eds), *The Routledge Handbook of Discourse Analysis*. London: Routledge.

Fox, H. (1994), *Listening to the World: Cultural Issues in Academic Writing*. Urbana, IL: National Council of Teachers of English.

Fraser, B. (1980), 'Conversational mitigation', *Journal of Pragmatics*, 14, 341–50.

— (1990), 'An approach to discourse markers', *Journal of Pragmatics*, 14, 383–95.

— (1999), 'What are discourse markers?' *Journal of Pragmatics*, 31, 931–52.

Freedman, A. (1989), 'Reconceiving genre', *Texte*, 8, 279–92.

— (1999), 'Beyond the text: Towards understanding the teaching and learning of genres', *TESOL Quarterly*, 33, 764–8.

Freedman, A. and Medway, P. (eds) (1994), *Genre and the New Rhetoric*. London: Taylor & Francis.

Fries, P. H. (2002), 'The flow of information in a written text', in P. H. Fries, M. Cummings, D. Lockwood and W. Spruidell (eds), *Relation and Functions Within and Across Language*. London: Continuum, pp. 117–55.

Fung, L. (2003), 'The use and teaching of discourse markers in Hong Kong: Students' production and teachers' perspectives' (PhD dissertation, University of Nottingham).

— (2011), 'Discourse markers in the ESL classroom: A survey of teachers' attitudes', *Asian EFL Journal*, 13, 199–248. Available at www.asian-efl-journal.com/June_2011_lf.php, accessed 15 December 2011.

Fung, L. and Carter, R. (2007), 'Discourse markers and spoken English: Native and learner use in pedagogic settings', *Applied Linguistics*, 28, 410–39.

Gardner, R. (1994), 'Conversation analysis: Some thoughts on its applicability to applied linguistics', *Australian Review of Applied Linguistics*, Series No. 11, 97–118.

— (2001), *When Listeners Talk: Response Tokens and Listener Stance*. Amsterdam: John Benjamins.

— (2004), 'On delaying the answer: Question sequences extended after the question', in R. Gardner and J. Wagner (eds), *Second Language Conversations*. London: Continuum, pp. 246–66.

Garfinkel, H. (1967), *Studies in Ethnometholdogy*. Cambridge: Polity Press.

Gee, J. P. (1993), *An Introduction to Human Language: Fundamental Concepts in Linguistics*. Englewood Cliffs, NJ: Prentice Hall.

— (1996), *Social Linguistics and Literacies: Ideology in Discourses*. London: Taylor and Francis.

— (2005), *An Introduction to Discourse Analysis: Theory and Method* (2nd edn). London: Routledge.

— (2011a), 'Discourse analysis: What makes it critical?' in R. Rogers (ed.), *An Introduction to Critical Discourse Analysis in Education* (2nd edn). Mahwah, NJ: Laurence Erlbaum, pp. 23–45.

— (2011b), *How to do Discourse Analysis: A Toolkit*. New York: Routledge.

Gibbs, N. and Scherer, M. (2009), 'The meaning of Michelle Obama', *Time*, 1 June 2009. Available at www.time.com/time/magazine/article/0,9171,1900228,00.html, accessed 22 August 2011.

Gibson, J. J. (1977), 'The theory of affordances', in R. E. Shaw and J. Bransford (eds), *Perceiving, Acting, and Knowing*. Hillsdale, NJ: Lawrence Erlbaum, pp. 67–82.

Gledhill, C. (2000), 'The discourse function of collocation in research article introductions', *English for Specific Purposes*, 19, 115–35.

Goffman, E. (1967), *Interaction Ritual: Essays on Face to Face Behaviour*. New York: Garden City.

— (1981), *Forms of Talk*. Philadelphia: University of Pennsylvania Press.

Goodwin, M. J. (1999), 'Constructing opposition within girls' games', in M. Bucholtz, A. Liang, and L. Sutton (eds), *Reinventing Identities: From Category to Practice in Language and Gender Research*, New York: Oxford University Press, pp. 388–409.

Gould, J. D., Conti, J. and Hovanyecz, T. (1983), Composing letters with a simulated listening typewriter', *Communications of the ACM*, 26, 295–308.

Grice, H. P. (1975), 'Logic and conversation', in P. Cole and J. L. Morgan (eds), *Syntax and Semantics 3: Speech Acts*. New York: Academic Press. Reprinted in A. Jaworski and N. Coupland (eds) (1999), *The Discourse Reader*. London: Routledge, pp. 76–88.

Grundy, P. (2008), *Doing Pragmatics* (3rd edn). London: Hodder.

Gu, Y. (1990), 'Politeness phenomena in modern Chinese', *Journal of Pragmatics*, 14, 237–57.

Hall, K. (1995), 'Lip service on the fantasy lines', in K. Hall and M. Bucholtz (eds), *Gender Articulated: Language and the Socially Constructed Self*. London: Routledge, pp. 183–216.

— (2000), 'Performativity', *Journal of Linguistic Anthropology*, 9, 184–7.

Halliday, M. A. K. (1971), 'Language in a social perspective', *Educational Review*, 23, 165–88. Reprinted in M. A. K. Halliday and J. J. Webster (eds) (2009), *Language and Society*, Volume 10 in the Collected Works of M. A. K. Halliday. London: Continuum, pp. 43–64.

— (1978), *Language as Social Semiotic: The Social Interpretation of Language and Meaning*. London: Edward Arnold.

— (1985), *An Introduction to Functional Grammar*. London: Edward Arnold.

— (1989a), 'Context of situation', in M. A. K. Halliday and R. Hasan. *Language, Context, and Text: Aspects of Language in a Social-semiotic Perspective*. Oxford: Oxford University Press, pp. 3–14.

— (1989b), *Spoken and Written Language*. Oxford: Oxford University Press.

— (1989c), 'Register variation', in M. A. K. Halliday and R. Hasan. *Language, Context, and Text: Aspects of Language in a Social-semiotic Perspective*. Oxford: Oxford University Press, pp. 29–43.

— (1990), 'Some grammatical problems in scientific English', *Australian Review of Applied Linguistics*, S(6), 13–37.

— (1998), 'Things and relations: Regrammaticalising experience as technical knowledge', in J. R. Martin and R. Veel (eds), *Reading Science: Critical and Functional Perspectives on Discourses of Science*. London: Routledge, pp. 183–235.

— (2009a), 'Context of culture and of situation', in J. J. Webster (ed.), *The Essential Halliday*. London: Continuum, pp. 55–84.

— (2009b), 'Text and discourse analysis', in J. J. Webster (ed.), *The Essential Halliday*. London: Continuum, pp. 362–402.

— (2009c), 'Grammatical metaphor', in J. J. Webster (ed.), *The Essential Halliday*. London: Continuum, pp. 116–158.

Halliday, M. A. K. and Hasan, R. (1976), *Cohesion in English*. London: Longman.

Halliday, M. A. K. and Matthiessen, C. (2004), *An Introduction to Functional Grammar* (3rd edn). London: Edward Arnold.

Hammersley, M. (2003), 'Conversation analysis and discourse analysis: Methods or paradigms?' *Discourse & Society*, 14, 751–81.

Hammond, J. and Macken-Horarick, M. (1999), 'Critical literacy: Challenges and questions for ESL classrooms', *TESOL Quarterly*, 33, 528–44.

Handford, M. (2010), 'What can a corpus tell us about specialist genres?' in M. McCarthy and A. O'Keeffe (eds), *The Routledge Handbook of Corpus Linguistics*. London: Routledge. pp. 255–69.

Harnden, T. (2009), 'Hillary Clinton: my husband Bill Clinton is not secretary of state', *The Telegraph*. Available at www.telegraph.co.uk/news/worldnews/northamerica/usa/6011874/Hillary-Clinton-my-husband-Bill-Clinton-is-not-secretary-of-state.html, accessed 8 April 2011.

Harney, A. (2009), *The China Price: The True Cost of Chinese Competitive Advantage*. London: Penguin.

Harrington, K., Litosseliti, L., Saunston, H. and Sunderland, J. (eds), (2008), *Gender and Language Research Methodologies*. Basingstoke, England: Palgrave MacMillan.

Harris, Z. (1952), 'Discourse analysis', *Language*, 28, 1–30.

— (1959), 'Linguistic transformations for information retrieval', in *Proceedings of the International Conference on Scientific Information*, Volume 2. Washington, DC: NAS-WRC, pp. 937–50

Harwood, N. (2005), '"We do not seem to have a theory . . . the theory I present here attempts to full this gap": Inclusive and exclusive pronouns in academic writing', *Applied Linguistics*, 26, 343–75.

Hasan, R. (1989a), 'The structure of a text', in M. A. K. Halliday and R. Hasan, *Language, Context and Text: Aspects of Language in a Social-Semiotic Perspective*. Oxford: Oxford University Press, pp. 52–69.

— (1989b), 'The texture of a text', in M. A. K. Halliday and R. Hasan, *Language, Context and Text: Aspects of Language in a Social-Semiotic Perspective*. Oxford: Oxford University Press, pp. 70–96.

— (2009), 'The place of context in a systemic functional model', in M. A. K. Halliday and J. J. Webster (eds), *Continuum Companion to Systemic Functional Linguistics*, London: Continuum, pp. 166–89.

Hatch, E. (1992), *Discourse and Language Education*. Cambridge: Cambridge University Press.

Higgens, C. (2008), 'The new Cicero', guardian.co.uk. Available at www.guardian.co.uk/world/2008/nov/26/barack-obama-usa1, accessed 7 February 2011.

Hilles, S. (2005), 'Contextual analysis a la Celce-Murcia', in J. Frodesen and C. Holten (eds), *The Power of Context in Language Teaching and Learning*. Boston, MA: Thomson/Heinle, pp. 3–12.

Hirsh, D. (2010), *Academic Vocabulary in Context*. Bern: Peter Lang.

Hirvela, A. and Belcher, D. (2001), 'Coming back to voice: The multiple voices and identities of mature multilingual writers', *Journal of Second Language Writing*, 10, 83–106.

Hoey, M. (1983), *On the Surface of Discourse*. London: Goerge Allen and Unwin.

— (2001), *Textual Interaction: An Introduction to Written Discourse Analysis*. London: Routledge.

Holmes, J. (1995), *Women, Men and Politeness*. London: Longman.

— (1997), 'Women, language and identity', *Journal of Sociolinguistics*, 1, 195–223.

— (2004), 'Power, lady, and linguistic politeness in Language and Women's Place', in M. Bucholtz (ed.), *Language and Woman's Place: Text and Commentaries*. Oxford: Oxford University Press, pp. 151–7.

— (2006), *Gendered Talk at Work*. Oxford: Blackwell.

— (2008), *An Introduction to Sociolinguistics* (3rd edn). Harlow: Longman.

Hood, S. (2004), 'Managing attitude in undergraduate writing: A focus on the introductions to research papers', in L. Ravelli and R. Ellis (eds), *Analyzing Academic Writing: Contextualised Frameworks*. London: Continuum, pp. 24–44.

— (2010), *Appraising Research: Evaluation in Academic Writing*. Basingstoke, England: Palgrave Macmillan.

Huckin, T. N. (1997), 'Critical discourse analysis', in T. Miller (ed.), *Functional Approaches to Written Text: Classroom Applications*. Washington, DC: United States Information Agency, pp. 78–92. Available at http://eca.state.gov/education/engteaching/pubs/BR/functionalsec3_6.htm, accessed 19 August 2011.

— (2002), 'Textual silence and the discourse of homelessness', *Discourse & Society*, 13, 347–72.

— (2010), 'On textual silences, large and small', in C. Bazerman, R. Krut, K. Lundford, S. McLeod, S. Null, P. Rogers and A. Stansell (eds), *Traditions of Writing Research*. New York: Routledge, pp. 419–31.

Hughes, R. and McCarthy, M. (1998), 'From sentence to discourse: Discourse grammar and English language teaching', *TESOL Quarterly*, 32, 263–87.

Humphrey, S., Martin, J., Dreyfus, S. and Mahboob, A. (2010), 'The 3x3: Setting up a linguistic toolbox for teaching and assessing academic writing', in A. Mahboob and N. Knight (eds), *Appliable Linguistics: Texts, Contexts, and Meanings*. London: Continuum, pp. 185–99.

Hunston, S. (2002), 'Pattern grammar, language teaching, and linguistic variation', in R. Reppen, S. M. Fitzmaurice and D. Biber (eds), *Using Corpora to Explore Linguistic Variation*. Amsterdam: John Benjamins, pp. 167–83.

Hutchby, I. (1996), 'Power in discourse: The case of arguments on a British talk radio show', *Discourse & Society*, 7, 481–97.

Hutchby, I. and Wooffitt, R. (2008), *Conversation Analysis: Principles, Practices and Applications* (2nd edn). Cambridge: Polity Press.

Hyland, K. (1998a), 'Persuasion and context: The pragmatics of academic metadiscourse', *Journal of Pragmatics*, 30, 437–55.

— (1998b), *Hedging in Scientific Research Articles*. Amsterdam: John Benjamins.

— (1999), 'Talking to students: Metadiscourse in introductory textbooks', *English for Specific Purposes*, 18, 3–26.

— (2001), 'Humble servants of the discipline? Self-mention in research articles', *English for Specific Purposes*, 20, 207–26.

— (2002a), 'Authority and invisibility: Authorial identity in academic writing', *Journal of Pragmatics*, 34, 1091–112.

— (2002b), 'Options of identity in academic writing', *ELT Journal*, 56(4), 351–8.

— (2004a), *Genre and Second Language Writing*. Ann Arbor: University of Michigan Press.

— (2004b), 'Graduates' gratitude: The generic structure of dissertation acknowledgements', *English for Specific Purposes*, 23, 303–24

— (2004c), *Disciplinary Discourses: Social Interactions in Academic Writing* (2nd edn). Ann Arbor: University of Michigan Press.

— (2005a), 'Digging up texts and transcripts: Confessions of a discourse analyst', in P. K. Matsuda and T. Silva (eds), *Second Language Writing Research: Perspectives on the Process of Knowledge Construction*. Mahwah, NJ: Lawrence Erlbaum, pp. 177–89.

— (2005b), *Metadiscourse: Exploring Interaction in Writing*. London: Continuum.

— (2005c), 'Stance and engagement: A model of interaction in academic discourse', *Discourse Studies*, 7, 173–92.

— (2008a), 'As can be seen: Lexical bundles and disciplinary variation', *English for Specific Purposes*, 27, 4–21.

— (2008b), 'Academic clusters: Text patterning in published and postgraduate writing', *International Journal of Applied Linguistics*, 18, 41–62.

— (2008c), '"Small bits of textual material": A discourse analysis of Swales' writing', *English for Specific Purposes*, 27, 143–60.

— (2009a), *Academic Discourse*. London: Continuum.

— (2009b), 'Corpus informed discourse analysis: The case of academic engagement', in M. Charles, D. Pecorari and S. Hunston (eds), *Academic Writing: At the Interface of Corpus and Discourse*. London: Continuum, 110–28.

— (2010), 'Community and individuality: Performing identity in applied linguistics', *Written Communication*, 27, 159–88.

— (2011a), 'Projecting an academic identity in some reflective genres', *Iberica, Journal of the European Association of Languages for Specific Purposes*, 21, 9–30.

— (2011b), 'Writing in the university: Education, knowledge and reputation', *Language Teaching*, DOI: 10.1017/S0261444811000036

— (2011c), 'The presentation of self in scholarly life: Identity and marginalization in academic homepages', *English for Specific Purposes*, 30, 286–97.

— (2012), *Disciplinary Identities: Individuality and Community in Academic Discourse*. Cambridge: Cambridge University Press.

Hyland, K. and Tse, P. (2004), '"I would like to thank my supervisor" Acknowledgments in graduate dissertations', *International Journal of Applied Linguistics*, 14, 259–75.

Hymes, D. (1964), 'Introduction: Towards ethnographies of communication', *American Anthropologist, New Series*, 66 (Part 2: The Ethnography of Communication), 1–34.

Hyon, S. (2001), 'Long term effects of genre-based instruction: A follow up study of an EAP reading course', *English for Specific Purposes*, 20, 417–38.

Ide, R. (1998), '"Sorry for your kindness": Japanese interactional rituals in public discourse', *Journal of Pragmatics*, 29, 509–29.

Ide, S. (1982), 'Japanese sociolinguistics: Politeness and women's language', *Lingua*, 57, 49–89.

Iedema, R. (2001), 'Analysing film and television: A social semiotic account of *Hospital: An Unhealthy Business*', in T. van Leeuwen and C. Jewitt (eds), *The Handbook of Visual Analysis*. Los Angeles: Sage, pp. 181–204.

Iley, C. (2010), 'Meet the cast', in W. Dean (ed.), *The Ultimate Guide to Mad Men*. London: Guardian Books, pp. 27–33.

Ivanic, R. (1998), *Writing and Identity: The Discoursal Construction of Identity in Academic Writing*. Amsterdam: John Benjamins.

Ivankova, N. V. and Cresswell, J. W. (2009), 'Mixed methods', in J. Heigham and R. A. Croker (eds), *Qualitative Research in Applied Linguistics*. Basingstoke, England: Palgrave Macmillan, pp. 135–61.

Jaworski, A. and Coupland, N. (2006), 'Introduction: Perspectives on discourse analysis', in A. Jaworski and N. Coupland (eds), *The Discourse Reader* (2nd edn). London: Routledge, pp. 1– 37.

Jefferson, G. (2004), 'Glossary of transcript symbols with an introduction', in G. H. Lerner (ed.), *Conversation Analysis: Studies from the First Generation*. Amsterdam: John Benjamin, pp. 13–31.

Jewitt, C. (2009a), 'An introduction to multimodailty', in C. Jewitt (ed.), *The Routledge Handbook of Multimodal Analysis*. London: Routledge, pp. 14–27.

— (2009b), 'Different approaches to multimodailty', in C. Jewitt (ed.), *The Routledge Handbook of Multimodal Analysis*. London: Routledge, pp. 28–39.

Johns, A. M. (1993), 'Written argumentation for real audiences: Suggestions for teacher research and classroom practice', *TESOL Quarterly*, 27, 75–90.

— (2008), 'Genre awareness for the novice student: An on-going quest', *Language Teaching*, 41, 237–52.

Johnstone, B. (2000), *Qualitative Methods in Sociolinguistics*. New York: Oxford University Press.

— (2002), *Discourse Analysis*. Oxford: Blackwell.

— (2007), *Discourse Analysis* (2nd edn). Oxford: Blackwell.

Jucker, A. (ed.) (1998), *Discourse Markers*. Amsterdam: John Benjamins.

Kadar, D. and Mills, S. (eds) (2011), *Politeness in East Asia*, Cambridge: Cambridge University Press.

Kandil, M. and Belcher, D. (2011), 'ESP and corpus-informed critical discourse analysis: Understanding the power of genres of power', in D. Belcher, A. M. Johns and B. Paltridge (eds), *New Directions in English for Specific Purposes Research*. Ann Arbor: University of Michigan Press, pp. 252–70.

Kaplan, R. B. (1966), 'Cultural thought patterns in intercultural education', *Language Learning*, 16, 1–20.

Kasper, G. (1997), 'Can pragmatic competence be taught?' Second Language Teaching and Curriculum Center, University of Hawaii. Available at http://nflrc.hawaii.edu/NetWorks/NW06, accessed 1 February 2011.

Kay, H. and Dudley-Evans, T. (1998), 'Genre: What teachers think', *ELT Journal*, 52, 308–14.

Kennedy, G. (1998), *An Introduction to Corpus Linguistics*. London: Longman.

KhosraviNik, M. (2005), 'The representation of refugees, asylum seekers and immigrants in British newspapers during the Balkan conflict (1999) and the British general election (2005)', *Discourse & Society*, 20, 477–98.

Kiesling, S. F. (2002), 'Playing the straight man: Displaying and maintaining male heterosexuality in discourse', in K. Campbell-Kibler, R. J. Podesva, S. J. Roberts and A. Wong (eds), *Language and Sexuality: Contesting Meaning in Theory and Practice*. Stanford, CA: CSLI Publications, pp. 249–66

Kim, H. (2008), 'The semantic and pragmatic analysis of South Korean and Australian English apologetic speech acts', *Journal of Pragmatics*, 40, 257–78.

King, M. P. (executive producer) (2001/2002), *Sex and the City* (Television series). New York: Home Box Office.

Kitzinger, C. (2000), 'Doing feminist conversation analysis', *Feminism and Psychology*, 10, 163–93.

— (2008), 'Developing feminist conversation analysis: A response to Wowak', *Human Studies*, 31, 179–208.

Kitzinger, C. and Frith, H. (1999), 'Just say no? The use of conversation analysis in developing a feminist perspective on sexual refusal', *Discourse & Society*, 10, 293–316.

Knapp, P. and Watkins, M. (2005), *Genre, Text, Grammar: Technologies for Teaching and Assessing Writing*. Sydney: University of New South Wales Press.

Knox, J. S. (2007), 'Visual-verbal communication on online newspaper home pages'. *Visual Communication*, 6, 19–53.

— (2009), 'Punctuating the home page: Image as language in an online newspaper', *Discourse and Communication*, 3, 145–72.

— (2010), 'Online newspapers: Evolving genres and evolving theory', in C. Coffin, T. Lillis and K. O'Holloran (eds), *Applied Linguistics Methods: A Reader*. London: Routledge, pp. 31–51.

— (forthcoming), 'Designing the news in an online newspaper: A systemic description', in A. Baldry and E. Montagna (eds), *Interdisciplinary Perspectives on Multimodality: Theory and Practice*. Proceedings of the Third International Conference on Multimodality. Campobasso, Italy: Palladino. Available at www.ling.mq.edu.au/about/staff/knox_john/knox_baldrychapter.pdf, accessed 24 August 2011.

Koch, H. (1996), *Casablanca: Script and Legend*. Woodstock, NY: Overlook Press.

Kongpetch, S. (2003), 'The implications of the genre-based approach on the teaching of English writing at the Department of Foreign Languages, Khon Kaen University in north-eastern Thailand' (PhD dissertation, Faculty of Education, University of Technology, Sydney).

— (2006), 'Using a genre-based approach to teach writing to Thai students: A case study', *Prospect*, 21, 3–33.

Koutsantoni, D. (2009), 'Persuading sponsors and securing funding: Rhetorical patterns in grant proposals', in M. Charles, D. Pecorari and S. Hunston (eds), *Academic Writing: At the Interface of Corpus and Discourse*. London: Continuum, pp. 37–57.

Kowal, S. and O'Connell, D. C. (1997), 'Theoretical ideals and their violation: Princess Diana and Martin Bashir in the BBC interview', *Pragmatics*, 7, 309–23.

Kress, G. (1991), 'Critical discourse analysis', *Annual Review of Applied Linguistics*, 11, 84–99.

— (1993), 'Against arbitrariness: The social production of the sign as a foundational issue in critical discourse analysis', *Discourse & Society*, 4, 169–91.

— (2010), *Multimodality: A Social Semiotic Approach to Contemporary Communication*. London: Routledge.

Kress, G. and van Leeuwen, T. (2006), *Reading Images: The Grammar of Visual Design* (2nd edn). London: Routledge.

Krzyzanowski, M. and Wodak, R. (2008), 'Multiple identities, migration and belonging: "Voices of migrants"', in C. R. Caldas-Coulthard and R. Iedema (eds), *Identity Trouble: Critical Discourse and Contested Identities*. Basingstoke, England: Palgrave Macmillan, pp. 95–119.

Kubota, R. (1997), 'A reevaluation of the uniqueness of Japanese written discourse: Implications for contrastive rhetoric', *Written Communication*, 14, 460–80.

Kurzon, D. (1996), 'The maxim of quantity, hyponymy and Princess Diana', *Pragmatics*, 6, 217–27.

Lakoff, R. T. (1990), *Talking Power*. New York: Basic Books.

Language Teaching review panel (2007), 'Call for papers: Replication studies', *Language Teaching*, 41, i.

— (2008), 'Replication studies in language learning and teaching: Questions and answers', *Language Teaching*, 41, 1–14.

Larsen-Freeman, D. (2003), *Teaching Language: From Grammar to Grammaring*. Boston, MA: Thomson Heinle.

Lave, J. and Wenger, E. (1991), *Situated Learning. Legitimate Peripheral Participation*. Cambridge: University of Cambridge Press.

Lea, M. and Street, B. (2006), 'The "academic literacies" model: Theory and applications', *Theory into Practice*, 45, 368–77.

Lee, D. A. (1997), 'Frame conflicts and competing construals in family argument', *Journal of Pragmatics*, 27, 339–60.

Lee, D. and Swales, J. M. (2006), 'A corpus-based EAP course for NNS doctoral students: Moving from available specialized corpora to self-compiled corpora', *English for Specific Purposes*, 25, 56–75.

Leech, G. (2007), 'Politeness: Is there an East-West divide?' *Journal of Politeness Research*, 3, 167–206.

— (2009), 'Forward: Studies in pragmatics and discourse analysis', in *Gu Yueguo's Anthology on Linguistics*. Beijing: Foreign Language Teaching and Research Press, pp. v–x.

Leki, I. (1997), 'Cross-talk: ESL issues and contrastive rhetoric', in C. Severino, J. C. Guerra and S. E. Butler (eds), *Writing in Multicultural Settings*. New York: Modern Language Association of America, pp. 234–44.

Lemke, J. L. (1992), 'Intertextuality and educational research', *Linguistics and Education*, 4, 257–67.

— (1995), *Textual Politics. Discourse and Social Dynamics*. London: Taylor and Francis.

Lewis, A. G. (1998), 'The political and educational implications of gender, class and race in Hollywood film: holding out for a female hero', unpublished MA thesis, McGill University, Canada.

Liddicoat, A. J. (2011), *An Introduction to Conversation Analysis* (2nd edn). London: Continuum.

Lillis, T. (2008), 'Ethnography as method, methodology, and 'deep theorizing'', *Written Communication*, 25, 353–88.

Lillis, T. and Curry, M. J. (2010), *Academic Writing in a Global Context: The Politics and Practices of Publishing in English*. London: Routledge.

Lillis, T. and Scott, M. (2007), 'Defining academic literacies research: Issues of epistemology, ideology and strategy', *Journal of Applied Linguistics*, 4, 5–32.

Lincoln, Y. and Guba, E. (1985), *Naturalistic Inquiry*. Beverly Hills, CA: Sage.

Litossoleti, L. (2006), *Gender & Language: Theory and Practice*. London: Hodder.

Liu, J. (2004), 'A study of Chinese ethnic minorities English writing from a contrastive rhetoric perspective' (MEd TESOL dissertation, University of Sydney).

— (2008), 'The generic and rhetorical structures of expositions in English by Chinese ethnic minorities: A perspective from intracultural contrastive rhetoric', *Language and Intercultural Communication*, 8, 2–20.

— (2010a), 'The blog as genre and performance: An analysis of Chinese A-list personal blogs' (PhD thesis, University of Sydney).

— (2010b), 'Gendered performances and norms in Chinese personal blogs', *Gender Forum. An Internet Journal for Gender Studies*, 30, 1–9. Available at www.genderforum.org/issues/de-voted/detailed-table-of-contents, accessed 8 March 2011.

Livia, A. and Hall, K. (1997), '"It's a girl!" Bringing performativity back into linguistics', in A. Livia and K. Hall (eds), *Queerly Phrased: Language, Gender, and Sexuality*. New York: Oxford University Press, pp. 3–18.

Lo Castro, V. (2003), *An Introduction to Pragmatics: Social Action for Language Teachers*. Ann Arbor: University of Michigan Press.

— (2011), 'Second language pragmatics', in E. Hinkel (ed.), *Handbook of Research in Second Language Teaching and Learning*, Volume 2. London: Routledge, pp. 319–44.

Luckmann, T. (2009), 'Observations on the structure and function of communicative genres', *Semiotica*, 173, 267–82.

Luke, A. (1996), 'Genres of power? Literacy education and the production of capital', in R. Hasan and G. Williams (eds), *Literacy in Society*. London: Longman, pp. 308–38.

Machin, D. (2007), *Introduction to Multimodal Analysis*. London: Hodder Arnold.

Machin, D. and Thornborrow, J. (2003), 'Branding and discourse: The case of Cosmopolitan', *Discourse & Society*, 14, 453–71.

Machin, D. and van Leeuwen, T. (2007), *Global Media Discourse: A Critical Introduction*. London: Routledge.

Maier, C. D. (2011), 'Structure and function in the generic staging of film trailers', in R. Piazza, F. Rossi and M. Bednarek (eds), *Telecinematic Discourse: Approaches to the Language of Films and Television Series*. Amsterdam: John Benjamins, pp. 141–58.

Malinowski, B. (1923), 'The problem of meaning in primitive languages', in C. K. Ogden and I. A. Richards (eds), *The Meaning of Meaning*. London: Routledge and Kegan Paul, 296–336.

— (1935), *Coral Gardens and their Magic* Volume II. London: George Allen and Unwin. Reprinted as *The Language of Magic and Gardening*. Bloomington, IN: Indiana University Press. 1967.

Mallinson, C. and Brewster, Z. W. (2005), '"Blacks and bubbas": Stereotypes, ideology, and categorization processes in restaurant servers' discourse', *Discourse & Society*, 16, 787–807.

Mao, L. R. (1994), 'Beyond politeness theory: "Face" revisited and renewed', *Journal of Pragmatics*, 21, 451–86.

Markee, N. (2000), *Conversation Analysis*. Mahwah, NJ: Lawrence Erlbaum.

Martin, J. R. (1984), 'Language, register and genre', in F. Christie (ed.), *Language Studies: Children's Writing: Reader*. Geelong, Victoria: Deakin University Press, pp. 21–9.

— (1992), *English Text. System and Structure*. Amsterdam: John Benjamins.

— (1993), 'Genre and literacy – modelling context in educational linguistics', *Annual Review of Applied Linguistics*, 13, 141–72.

— (2001), 'Language, register and genre', in A. Burns and C. Coffin (eds), (2001), *Analyzing English in a Global Context*. London: Routledge, pp. 149–66.

— (2011), 'Systemic functional linguistics', in K. Hyland and B. Paltridge (eds), *Continuum Companion to Discourse Analysis*. London: Continuum, pp. 101–19.

Martin, J. R. and Rose, D. (2007), *Working with Discourse: Meaning Beyond the Clause* (2nd edn). London: Continuum.

— (2008), *Genre Relations: Mapping Culture*. London: Equinox.

Martin, J. R. and White, P. R. R. (2005), *The Language of Evaluation: Appraisal in English*. London: Palgrave Macmillan.

Mason, J. (2006), 'Mixing methods in a qualitatively driven way', *Qualitative Research*, 6, 9–25.

Matsumoto, Y. (1989), 'Politeness and conversational universals – observations from Japanese', *Multilingua*, 8, 207–22.

Mauranen, A. (2001), 'Reflexive academic talk: Observations from MICASE', in R. C. Simpson and J. M. Swales (eds), *Corpus Linguistics in North America: Selections from the 1999 Symposium*. Ann Arbor: University of Michigan Press, pp. 165–78.

Mautner, G. (2005a), 'Time to get wired: Using web-based corpora in critical discourse analysis', *Discourse & Society*, 16, 809–28.

— (2005b), 'The entrepreneurial university: A discursive profile of a higher education buzzword', *Critical Discourse Studies*, 2, 95–120.

McCarthy, M. (1991), *Discourse Analysis for Language Teachers*. Cambridge: Cambridge University Press.

— (1994), 'It, this, and that', in M. Coulthard (ed.), *Advances in Written Text Analysis*. London: Routledge, pp. 266–75.

— (1998), *Spoken Language and Applied Linguistics*. Cambridge: Cambridge University Press.

— (2001), *Issues in Applied Linguistics*. Oxford: Oxford University Press.

McCarthy, M. and Carter, R. (2001), 'Size isn't everything: Spoken English, corpus, and the classroom', *TESOL Quarterly*, 35, 337–40.

McConnell-Ginet, S. (2011), *Gender, Sexuality, and Meaning: Linguistic Practice and Politics*. Oxford: Oxford University Press.

McHoul, A. (1991), 'ReadingS', in C. Baker and A. Luke (eds), *Towards a Critical Sociology of Reading Pedagogy*. Amsterdam: John Benjamins, pp. 191–210.

McKenna, B. (2004), 'Critical discourse studies: Where to from here?' *Critical Discourse Studies*, 1, 9–39.

Meadows, B. (2009), 'Nationalism and language learning at the US/Mexico Border: An ethnographically-sensitive critical discourse analysis of the reproduction of nation, power, and privilege in an English language classroom' (PhD dissertation, University of Arizona).

Meadows, B. and Waugh, L. (2010), 'Identity and power in online communities of practice: Working in the extreme margins of a celebrity gossip blogsite', in J. Watzke, P. Chamness Miller and M. Mantero (eds), *Readings in Language Studies*, Volume Two. St Louis, MO: International Society for Language Studies, pp. 185–200.

Mean, L. (2001), 'Identity and discursive practice: Doing gender on the football pitch', *Discourse & Society*, 12, 789–815.

Mendoza-Denton, N. (1999), 'Turn initial *no*: Collaborative opposition among Latina adolescents', in M. Bucholtz, A. C. Liang and L. A. Sutton (eds), *Reinventing Identities: The Gendered Self in Discourse*. New York: Oxford University Press, pp. 273–92.

— (2007), 'Sociolinguistic extensions of exemplar theory: Comments of Flege, Khattab, and Darcy, Peperkamp and Dupopux', in J. Cole and J. Hualde (eds), *Laboratory Phonology 9*. Berlin: Mouton de Gruyter, pp. 443–54.

— (2008), *Homegirls: Language and Cultural Practice among Latina Youth Gangs*. Boston: Wiley Blackwell.

Meyerhoff, M. (2002), 'Communities of practice', in J. Chambers, P. Trudgill and N. Schilling-Estes (eds), *The Handbook of Language Variation and Change*. Malden, MA: Blackwell, pp. 526–48.

— (2011), *Introducing Sociolinguistics* (2nd edn). London: Routledge.

MICASE (nd), 'Research and development activities'. Available at http://micase.elicorpora.info, accessed 1 February 2011.

Miller, C. R. (1984), 'Genre as social action', *Quarterly Journal of Speech, 70*, 151–67. Reprinted in A. Freedman and P. Medway (eds) (1994). *Genre and the New Rhetoric*, London: Taylor & Francis, pp. 23–42.

Miller, C. R. and Bazerman, C. (2011), 'Gêneros textuais (Genres)'. Available at www.nigufpe.com.br/serie-bate-papo-academico-vol-1-generos-textuais, accessed 12 September 2011.

Mills, S. (1997), *Discourse*. London: Routledge.

— (2003), *Gender and Politeness*. Cambridge: Cambridge University Press.

— (2008), *Language and Sexism*. Cambridge: Cambridge University Press.

— (2010), 'Impoliteness in a cultural context', *Journal of Pragmatics*, 41, 1047–60.

Mills, S. and Mullany, L. (2011), *Language, Gender and Feminism*. London: Routledge.

Milne, A. A. (1988), *Winnie-the-Pooh*. London: Methuen & Co.

Mitchell, T. F. (1957), 'The language of buying and selling in Cyrenaica', *Hesperis*, 44, 31–71. Reprinted in T. F. Mitchell (1975), *Principles of Firthian Linguistics*. London: Longman, pp. 167–200.

Moerman, M. (1988), *Talking Culture: Ethnography and Conversation Analysis*. Philadelphia: University of Pennsylvania Press

Molle, D. and Prior, P. (2008), 'Multimodal genre systems in EAP writing pedagogy: reflecting on a needs analysis', *TESOL Quarterly*, 42, 541–66.

Montgomary, M. (2011), 'Discourse and the news', in K. Hyland and B. Paltridge (eds), *Continuum Companion to Discourse Analysis*. London: Continuum, pp. 199–212.

Moreno, A. (2008), 'The importance of comparable corpora in cross-cultural studies', in U. Connor, E. Nagelhout and W. Rozycki (eds), *Contrastive Rhetoric: Reaching to Intercultural Rhetoric*. Amsterdam: Benjamins, pp. 25–41.

Mori, J. (2002), 'Task design, plan, and development of talk-in-interaction: A select study of small group activity in a Japanese classroom', *Applied Linguistics*, 23, 323–47.

Morrish, L. and Leap, W. (2007), 'Sex talk: Language, desire, identity and beyond', in H. Sauntson and S. Kyratzis (eds), *Language, Sexualities, Desires: Cross-Cultural Perspectives*. Basingstoke, England: Palgrave Macmillan, pp. 17–40.

Morrish, L. and Saunston, H. (2007), 'Introduction', in L. Morrish and H. Saunston (eds), *New Perspectives on Language and Sexual Identity*. Basingstoke, England: Palgrave Macmillan, pp. 1–24.

Morse, J. (2010), 'Simultaneous and sequential qualitative and mixed methods designs', *Qualitative Inquiry*, 16, 483–91.

Morton, A. (1999), *Monica's Story*. New York: St Martin's Press.

Mullany, L. (2002), '"I don't think you want me to get a word in edgeways do you John?" Re-assessing (im)politeness, language and gender in political broadcast interviews', *Working Papers on the Web*, 3. Available at http://extra.shu.ac.uk/wpw/politeness/mullany.htm, accessed 1 February 2011.

Murachver, T. and Janssen, A. (2007), 'Gender and communication in context', in A. Weatherall, B. M. Watson and C. Gallois (eds), *Language, Discourse & Social Psychology*. Basingstoke, England: Palgrave Macmillan, pp. 185–205.

Nakane, I. (2005), 'Negotiating silence and speech in the classroom', *Multilingua*, 24, 75–100.

— (2007), *Silence in Intercultural Communication: Perceptions and Performance*. Amsterdam: John Benjamins.

Nakanishi, M. (1998), 'Gender enactment on a first date: A Japanese sample', *Women and Language*, 21, 10–17.

Negra, D. (2004), 'Quality postfeminism? Sex and the single girl on HBO', *Genders*. Available at www.genders.org/g39/g39_negra.html, accessed 8 March 2011.

Nesbitt, D., Nesbitt, J. and Uchimaru, K. (1990), *Contact Japanese: Communicating in Japanese*. Auckland: New House Publishers.

Nesi, H. (2001), 'A corpus-based analysis of academic lectures across disciplines', in J. Cotterill and A. Ife (eds), *Language across Boundaries*. London: BAAL in association with Continuum Press, pp. 201–18.

— (2011), 'BAWE: An introduction to a new resource', in A. Frankenberg-Garcia, L. Flowerdew and G. Aston (eds), *New Trends in Corpora and Language Learning*. London: Continuum, pp. 213–28.

North, S. (2005), 'Disciplinary variation in the use of theme in undergraduate essays', *Applied Linguistics*, 26, 431–52.

O'Halloran, K. L. (2004), 'Visual semiosis in film', in K. Halloran (ed.), *Multimodal Discourse Analysis: Systemic Functional Perspectives*. London: Continuum, pp. 109–30.

— (ed.) (2004), *Multimodal Discourse Analysis: Systemic Functional Perspectives*. London: Continuum.

— (2011), 'Multimodal discourse analysis', in K. Hyland and B. Paltridge (eds), *Continuum Companion to Discourse Analysis*. London: Continuum, pp. 120–37.

O'Loughlin, K. (1989), 'Routine beginnings: Telephone openings in Australia', *Melbourne Papers in Applied Linguistics*, 1, 27–42.

O'Shannessy, C. (1995), 'Pre-court barrister–client interactions: An investigation' (MA thesis, Department of Linguistics and Applied Linguistics, University of Melbourne).

Ochs, E. (1992), 'Indexing gender', in A. Duranti and C. Goodwin (eds), *Rethinking Context: Language as an Interactive Phenomenon*. Cambridge: Cambridge University Press, pp. 335–58.

Ohashi, J. (2000), 'Thanking, giving and receiving in Japanese: A cross-cultural pragmatic investigation' (PhD thesis, Department of Linguistics and Applied Linguistics, University of Melbourne).

— (2003), 'Japanese culture specific face and politeness orientation: A pragmatic investigation of yoroshiku onegaishimasu', *Multilingua*, 22, 257–74.

— (2008), 'Linguistic rituals for thanking in Japanese: Balancing obligations', *Journal of Pragmatics*, 40, 2150–74.

Ohashi, J., Ohashi, H. and Paltridge, B. (2008), 'Finishing the dissertation while on tenure track: Enlisting support from inside and outside the academy', in C. Casanave and X. Li (eds), *Learning the Literacy Practices of Graduate School: Insiders' Reflections on Academic Enculturation*. Ann Arbor: University of Michigan Press, pp. 218–39.

Ooi, V. B. Y. (2001), 'Investigating and teaching genres using the World Wide Web', in M. Ghadessy, A. Henry and R. L. Roseberry (eds), *Small Corpus Studies and ELT*. Amsterdam: John Benjamins, pp. 175–203.

Orr, J. (1996), 'A comparative investigation into the structure of arguments: Frame semantics and conversation analysis' (MA thesis, Department of Linguistics and Applied Linguistics, University of Melbourne).

Otsuji, E. (2010), '"Where am I from?": Performative and 'metro' perspectives of origin', in D. Nunan and J. Choi (eds), *Language and Culture: Reflective Narratives and the Emergence of Identity*. London: Routledge, pp. 186–93.

Page, R. E. (2003), '"Cherie: lawyer, wife, mum": Contradictory patterns of representation in media reports of Cherie Booth/Blair', *Discourse & Society*, 14, 559–79.

Painter, C. and Martin, J. R. (forthcoming), 'Intermodal complementarity: Modelling affordances across verbiage and image in children's picture book'. *Ilha do Desterro: A Journal of English Language, Literatures in English and Cultural Studies* (Special Issue on Multimodality).

Painter, C., Martin, J. R. and Unsworth, L. (2012), *Reading Visual Narratives: Image Analysis of Children's Picture Books*. London: Equinox.

Paltridge, B. (1996), 'Genre, text type and the language learning classroom', *ELT Journal*, 50, 237–43.

— (1998), 'Get your terms in order', in P. Master and D. Brinton (eds), *New Ways in English for Specific Purposes*. Alexandra, VA: TESOL, pp. 263–6.

— (2001), *Genre and the Language Learning Classroom*. Ann Arbor: University of Michigan Press.

— (2002a), 'Genre, text type and the EAP classroom', in A. M. Johns (ed.), *Genre in the classroom: Multiple perspectives*. Malwah, NJ: Lawrence Erlbaum, pp. 73–90.

— (2002b), 'Thesis and dissertation writing: An examination of published advice and actual practice', *English for Specific Purposes*, 21, 125–43.

— (2004), 'The exegesis as a genre: An ethnographic examination', in L. Ravelli and R. Ellis (eds), *Analyzing Academic Writing: Contextualised Frameworks*. London: Continuum, pp. 84–103.

— (2006), *Discourse Analysis: An Introduction*. London: Continuum.

— (forthcoming), 'Genre and English for specific purposes', in B. Paltridge and S. Starfield (eds), *Handbook of English for Specific Purposes*. Boston: Blackwell.

Paltridge, B. and Starfield, S. (2007), *Thesis and Dissertation Writing in a Second Language*. London: Routledge.

— (2011), 'Research in English for specific purposes', in Eli Hinkel (ed.), *Handbook of Research in Second Language Teaching and Learning*, Volume 2. London: Routledge, pp. 106–21.

Paltridge, B., Harbon, L., Hirsh, D., Phakiti, A., Shen, H., Stevenson, M. and Woodrow, L. (2009), *Teaching Academic Writing: An Introduction for Teachers of Second Language Writers*. Ann Arbor: University of Michigan Press.

Paltridge, B., Starfield, S., Ravelli, L. and Nicholson, S. (2011), 'Doctoral writing in the visual and performing arts: Issues and debates', *International Journal of Art and Design Education*, 30, 88–101.

Paltridge, B., Starfield, S., Ravelli, L., Nicholson, S. and Tuckwell, K. (2011), 'Doctoral writing in the visual and performing arts: Two ends of a continuum', *Studies in Higher Education*. DOI: 10.1080/03075079.2011.562285.

Paltridge, B., Thomas, A. and Liu, J. (2011), 'Genre, performance and Sex and the City', in R. Piazza, F. Rossi and M. Bednarek (eds), *Telecinematic Discourse: Approaches to the Language of Films and Television Series*. Amsterdam: John Benjamins, pp. 249–62.

Paltridge, B. and Wang, W. (2010), 'Researching discourse', in B. Paltridge and A. Phakiti (eds), *Companion to Research Methods in Applied Linguistics*. London: Continuum, pp. 256–73.

— (2011), 'Contextualising ESP research: Media discourses in China and Australia', in D. Belcher, A. M. Johns and B. Paltridge (eds), *New Directions in English for Specific Purposes Research*. Ann Arbor: University of Michigan Press, pp. 25–43.

Pavlenko, A. and Norton, B. (2007), 'Imagined communities, identity, and English language learning', in J. Cummins and C. Davison (eds), *International Handbook of English Language Teaching* (Part 2). New York: Springer, pp. 669–80.

Peng, H. (2010), *Chinese PhD Thesis Acknowledgements: A Communities of Practice Perspective*. Bern: Peter Lang.

Pennycook, A. (2004), 'Performativity and language studies', *Critical Inquiry in Language Studies*, 1, 1–26.

— (2007), *Global Englishes and Transcultural Flows*. London: Routledge.

— (2010), *Language as a Local Practice*. London: Routledge.

— (2011), Roundtable on language and identity. Symposium on Language and Identity across Modes of Communication, 22 November, University of Sydney.

Phillips, L. and Jorgenson, M. W. (2002), *Discourse Analysis as Theory and Method*. London: Sage.

Phillips, S. U. (1983), *The Invisible Culture: Communication in Classroom and Community on the Warm Springs Indian Reservation*. Prospect Heights, IL: Waveland Press.

Piazza, R., Rossi, F. and Bednarek, M. (eds) (2011), *Telecinematic Discourse: Approaches to the Language of Films and Television Series*. Amsterdam: John Benjamins,

Poos, D. and Simpson, R. C. (2002), 'Cross-disciplinary comparisons of hedging: Some findings from the Michigan Corpus of Academic Spoken English', in R. Reppen, S. M. Fitzmaurice and D. Biber (eds), *Using Corpora to Explore Linguistic Variation*. Amsterdam: John Benjamins, pp. 3–23.

Prior, P. (forthcoming), 'Multimodality and ESP research', in B. Paltridge and S. Starfield (eds), *Handbook of English for Specific Purposes*. Boston: Blackwell.

Reiff, M. J. and Bawarshi, A. (2011), 'Tracing discursive resources: How students use prior genre knowledge to negotiate new writing contexts in first-year composition', *Written Communication*, 28, 312–37.

Reinhart, S. (2002), *Giving Academic Presentations*. Ann Arbor: University of Michigan Press.

Reppen, R. (2010), *Using Corpora in the Language Classroom*. Cambridge: Cambridge University Press.

Reppen, R. and Simpson, R. (2002), 'Corpus linguistics', in N. Schmitt (ed.), *An Introduction to Applied Linguistics*. London: Arnold, pp. 92–111.

Resende, V. M. (2009), '"It's not a matter of inhumanity": A critical discourse analysis of an apartment building circular on "homeless people"', *Discourse & Society*, 20, 363–79.

Richards, J. C. and Schmidt, R. (2010), *Longman Dictionary of language Teaching and Applied Linguistics* (4th edn). Harlow, UK: Longman.

Richardson, K. (2010), *Television Dramatic Dialogue: A Sociolinguistic Study*. Oxford: Oxford University Press.

Richardson, K. F. (2000), '"Suffer in your jocks, ya dickhead": Solidarity and the construction of identity in an Australian university cricket club magazine' (MA thesis, Department of Linguistics and Applied Linguistics, University of Melbourne).

Riggenbach, H. (1999), *Discourse Analysis in the Language Classroom*. Volume 1: The Spoken Language. Ann Arbor: University of Michigan Press.

Rogers, R. (2004), 'Setting an agenda for critical discourse analysis in education', in R. Rogers (ed.), *An Introduction to Critical Discourse Analysis in Education*. Mahwah, NJ: Laurence Erlbaum, pp. 237–54.

— (ed.) (2011), *An Introduction to Critical Discourse Analysis in Education* (2nd edn). London: Routledge.

Rosch, E. (1978), 'Principles of categorization', in E. Rosch and B. B. Lloyd (eds), *Cognition and Categorization*. Hillsdale, NJ: Lawrence Erlbaum, pp. 27–48. Available at www.commonweb.unifr.ch/artsdean/pub/gestens/f/as/.../9778_083247.pdf, accessed 26 September 2011.

— (1983), 'Prototype classification and logical classification: The two systems', in E. K. Scholnick (ed.), *New Trends in Conceptual Representation: Challenges to Piaget's Theory?* Hillsdale, NJ: Lawrence Erlbaum, pp. 73–86.

Rose, D. (2012), 'Genre in the Sydney school', in J. P. Gee and M. Handford (eds), *The Routledge Handbook of Discourse Analysis*. London: Rouledge, pp. 209–25.

Rose, D. and Martin, J. R. (2012), *Learning to Write/Reading to Learn: Genre, Knowledge and Pedagogy in the Sydney School*. London: Equinox.

Rothery, J. and Stenglin, M. (2000), 'Interpreting literature: The role of appraisal', in L. Unsworth (ed.), *Researching Language in Schools and Communities: Functional Linguistic Perspectives*. London: Cassell, pp. 222–43.

Sacks, H. (1992), *Lectures on Conversation* (2 vols). Oxford: Basil Blackwell.

— (2004), 'An initial characterisation of the organisation of turn taking for conversation', in G. H. Lerner (ed.), *Conversation Analysis: Studies from the First Generation*. Amsterdam: John Benjamin, pp. 35–42.

Sacks, H., Schegloff, E. A. and Jefferson, G. (1978), 'ŒA simplest systematics for the organisation of turn taking for conversation', in J. Schenkein (ed.), *Studies in the Organisation of Conversational Interaction*. New York: Academic Press, pp. 7–55.

Samraj, B. (2005), 'An exploration of a genre set: Research article abstracts and introductions in two disciplines', *English for Specific Purposes*, 24, 141–56.

Santos, T. (1989), 'Replication in applied linguistics research', *TESOL Quarterly*, 23, 699–702.

Sartain, S. (1995), 'Letter to the editor', *The Sunday Age*, 30 April 1995, p. 16.

Saunston, H. and Kyratzis, S. (eds) (2007), *Language, Sexualities and Desires: Cross-Cultural Perspectives*. Basingstoke, England: Palgrave Macmillan.

Saville-Troike, M. (2003), *The Ethnography of Communication: An Introduction* (3rd edn). Malden, MA: Blackwell.

Schegloff, E. (1986), 'The routine as achievement', *Human Studies*, 9, 111–52.

— (1997), 'Whose text? Whose context?' *Discourse & Society*, 8, 165–87.

— (2004), 'Answering the phone', in G. H. Lerner (ed.), *Conversation Analysis: Studies from the First Generation*. Amsterdam: John Benjamins, pp. 63–107.

Schegloff, E. A. (2007), 'A tutorial on membership categorization', *Journal of Pragmatics*, 39, 462–82.

Schegloff, E. and Sacks, H. (1973), 'Opening up closings', *Semiotica*, 7, 289–437.

Schegloff, E., Koshik, I., Jacoby, S. and Olsher, D. (2002), 'Conversation analysis and applied linguistics', *Annual Review of Applied Linguistics*, 22, 3–31.

Schiffrin, D. (1987), *Discourse Markers*. Cambridge: Cambridge University Press.

— (1994), *Approaches to Discourse*. Oxford: Blackwell.

— (2001), 'Discourse markers', in D. Schiffrin, D. Tannen and H. E. Hamilton (eds), *The Handbook of Discourse Analysis*. Malden, MA: Blackwell, pp. 54–75.

Schmidt, R. (1983), 'Interaction, acculturation, the acquisition of communicative competence?' in N. Wolfson and E. Judd (eds), *Sociolinguistics and TESOL*, Rowley, MA: Newbury House. Available at http://ebookbrowse.com/schmidt-interaction-acculturation-and-the-acquisition-of-communicative-competence-pdf-d62293427, accessed 10 March 2011.

Schryer, C. (1993), 'Records as genre', *Written Communication*, 10, 200–34.

— (2002), 'Genre and power: A chronotopic analysis', in R. Coe, L. Lingard and T. Teslenko (eds), *The Rhetoric and Ideology of Genre: Strategies for Stability and Change*. Cresskill, NJ: Hampton Press, pp. 73–102.

— (2011), 'Investigating texts in their social contexts: The promise and peril of rhetorical genre studies', in D. Starke-Meyerring, A. Paré, N. Artemeva, M. Horne and L. Yousoubova (eds), *Writing in Knowledge Societies. Perspectives on Writing*. Fort Collins, CO: The WAC Clearinghouse and Parlor Press, pp. 31–52. Available at http://wac.colostate.edu/books/winks/, accessed 2 April 2012.

Scollon, R. and Wong-Scollon, S. (2001), *Intercultural Communication: A Discourse Approach* (2nd edn). Oxford: Blackwell.

Scott, M. (2004), *Wordsmith Tools* (version 4). Oxford: Oxford University Press.

Scott, M. and Groom, N. (1999), 'Genre-based pedagogy: Problems and possibilities', in P. Thompson (ed.), *Issues in EAP Research and Writing Instruction*. Reading: Centre for Applied Language Studies, University of Reading, pp. 18–27.

Searle, J. R. (1969), *Speech Acts*. London: Cambridge University Press.

Shalom, C. (1997), 'That great supermarket of desire: Attributes of the desired other in personal advertisements', in K. Harvey and C. Shalom (eds), *Language and Desire: Encoding Sex, Romance and Intimacy*. London: Routledge, pp. 186–203.

Sheridan, G. (2001), 'US should now take careful aim', *The Australian*, 13 September 2001, p. 19.

Sigley, R. and Holmes, J. (2002), 'Looking at girls in corpora of English', *Journal of English Linguistics*, 30, 138–57.

Sinclair, J. (2001), 'Preface', in M. Ghadessy, A. Henry and R. L. Roseberry (eds), *Small Corpus Studies and ELT*. Amsterdam: John Benjamins, pp. vii–xv.

— (2004), *Trust the Text: Language, Corpus and Discourse*. London: Routledge.

Smart, G. (forthcoming), 'Argumentation across web-based organizational discourses: The case of climate change', in S. Sarangi and C. Candlin (eds), *Handbook of Communication in Organisations and Professions*. Berlin: Mouton De Gruyter.

Spencer-Oatey, H. (2008), 'Face, (im)politeness and rapport', in H. Spencer-Oatey (ed.), *Culturally Speaking: Culture, Communication and Politeness Theory*. London: Continuum, pp. 11–47.

Spender, D. (1980), *Man Made Language*. London: Routledge and Kegan Paul.

Starfield, S. (2010), 'Ethnographies', in B. Paltridge and A. Phakiti (eds), *Continuum Companion to Research Methods in Applied Linguistics*. London: Continuum, pp. 50–65.

Stevens, K. and Asmar, C. (1999), *Doing Postgraduate Research in Australia*. Melbourne: Melbourne University Press.

Stokoe, E. H. (2003), 'Mothers, single women and sluts: Gender, morality and membership categorization in neighbour disputes', *Feminism & Psychology*, 13, 317–44.

Storch, N. (2001a), 'How collaborative is pair work? ESL tertiary students composing in pairs', *Language Teaching Research*, 5, 29–53.

— (2001b), 'An investigation into the nature of pair work in an ESL classroom and its effect on grammatical development' (PhD thesis Department of Linguistics and Applied Linguistics, University of Melbourne).

Street, B. (2010), 'Academic literacies: New directions in theory and practice', in J. Maybin and J. Swann (eds), *The Routledge Companion to English Language Studies*. London: Routledge, pp. 232–42.

Street, B., Pahl, K. and Rowsell, J. (2009), 'Mulitmodality and new literacy studies', in C. Jewitt (ed.), *The Routledge Handbook of Multimodal Analysis*. London: Routledge, pp. 191–200.

Stubbs, M. (1996), *Computer-assisted Studies of Language and Culture*. Oxford: Blackwell.

— (1997), 'Whorf's children: Critical comments on critical discourse analysis (CDA)', in A. Ryan and A. Wray (eds), *Evolving Models of Language*. Clevedon: Multilingual Matters, pp. 100–16.

— (2004), 'Corpus-assisted text and corpus analysis: Lexical cohesion and communicative competence', in D. Schiffrin, D. Tannen and H. E. Hamilton (eds), *The Handbook of Discourse Analysis*. Oxford: Blackwell, pp. 304–20.

Subrahmanyam, K., Greenfield, P. M. and Tynes, B. (2004), 'Constructing sexuality and identity in an online teen chat room', *Applied Developmental Psychology*, 25, 651–66.

Sunderland, J. (2010), 'Research questions in linguistics', in L. Litosseliti (ed.), *Research Methods in Linguistics*. London: Continuum, pp. 9–28.

Sunderland, J. and Litosseliti, L. (2002), 'Gender identity and discourse analysis: Theoretical and empirical considerations', in J. Sunderland and L. Litosseliti (eds), *Gender Identity and Discourse Analysis*. Amsterdam: John Benjamins, pp. 1–39.

Swales, J. M. (1981), 'Aspects of article Introductions', *Aston ESP Research Reports*, 1. Language Studies Unit. University of Aston at Birmingham. Reprinted 2011, University of Michigan Press.

— (1990), *Genre Analysis: English in Academic and Research Settings*. Cambridge: Cambridge University Press.

— (1993), 'Genre and engagement', *Revue Belge de Philologie et d'Histoire*, 71, 689–98.

— (1996), 'Occluded genres in the academy: The case of the submission letter', in E. Ventola and A. Mauranen (eds), *Academic Writing: Intercultural and Textual Issues*. Amsterdam and Philadelphia: John Benjamins, pp. 45–58.

— (1998), *Other Floors, Other Voices: A Textography of a Small University Building*. Mahwah, NJ: Lawrence Erlbaum.

— (2000), 'Languages for specific purposes', *Annual Review of Applied Linguistics*, 20, 59–76.

— (2003), 'Is the university a community of practice?' in S. Sarangi and T. van Leeuwen (eds), *Applied Linguistics and Communities of Practice*. London: Continuum, pp. 203–16.

— (2004), *Research Genres: Explorations and Applications*. Cambridge: Cambridge University Press.

Swales, J. M. and Feak, C. B. (2000), *English in Today's Research World: A Writing Guide*. Ann Arbor: University of Michigan Press.

— (2009), *Abstracts and the Writing of Abstracts*. Ann Arbor: University of Michigan Press.

— (2011), *Navigating Academia: Writing Support Genres*. Ann Arbor: University of Michigan Press.

Swales, J. M. and Malczewski, B. (2001), 'Discourse management and new episode flags in MICASE', in R. Simpson and J. M. Swales (eds), *Corpus Linguistics in North America: Selections from the 1999 Symposium*. Ann Arbor: University of Michigan Press, pp. 145–64.

Swales, J. M. and Rogers, P. (1995), 'Discourse and the projection of corporate culture: The mission statement', *Discourse & Society*, 6, 223–42.

Swann, J. (2002), 'Yes, but is it gender?' in L. Litosseliti and J. Sunderland (eds), *Gender Identity and Discourse Analysis*. Amsterdam: John Benjamins, pp. 43–67.

Swann, J., Deumert, A., Lillis, T. and Mesthrie, R. (2004), *A Dictionary of Sociolinguistics*. Edinburgh: Edinburgh University Press.

Taguchi, N. (2011), 'Teaching pragmatics: Trends and issues', *Annual Review of Applied Linguistics*, 31, 289–310.

Tanaka, K. (1997), 'Developing pragmatic competence: A learners-as-researchers approach', *TESOL Journal*, 6, 14–18.

Tardy, C. M. (2003), 'A genre system view of the funding of academic research', *Written Communication*, 20, 7–36.

— (2006), 'Researching first and second language genre learning: A comparative review and a look ahead', *Journal of Second Language Writing*, 15, 79–101.

— (2011), 'Genre analysis', in K. Hyland and B. Paltridge (eds), *Continuum Companion to Discourse Analysis*. London: Continuum, pp. 54–68.

Taylor, S. (2001), 'Evaluating and applying discourse analytic research', in M. Wetherall, S. Taylor and S. J. Yates (eds), *Discourse as Data: A Guide for Analysis*. London: Sage, pp. 311–30.

Teo, P. (2005), 'Mandarinizing Singapore: A critical analysis of slogans in Singapore's "Speak Mandarin" Campaign', *Critical Discourse Studies*, 2, 121–42.

Thomas, A. (2004), 'Digital literacies of the cybergirl', *E-Learning*, 1, 358–82.

— (2007), *Youth Online: Identity and Literacy in the Digital Age*. New York: Peter Lang.

Thomas, J. (1983), 'Cross cultural pragmatic failure', *Applied Linguistics*, 4, 91–112.

— (1995), *Meaning in Interaction. An Introduction to Pragmatics*. London: Longman.

Thompson, G. (2004), *Introducing Functional Grammar* (2nd edn). London: Arnold.

Thornborrow, J. (2001), 'Questions, control and the organization of talk in calls to a radio phone-in', *Discourse Studies*, 1, 119–43.

Threadgold, T. (1989), 'Talking about genre: Ideologies and incompatible discourses', *Cultural Studies*, 3, 101–27.

— (2003), '"Cultural studies, critical theory and critical discourse analysis" Histories, remembering and futures', *Linguistik Online*, 14, 2. Available at www.linguistik-online.com/14_03/threadgold.html, accessed 1 February 2011.

Thurlow, C., Lengel, L. and Tomic, A. (2004), *Computer Mediated Communication: Social Interaction and the Internet*. London: Sage.

Thurstun, J. and Candlin, C. N. (1997), *Exploring Academic English: A Workbook for Students' Essay Writing*. Sydney: National Centre for English Language Teaching and Research, Macquarie University.

Tognini-Bonelli, E. (2004), 'Working with corpora: Issues and insights', in C. Coffin, A. Hewings and K. O'Lalloran (eds), *Applying English Grammar: Functional and Corpus Approaches*, London: Arnold, pp. 11–24.

Toolan, M. (1997), 'What is critical discourse analysis and why are people saying such terrible things about it?' *Language and Literature*, 6, 83–103.

Trautner, M. N. (2005), 'Doing gender, doing class: The performance of sexuality in exotic dance clubs', *Gender and Society*, 19, 771–88.

Tribble, C. (2002), 'Corpora and corpus analysis: New windows on academic writing', in J. Flowerdew (ed.), *Academic Discourse*. London: Longman, pp. 131–49.

Truss, L. (2003), *Eats, Shoots & Leaves*. London: Profile Books.

Tsang, D. (2000), 'Notes on queer "n" Asian virtual sex', in D. Bell and B. Kennedy (eds), *The Cybercultures Reader*. London: Routledge, pp. 432–7.

Tse, P. and Hyland, K. (2008), '"Robot Kung fu": Gender and professional identity in biology and philosophy reviews', *Journal of Pragmatics*, 40, 1232–48.

Uchida, A. (1992), 'When "difference" is "dominance": A critique of the "anti-power-based" cultural approach to sex differences', *Language in Society*, 21, 547–68.

Uhrig, K. (2012), 'Business and legal case genre networks: Two case studies', *English for Specific Purposes*, 31, 127–36.

van Dijk, T. A. (1991), *Racism and the Press*. London: Routledge.

— (1998), *Ideology*. London: Sage.

— (2008), *Discourse and Context: A Sociocognitive Approach*. Cambridge: Cambridge University Press.

— (2009), *Society and Discourse: How Social Contexts Influence Text and Talk*. Cambridge: Cambridge University Press.

— (2011), 'Discourse studies and hermeneutics', *Discourse Studies*, 13, 609–21.

van Leeuwen, T. (2005a), *Introducing Social Semiotics*. London: Routledge.

— (2005b), 'Multimodality, genre and design', in S. Norris and R. H. Jones (eds), *Discourse in Action: Introducing Mediated Discourse Analysis*. London: Routledge, pp. 73–94.

van Noppen, J.-P. (2004), 'CDA: A discipline come of age?' *Journal of Sociolinguistics*, 8, 107–26.

Vande Kopple, W. (1985), 'Some exploratory discourse on metadiscourse', *College Communication and Composition*, 36, 82–93.

Varis, P., Wang, X. and Du, C. (2011), 'Identity repertoires on the Internet: Opportunities and constraints', *Applied Linguistics Review*, 2, 265–84.

Venables, T. and Yeuh, L. (2006), 'The China effect', *CentrePiece*. Available at www.cep.lse.ac.uk/pubs/download/CP208.pdf, accessed 27 April 2011.

Ventola, E. (1984), 'Orientation to social semiotics in foreign language teaching', *Applied Linguistics*, 5, 275–86.

— (1987), *The structure of social interaction: A systemic approach to the semiotics of service encounters*. London: Frances Pinter

Verschueren, J. (1999), *Understanding Pragmatics*. London: Arnold.

Villa, A. and Barrios, V. (1978), *Adventures in Mexican Cooking*. San Francisco: Ortho Books.

Virtanen, T. (2009), 'Discourse linguistics meets corpus linguistics: Theoretical and methodological issues in the troubled relationship', in A. Renouf and A. Kehoe (eds), *Corpus Linguistics: Refinements and Reassessments*, Amsterdam: Rodopi, pp. 49–65.

Walker, J. (1997), 'Restaurateur shows food critic the door', *The Weekend Australian*, 7–8 June 1997.

Wang, H.-C. (2009), 'Language and ideology: Gender stereotypes of female and male artists in Taiwanese tabloids', *Discourse & Society*, 20, 747–74.

Wang, W. (2002), 'A contrastive analysis of letters to the editor in English and Chinese' (MEd dissertation, University of Sydney).

— (2004), 'A contrastive analysis of letters to the editor in Chinese and English', *Australian Review of Applied Linguistics*, 27, 72–88.

— (2006a), 'Newspaper commentaries in China and Australia: A contrastive genre study', in U. Connor and E. Nagelhout (eds), *Contrastive Rhetoric: Reaching to Intercultural Rhetoric*. London: Equinox, pp. 171–91.

— (2006b), 'Editorials on terrorism in Chinese and English: A contrastive genre study' (PhD thesis, University of Sydney).

— (2007), *Genre across Languages and Cultures: Newspaper Commentaries in China and Australia*. Saarbruecken, Germany: VDM Verlag Dr. Müller.

Watts, R. (2003), *Politeness*. Cambridge: Cambridge University Press.

Weatherall, A. (2002), *Gender, Language and Discourse*. London: Routledge.

Weissberg, R. and Buker, S. (1990), *Writing up Research. Experimental Report Writing for Students of English*. Englewood Cliffs, NJ: Prentice Hall Regents.

Wenger, E. (1998), *Communities of Practice: Learning, Meaning and Identity*. Cambridge: Cambridge University Press.

— (2006), *Communities of Practice: A Brief Introduction*. Available at www.ewenger.com/theory, accessed 2 April 2012.

West, C. and Zimmerman, D. H. (1983), 'Small insults: A study of interruptions in cross-sex conversations between unacquainted persons', in B. Thorne, C. Kramerae and N. Henley (eds), *Language, Gender & Society*. Rowley, MA: Newbury House, pp. 103–18.

Wetherell, M. (1998), 'Positioning and interpretative repertoires: Conversation analysis and post-structuralism in dialogue', *Discourse & Society*, 19, 387–412.

— (2001), 'Themes in discourse research: The case of Diana', in M. Wetherell, S. Taylor and S. J. Yates (eds), *Discourse Theory and Practice: A Reader*. London: Sage, pp. 14–28.

White, P. R. R. (1998), 'Telling Media Tales: The News Story as Rhetoric', PhD dissertation, Department of Linguistics, University of Sydney. Available at www.grammatics.com/appraisal/whiteprr_phd.html, accessed 18 April 2011.

— (2005), *The Appraisal Website*. Available at www.grammatics.com/appraisal/index.html, accessed 18 April 2011.

Widdowson, H. G. (1995), 'Discourse analysis: A critical view', *Language and Literature*, 4, 157–72.

— (1998), 'Review article: The theory and practice of critical discourse analysis', *Applied Linguistics*, 19, 136–51.

— (2000), 'The limitations of linguistics applied', *Applied Linguistics*, 21, 3–25.

— (2004), *Text, Context, Pretext: Critical Issues in Discourse Analysis*. Oxford: Blackwell.

Wierzbicka, A. (2003), *Cross-Cultural Pragmatics: The Semantics of Human Interaction* (2nd edn). Berlin and New York: Mouton de Gruyter.

Wilkinson, S. and Kitzinger, C. (2007), 'Conversation analysis, gender and sexuality', in A. Weatherall, B. M. Watson and C. Gallois (eds), *Language, Discourse & Social Psychology*. Basingstoke, England: Palgrave Macmillan, pp. 206–30.

Williams, H. (2008), 'Barack Obama. This is your victory', in H. Williams (ed.), *In Our Time: The Speeches that Shaped the Modern World*. London: Quercus Publishing, pp. 205–9.

Wingate, U. and Tribble, C. (2011), 'The best of both worlds?' Towards an English for Academic Purposes/Academic Literacies writing pedagogy', *Studies in Higher Education*, DOI: 10.1080/03075079.2010.525630.

Wiseman, R. (1994), *Defending Ourselves: A Guide to Prevention, Self-Defence, and Recovery from Rape*. New York: Farrar, Straus and Giroux.

Wodak, R. (1996), *Disorders of Discourse*. London: Longman.

— (1997), 'Das Ausland and anti-Semitic discourses: The discursive construction of the Other', in S. Riggens (ed.), *The Language of Politics and Exclusion*. London: Sage, pp. 65–87.

Wooffitt, R. (2005), *Conversation Analysis and Discourse Analysis: A Comparative and Critical Introduction*. London: Sage.

Wray, A. and Bloomer, A. (2006), *Projects in Linguistics: A Practical Guide to Researching Language* (2nd edn). London: Hodder Arnold.

Yang, L. (1997), 'An Analysis of Opening Sequences in Chinese Telephone Calls' (MA thesis, Department of Linguistics and Applied Linguistics, University of Melbourne).

Yates, J. and Orlikowski, W. (2007), 'The powerpoint presentation and its corollaries: How genres shape communicative action in organizations', in M. Zachry and C. Thrall (eds), *Communicative Practices in Workplaces and the Professions: Cultural Perspectives on the Regulation of Discourse and Organizations*. Amityville, NY: Baywood, pp. 67–92.

Zhang, J. (1986), *Love Must Not be Forgotten*. Beijing: China Books and Periodicals.

Zhang, L. (2008), 'Mao's new tailor: Sui Jianguo', *Artzine: A Chinese Contemporary Art Portal*. Available at www.artzinechina.com/display.php?a=89, accessed 2 September 2011.

Zhang, Q. (2005), 'A Chinese yuppie in Beijing: Phonological variation and the construction of a new professional identity', *Language in Society*, 34, 431–66.

— (2008), 'Rhotacization and the 'Beijing Smooth Operator': The meaning of a sociolinguistic variable', *Journal of Sociolinguistics*, 12, 210–22.

— (2012), 'Carry shopping through to the end': Linguistic innovation and social distinction in Chinese television medium', in J. M. Hernández-Campoy and J. A. Cutillas-Espinosa (eds), *Style-shifting in Public: New Perspectives on Stylistic Variation*. Amsterdam: John Benjamins, pp. 205–24.

Zhang, Y. (2005), House of Flying Daggers: Director's statement. Available at www.sonyclassics.com/houseofflyingdaggers/flashsite.html, accessed 28 October 2011.

Index

Page numbers in **bold** denote tables.